CW01510412

Netflix's *Chilling Adventures of Sabrina*

Netflix's *Chilling Adventures of Sabrina*

Hell's Under New Management

Edited by Cori Mathis, Stephanie A. Graves, and Melissa Tyndall

LEXINGTON BOOKS
Lanham • Boulder • New York • London

Published by Lexington Books
An imprint of The Rowman & Littlefield Publishing Group, Inc.
4501 Forbes Boulevard, Suite 200, Lanham, Maryland 20706
www.rowman.com

86-90 Paul Street, London EC2A 4NE

British Library Cataloguing in Publication Information Available

Library of Congress Cataloging-in-Publication Data

Names: Mathis, Cori, 1984- editor. | Graves, Stephanie A., 1978- editor. | Tyndall, Melissa, 1982- editor.
Title: Netflix's *Chilling adventures of Sabrina* : Hell's under new management / edited by Cori Mathis, Stephanie A. Graves, and Melissa Tyndall.
Description: Lanham : Lexington Books, 2023. | Includes bibliographical references and index. | Summary: "This interdisciplinary edited collection examines multiple themes found within the popular Netflix series *Chilling Adventures of Sabrina*. Chapters on topics such as genre, postmodernism, adaptation, history, fashion, and ideology offer new insights and contextualize the series within contemporary teen television"-- Provided by publisher.
Identifiers: LCCN 2022059567 (print) | LCCN 2022059568 (ebook) | ISBN 9781666929782 (cloth) | ISBN 9781666929799 (ebook)
Subjects: LCSH: Chilling adventures of Sabrina (Television program) | Spellman, Sabrina (Fictitious character) | Fantasy television programs--United States--History and criticism. | Witches on television. | Witchcraft on television. | Feminism on television.
Classification: LCC PN1992.77.C47825 N48 2023 (print) | LCC PN1992.77.C47825 (ebook) | DDC 791.45/72--dc23/eng/20230123
LC record available at https://lccn.loc.gov/2022059567
LC ebook record available at https://lccn.loc.gov/2022059568

Cori Mathis: For Donald Andrews, who taught me to love literature's complexity and modeled the life of the mind, and for David Lavery, who insisted I had a talent for this work and cleared a path for me to do it.

Stephanie A. Graves: For David Lavery—who said I could.

Melissa Tyndall: For my spouse, without whom this Gothic Mother would have no time to write.

Contents

Acknowledgments

This volume arose from a roundtable discussion at the 2021 meeting of the Popular Culture Association, which three Nashville-based colleagues and friends saw as an opportunity to come to an understanding of *Chilling Adventures of Sabrina*, a text that each of them found fascinating in different ways but were equally unable to fully explain. The roundtable's warm, engaged audience led to such a stimulating conversation that the later suggestion of an edited collection on the series seemed like the most obvious next step.

It may have been obvious, but this collection took over a year to realize. We'd like to thank our contributors for their patience and hard work throughout the process; for many of them, television is not their primary area of study, and their openness to revisions was greatly appreciated.

We must also acknowledge the contributions of our respective universities and colleagues, in particular the departments of Cinematic Arts and English and Modern Languages at Lipscomb University, with which Cori is affiliated. Along with the University's librarians, they provided a great deal of support that assured this project would be completed in a timely manner.

And, finally, we'd like to thank our editor at Lexington Books, Judith Lakamper, for reaching out to us after our roundtable discussion and encouraging us to propose this collection. We have all learned a great deal from this process and appreciate your confidence in us.

Introduction

Something Wickedly Different This Way Comes: Netflix's Chilling Adventures of Sabrina

Cori Mathis, Stephanie A. Graves, and Melissa Tyndall

In the fall of 2020, we found ourselves in a similar position as many academics across the globe: trying to decide what, among the dozens of texts we each examined during the isolation of the COVID-19 pandemic, would provide significant engagement for Zoom conference attendees at an upcoming national conference. Soon, we realized that even when discussing more likely options from our respective specialties, we kept returning to an ongoing conversation: just what was happening in *Chilling Adventures of Sabrina* (*CAoS*), which had released its first season on Netflix that October. We knew it felt like few teen dramas or Gothic series to date, but why? Our attempt to determine what was at work in the series led to even more questions, ending in this volume, in which scholars from all over the world and a wide variety of academic disciplines wrestle with the complexities, both welcome and troubling, of *CAoS*. This project does not attempt to address all of the facets of the text; instead, we focus on five general areas of inquiry in hopes that these examinations will function as both a foundation and a springboard for further insight into the series. There are many lenses through which one can read the text, unlike many teen dramas or horror television shows, and that hybridity makes *Chilling Adventures of Sabrina* a fruitful site for academic exploration.

A SHORT OVERVIEW OF THE HISTORY
OF SABRINA SPELLMAN

On October 26, 2018, Netflix released the first season of *Chilling Adventures of Sabrina,* a series centered around Sabrina the Teenage Witch, a character from Archie Comics. Sabrina originated in the October 1962 issue of *Archie's Mad House* (1959–82), an Archie series that featured zanier, less "realistic" stories that often made no sense at all. The character proved popular, and Sabrina began to appear in other Archie Comics series, was adapted into an animated television show, and then got her own series, *Sabrina the Teenage Witch*, in 1971, which was continuously published until 1983. Sabrina returned to American youth popular culture in 1996, when Melissa Joan Hart began portraying the character, first in a Showtime movie and then in the well-known sitcom (ABC, 1996–2000/The WB, 2000–03) *Sabrina the Teenage Witch*. The series changed a number of details from the original comics; while they explain that Sabrina was created by her aunts, Hilda and Zelda Spellman, as the result of a spell gone awry and was always aware of her powers (though sometimes not in control of them), the sitcom's Sabrina is a half-mortal who learns of her witch heritage on her sixteenth birthday and is living with her aunts while her divorced parents are supposedly traveling. The 1990s iteration also enhances Salem the cat; instead of being a simple witch's familiar, he is a wisecracking witch named Salem Saberhagen, trapped in the body of a cat as punishment for his attempts at world domination. As a result of the popularity of this series, Archie Comics rebooted *Sabrina the Teenage Witch*, and the character has appeared in multiple titles since then.

In 2013, as part of their continued efforts at reviving and contemporizing the brand, Archie Comics began to release darker, more adult stories featuring Archie and his pals. These tales—which take place outside of the main Archie continuity and were later collected under the newly established Archie Horror imprint—cast the teens as zombies, werewolves, vampires, and witches. In the first of these series, Roberto Aguirre-Sacasa and Francesco Francavilla's *Afterlife with Archie* (2013–present), Sabrina tries to help Jughead bring his dog, Hot Dog, back to life after he is run over by a car. Unfortunately, the spell goes awry, and Hot Dog comes back as a zombie, eventually biting Jughead and beginning a zombie apocalypse. Aguirre-Sacasa also created a companion series with Robert Hack, *Chilling Adventures of Sabrina* (2014–present), which follows Sabrina Spellman as she must choose between her witch and mortal lives upon the occasion of her sixteenth birthday. The comic casts the Spellman family as members of the Church of Night—witches who have received their powers in exchange for worshiping Satan—with Sabrina's father, Edward, as a high-ranking and deeply corrupt member of its clergy, and features murder, cannibalism, and incest as major parts of the narrative.

2013 also saw renewed interest in screen versions of the Archie universe, which reflected the great success of the Archie Horror titles. Capitalizing on the comic's newfound relevance, Roberto Aguirre-Sacasa pitched an Archie feature film that, after some development issues, was reimagined as a television series for The CW. When *Riverdale* (2015–present) premiered, it enjoyed almost instantaneous popularity, propelling its central cast—who, with the exception of Cole Sprouse, were unknown when the series began—into teen idolhood reminiscent of that enjoyed by the stars of *Beverly Hills, 90210* (FOX, 1990–2000). As the first in the so-called "Archieverse," which also includes *Chilling Adventures of Sabrina* and *Katy Keene* (The CW, 2020), *Riverdale* makes a compelling case for the continued relevance of Archie Andrews and his friends as it uses a variety of genre-based approaches from *film noir* to fantasy to represent the complexities of contemporary adolescence.

As a companion series to *Riverdale*—and one recently confirmed to exist in the same universe—*Chilling Adventures of Sabrina* follows much of the pattern established by that series, functioning primarily as a teen drama but pulling elements from multiple genres and taking place in a slightly alternate universe from our own, one which feels dreamlike and unstuck in time and makes even more kinds of characters and stories possible. If one were to describe *Chilling Adventures of Sabrina*, terms like "horror" and "Gothic" would likely come first—it *is* a series in which the main character is a witch from a coven that practices ritual cannibalism and worships Satan. However, it is also a teen drama, providing rich portraits of contemporary teens and their worries, and a family drama in which two middle-aged sisters come to a true understanding of their own power, needs, and destinies separate from each other. It is a supernatural drama whose characters traverse multiple planes of existence, manipulate time and space, and battle cosmic forces from alternate dimensions. It is a number of things all at once, reflecting the increasing transgenericism of the contemporary television landscape, which makes it a fecund text in terms of different scholarly approaches.

AREAS OF INQUIRY

In this volume's first section, the authors attempt to provide some context on witchcraft in the series. While witches across media types have been played for comedy in the past, films like *The Witch* (2015) and series like *Chilling Adventures of Sabrina* have swung the pendulum back toward darker, more complicated images of the witch, one that hearkens back to historical views and positions the character to function effectively as a cultural symbol. As Farhana Irshad illustrates in "The Revised Image of the Witch: Historical Archetypes Revamped for the Contemporary Online Audience" and Diana Celeste Etain and Cori Mathis further explore in "The Inclusive Witch in *Chilling Adventures of Sabrina*," there have been a number of perceptions of witches and witchcraft throughout history, but the vision of the Satanic witch has persevered since the publication of the *Malleus Maleficarum* in the late 15th century. In an American context, Puritanical views of witchcraft—where witches are threats ostensibly because they are instruments of the Devil in his war against Christians—may have been muted after the infamous Salem witch trials, but the connection remains in cultural memory. As such, media representations have historically reflected a tension between beliefs of witches as dangerous and evil and emerging understandings of peaceful practice. Additionally, the increasing influence of feminism has necessitated a revision in how witches are portrayed in order to appeal to viewers who understand the connections between the two. Continuing in this vein, in their chapter, "Controlling the Female Body: Foucault, Catholic Ireland, and *Chilling Adventures of Sabrina*," Shannon Hughes Spence and Cori Mathis argue that the series can be read as a parallel text to the real-life experience of Irish feminist witches, who have suffered a wide variety of patriarchal surveillance and control under the Catholic Church, particularly after the establishment of the Irish Free State. Similarly, the Church of Night, as a result of the misogynistic beliefs of its clergy, oppresses and polices its female members, a key factor in Sabrina and her fellow witches' rebellion over the course of the series.

Authors Tp Coughlin, Alice Capstick, and Luisa Fernanda Grijalva-Maza take on the distinctly feminist concerns of *Chilling Adventures of Sabrina*, arguing for the variety of ways it both contributes to the work of feminism and reflects some contemporary concerns regarding widespread, popular understandings and practices of the same. Tp Coughlin's essay, "Proliferating Feminisms and the Irruption of the Material in *Chilling Adventures of Sabrina*," takes the position that the series does not attempt to enter the feminist project at all; in fact, it deliberately features a variety of feminisms as a way of reflecting the current moment, wherein feminism is suffering from a lack of unification and young people's secondhand, popular culture-influenced understanding of its message and goals. Naturally, Coughlin argues, using the figure of The Uninvited as one key example of this concern, there will exist a tension in the series that leads scholars to argue firmly for its feminist stance or lack thereof. Alice Capstick uses literary Satanism to come to an understanding of the series' feminist concerns in "The Devil You Know? Feminism and Postmodern Pastiche of Satanism and the Infernal in *Chilling Adventures of Sabrina*." In her essay, Capstick reminds us that while literature offers some significant and enduring depictions of Satan as the great rebel against the establishment, because these images are so prevalent in our cultural memory, they can be nothing but oppressively patriarchal; however, the postmodern work of pastiche provides a path toward feminist rebellion. In this way, the postmodern infernal tradition allows for a true critique of patriarchal institutions and perspectives. Luisa Fernanda Grijalva-Maza identifies another feminist argument in the text in her "Giving Satanic and Divine Patriarchy a Run for Their Money: Hybridity, Liminality, and Female Empowerment in *Chilling Adventures of Sabrina*." In this chapter, Grijalva-Maza posits that it is not just Sabrina's liminality—her in-between state of transition between the mortal and witch worlds—that allows her to effectively fight the patriarchal forces around her, it is her hybridity. As a half-mortal, half-witch hybrid, Sabrina is able to navigate both worlds effectively, leveraging her talents in one against the enemies of the other while still calling upon whatever power she naturally has in that space. Additionally, Sabrina becomes more powerful as a result of this navigation, leading to a state of full liminality in which she rejects the call to choose one identity over another, which influences those around her to pursue their own empowerment.

Much of *Chilling Adventures of Sabrina*'s narrative surrounds ideas of binarities and duality, and its characters spend considerable time wrestling with questions of identity, especially when their senses of self clash with pre-established, outdated norms. In "From Having to Choose to Being Chosen: Analyzing Sabrina as a Mixed (Race) Being," Lisa Delacruz Combs, Nicole Neifert, and Marc P. Johnston-Guerrero explore the ways in which Sabrina, though not racially mixed, reflects common tropes and ideas found in multiracial representations, particularly ideas of in-betweenness, being forced to choose between identities, and her positioning as a savior figure toward the end of the series. As a White woman coded as a mixed being, Sabrina's characterization highlights some of the dangerous messages perpetuated by outdated, assimilationist narratives of mixedness. Co-editor Stephanie A. Graves also calls attention to the ways in which the series should be read in relation to identity. In "'I want freedom and power': The Allegory of Queer Rhetoric in *Chilling Adventures of Sabrina*," she posits that the world of Greendale is explicitly created in opposition to dominant norms, frustrating discrete compartmentalizing of identities, rejecting *de rigueur* acceptance of patriarchal control, and repudiating heteronormative hegemony. The series, Graves argues, not only includes positive representation of queer characters within the text but also acts as an allegory of the transformative power of queer resistance through multiple sites of queer rupture. Laura Davidel contends in "Empowering Liminality in *Chilling Adventures of Sabrina*" that the series positions resistance as connected to identity—namely, that Sabrina's identity as a liminal being empowers her to fight for social justice and upset the patriarchal systems in both the mortal and witch worlds. In Sabrina's struggle for agency and autonomy, she reflects the real-life experiences of the series' target audience.

Chilling Adventures of Sabrina also offers compelling explorations of gender and gender performance. In her essay, "'I'm sick of being the afterthought, the joke': Hilda Spellman's Empowering Domesticity in Netflix's *Chilling Adventures of Sabrina*," Katie E. Cline discusses the ways in which Sabrina's aunt Hilda, as a woman with talents and preferences toward more traditional, domestic pursuits, represents a group typically undervalued in modern feminism. Not only does Hilda truly enjoy cooking, knitting, and romance novels, she uses these hobbies as pathways to empowerment and even as weapons, when necessary, since Hilda is underestimated by those with more traditionally masculine power, especially other women. Co-editor Melissa Tyndall identifies another element of tension in her essay, "The Gothic Mother and Daughter in *Chilling Adventures of Sabrina*," arguing that, as a Gothic text, the series has a complicated relationship with both mothers and mothering as a concept. In Greendale, biological or adoptive mothers are often dead or completely absent, and if they do appear on-screen, they are monstrous in some fashion and do not beget daughters, only sons. Tyndall also notes that, while surrogate mothers do feature in the narrative—as Zelda and Hilda Spellman have stepped in to raise Sabrina after the death of their brother and sister-in-law and also mother Ambrose—their resistance to patriarchal norms ensures that they are continually punished for their duality until the Church of Night is abolished. However, their example helps facilitate cycle-breaking decisions from their surrogate daughters, ensuring that the next generation will not suffer in the same ways. To close this section, David Rosen offers a close reading of the many incidents of consumption that can be found within the series in his essay, "Devouring Women, Consuming Men: Cats, Mice, and the World of Sabrina Spellman." Unless viewers have a deep familiarity with Renaissance literature, they may miss the symbolism of cats, mice, and consumption in the series, and Rosen argues that this literary tradition informs *Chilling Adventures of Sabrina*'s narrative. In their acts of consumption, characters such as Ambrose, Lilith, and Sabrina illuminate the series' interest in the instability of identity.

We conclude this volume with a set of essays that examine the generic and cultural implications of the series' formal choices. *Chilling Adventures of Sabrina* makes use of visual and narrative generic markers that make easy categorization of the series difficult, and its intertextual elements make space for a variety of perspectives about the work being done in the text. Co-editor Cori Mathis's chapter, "'What's needed here is a fundamental shift in thinking': *Chilling Adventures of Sabrina* and the Complexities of the Teen Drama," contends that the series occupies a particularly relevant space in the genre as a strong example of its increasing transgenericism. In this analysis, Mathis provides an overview of the formal and thematic concerns at work in the teen drama and argues that, to draw the continued attention of teenagers who have a wide variety of narratives to engage with at any given moment, these series must reproduce that variety via a generic flexibility that reflects the interests and experiences of its target audience. *Chilling Adventures of Sabrina*, as a series that pulls from multiple traditions, is a strong example of how contemporary teen dramas attempt to negotiate this requirement. Lori Bindig Yousman also examines the generic aspects of the series in "The Legacy, Liberation, and Limitations of Gender and Genre in *Chilling Adventures of Sabrina*," where she observes that, as a teen drama, the series becomes embroiled in the genre's complicated history with representations of gender. In some ways, Bindig Yousman argues, the narrative is progressive in its gender politics, confronting sexist tropes about female friendship and acknowledging the importance of intersectional concerns. However, *Chilling Adventures of Sabrina* also reinforces limiting and harmful perspectives, including placing romance at the top of a young woman's priorities and encouraging martyrdom. Daria Romanova and Maggie Webster focus on another key element of teen dramas in their essay, "Anachronistic Bricolage and Eternal Autumn Aesthetic in *Chilling Adventures of Sabrina*," addressing the unique approach the series' production team has taken to the characters' wardrobe and production design as a whole. These choices situate the show within the larger cultural phenomenon of vintage and nostalgia and, by extension, reflect the real-life aesthetics of contemporary witchcraft. Finally, Alissa Burger articulates a parallel element in the text as she explores the ways in which the many iterations of Sabrina Spellman impact the reception of this series in "Intersecting Narratives and the *Book*(s) *of the Beast*: The Multiplicity of Textual Engagements and *Chilling Adventures of Sabrina*." The success of the Sabrina the Teenage Witch character over the past sixty years has led to a number of approaches to her story across media, and the multiverse that has arisen alongside these stories allows us to interrogate not only the material presented but the very idea of narrative itself. In particular, the intertextual components of the series paired with its horror elements make for a dynamic reading experience that encourages the questioning and revision of narrative and characterization in the Archieverse as a whole, offering viewers the chance to experience a multitude of realities at once. In much the same way, this collection does not argue that there is one way to read *Chilling Adventures of Sabrina*, nor that the essays collected here represent all that could or should be said about the series. Though we have had to limit the volume's exploration to a few themes, we look forward to the conversation these chapters will inspire.

PART 1

"A girl who was half-witch, half-mortal"

The Witches of Greendale

Chapter 1

The Revised Image of the Witch

Historical Archetypes Revamped for the Contemporary Online Audience

Farhana Irshad

With the rise of subscription video-on-demand (SVoD) services such as Netflix, Amazon Prime, Hulu, and Disney+, audiences can now choose how and when they consume their television. With this autonomy comes the increased ability and option to binge-watch a series, and this newer, now normalized, form of viewing enables audiences' narrative transportation to be elevated to a new level. The journey audiences take when watching television is a process where consuming a text allows them to access their thoughts and experiences, a specific process that Melanie Green and Timothy Brock describe as becoming "absorbed into a story or transported into a narrative world."[1] This level of narrative transportation can be increased and "sped-up" by binge-watching. In their article "An Experimental Examination of Binge Watching and Narrative Engagement," Sarah Erikson, Sonya Dal Cin, and Hannah Byl found that "binge watching maximizes exposure to a narrative within a short period while also minimizing interruption and other intervening factors. Some viewers have even defined an experience as a binge only when they were transported into a narrative."[2] To support these newer forms of viewing, SVoD services must now integrate a more detailed and engaging narrative into their new releases to promote a higher level of continuous immersion by encouraging audience connection to the characters on-screen. As Zachary Snider explains in *The Netflix Effect*, "we crave intimacy and emotional connection with characters and their 'truthful' stories; then, once we've garnered this intimacy a few episodes in [. . .] binge-watching is underway."[3]

Chilling Adventures of Sabrina (Netflix, 2018–20) uses a variety of genres that include horror, thriller, drama, mystery, and the supernatural to appeal to a wide range of audiences. The series also provides us with a contemporary representation of the traditional witch on-screen. Streaming audiences positively received the series, which led to Netflix featuring *CAoS* as a recommendation on its homepage. Although *CAoS* shares the same name and inspiration as the 1996 series *Sabrina the Teenage Witch* (ABC, 1996–2000/ The WB, 2000–03), its narrative steers away from its predecessor's light, teen comedy style and adopts a darker narrative that presents itself as an homage to the historical archetypes of witches. These revised images of the witch allow viewers to understand the context of the characters on-screen as well as how they might define their own identity as a witch. This chapter will discuss how these characters have evolved and/or removed themselves from previously established images of witches yet still demonstrate an attachment to the historical archetypes present within the witch-hunting era. This provides the audience with a world that they are transported to by the narrative, one which can support a pre-existing image of witches that the audience may already have—such as character types, tropes, and narrative arcs—but also challenges and revises these ideas to suit the context of the series and current society.

TEENAGER OR WITCH?

The influence of the traditional image on the contemporary portrayal of the witch is perhaps linked to our interests in an older world. Paul Wells comments that while "fairy tales, folktales, and gothic romances articulated the fears of the 'old' world, the contemporary horror film has defined and illustrated the phobias of a 'new' world characterized by a rationale of industrial, technological, and economic determinism."[4] Similarly, *Chilling Adventures of Sabrina* takes a revisionist approach to the previously established archetypes and caters to a contemporary audience. In the series, Sabrina Spellman (Kiernan Shipka) and her family are not represented as exact replicas of the historical image of the witch, at least not as the typical "enemy" against society. Instead, the first season of *CAoS* focuses on Sabrina's unwavering stance against adopting what she considers barbaric practices within her coven and her refusal to sign away her name to the Dark Lord's *Book of the Beast*, along with highlighting her keen use of her inherited magics.

We first see Sabrina portrayed in a traditional teenage setting within the horror/thriller genre: watching a horror film, *Night of the Living Dead* (George A. Romero, 1968). Sabrina enjoys the gore displayed on the screen while her friends jump in fear; later, at Dr. Cerberus's, they good-naturedly argue about the film's meaning. After her boyfriend, Harvey Kinkle (Ross Lynch), drops her off at home, Sabrina is elated by her evening and demonstrates this by using her magic—our first sign of magic within the show—establishing Sabrina's character as a teenager first and a witch second. This theme continues throughout the first season as we follow Sabrina's battle between choosing a life as a teenager in high school or as a witch in a coven.

Largely, Sabrina is motivated to stay in her mortal school to maintain her friendships—something she would have to give up once she signs her name in the Dark Lord's *Book of the Beast* on her sixteenth birthday. Sabrina is reluctant to reveal her identity as half-mortal and half-witch to her friends and later asks her aunts if she can postpone her Dark Baptism, as she feels committed to her mortal life. When they refuse, Sabrina asks instead to speak to someone to discuss her concerns and doubts about becoming a witch before she commits to the Church of Night. A lot of her doubts—really, her fear—about signing her name stems from established historical tropes and imagery of witches. Whether this is from experiences in her mortal life, perhaps through her knowledge of horror films or ignorance of how her witch-aunts live, Sabrina's reluctance and fear surrounding joining the Church of Night and practicing witchcraft more openly is a key part of the first season's storyline.

Sabrina's misunderstanding of what it means to be a witch remains consistent throughout the first season, despite the positive examples and diverse types of witches in her life. Her aunts, Zelda (Miranda Otto) and Hilda Spellman (Lucy Davies), who in the mortal world manage the Spellman Sisters Mortuary, are accomplished witches; they take on diverse roles throughout the series, which reflects their characters' deep complexity. For example, the aunts' various roles include matriarch, mother, High Priestess, and Directrix, as well as being powerful witches with their preferred ways of practicing their magic. Despite having these complex and positive representations of witches at home, Sabrina's continued misunderstanding of her witch heritage and identity is marred by what mortal society assumes witches to be. Sabrina provides an outsider's perspective of the coven as she continually questions and opposes various aspects of their practice. Equally, audiences have their image of witches that has been established from various representations of the female monster across media. However, despite adaptations to suit modern audiences and genres, the essence of the archetype remains consistent and bears a strong resemblance to the historical image of witches.

HISTORICAL IMAGES OF WITCHES
AND THE INFLUENCE OF *HÄXAN*

The established image of the witch in America is rooted in the witchcraft accusations and trials of the mid-to-late sixteenth century. The rise in trials of those accused as witches were led by fear, doubt, and often prejudice. Some of these accusations may have been a consequence due to the state of the Church of England. Peter Elmer writes that the group's "need to punish witches helped to purge and redefine the boundaries of the new confessional state."[5] As the Puritans promoted the persecution of witches through the idea that they lived in sin and were consumed with the dark arts, a shared image of the witch emerged in society. Witches were assumed, as Helen Berger and Douglass Ezzy found in their research, to be a "hooked nosed, green skinned, hexing maniac with a black hat on."[6] This dark image of the witch has been perpetuated within popular culture in most forms of media and traditional texts. Their image of ugliness presents itself as a metaphor for their evil, contaminated souls; dark, sinful deeds; hatred for regular people; and need for vengeance. The witch's reputation and association with the so-called dark arts allow audiences to recognize them as the enemy or as the antagonists. By extension, the image becomes associated with fear due to what a witch might do to an individual, such as physically harming them.

The image of the witch in the horror genre has continued to be an abject figure, an image that creates feelings of fear, anxiety, and disgust which often, as Cynthia Freeland has discussed, "stimulates more complex emotional and intellectual responses"[7] to the narrative, *mise-en-scéne*, or characters on-screen. Although this image can be seen as damaging and detrimental to those who identify as witches in real life, it does, however, offer another representation. This abject image of the witch can also be viewed as a positive, even complex, role through the lens of their sexuality and/or menstruation. Barbara Creed, the author of *The Monstrous-Feminine,* writes that a witch's "devil powers are seen as part of her 'feminine' nature."[8] Though this image is often considered horrifying, in the context of psychoanalytical theory, it has become associated with empowerment, and, in *CAoS*, the empowered witch image is attached to strong female characters.

Furthermore, the abject witch in horror, as Creed discusses, is often the "transgressive woman: *femme fatale,* witch, bitch, hysteric, nymphomaniac."[9] It is these archetypes of female characters that dominate the screen in a way that creates fear in male audiences. Creed also goes on to say that this is connected to the "problem of sexual difference and castration," which is a result of a "patriarchal and phallocentric ideology."[10] The first images of witches on-screen were based on the only available sources that featured witches:

folklore, books, and historical images and events from the witch-hunting era. In a way, folklore helped inspire the fear of witches in society, which later translated to the fear of witches on-screen. These historical images of the witch are also present within *Chilling Adventures of Sabrina*. The witches in *CAoS* are not "hooked-nosed hexing maniac" witches but share similarities to historical practitioners through their expertise in topics such as sexuality, childbirth, and herbal remedies. There are elements within *CAoS* that are inspired by the historical representation of witches, including Satanic rituals, cannibalism, and human sacrifices, whilst simultaneously revising, and rejecting various aspects of that traditional image.

As hinted by the film's poster in Sabrina's bedroom, *Häxan* (Benjamin Christensen, 1922) is worth mentioning due to its adaptation of historical images of the witch to the screen. *Häxan* was the first film to represent the witch on-screen and set a precedent for the images we still associate with witches today; it has certainly influenced *CAoS*. *Häxan* is a silent film that exhibits a range of both factual and fictional takes of witches and witchcraft through the ages, spanning from medieval times to the period of the film's release. The film used the *Malleus Maleficarum* as its primary reference, a fifteenth-century text that provided a criterion for identifying a witch during the witch-hunting era. *Häxan* adapts some of the medieval illustrations within the text, including those depicting various acts that witches were believed to take part in, such as flying; cannibalism and using human body parts for spell work; brewing potions in cauldrons; causing harm to crops and cattle; burning villages; cursing people with diseases; meeting in councils; and dancing naked with the Devil. Before *Häxan,* the only other representation of witches was in medieval illustrations and texts—thus giving *Häxan*, as Tanya Krzywinska writes in *A Skin for Dancing in: Possession, Witchcraft and Voodoo in Film*, a "certain prototypical status."[11] *Chilling Adventures of Sabrina*, like other television series, books, films, and other media before it, pulls much of its imagery of witches from the *Malleus Maleficarum* and *Häxan*—whether it is intentional or not. With battles against the angelic witch-hunters, acting on vengeance, and creating curses, *CAoS* does not steer far from traditional images and understandings of witches.

One aspect of this traditional image is that of the age and/or aging of the witch. In "Evil Imaginings and Fantasies: Child-Witches and the End of the Witch Craze," Lyndal Roper notes that the witch-hunts "offered a clear way of dealing with evil, by locating the source of evil in an old woman."[12] Their age presents a connection to the primordial world, implying that these witches are as old as time; they are immortal and thus a continual threat to society. Likewise, in "Chapter Three: The Trial of Sabrina Spellman" (1:3), we learn that, although not crones, Hilda and Zelda are much older than their current appearance would suggest, because witches live longer than mortals—a trait borrowed from folklore. Despite being contemporary witches for the modern audience, elements of Hilda and Zelda's image remain consistent with historical archetypes.

The newer revisionist, revolutionary representations of the witch seen in modern media are perhaps due to, as Tanya Krzywinska argues, the "presence and evolution of feminist ideas within the field of popular culture."[13] Due to this presence, more complex and dynamic roles are available for women in film, and the role of the witch has evolved similarly. In *Mass Media and Religious Identity: A Case Study of Young Witches*, Helen Berger and Douglas Ezzy explain that witchcraft is now viewed as a religious identity due to the development of Wicca, a Neo-Pagan religion, a little over a century ago.[14] Berger and Ezzy found that contemporary portrayals help, particularly for young witches, "to legitimize their religion, providing a framework or cultural backdrop within which they begin to explore Witchcraft and develop their religious identities."[15] The way witches are represented in media has shifted from previous depictions, but that does not necessarily mean that all representations of witches on-screen are now ambassadors for the identity; on the contrary, they are far from it. Specific codes and conventions of the horror genre influence those representations and, as Helen Berger and Douglass Ezzy discuss, perhaps result in young witches seeing "media representations as inaccurate and, therefore, something to respond against,"[16] rather than something that wholly represents themselves on the screen. On the other hand, there are portrayals of women in film who happen to be/become witches within the narrative of the film yet live otherwise ordinary lives, providing a character with whom the audience can relate and identify by placing the witches in a familiar "framework of cultural backdrop."[17] *Chilling Adventures of Sabrina* follows such a pattern, placing the Spellman witches in an otherwise normal environment—one in which Sabrina is able to explore, rather than simply accept, her witch heritage.

THE SPELLMAN WITCHES AND THE REVISED WITCH

Sabrina Spellman displays reservations about becoming a witch, despite having two aunts who are multidimensional characters and offer positive representations of what that means. Zelda, the eldest of Sabrina's two aunts, acts as the matriarch of the Spellman family. After the death of her brother, Edward Spellman (Georgie Daburas), the previous High Priest of the Church of Night and Sabrina's father, Zelda attempts to maintain the family's status and continually imposes the expectations of the Spellman name onto her niece, Sabrina. However, Zelda, although a staunch traditionalist—as displayed through her devotion to the Dark Lord and her experience and expertise in witch history and tradition—often reveals her softer maternal side throughout the series. Zelda's maternal love for Sabrina often makes her ignore traditional witch values to protect Sabrina and the family. With this revised image of the witch, there is much more flexibility in characterization; it provides insight into the characters' motives and can further guide the narrative as audiences continue to be absorbed into the story.

However, we as the audience do not fear the Spellman aunts, as previous images would encourage us to do. Instead, they become audience favorites due to the complex nature of their characters and the support they provide to Sabrina and her mortal friends—all while demonstrating their magical prowess. The aunts are stern, but comforting, maternal influences on Sabrina. What is not provided by the aunts is the fear Sabrina holds for signing her name in the *Book of the Beast.* Based on Sabrina's experience with witchcraft and her positive female examples at home, it may be assumed that Sabrina would wholeheartedly become a witch without any reservations. However, that is not the case, and it appears that, since Sabrina is half-mortal and sub-ject to the forces of those ideologies, she may have adopted the mortal fears of witches, all of which stem from the *Malleus Maleficarum* and other early cultural images of witches.

A large part of *CAoS*'s first season involves Sabrina battling against her identity as a witch. Her decision to finally sign Satan's book is due to her inability to stop the Greendale Thirteen—witches executed early in Greendale's history who have been resurrected and set upon the town. Consequently, Sabrina signs the *Book of the Beast* in the presence of the Dark Lord because she needs more power and is only able to access it when she becomes a witch. Once granted her powers, she faces the Greendale Thirteen and burns them with hellfire. This is another nod to the historical archetypes of a woman trading herself for power (especially as demonstrated within *Häxan*)—Sabrina needs power and therefore signs her name away.

Furthermore, Sabrina exhibits her reluctance through her continued disap-proval of various rituals practiced within the Church of Night. Within the first episode, "Chapter One: October Country" (1:1) the Spellman aunts question Sabrina about whether she has been "defiled" by Harvey and stress that "[w]itch law forbids novitiates from being anything less than virginal."[18] However, "Chapter Fourteen: Lupercalia (2:3)," focuses on the "witch's Valentine's Day," i.e., Lupercalia—a festival to celebrate lust and fertility. Here, Zelda passionately educates her niece regarding the sensuality of the festival, and Sabrina shares that she may not be ready for sex, to which Zelda retorts, "What better time to start?"[19] Zelda also shares that the festival does not hold any "shame or regret" as Sabrina's mortal ideologies may suggest, linking her worries to another significant aspect of the historical image of witches that relies on the assumed sexuality and gender of the witch. In the era of witch-hunting, a girl reaching puberty or womanhood was more likely to be accused of practicing witchcraft or having an association with the Devil than a boy of the same age. The historical condemnation of witches in society is a result of, as Barbara Creed writes, "an order which has defined women's sexuality as the source of all evil and menstruation as the sign of sin."[20] The danger associated with female witches has a clear connection to their sexual practices, sexual orientation, and femininity. This stereotype is readily attached to gender and offers a dated, patriarchal view of what a witch is based on the gender roles historically assigned to women. It presents a negative view of women who were perhaps confident in and adventurous with their sexuality—a trait often also assigned to witches. Instead of reflecting this perspective, *Chilling Adventures of Sabrina* uses the Lupercalia storyline to promote ideologies of gender and sexuality for contemporary audiences, especially through the inclusion of an open and honest discussion that Sabrina has with her aunts about sex and relationships. Taking a dated ideology about women and/or witches and revising it to suit contemporary audiences and their expectations of the teen drama is a continuous theme in *CAoS*.

Many representations of witches, whether on-screen or literary, reflect the *Malleus Maleficarum* and *Häxan*'s original depictions and imagery, and equally, many of those representations of witches adapt and/or reject historical images of the witch and revise them for their respective cultures and audiences. However, few address the religious component of these narratives the way *Chilling Adventures of Sabrina* does. For example, in "Chapter Six: An Exorcism in Greendale" (1:6), Ms. Wardwell advises Sabrina that they will need to perform an exorcism to save Susie's uncle, Jesse Putnam (Jason Beaudoin), who has been possessed by a demon for years and, until the events of this episode, has lain catatonic in the Putnam home. In the same episode, Sabrina asks Father Blackwood about exorcisms during a class within the Academy of Unseen Arts, to which Father Blackwood replies that exorcisms are traditionally done by the "false church which calls on the false God."[21] Nonetheless, Sabrina, Ms. Wardwell, and Hilda set out to perform the first exorcism led by witches. Sabrina calls out names such as Hecate, Artemis, and Luna (all names historically linked to witchcraft and/or occult activity). Zelda then arrives and promptly calls out to the female ancestors of the Spellman family. The exorcism spell they perform, which Sabrina's father (Edward Spellman) created, pulls power from the individual witch casting the exorcism as well as those she calls upon and cements exorcism as a practice of the Church of Night.

Furthermore, though Sabrina's coven gains their gift of power from the Dark Lord after signing his book, they later face issues after her real father is revealed to be Lucifer, not Edward Spellman. After Lucifer threatens them, the coven directs their prayers toward Lilith instead, and when they dethrone and imprison Lucifer, he takes away their power to punish them for their betrayal. In pursuit of a new power source in "Chapter Twenty-Eight: Sabrina Is Legend" (3:8), Zelda rediscovers Hecate in her time of need. Hecate, the Three-in-One, represents the Maiden, Mother, and Crone, which Zelda explains represents both the three phases of the moon and the three parts of a witch's life. When Hilda is unable to resurrect herself from the Cain Pit, as she usually does when killed and buried there, Zelda, surrounded by female witches in the coven, asks Hecate to provide them with "the powers that have been denied us."[22] After struggling with their power for so long, the coven becomes successful after they dedicate their worship to Hecate, and, in doing so, rebuke the patriarchal power structure of the Church of Night. These "powers that have been denied" and the witch's femininity and gender are steady figures in the series.

Similarly, Zelda holds up her femininity and heritage in her work as coven midwife, a role historically connected to accusations of witchcraft due to its proximity to and support of female reproductivity and sexuality and often a knowledge of herbal remedies. Traditionally, the witch "was a healer and practitioner of various forms of magic that made her popular in the community, but this increasingly signaled her as a danger."[23] Here, again, the series upends this view. Zelda is shown to be revered for her role as a midwife; in fact, Father Blackwood states that she has never lost a baby. However, as Blackwood's wife gives birth to twins—one girl and one boy—Zelda begins to fear what Blackwood might do to the girl based on his archaic, misogynistic ideologies. Zelda abducts the girl and lets Blackwood believe only the boy survived, setting herself up for a dangerous confrontation later in the series.

"THEY ALWAYS THINK I'M MEEK AND MILD": OTHER TYPES OF FEMALE POWER

Although Zelda is presented as a traditionalist, which may suggest that she upholds the same archaic beliefs regarding women, she does not. After Blackwood releases his new tenets of the Church of Judas (named after his surviving son and shown to be regressive, misogynistic, and limiting of the abilities and roles of the female witches within the coven), Zelda and the coven rise against Blackwood and his followers. This results in Zelda naming herself as the High Priestess and Directrix of the Academy, after which she immediately recruits her sister, Hilda, to oversee the curriculum.

Hilda Spellman offers a contrasting image to Zelda. We first see Hilda as a caregiver, serving a plate of food to Sabrina at breakfast while offering a remedy to help her sleep, and we continue to see this dynamic in the family. For example, in "Chapter One: October Country" (1:1), Hilda serves Sabrina and Ambrose food and drink while Zelda reads her paper at the table, drinking tea and smoking—an image that parallels television shows showcasing the nuclear family. In this case, it suggests that Zelda has taken on the role of the father, the head of the family, whilst Hilda takes on the role of the mother who builds their home. Paired with Hilda's kind and gentle nature, this image of Hilda is continually perpetuated throughout the series and their battles repeatedly depend on her "kitchen magic" prowess. For example, Hilda bakes a cake laced with a truth spell for Lady Constance Blackwood (Alvina August) to reveal her recent spells. Hilda also later bakes a cake to influence the thoughts of the witch council. However, despite Hilda's powers and capabilities, as shown when she manages the protection spell alone at Baxter High at the end of season one, she is still seen to be a maternal and homely character rather than a powerful matriarch like her sister. This is due to the portrayal of her abilities, which are shown to be primarily kitchen magics, identified as female-oriented witchcraft within the series, as opposed to male-oriented magics, such as conjuring.

With Hilda's talent for the more "homely" magics, such as calming balms and cleansing drinks, she seems almost harmless. However, as we see throughout the series, Hilda faces the opponents who threaten her family and doubt her skills with a vengeance that is unmatched and almost morbid in nature. An example of this is in "Chapter Twenty-Eight: Sabrina Is Legend" (3:8), when Hilda is cursed to become a human-sized spider by the Pagan witch Circe, later harming her partner, Dr. Cerberus (Alessandro Juliani). After recovering from her curse, Hilda then confronts Circe alone when the coven attacks the Pagan witches. Using a voodoo doll of Circe that she created herself, Hilda twists the Circe-doll to force Circe's actual limbs to twist. Hilda then says that she wants "to show [Circe] some of [her] other talents,"[24] and kills Circe with one final turn of the doll's neck. Circe's morbid death demonstrates the frustration Hilda has with people assuming who she is or what she is capable of, tying Hilda to the key trope within the female witch archetype: vengeance.

Vengeance is a theme throughout the series and is another example of how *CAoS* reflects the historical archetypes of the witch. A clear reference to this element can be found in the Weird Sisters, Prudence (Tati Gabrielle), Agatha (Adeline Rudolph), and Dorcas (Abigail Cowen)—witch orphans living at the Academy. In "Chapter Two: The Dark Baptism" (1:2), the Weird Sisters are summoned to support Sabrina and join in an act of vengeance against four mortal boys who had pulled up Theo (who, at the time, was still going by Susie) Putnam's shirt to see if they had breasts; at this point, Theo has not yet fully addressed the question of their gender identity in public or in private, but the suspicion of difference is enough for these bullies. In Theo's defense, the Weird Sisters and Sabrina use their sexuality to lure the boys into the Greendale mines and bewitch them into removing their clothes. The Weird Sisters take their vengeance further and remove the boys' "boyhood," stating that they will not be "rising to the occasion"[25] any time soon. With their "boyhoods" now presented in the form of birds in a cage, the boys will be impotent until the birds are released, and this act of vengeance results in a form of castration—an important component of this encounter, as it references a common fear steeped in the concept of the monstrous and female witches. While fears of witches historically included failed crops, sickness, the plague, and death, impotence and castration were held as a significant fear of witches' potential power, which categorized them as a female monster. Furthermore, as Barbara Creed suggests, there is a link between a "man's fear of woman to his infantile belief that the mother is castrated," which further demonizes witches.[26]

The use of castration within *CAoS*, as well as other key signifiers of and tropes related to witchcraft—such as cursing humans, performing glamours, summoning familiars, and bewitching men—all point to the historical archetypes of witches, even as much of the narrative attempts to move past them. The well-known images that we now associate with witches, even a hundred years after the first on-screen representation, have become so embedded into Western society that modern, revised depictions ultimately do not stray too far from those historical conventions for fear they may no longer be associated with what audiences believe possible and natural in these stories. With the revised witches presented within *CAoS*, contemporary viewers can relate to the characters on-screen through its modernized take on the image of the witch while still seeing aspects of earlier representations that feel more familiar. *CAoS* presents these witches—who were historically shown to be monsters and were continually misunderstood—as progressive, inclusive characters in its world, providing a useful revision of the witch in comparison to historical approaches to these characters.

The diverse images of the witch are a key narrative device within *Chilling Adventures of Sabrina*, and despite existing in a world where witches and magic exist, the witch's gender is still a significant factor regarding their treatment and level of respect from certain circles. However, this is not the case for the female witches in the series. These women are aware of the various images and roles traditionally attached to witches and the ways in which they are helpful or harmful to them. The witches' journey in questioning their worship of the Dark Lord—and later Lilith, followed by Hecate—highlights their need for a source of power that reflects themselves in their perceived identity as female witches. Concluding their exploration by worshipping Hecate—the three-part goddess who represents the three phases of a witch's life—speaks to the various identities of witches presented within *CAoS* and is a stark contrast to the coven's previous male-dominated patriarchy.

The witches in *Chilling Adventures of Sabrina* reflect the traditional arche-types of the witch but have revised them to suit current societal views and the modern audience. This enables contemporary audiences, particularly those who are new to the genre, to recognize the witch archetype based on their preconceived image of a witch from childhood tales and/or previous media yet remain comfortable with its deployment, because although the witches of *Chilling Adventures of Sabrina* still fit those historical stereotypes—such as worshipping the Devil, curses, glamours, and human sacrifices—the series provides further context. These witches are not just women captivated by the Devil and made to sign his book for power, beauty, or vengeance. They are complex women with individual desires who have been able to meet their needs through their decision to become a witch and their subsequent varied types of practice. As demonstrated by the opposing images of Sabrina's aunts and the Weird Sisters, the image of the witch is not static. The witches of *CAoS* pay homage to traditional tropes of the archetype, particularly that of vengeance. With centuries of folklore, literature, and now on-screen depic-tions of the archetype, creating an entirely new image of the witch may be too far removed from audiences' expectations and genre-based understandings of the female monster. Instead, as *Chilling Adventures of Sabrina* has done, it may be enough to adapt the image to suit the needs of different genres and, in doing so, provide multi-layered characters that supersede the potentially misleading label of "witch."

BIBLIOGRAPHY

Baxstrom, Richard, and Meyers, Todd. *Realizing the Witch: Science, Cinema, and the Mastery of the Invisible*. New York: Fordham University Press, 2015.

Berger, Helen, and Ezzy, Douglas. "Mass Media and Religious Identity: A Case Study of Young Witches," *Journal for the Scientific Study of Religion* 48, no. 3 (September 2009): 501–508. doi.org/10.1111/j.1468-5906.2009.01462.x

Chilling Adventures of Sabrina, Season 1, episode 1, "Chapter One: October Country." Directed by Lee Toland Krieger, written by Roberto Aguirre-Sacasa, featuring Kiernan Shipka, Miranda Otto, Lucy Davis, and Chance Perdomo. Released October 26, 2018, Netflix, www.netflix.com/watch/80230071?trackID =200257859.

———, Season 1, episode 2, "Chapter Two: The Dark Baptism." Directed by Lee Toland Krieger, written by Roberto Aguirre-Sacasa, featuring Kiernan Shipka, Miranda Otto, Lucy Davis, and Richard Coyle. Released October 26, 2018, Netflix, www.netflix.com/watch/80230072?trackId=200257859.

———, Season 1, episode 6, "Chapter Six: An Exorcism in Greendale." Directed by Rachel Talalay, written by Joshua Conkel and MJ Kaufman, featuring Kiernan

Shipka, Miranda Otto, Lucy Davis, and Michelle Gomez. Released October 26, 2018, Netflix, www.netflix.com/watch/80230072?trackId=200257859.

———, Season 2, episode 3, "Chapter Fourteen: Lupercalia." Directed by Salli Richardson-Whitfield, written by Oanh Ly, featuring Kiernan Shipka, Miranda Otto, Lucy Davis, and Gavin Leatherwood. Released April 5, 2019, Netflix, www.netflix.com/watch/80230072?trackId=200257859.

———, Season 3, episode 8. "Chapter Twenty-Eight: Sabrina Is Legend." Directed by Rob Seidenglanz, written by Roberto Aguirre-Sacasa and Daniel King, featuring Kiernan Shipka, Miranda Otto, Lucy Davis, and Sam Corlett. Released January 24, 2020, Netflix, www.netflix.com/watch/81062659?trackId=200257859.

Creed, Barbara. *The Monstrous-Feminine: Film, Feminism, Psychoanalysis*. London: Routledge, 1993.

Elmer, Peter. *Witchcraft, Witch-hunting, and Politics in Early Modern England*. Oxford: Oxford University Press, 2016.

Erikson, Sarah E., Dal Cin, Sonya, and Byl, Hannah. "An Experimental Examination of Binge Watching and Narrative Engagement," *Social Sciences* 8, no. 1: 19 (January 2019): 2–9. doi.org/10.3390/socsci8010019.

Federici, Silvia. *Witches, Witch-Hunting, and Women*. Oakland, CA: PM Press, 2018.

Freeland, Cynthia. *The Naked and the Undead*. Oxford: Westview Press, 2000.

Green, Melanie. C., and Brock, Timothy C. "The Role of Transportation in the Persuasiveness of Public Narratives," *Journal of Personality and Social Psychology*, 79, no. 5 (November 2000): 701–21.

Krzywinska, Tanya. *A Skin for Dancing in: Possession, Witchcraft and Voodoo in Film*. Trowbridge, UK: Flicks Books, 2000.

Mackay, Christopher, and Institoris, Heinrich. *The Hammer of Witches*. Cambridge: Cambridge University Press, 2014.

Mallan, Kerry M. "Witches, Bitches, and *Femmes Fatales*: Viewing the Female Grotesque in Children's Film," *Papers*: *Explorations into Children's Literature* 10, no. 1 (April 2000): 26–35.

Roper, Lyndal. "'Evil Imaginings and Fantasies': Child-Witches and the End of the Witch Craze," *Past & Present* 167 (May 2000): 107–39.

Snider, Zachary. "The Cognitive Psychological Effects of Binge-Watching," in *The Netflix Effect: Technology and Entertainment in the 21st Century,* edited by Kevin McDonald and Daniel Smith-Rowsey, 117–28. New York: Bloomsbury, 2016.

Wells, Paul. *The Horror Genre: from Beelzebub to Blair Witch*. London: Wallflower. 2004.

NOTES

1. Melanie C. Green and Timothy C. Brock, "The Role of Transportation in the Persuasiveness of Public Narratives," *Journal of Personality and Social Psychology* 79, no. 5 (2000): 700.

2. Sarah E. Erikson, Sonya Dal Cin, and Hannah Byl, "An Experimental Examination of Binge Watching and Narrative Engagement," *Social Sciences* 8, no. 1 (2019): 3. doi.org/10.3390/socsci8010019.

3. Zachary Sider, "The Cognitive Psychological Effects of Binge-Watching," in *The Netflix Effect: Technology and Entertainment in the 21st Century*, eds. Kevin McDonald and Daniel Smith-Rowsey (New York: Bloomsbury, 2016), 123.

4. Paul Wells, *The Horror Genre: from Beelzebub to Blair Witch* (London: Wallflower, 2004), 3.

5. Peter Elmer, *Witchcraft, Witch-hunting, and Politics in Early Modern England* (Oxford: Oxford University Press, 2016), 16.

6. Helen Berger and Douglas Ezzy, "Mass Media and Religious Identity: A Case Study of Young Witches," *Journal for the Scientific Study of Religion* 48, no. 3 (September 2009): 509. doi.org/10.1111/j.1468-5906.2009.01462.

7. Cynthia Freeland, *The Naked and the Undead* (Oxford: Westview Press, 2000), 273.

8. Barbara Creed, *The Monstrous-Feminine: Film, Feminism, Psychoanalysis* (London: Routledge, 1997), 76.

9. Mallan, Kerry M., "Witches, Bitches, and Femmes Fatales: Viewing the Female Grotesque in Children's Film," *Papers: Explorations into Children's Literature,* 10, no. 7 (April 2000): 1.

10. Creed, *The Monstrous-Feminine*, 2.

11. Tanya Krzywinska, *A Skin for Dancing In: Possession, Witchcraft and Voodoo in Film* (Trowbridge, UK: Flicks Books, 2000), 8.

12. Lyndal Roper, "'Evil Imaginings and Fantasies': Child-Witches and the End of the Witch Craze," *Past & Present* 167 (May 2000): 123.

13. Tanya Krzywinska, *A Skin for Dancing In*, 117.

14. Berger and Ezzy, "Mass Media and Religious Identity," 502.

15. Berger and Ezzy, "Mass Media and Religious Identity," 501.

16. Berger and Ezzy, "Mass Media and Religious Identity," 502.

17. Berger and Ezzy, "Mass Media and Religious Identity," 501.

18. *Chilling Adventures of Sabrina*, season 1, episode 1, "Chapter One: October Country," written by Roberto Aguirre-Sacasa, directed by Lee Toland Krieger, 2018, Netflix, 00:42:00.

19. *Chilling Adventures of Sabrina*, season 2, episode 3, "Chapter Fourteen: Lupercalia," written by Oanh Ly, directed by Salli Richardson-Whitfield, 2019, Netflix, 00:03:03.

20. Creed, *The Monstrous-Feminine*, 74.

21. *Chilling Adventures of Sabrina*, season 1, episode 6, "Chapter Six: An Exorcism in Greendale," written by Joshua Conkel and MJ Kaufman, directed by Rachel Talalay, 2018, Netflix, 00:29:15.

22. *Chilling Adventures of Sabrina*, season 3, episode 8, "Chapter Twenty-Eight: Sabrina Is Legend," directed by Rob Seidenglanz, written by Roberto Aguirre-Sacasa and Daniel King, featuring Kiernan Shipka, Miranda Otto, Lucy Davis, and Sam Corlett, released January 24, 2020, on Netflix, www.netflix.com/watch/81062659?trackId=200257859: 00:26:22.

23. Silvia Federici, *Witches, Witch-Hunting, and Women* (Oakland, CA: PM Press, 2018), 20.

24. *Chilling Adventures of Sabrina*, season 3, episode 8, "Chapter Twenty-Eight: Sabrina Is Legend": 00:37:50.

25. *Chilling Adventures of Sabrina*, season 1, episode 2, "Chapter Two: The Dark Baptism," directed by Lee Toland Krieger, written by Roberto Aguirre-Sacasa, featuring Kiernan Shipka, Miranda Otto, Lucy Davis, and Richard Coyle, released October 26, 2018, on Netflix, www.netflix.com/watch/80230072?trackId=200257859: 00:24:00.

26. Creed, *The Monstrous-Feminine*, 1.

Chapter 2

The Inclusive Witch in *Chilling Adventures of Sabrina*

Diana Celeste Etain and Cori Mathis

No word inspires alarm and intrigue quite like "witch." Witches can heal or hex, and their motives remain elusive and sinister to those who fear them. Surprisingly, the modern-day spiritual movements that have adopted the term and the individuals who have deemed themselves witches have no singular, widely accepted definition for the descriptor. *Chilling Adventures of Sabrina* (Netflix, 2018–20) explores the breadth of connotations associated with "witch" by seemingly reinforcing but ultimately deconstructing and reframing the negative stereotypes associated with it. Throughout the series, the portrayal of witches associates the term with empowerment and inclusivity, and in this way, *Chilling Adventures of Sabrina* (*CAoS*) emphasizes the importance of moving towards social justice, primarily by using Sabrina's experiences as witch-mortal hybrid to stress how prejudices and preconceptions act as obstacles to progress and the creation of an equitable culture of belonging. However, Sabrina's lack of acceptance of her half-mortal, half-witch nature highlights a key tension between historical and largely patriarchal views of witches and the present-day feminist portrayal of the witch as a symbol for empowerment.

MIRRORING THE HISTORICAL WITCH IMAGE

Historians of witchcraft and its surrounding beliefs have long established that the early modern period marked a significant change in perspectives regarding witches and that witches and witchcraft during this time should not be equated with what the terms meant in the ancient world.[1] Early Christian theologians had not provided a positive view of what was typically termed "sorcery," especially considering its representation in the Old Testament. However, as scholars have often pointed out, the translation of Exodus 22:18 and 1 Samuel 28:1–25 shifts throughout history, but the Old Testament pulls from ancient perspectives on witchcraft; these people saw the practice as having a multiplicity of approaches, only some of which were deliberately harmful to others or attempted to usurp divine authority over life and death and were therefore condemned. The use of the word "witch" in the King James Version, for example, eliminates the nuance found in the original Hebrew, which can be interpreted in more than one way and points to a concern with the intention and impact of spellcasting: evil intentions, necromancy, etc.[2] As Laura Apps and Andrew Gow explain, this imperfect translation simply topped off a slowly developing theological trend: "the night-flying witch who made a pact with the Devil and worshipped him in exchange for supernatural powers was a learned, cumulative construct that developed over centuries of Christian demonisation [*sic*] of heretics and sorcerers."[3] The increasing acceptance of a definition of all witchcraft as evil and demonic led to the witch trials of the early modern period and gave rise to the Satanic image of the witch that lingers in our contemporary collective consciousness—one that can primarily be located in a medieval witch-hunting manual.

1486's *Malleus Malificarum* (or *The Hammer of the Witches*) offers a perspective on witches and witchcraft that still resonates today. In this treatise, Dominican monk and Inquisitor Heinrich Kramer, who published the work under his Latinized name, Henricus Institoris, argues that the witches of his period—and, arguably, all witches throughout time—are Satanic allies who devote themselves to plaguing godly souls and communities. Kramer also discusses witches' rituals and practices, noting that they make a "ceremonial vow" to "renounce the Most Christian Faith and Worship." In addition to this promise, they are asked "to turn any other people, of both sexes, into the demon's associates."[4] Throughout the *Malleus Maleficarum*, Kramer works hard to eliminate any visions of witches as wise women and conflates Paganism with Satanism, tying witches so closely to devil worship that the image persists to this day.

While *Chilling Adventures of Sabrina* is clear that Paganism and Satanism are not interchangeable, the series does attach to its protagonist a number of the practices Kramer details. Because the Spellmans, along with their coven, are acolytes of Satan (Luke Cook)—also known as Lucifer, or the Dark Lord—in *CAoS*'s mythology, the demonic baptism Kramer describes plays out in the first season of the series. In "Chapter Two: The Dark Baptism" (1:2), Sabrina Spellman (Kiernan Shipka) is faced with her dreaded Dark Baptism. She enters the woods at midnight for the ritual and is asked to sign her name with her own blood in the Dark Lord's *Book of the Beast*, thus committing herself to him and the Church of Night. However, Sabrina hesitates when she learns that inherent in signing the book is the agreement that her soul will belong to the Dark Lord and that she will be required to serve him. Sabrina sees her deceased mother beckoning her to leave, and she defies Father Faustus Blackwood's (Richard Coyle) increasingly urgent commands to sign the book, asserting: "There is another path for me, just as there was for my father and mother. A third way. And even if there isn't, my name is Sabrina Spellman, and I will *not* sign it away!"[5] In rejecting her destined Dark Baptism, Sabrina is able to keep her autonomy and soul intact, and through her questioning of the requirements attached to the ritual, the Satanic, patriarchal witch society in which Sabrina lives begins to unravel. Clearly, the elements of the Dark Baptism align with the Satanic imagery that led to fear-mongering and witch burnings in the Middle Ages, which establishes a tension between the otherwise progressive messages promoted by the series and expected by its target audience, millennial and Gen Z young adults who have grown up with positive representations of the witch. However, a look back at the experiences of just a generation before reveals a likely influence on this choice.

Our contemporary version of the Satanic, evil witch comes from the Satanic Panic of the 1970s and 1980s. In his study of the moral panic over fantasy role-playing games, Joseph Laycock describes the social unease related to anything deemed "occult" during the 1980s and the assertions of the prominent anti-occult activist Patricia A. Pulling. After her son Irving died by suicide, Pulling claimed that a curse received during his *Dungeons and Dragons* roleplay was to blame and founded an organization known as B.A.D.D. (Bothered About *Dungeons and Dragons*), to combat its popularity. However, her time as a respected moral leader was relatively short, as Laycock explains:

> Pulling's authority as an expert was finally challenged in 1989, when she announced that approximately 8 percent of the population of Richmond was "involved with Satanic worship at some level." A reporter questioned this statistic, pointing out that 8 percent of the population equaled 56,000 people. This meant that Richmond was home to more Satanists than Methodists. Pulling responded that her figure concerned not just Satanists but also "occultists," including New Agers, witches, and others.[6]

Pulling's assertions reflect the fear-mongering of her day. All occultists, witches, and New Agers alike, were in league with the Devil. Satanists were everywhere, and they wanted to entice your children to the dark side. B.A.D.D. also distributed pamphlets warning of dangerous Satanic influences in communities across America. One pamphlet titled "Dungeons and

Dragons—Witchcraft Suicide Violence" details the concerns expressed by the group and argues that "we cannot afford to overlook a 'game' that teaches witchcraft, Satan worship [,] and a cult-like religion [,] not to mention specific suicide phrases."[7] To B.A.D.D., witchcraft was inherently Satanic in nature and found in seemingly innocuous cultural products like *Dungeons and Dragons*. Even worse, it was not just the game which promoted the occult in American life, the group asserted: witchcraft received governmental recognition as a religion, making it even more insidious. B.A.D.D.'s position that *Dungeons and Dragons* was a medium for teaching the ideals of a religion that was against Christianity—a position that reflects B.A.D.D.'s connections to the fundamentalist, right-wing worldview of the Religious Right—rang true to many Americans.

The notion that society, particularly the government, grants witchcraft the same protections as other faiths troubled B.A.D.D., and they described fantasy as a tool for the dissemination of the occult practices which they believed increased the risks of suicide in the young people who played it.[8] The assumption that fantasy found in gameplay is one reason why youth attempt suicide was a direct way of advocating for the conformist thought developed and promoted in right-wing circles, and this perspective survives today, especially among many conservative Christian groups—the later furor over *Harry Potter* was another version of this outcry from B.A.D.D. and its supporters. However, a more nuanced analysis shows that fantasy allows individuals to find creative ways of expressing themselves and solving problems, and an excess of creativity and critical thinking poses a direct challenge to those fundamentalist beliefs which rely on limiting dissent and differing opinions. B.A.D.D.'s choice to create pamphlets to perpetuate their close-minded ideology stresses their dedication to spreading their views throughout America. The pamphlets are quick reads—generally less than fifty pages—and sensational language, including the repeated use of "witchcraft," "violence," and "suicide," drew attention. At the time, the pamphlets appeared to be credible sources of information, despite their provocative language and ludicrous claims, and it is easy to see how they influenced readers to believe that something as mundane as a role-playing game was contributing to larger societal issues. Because of the continued pervasiveness of this rhetoric in conservative circles, especially the Religious Right, anything involving magic or witches is more likely to be identified as Satanic and harmful.

In many ways, *Chilling Adventures of Sabrina* affirms the conservative view that associates the witch with demonic forces. For example, Sabrina's aunt Zelda Spellman (Miranda Otto) is particularly renowned for her dedication to the Dark Lord. In "Chapter Two: The Dark Baptism" (1:2), Zelda tells Sabrina to stay to home from school and read her Satanic Bible to prepare for her Dark Baptism. It is clear that Zelda wants Sabrina to follow the doctrine of the Church of Night and give herself to the Dark Lord through the sign-ing of her name in his book. The act of giving oneself over to the Dark Lord in exchange for power is reminiscent of B.A.D.D.'s claims. Though signing one's name in the *Book of the Beast* appears on the surface to be a medium for gaining power and autonomy in one's life, it is, as Sabrina intuits and Father Blackwood confirms, actually the first step in relinquishing one's agency to the Devil. The power gained from the Dark Baptism is not an activation of earth-connected, positive magic but instead comes from a demonic source that is invited to interfere in the witch's life in perpetuity once she completes the ceremony. Additionally, the imagery is not just evocative, it is jarring and gory: blood spills over an altar in the barely moonlit woods, with the members of the Church of Night primarily dressed in black while Sabrina wears white, as if she were a virginal sacrifice from a different time, her innocence given away for the wants and needs of men and under ecclesiastical constraints that benefit everyone but her. Father Blackwood's insistence that Sabrina sign her name goes far beyond a recommendation from a member of the clergy; he leads the Church of Night members to chase after Sabrina when she runs from the altar and refuses to sign her name. In this scene that exemplifies the patriarchal nature of and leadership structure initially found in the Church of Night at the beginning of the series, Blackwood is quite literally chasing after to Sabrina in an effort to control her. The fact that Sabrina is able to escape after Blackwood feels threatened foreshadows the eventual feminist turn of the series, which begins in earnest with a particularly appropriate storyline toward the end of the first season—one that reveals that the misogyny in the Church of Night is even worse than it first appears.

Despite witches typically being understood by modern viewers as a femi-nist symbol, the Church of Night does not have many women in leadership roles as *Chilling Adventures of Sabrina* opens; in fact, their default belief is that men in the coven should occupy those positions over women, no mat-ter who might be more suited to the role or more competent overall. Father Blackwood, as High Priest of the Church of Night, works hard to reinforce this belief, especially in his own home. In "Chapter Ten: The Witching Hour" (1:10), Lady Blackwood (Alvina August) gives birth to twins, a girl and a boy. Aware of the girl's likely future with her father—especially as she is technically the heir, having been born first—Zelda tells Blackwood that the twin boys he expected has become only one son, spinning a story wherein the surviving twin, Judas, was so strong even in utero that he overpowered and absorbed his brother. Blackwood is thrilled to hear this, and his distraction allows Zelda to smuggle the girl away. Blackwood's daughter—whom Zelda names Letitia but who is later renamed Judith when her father discovers her existence—would have been an inappropriate successor in Blackwood's perspective simply due to her gender. His expectation is that Judas will lead the Church of Night into a new, increasingly patriarchal era where women witches will live in subjugation to the men in the church; he calls upon Prudence Night (Tati Gabrielle), his secret daughter from a previous relationship, to care for Judas and reinforce Blackwood's teachings. Additionally, he plans to marry Judith to her twin, thereby keeping the Blackwood bloodline pure. Blackwood's insistence on positioning women as pawns in his master plan rather than autonomous beings is a major component of his character; his victims likely cannot be numbered, but the series revisits his crimes against his wife and daughters often, especially as his misogyny becomes more and more blatant.

NEGOTIATING DIAMETRICALLY OPPOSED IDEOLOGIES

The same episode that sees the Blackwood twins' birth features Lilith (Michelle Gomez)—also known as Madam Satan and currently occupying the body of Sabrina's teacher Mary Wardwell—as the narrator of sorts, offering the story of some especially significant and recent events to an initially unseen listener. At the end of her tale, she explains just who she really is to her captive audience, detailing her plans for Sabrina and declaring that is she is the "future Queen of Hell."[9] The presence of Lilith in the series helps build the groundwork for the pro-feminist stance that series later takes. In her article "Lilith," Chani Nicholas gives context regarding and insight into cultural and historical representations of Lilith, asserting: "[Lilith] has been used by the patriarchy to exemplify the punishment dealt out to any woman who is autonomous and awakened to their female sexual power. Jungians call her our unincorporated female *shadow* for she, and figures like her, becomes a basin for humanity to deposit our collective fears of the dark."[10] Lilith's portrayal in *CAoS* most certainly embodies those patriarchal fears. In "Chapter Five: Dreams in a Witch House" (1:5), Lilith is revealed to be the mother of all demons, which means she has a number of terrifying powers through her connections to them. She is able to see through the mirrors in the Spellman's mortuary and enters Sabrina's dream—a nightmare from one of her demonic children. Like the feared, so-called demonic witches in history, Lilith has powers that give her the ability to see what would be otherwise unknown to her. She can influence and communicate with others through the incorporeal realm of dreams, just as witches were accused of meeting for the Black Sabbath in the astral realm. Lilith is ever-present, even when Sabrina herself is unaware of Lilith's presence. Initially, she does not appear to be an ally to or at all involved with the feminist cause, as Lilith's purpose during the first season is to use her power to fulfill the Dark Lord's will by convincing

Sabrina to sign away her soul and free will to him. However, the more the series diverges from the image of the Satanic witch, so do Lilith's motivations, and her characterization grows ever more complex as she confronts the realities of her relationship with Lucifer and the effect it has had on her.

Societal fears of powerful women and witches are also evident in the characterization of Sabrina's friend Rosalind "Roz" Walker (Jaz Sinclair). A key plot point of *CAoS* is Roz's medical condition that will eventually cause blindness. In "Chapter Seven: Feast of Feasts" (1:7), Roz visits her grandmother, Ruth Walker (L. Scott Caldwell)—who is blind due to the same condition—to ask her about their family history for a project Ms. Wardwell has assigned, and Nana Ruth explains that there is more to their illness than genetics: "Generations ago, our kin accused a woman of being a witch. The other witches in Greendale, they cursed us Walker women with blindness. [. . .] I don't know if being cursed gave us the Cunning or it simply brought out what was already there. But I do know, you will lose your vision. But with the Cunning, you'll be able to see things that others cannot. And that will save your life."[11] Historically, the term "Cunning" is free from the religious connotations inherent in the word "witch," thus allowing those who associated themselves with the former term but would normally be considered witches to avoid the danger inherent in that label.[12] In aligning the Walker women and their progressive, open perspectives with the cunning folk, *CAoS* establishes a variety of ways to practice witchcraft and brings into sharp relief the deficiencies and prejudices found in the Church of Night.

Roz's grandmother suggests that the Cunning is the ability to see the world in a way that is unbridled by cultural expectations or preconceptions. For example, in "Chapter Seventeen: The Missionaries" (2:6), the Order of the Innocents, a group of angelic—presumably Christian—witch-hunters, comes to Greendale with the goal of killing all of the witches in the Church of Night. One of them, Jerathmiel (Spencer Treat Clark), poses as a missionary and visits Sabrina at the Spellman Mortuary; at the same time, Roz's Cunning warns her of Jerathmiel's intent to kill Sabrina, who seems oblivious to the threat the angel poses to her. Roz quickly calls Sabrina, who ultimately lives due to Roz's Cunning. Notably, the Cunning does not show a bias against Sabrina for effectively being a Satanist, nor does it show a preference for the Christian missionary/angel. The Cunning appears to show what will happen to those Roz is close with, regardless of the belief system or faith tradition of those involved in her visions. Significantly, the Cunning appears at the onset of blindness, thus establishing a direct correlation between the ability and the metaphorical eye, which in this context is understood to be a higher, or spiritual level of perception.[13] Roz's Cunning is excellent example of the metaphorical eye because it shows her visions that contain information that goes beyond what she should be able to gain through the five senses all humans typically possess.

Eventually, the Cunning is confirmed to be another term for "witch" in the diegesis of *Chilling Adventures of Sabrina*. In "Chapter Thirty-One: The Weird" (4:3), Roz's grandmother—now in spirit form after her death—visits Roz and explains that the Walker women only used the word "Cunning" to separate themselves from the stigma associated with the word "witch," reflecting the traditional real-life reasoning for favoring one over the other: the belief that Christians could not also be witches because that would align them with the Devil. Historian James W. Baker gives insight into this distinction, noting: "[p]ublic opinion on the Cunningfolk [*sic*] was ambiguous to say the least. [. . .] Cunning women, wise men, blessers, conjurors, and currens (a few of the many names for white witches[14]) were regularly veiled from the pulpit and secretly supported by the populace."[15] Just as the Cunning is not partial to any one demographic, the cunning folk are perceived as neutral. The ambiguous nature of their abilities meant that they could blend into Christian society more readily than the perceived demonic witches, even if some of their talents were more obviously contrary to the widely accepted version of the faith.

The Walker women have long negotiated a tension between their Christian practice and magical abilities; from what the series reveals, the Walkers belong to the evangelical tradition, which typically denounces all types of psychic ability as demonic, since knowledge of the future belongs solely to God. As such, Roz must carve a new path for herself, integrating the complexities of her lived experience with what she has been taught to believe when the precognitive nature of the Cunning becomes increasingly evident. In "Chapter Thirty-One: The Weird" (4:3), Roz is classified as a "seer" alongside her new status as a witch. The *Malleus Maleficarum* gives clear information regarding seers or "diviners":

> The varieties of the first kind of divination, the one that takes place through the explicit invocation of demons, are conjuring, divination by dreams, divination by the dead, Pythian divination, divination by earth, divination by water, divination by air, divination by fire and the religious practice of soothsayers. Next, the varieties of the second kind are horoscope casters, haruspices, augurs, omen watchers, diviners by hand and diviners by shoulder bone. [. . .] Finally, the third variety [. . .] is called the divination of dreams. (242–44)

This absorption of precognition into witchcraft as a whole alongside the typically harsh cultural view of both witches and diviners places the Christian Roz in a precarious situation. The women of her family had used the word Cunning with the goal of avoiding the stigma and persecution of witches that may have been caused, at least in part, by the vivid descriptions found in the *Malleus Maleficarum* and other portrayals of evil witches. Now, Roz must reconcile her family's Christian beliefs with the undeniable fact that she is a witch—and a hereditary one at that—and is left to question her worldview and preconceptions surrounding the term "witch."

While Roz struggles with her newfound understanding of her connection to witchcraft, she begins to move toward a place of self-determination. Her inherited Cunning power is not one that she consciously pursues or asks for; instead, the Cunning appears alongside her vision loss as an extra obstacle for her to overcome. Rather than ignore this challenge, Roz decides to embrace the Cunning, determining for herself how it will influence her choices and her connection to her witch ancestry, which adds new depth to her character. By framing Roz as the first Walker woman who gets to live openly as a witch, *Chilling Adventures of Sabrina* gestures to the idea of healing generational wounds caused by societal oppression through unashamedly embracing one's diverse heritage and makes Roz's character a symbol of progress within the series.

EMBRACING THE DARK MOTHER— AND PROGRESSIVISM

By the end of the twentieth century, popular culture at large no longer saw witches as necessarily tied to the Devil's service, though the idea has certainly not died out. However, more people are aware that the idea that witches are handmaids of Satan and thus inherently evil is a patriarchal misconception that took root during the early modern period due to the popularity of the *Malleus Maleficarum* in Christian Europe. Fewer might understand what witches would worship instead, and *Chilling Adventures of Sabrina* attempts to provide some possible answers to that question in the last half of the series. In "Chapter Thirty-One: The Weird" (4:3), the Plague Kings—higher-level demons who have been attempting to dethrone and even kill Sabrina in an attempt to keep a half-witch from ruling Hell—come after Lilith and her child, in this case finding the illegitimacy of the baby a disqualification to sit on the throne of Hell. In their stand against the Plague Kings, the witches are adamant that their power no longer stems from the Dark Lord. Instead, Zelda calls on the goddess Hecate, the Dark Mother and the Three-in-One, to protect Lilith as she gives birth to her son, asking Hecate to let the small group of witches assembled around Lilith share her pain. When the Plague Kings arrive to take the baby back to Caliban—the Prince of Hell and hus-band of Sabrina Morningstar, a time paradox copy of Sabrina Spellman who is ruling Hell in her place to allow Sabrina to stay on Earth—the witches rise up, calling down Hecate's power to defeat them and once and for all breaking with Lucifer and the Church of Night. The message of this scene is clear—the witches of Greendale will no longer bend to the misogyny of Lucifer and his acolytes or subscribe to the destructive ideologies that have haunted the image of the witch for centuries. In taking a stance against the Dark Lord and choosing instead to embrace the Dark Mother, the witches are reclaiming their own autonomy. The cathartic anger they send to the Plague Kings for the sake of protecting Lilith symbolizes a new, deeply feminist way to celebrate their power as independent women and witches.

The Church of Night, especially under the rule of Father Faustus Blackwood, is strictly and toxically patriarchal. For the women witches who suffered under this system, belonging to a new belief and power structure that does not view them as lesser than men gives them the freedom to question and upend the existing top-down hierarchy and poisonous values of the Church of Night. They begin this deconstruction through protecting Lilith, the first witch and one who internalized those values so deeply that she originally appears in the narrative to tempt Sabrina down the Path of Night, thus cementing Lucifer's plans for his daughter and shoring up his abusive leadership in Hell. In many ways, this Lilith recalls the one of Jewish tradition, who was made for Adam first, before Eve, but left Adam when he attempted to make her submit and later married Samael—the personal name for Satan in many Judeo-Christian perspectives—and became the mother of demons.[16] Madam Satan, despite her moniker, deeply resents Lucifer for his insistence on her submission and ultimately rebels by helping Sabrina reject her father's plans for her life, leading to a slowly increasing level of alliance with the Greendale witches. In "Chapter Thirty-One: The Weird" (4:3), Lilith gives birth to Adam and is immediately protected by the witches, cementing their bond; no longer enemies, they provide her comfort and support, even when she kills her son to save him from Lucifer's influence. Creating a new normal that subverts cultural ideologies and imaginings in favor of a more inclusive environment mirrors the modern-day witchcraft movement.

Discussing the diversity of modern-day witchcraft, Titus Hjelm explains that "[e]specially after the 1980s, there has been an increased eclecticism in witchcraft, with a growing number of groups and individuals calling themselves witches and Wiccans, but ignoring most of the pioneers' teachings or combining them with other contemporary Pagan beliefs and practices."[17] The practice of witchcraft and the spiritual or religious beliefs that may accompany it are diverse. Likewise, the earlier-discussed revelation that Sabrina's mortal—and now psychic—friend Roz is actually a witch from a Christian background calls into question what it really means to identify as a "witch." The series includes Satanic witches, Pagan witches, Christian witches, and Vodou practitioners; the sheer number of spiritual movements and established traditions that identify with the term "witch" makes it nearly impossible to limit its use to only one, turning the witch identity into one of individuality and diversity rather than a monolith—each witch gets to decide what it means to them. Unlike the days when all witches supposedly met on the Black Sabbath to worship the Devil and tempt the innocent, the witches in the series can choose to protect the innocent from harm or advocate for social change, and with the formation of the Order of Hecate and the rise of Sabrina Spellman, they are encouraged to do so. In their book *Dead Blondes and Bad Mothers: Monstrosity, Patriarchy, and the Fear of Female Power*, Jude Ellison Sady Doyle asserts that "[w]itchcraft is not just a *form* of power for these girls, it's more or less the only power they have; magic is the voice of the marginalized responding to their oppression."[18] To this end, Sabrina uses her status as a powerful witch to enact social changes in both her mundane and mystical lives. This reality threatens the patriarchal status quo of the series, creating division between those who embrace these changes and those who want to further restrict the power of those who challenge it.

Essentially, *Chilling Adventures of Sabrina* can be read as a vessel through which the cultural stereotypes of witchcraft and even women themselves are examined and challenged. The patriarchal and Satanic start of the series, while jarring, is the first way that the series undermines the toxic historical claims regarding the witch. If the vivid, over-the-top imagery and depiction of witches' lives as one long, sometimes melodramatic pursuit of justice—primarily among themselves—helps to unravel the cultural image of Satanic witches of years past, then the question remains: What does it mean to be a witch according to *Chilling Adventures of Sabrina*? While it is undeniable that the series stresses that the answer to this question is determined by the individual, Sabrina's development as the titular character of the series provides a plethora of examples that can provide further insight.

Sabrina often uses her powers to help her friends, but these are no ordinary favors. Though she sometimes struggles with unexpected outcomes of her spells and charms in the beginning of the series, overall, her interventions with her friends typically work out in the end, but they tend to come with personal consequences. In fact, considering the ways in which the series positions Sabrina as a savior through her continued fight for justice and true kindness of spirit—not to mention the ultimate ending of the series—her actions can be read another way. Notably, in "Chapter Eighteen: The Miracles of Sabrina Spellman" (2:7), she cures Roz of her blindness. This act is not just a display of Sabrina's powerful witch nature; it can also be read as Sabrina-the-Christ-figure helping the blind to see. However, it is Sabrina's actions in the series finale that make the most definitive statement about her place in the universe and her feelings toward the others in it. In "Chapter Thirty-Six:

At the Mountains of Madness" (4:8), Sabrina sacrifices herself to save not only Greendale but the entire world from the Void, the final Eldritch Terror, which is on the path to consume the celestial, earthly, and infernal realms. In the group's initial attempt to stop the Void, Sabrina accidentally takes some of it in, later absorbing some foes in battle, including Caliban and a demon-possessed Mr. Kinkle (Christopher Rosamond). Fearful of who she might take next due to her lack of control of the Void's primordial powers, Sabrina teleports herself to the Mountains of Madness, an unholy place in the earthly realm where she eventually runs into Father Blackwood, who initially released the Eldritch Terrors and plans to see it through to the end. Realizing that there is no way to rescue the people absorbed by the Void and stop Blackwood's intended ritual to bring the Void into himself at the same time, Sabrina sacrifices herself, reinforcing her savior role in the series. After her death, Sabrina is last seen in the Sweet Hereafter, an afterlife comprised of a white room with three enormous paintings and a viewing bench, where she peacefully rests until Nick arrives, having died by suicide in order to be with her again. Ultimately, Sabrina is resurrected in the *Riverdale* universe, serving a similar, though supporting, function for Archie Andrews and his friends. *Chilling Adventures of Sabrina*'s culmination in Sabrina's death and reward reinforces the series' eventual move toward defining a witch as someone who uses their magical knowledge and gifts to act in the best interest of others. In this quiet scene, *CAoS* completes the turn away from the dark, shadowy opening and Satanic imagery of its beginning, placing Sabrina at the center of a softly lit white room, outfitting her in a white-on-white ensemble—even her iconic black headband is now white—to align her with ideas of purity, which in this case is symbolic of purifying the patriarchal misconceptions of the witch.

The shift in tone from the start of the series to the end of the series mirrors the progression of the witch from evil, Satanic puppet to selfless, inclusive heroine. Through Sabrina's death, all is right with Greendale, save for her absence. The distress Sabrina's passing causes those she left behind is notable because, despite having the abilities of a witch, Sabrina herself is half-witch, half-mortal. Sabrina's hybridity places her at odds with those around her as she is never able to be fully a part of the mortal realm or the witch realm. Throughout the series, Sabrina finds herself torn between her heritage and her friends. The students at the Academy of Unseen Arts do not readily accept her because she is not a full witch, and her mortal friends have difficulty understanding her because they have not lived in the witch realm. What results from Sabrina's hybridity is the one difference that cannot fully be reconciled as the series progresses. In fact, she spends most the series going back and forth between the Academy of Unseen Arts and Baxter High School. Her dual nature forces her to choose between the mundane and the mystical. Even then, she stands out, regardless of which side of her dual nature she chooses at any given point. Her family wants her to fully embrace her witch heritage while her friends want her to remain with them. Her hybridity in both of these scenarios does not place her in the good graces of either her family or her friends. For a series that makes it a priority to include Christian witches, Satanic witches, Pagan witches, and Vodou practitioners, Sabrina's unique status as a hybrid witch is never accepted by those around her. Sabrina's funeral is seemingly the first time that she is fully appreciated for *who* rather than *what* she is. Throughout the series, Sabrina's status as half-witch, half-mortal determines how she is perceived by others. As a half-witch, she is seen as less powerful than others who are full witches. Despite being a Spellman and the daughter of a powerful former High Priest of the Church of Night, Sabrina constantly has to prove her power and her worth. This tension, too, is a key component of the text and explored in other chapters in this collection, so we will not belabor the point here but point out that in a teen horror series, the inability to fully belong typically has deadly consequences for young women, who often find themselves sacrificing their lives for others, much like Sabrina does. Still, by the end of the series, some revision of previous harmful representations has occurred: the term "witch" has taken on new and varied meanings, as exemplified by Roz, the Order of Hecate, and even Lilith, but Sabrina finds her witch identity must ultimately be coupled with loss in order to be fully welcomed by both witches and mortals. The inability of Sabrina's character to find true acceptance suggests the interpretation of the word "witch" is a symbol of feminist empowerment connected to a still-evolving movement that, even as it fights for the rights and acknowledged dignity of its members in the larger world, may still be working to become more accepting of difference within the group itself.

BIBLIOGRAPHY

Bailey, Michael. "From Sorcery to Witchcraft: Clerical Conceptions of Magic in the Later Middle Ages," *Speculum* 76, no. 4 (October 2001): 960–90. doi.org/10.2307/2903617.

Baker, James W. "White Witches: Historic Fact and Romantic Fantasy." In *Magical Religion and Modern Witchcraft*, edited by James R. Lewis, 171–92. Albany, NY: State University of New York Press, 1996.

Chilling Adventures of Sabrina, Season 1, episode 2, "Chapter Two: The Dark Baptism." Directed by Lee Toland Krieger, written by Roberto Aguirre-Sacasa, featuring Kiernan Shipka, Miranda Otto, and Lucy Davis, and Richard Coyle. Released October 26, 2018, Netflix, https://www.netflix.com/watch/80230072?trackId=200257859.

———, Season 1, episode 3, "Chapter Three: The Trial of Sabrina Spellman." Directed by Rob Seidenglanz, written by Ross Maxwell, featuring Kiernan Shipka, Miranda Otto, Lucy Davis, and Ross Lynch. Released October 26, 2018, Netflix, https://www.netflix.com/watch/80230073?trackId=200257859.

———, Season 1, episode 4, "Chapter Four: Witch Academy." Directed by Rob Seidenglanz, written by Diana Thorland, featuring Kiernan Shipka, Miranda Otto, Lucy Davis, and Richard Coyle. Released October 26, 2018, Netflix, https://www.netflix.com/watch/80230074?trackId=200257859.

———, Season 1, episode 5, "Chapter Five: Dreams in a Witch House." Directed by Maggie Kiley, written by Matthew Barry, featuring Kiernan Shipka, Miranda Otto, Lucy Davis, and Chance Perdomo. Released October 26, 2018, Netflix, https://www.netflix.com/title/80223989.

———, Season 1, episode 7, "Chapter Seven: Feast of Feasts." Directed by Viet Nguyen, written by Oanh Ly, featuring Kiernan Shipka, Miranda Otto, Lucy Davis, and Tati Gabrielle. Released October 26, 2018, Netflix, https://www.netflix.com/watch/80230077?trackId=200257859.

———, Season 1, episode 10, "Chapter Ten: The Witching Hour." Directed by Rob Seidenglanz, written by Roberto Aguirre-Sacasa and Ross Maxwell, featuring Kiernan Shipka, Miranda Otto, Lucy Davis, and Chance Perdomo. Released October 26, 2018, Netflix, https://www.netflix.com/watch/80230080?trackId=200257859.

———, Season 2, episode 2, "Chapter Thirteen: The Passion of Sabrina Spellman." Directed by Michael Goi, written by MJ Kaufman and Christina Ham, featuring Kiernan Shipka, Miranda Otto, Lucy Davis, and Lachlan Watson. Released April 5, 2019, Netflix, https://www.netflix.com/watch/80230083?trackId=200257859.

———, Season 2, episode 6, "Chapter Seventeen: The Missionaries." Directed by Rob Seidenglanz, written by Donna Thorland, featuring Kiernan Shipka, Miranda Otto, and Lucy Davis, and Spencer Treat Clark. Released April 5, 2019, Netflix, https://www.netflix.com/watch/80230087?trackId=14277283.

———, Season 2, episode 7, "Chapter Eighteen: The Miracles of Sabrina Spellman." Directed by Antonio Negret, written by Christianne Hedtke & Lindsay Calhoon Bring, featuring Kiernan Shipka, Miranda Otto, Lucy Davis, and Chance Perdomo. Released April 5, 2019, https://www.netflix.com/watch/80230088?trackId=200257859.

———, Season 4, episode 3, "Chapter Thirty-One: The Weird." Directed by Lisa Soper, written by Jenina Kibuka, featuring Kiernan Shipka, Miranda Otto, Lucy Davis, and Jaz Sinclair. Released December 31, 2020, Netflix, https://www.netflix.com/watch/81062662?trackId=200257859.

———, Season 4, episode 8, "Chapter Thirty-Six: At the Mountains of Madness." Directed by Rob Seidenglanz, written by Roberto Aguirre-Sacasa, featuring Kiernan Shipka, Miranda Otto, Lucy Davis, and Gavin Leatherwood. Released December 31, 2020, Netflix, https://www.netflix.com/watch/81062667?trackId=200257859.

Doyle, Jude Ellison Sady. *Dead Blondes and Bad Mothers: Monstrosity, Patriarchy, and the Fear of Female Power.* Brooklyn, NY: Melville House, 2019.

Farrar, Janet and Stewart Farrar. *The Witches' Goddess*. Newton Abbot, UK: David & Charles Press, 2012.

Hjelm, Titus. "United in Diversity, Divided from Within: The Dynamics of Legitimation in Contemporary Witchcraft." In *Polemical Encounters: Esoteric Discourse and Its Others*, edited by Olav Hammer and Kocku von Stuckrad, 291–309. Leiden, Netherlands: Brill, 2007.

Johnston, Hannah E. "Of Teens and Tomes: The Dynamics of Teenage Witchcraft and Teen Witch Literature." In *Handbook of Contemporary Paganism*, edited by Murphy Pizza and James Lewis, 509–38. Leiden, Netherlands: Brill, 2009.

Laycock, Joseph P. "Satanic Panic: 1982–1991." In *Dangerous Games: What the Moral Panic over Role-Playing Games Says about Play, Religion, and Imagined Worlds*, 101–36. Oakland, CA: University of California Press, 2015.

Mackay, Christopher S. and Heinrich Institoris. *The Hammer of Witches: A Complete Translation of the Malleus Maleficarum.* Cambridge: Cambridge University Press, 2009.

Nicholas, Chani. "Lilith." In *Encyclopedia of Psychology and Religion*, 2nd edition, edited by David A. Leeming, 1029–32. Boston: Springer, 2014. https://doi.org/10 .1007/978-1-4614-6086-2.

Peters, Edward. *The Magician, the Witch, and the Law*. Philadelphia: University of Pennsylvania Press, 1978.

Pulling, Pat A., Pat Dempsey, and Mary Dempsey. *Dungeons and Dragons— Witchcraft Suicide Violence*. Richmond, VA: B.A.D.D., 1985. https://archive.org/ details/dungeons_and_dragons-witchcraft_suicide_violence.

Tangherlini, Timothy R. "'How Do You Know She's a Witch?'": Witches, Cunning Folk, and Competition in Denmark." *Western Folklore* 59, no. 3/4 (2000): 279– 303. https://www.jstor.org/stable/1500237.

NOTES

1. Edward Peters, *The Magician, the Witch, and the Law* (Philadelphia: University of Pennsylvania Press, 1978), 170.

2. Michael D. Bailey, "From Sorcery to Witchcraft: Clerical Conceptions of Magic in the Later Middle Ages," *Speculum* 76, no. 4 (2001): 960–90. https://doi.org/10 .2307/2903617.

3. Laura Apps and Andrew Gow, "Conceptual Webs: The Gendering of Witchcraft," in *Male Witches in Early Modern Europe* (Manchester: Manchester University Press, 2003), 119.

4. Christopher S. Mackay and Heinrich Institoris, *The Hammer of Witches: A Complete Translation of the Malleus Maleficarum* (Cambridge: Cambridge University Press, 2009), 283. https://doi.org/10.1017/CBO9780511626746.

5. *Chilling Adventures of Sabrina*, season 1, episode 2, "Chapter Two: The Dark Baptism," directed by Lee Toland Krieger, written by Roberto Aguirre-Sacasa, released October 26, 2018, on Netflix, https://www.netflix.com/watch/80230072 ?trackId=200257859: 00:47:45.

6. Joseph P. Laycock, "Satanic Panic: 1982–1991," in *Dangerous Games: What the Moral Panic over Role-Playing Games Says about Play, Religion, and Imagined Worlds* (Oakland: University of California Press, 2015), 119.

7. Mary Dempsey, Pat Dempsey, and Pat A. Pulling. *Dungeons and Dragons: Witchcraft Suicide Violence*, Richmond, VA: B.A.D.D., 1985. https://archive.org/details/dungeons_and_dragons-witchcraft_suicide_violence.

8. Dempsey, Dempsey, and Pulling, *Dungeons and Dragons*.

9. *Chilling Adventures of Sabrina*, season 1, episode 10, "Chapter Ten: The Witching Hour," directed by Rob Seidenglanz, written by Roberto Aguirre-Sacasa and Ross Maxwell, released October 26, 2018, on Netflix, https://www.netflix.com/watch/80230080?trackId=200257859: 01:00:15.

10. Chani Nicholas, "Lilith," in *Encyclopedia of Psychology and Religion*, 2nd ed., ed. by David A. Leeming (Boston: Springer, 2014), 1029. https://doi.org/10.1007/978-1-4614-6086-2.

11. *Chilling Adventures of Sabrina*, season 1, episode 7, "Chapter Seven: Feast of Feasts," directed by Viet Nguyen, written by Oanh Ly, released October 26, 2018, on Netflix, https://www.netflix.com/watch/80230077?trackId=200257859: 00:33:05.

12. Timothy Tangherlini discusses the use of the term "Cunning" in his article titled, "How Do You Know She's a Witch?" Witches, Cunning Folk, and Competition in Denmark." He asserts that "Cunning folk were apparently quite adept at keeping their names clean during the time of the witchcraft trials, perhaps because they spent considerable effort in deflecting narrative assaults" (296).

13. Some witches or other practitioners of the occult or metaphysics refer to this as the "Third Eye." The Third Eye is sometimes considered one of the chakras and it is believed to see the universe from a spiritual point of view. The perspective of the Third Eye is organic and it perceives the realities of the universe in a way that is free from human preconceptions and limitations. Connecting with the Third Eye is to attempt to gather information from the universe that cannot be obtained by mundane means. In other words, the information obtained through the Third Eye is psychic in nature.

14. The term "white witches" in this context refers to witches who practice "white" magic, or adhere to a magical practice that refrains from inflicting or causing harm to others. White magic can also refer to magic that is intended to heal someone.

15. James W. Baker, "White Witches: Historic Fact and Romantic Fantasy," in *Magical Religion and Modern Witchcraft*, edited by James R. Lewis (Albany, NY: State University of New York Press, 1996), 180–81.

16. Janet Farrar and Stewart Farrar discuss Lilith in their book *The Witches' Goddess*. They explain that "Adam's first wife was Lilith. Yahweh created them both at the same time. But Lilith refused to subordinate herself to Adam, or the male God [. . .] she is a patroness of witches; but where Hecate is visualized as an old crone, Lilith is instead the enticing sorceress, the beautiful vampire, the *femme fatale*" (131–32).

17. Titus Hjelm, "United in Diversity, Divided from Within: The Dynamics of Legitimation in Contemporary Witchcraft," in *Polemical Encounters: Esoteric*

Discourse and its Others (Leiden, The Netherlands: Brill, 2007), 298. https://doi.org/10.1163/ej.9789004162570.i-326.79.

18. Jude Ellison Sady Doyle. *Dead Blondes and Bad Mothers: Monstrosity, Patriarchy, and the Fear of Female Power* (Brooklyn, NY: Melville House, 2019), 220.

Chapter 3

Controlling the Female Body

Foucault, Catholic Ireland, and
Chilling Adventures of Sabrina

Shannon Hughes Spence and Cori Mathis

In "Chapter One: October Country" (1:1), *Chilling Adventures of Sabrina* (*CAoS*) introduces Ms. Mary Wardwell (Michelle Gomez), a timid teacher at Greendale's Baxter High. As she is driving home, she must abruptly stop her car to avoid hitting a mysterious young woman (Jenna Berman) who appears in the middle of the road. Ms. Wardwell brings the young woman home with her, and, after hearing the young woman's charge that "the woods attacked [her]," begins to tell her about the lesser-known witch hunts in Greendale, which, according to legend, left thirteen angry female witch spirits in the forest. At this point in the episode, it becomes clear that this is no legend. The young woman performs a possession ritual, and Ms. Wardwell becomes Madam Satan, or Lilith, the Dark Lord's right-hand woman, who is tasked with bringing Sabrina Spellman (Kiernan Shipka) down the Path of Night, therefore preparing Sabrina for the Dark Lord's plans for her.[1] This terrifying incident is but the first in a long series of attacks against women in the Church of Night, each of which brings to mind the historical connections to the attacks upon women from Catholic and Protestant churches during the fifteenth and seventeenth centuries.[2] Additionally, the surveillance and control the Church of Night exerts over witches recalls a similar effort from the Catholic Church after the establishment of the Irish Free State to regulate female bodies.[3] While *Chilling Adventures of Sabrina*'s source text does not explicitly reference this real-life systemic oppression, any viewer familiar with Irish history and Foucault's theory of surveilling and controlling rebellious bodies[4] cannot help but find clear parallels.

PATRIARCHAL POWER STRUCTURES

Witchcraft was once defined by the religious-historical definition of making a pact with the Devil in which one's soul was exchanged for power, with the Devil ultimately utilizing his agent to wreak havoc against traditional Christian teachings.[5] Therefore, witches were agents of Satan, "men and women who had renounced their covenant with God to make a pact with the Devil."[6] Witchcraft was officially condemned by the Catholic Church on December 5, 1484, with the papal bull *Summis desiderantes affectibus*. The bull outlined a witch as any person who deviated from the Catholic faith, engaged in sexual acts with demons, and/or performed incantations, spells, conjurations, and other charms.[7] The decree went on to associate contraception and abortion with witchcraft.[8] Shortly after issuing the papal bull, Pope Innocent VIII authorized Jakob Sprenger, dean of the University of Cologne, and Heinrich Kramer, a professor of theology at the University of Salzburg, to eradicate the heresy of witchcraft, resulting in their misogynistic book *Malleus Maleficarum* (*Hammer of the Witches*) in 1486.[9]

Witchcraft was not only seen as a crime against the Catholic Church, but was soon considered a legal crime. Elizabeth I's witchcraft law in 1586 saw a one-year prison sentence for those found guilty of witchcraft in the United Kingdom and Ireland, with a second guilty verdict being punishable by death. However, Ireland did not adopt the harsher 1604 Witchcraft Act brought forward by the Westminster Parliament, which saw any and all acts of witchcraft as punishable by death.[10] Similar laws began to emerge in other parts of Europe as witch panic began to spread. Witch panic, the deeply rooted fear within Christian society that the Devil would lead people astray with ungodly temptations to bestow powers upon his agents that could bring harm and death to communities,[11] engulfed mainland Europe, Great Britain, and the American colonies during the fifteenth and seventeenth centuries. Although the spread of witch panic can be attributed to a variety of economic, social, and religious factors, it is important to underscore the significance of gender and sexuality in witchcraft accusations as 70–80 percent of the 40,000 people persecuted as witches were women.[12] The view of the common witch may have its origin in gender stereotyping. The necromancer, who was typically an elite man, conjured demons to command them to perform magical acts to conduct his bidding. The simple witch, on the other hand, was usually a woman due to the weak nature of the female spirit. She was not considered savvy and was merely an agent of the Devil, acting only to do his bidding to satisfy her voracious desires and carnal appetite.[13] Some argue that women were predominantly targeted as witches, as "female sexuality was centered as a culprit" of witchcraft.[14] This argument is reinforced by the oftentimes sexual content of the accusations against women.[15] Accusations of a sexual nature were in direct opposition to the social norms women were expected to follow at the time, such as modesty and obedience.[16] These rigid requirements left little room for the expression of sexuality, and any such expressions came with a severe penalty. The fear of women engaging in such diabolical sexual acts and the effects such acts would have on Christian societies is exemplified in the witchcraft accusations against Florence Newton and the wife of James Maxwell.

Like Sarah Good in Salem,[17] Florence Newton's crime stemmed from begging.[18] During the Christmas of 1660, Newton called on the house of John Pyne, a Youghal nobleman in Cork, Ireland, and requested a piece of beef. When Pyne's servant, Mary Longdon, refused Newton the piece of meat, Newton claimed "thou hads't as good given it me."[19] This remark was later assumed to be an evil curse. Upon Newton and Longdon meeting a week later, Newton kissed Longdon and insisted the two remain friends, despite the previous quarrel. Within the month, Longdon became ill with violent fits, vomiting household objects. Longdon's fits were exacerbated when Newton was brought to approach her, a common occurrence in victims of a bewitching. Newton was arrested in the March of 1661 and her trial was set for September of the same year. Whilst in prison, Newton claimed that she was not responsible for Longdon's illness, despite being subjected to a series of brutal tests and other torture in order to produce a confession. Newton's situation was worsened when she was accused of causing the death of her prison guard, David Jones. During Newton's trial in September 1661, Jones's widow claimed that Newton kissed David Jones's hand through the bars of her prison cell. He quickly developed shooting pains in his arms and subsequently died while screaming Newton's name on his death bed. Newton's fate remains unknown as the court papers of her sentencing were lost. With two counts of witchcraft against her, it is speculated that she would have been sentenced to death.[20] On a similar note, and at the opposite end of Ireland, the wife of James Maxwell of Armagh (her name is unknown) was drowned during the winter of 1641. Mrs. Maxwell's murder was attributed to a local man claiming to have suffered severe misfortune after she kissed him. This implied not only that Mrs. Maxwell was adulterous—she was also clearly a witch.[21] Witchcraft accusations in Ireland (and more generally in Europe) involving kissing or displays of overt female sexuality were taken more seriously by male elites as it represented unregulated female touch, which, when not under the control of the Church or State, was a potent threat to patriarchal power structures.[22]

In the West, witch trials may seem like a barbaric stain on society and relegated to a few paragraphs within history books. However, *CAoS* reminds the audience of the horror of the real-life witch trials that saw the systematic murder of thousands of people during the fifteenth and seventeenth centuries. Furthermore, *CAoS* shows how the trepidation around strong and potentially uncontrollable women can be replicated within modern settings under oppressive patriarchal power structures, such as the Church of Night. By attempting to regulate and control female bodies, the Church of Night within *CAoS* mirrors the same anxiety of Christian churches during the witch trials surrounding the potential power of women to threaten the established patriarchal order.

HISTORICAL CONNECTIONS IN *CHILLING ADVENTURES OF SABRINA*

CAoS takes an interesting and opposing view to how witchcraft has been recently characterized within modern film and television shows. For example, *Practical Magic* (Griffin Dunne, 1998) represents magic and witchcraft as nature-based practices, with one protagonist, Sally Owens (Sandra Bullock), firmly stating, "There's no Devil in the craft."[23] Similarly, in *The Craft* (Andrew Fleming, 1996), witchcraft is seen as an earth-based practice of nature worship.[24] Such Devil-free depictions are somewhat reflective of the contemporary spiritual practice of witchcraft practiced by people in the twenty-first century. However, the depiction of witchcraft in *CAoS* is similar to the type of witchcraft that was feared during the time of the witch hunts. The witches and warlocks in *CAoS* receive their powers from Satan and carry out his wishes, reflecting how people living during the witch hunt period assumed witches received their powers. Moreover, throughout the entirety of *CAoS*, there are multiple references to the real-life witch trials and witch panic that occurred during the fifteenth and seventeenth centuries.

A subtle reference to the fear and rumors disseminated by *Malleus Maleficarum* is evident in "Chapter Two: The Dark Baptism" (1:2).[25] When Sabrina wishes to teach a group of football bullies a lesson, she seeks advice from Ms. Wardwell. Ms. Wardwell encourages Sabrina to enlist the help of three other girls to take on the four football players to seek revenge by simply scaring them. Sabrina approaches her fellow witches, the Weird Sisters—Prudence (Tati Gabrielle), Agatha (Adeline Rudolph), and Dorcas (Abigail Cowen) Night—for help. While assisting Sabrina, the Weird Sisters go rogue and take the boys' genitals (which they later return). This once again calls to mind the anxiety that was disseminated through the publication of *Malleus Maleficarum*, that witches were capable of removing penises.

In the following episode, "Chapter Three: The Trial of Sabrina Spellman" (1:3),[26] the historic events of the witch trials are ingeniously referenced. When Sabrina expresses her conflicting desire to retain her mortal life but also engage with her witch side, as she is both mortal and witch, it is decided that a trial will decide her fate. During the trial, Father Faustus Blackwood (Richard Coyle)—who is head of the witch school, the Academy of Unseen Arts, as well as the Church of Night—states that Sabrina will be bound and dropped into the river. If she floats, she is a witch. If she drowns, she is mortal. Subjecting those who were accused of witchcraft to a trial by water was common during the witch trials.[27] Alternatively, Sabrina must submit to being stripped and examined, in full view of the coven, for a witch's mark on her body. During the centuries when the witch trials were at their peak, those who were accused of witchcraft were stripped, completely shaved, and pricked with needles in physical examinations in front of local nobles and priests to search for the Devil's mark on their bodies.[28] Later in "Chapter Thirty-Two: The Imp of the Perverse" (4.4), Blackwood uses the Perverse, an Eldritch Terror, to create a world in which he is Emperor of Greendale and has persuaded mortals to join his witch-hunting army via historical stereotypes popular during the witch trials. This warped reality is so similar to that historical moment that Nick Scratch (Gavin Leatherwood) ends up on trial for witchcraft and is pressed by stones, much like Giles Corey was in Salem.[29]

The historical reasons for these punishments are also utilized in the series. In "Chapter Seven: Feast of Feasts" (1:7),[30] Sabrina's aunt Zelda (Miranda Otto) informs Sabrina that the Spellman family is one of fourteen families within the Church of Night that has been chosen to participate in the annual celebration of Feast of Feasts, which, as Zelda explains, "is meant to honor the single greatest sacrifice a witch ever made to save her coven."[31] Aunt Zelda, Aunt Hilda (Lucy Davis), and Sabrina's cousin Ambrose (Chance Perdomo), tell the story of Freya, a queen of witches who sacrificed herself and her body so her coven would have sustenance during the winter months. In the Feast, which functions as part memorial to Freya's sacrifice and part devotional ritual to the Dark Lord, one representative of each of the fourteen families is put forward to enter into a lottery. However, only women are eligible because, as Zelda adds, "It is the Dark Lord's will."[32] When the representative's name is pulled from the lottery, the winner, known as the Queen of the Feast, becomes the main course. While Sabrina is appalled by the idea of this cannibalistic celebration, some members of the coven embrace this culture of self-sacrifice. Prudence, for example, is excited to have been chosen to participate in the lottery; when Sabrina asks if Prudence wants to be sacrificed, Prudence replies, "more than I've wanted anything in my life."[33] As this plotline resolves, some of the witches in *CAoS* do engage in cannibalism, and the horror invoked by the dark nature of such a storyline replicates the horror people of the fifteenth to seventeenth centuries would have felt about people accused of witchcraft, who were also considered to engage in cannibalism. The notion originated from earlier Christian anti-heretical polemic and folklore surrounding blood-sucking vampires and werewolves. Through theological and legal frameworks, judicial trials, and folklore, cannibalism became a European metaphor for otherness and intrinsically associated with the malefic witch.[34] Additionally, witches were hunted as a type of Christian imperative in this period, referenced in "Chapter Thirty-Two: The Imp of the Perverse" (4:4).[35] When Sabrina approaches her house, "Thou shalt not suffer a witch to live" is spray painted on the outside of her home. This quotation, from Exodus 22:18 in the King James Bible, was used to further justify the capital punishment of witches.[36]

The horror of the real-life witch trials that *CAoS* cleverly conveys in a subtle manner underscores how the female body was treated as both inferior and a threat during the witch trials and also within the Church of Night. Considering that the Greendale Thirteen consisted of only witches and that the participants within the cannibalistic annual Feast of Feasts can only consume a witch, it can be argued that the male leaders of the Church of Night view female bodies as more expendable and witches as less powerful. These women are constructed as inferior while simultaneously remaining a threat to men. There is a juxtaposition between the strong women who are members of the Church of Night and the archaic and sexist rules that the male leaders impose on those who follow them. Under these leaders and their real-life counterparts, the female body requires continuous containment and control and is subjected to disciplinary techniques, such as trial by water, a search for a witch's mark, ex-communication, or an annual sacrifice during the Feast of Feasts. With the Foucauldian themes of containment, control, surveillance, and sacrifice of female bodies prominent during both the witch trials and within *CAoS*, it is impossible for anyone who is familiar with Irish women's history to deny the connections to specific periods in Catholic Ireland. It is therefore reasonable to draw comparisons to how the female body was regulated and controlled in Ireland after the establishment of the Irish Free State.

SEXUALITY, PURITY, AND CONTROL

The control and surveillance of female bodies due to the fear of women threatening the established order of patriarchal power structures was evident in both Catholic and Protestant churches during the witch trials and within the Church of Night in *CAoS*. However, such control and surveillance of female bodies was also prevalent after the establishment of the Irish Free State, which saw Irish national identity become intertwined with concepts of purity and shame.

The Declaration of the Irish Republic in 1916 symbolically shed several hundred years of colonization that Ireland experienced at the hands of the British Empire while simultaneously signifying a pivotal change in the social norms surrounding the perception of a woman's place in society. With ambitious and powerful women fighting alongside their male counterparts in the 1916 rebellion to end 800 years of colonization, it was believed that once an Irish Free State was established in the 1920s, women's position within society would change for the better. Unfortunately, the advancement of women's rights within Ireland was short-lived as anxieties surrounding the need to create an image of an independent and competent new Irish Free State that was distinct from the British Empire began to take hold.[37] In this attempt to establish itself as a competent post-colonial state, a close relationship between the State and the Catholic Church was decided upon as the most effective way to create the intended image. Unfortunately, this relationship only exacerbated the already marginalized status of women. As the next decade progressed, the right-wing traditionalist values of *Fianna Fáil* (a prominent Irish political party) and the conservative morals of the Catholic Church dominated the political landscape, with the Irish government incorporating several Catholic principles into legislation. These pieces of legislation exemplified how the female body was controlled and surveilled by both the State and the Catholic Church. Such pieces of legislation consisted of requiring women to retire from their positions as civil servants when they married, officially stating that a woman's place was within the home, banning contraception, and outlawing abortion, to name a few.[38] To say Irish women had a lack of choice under a patriarchal power structure would be an understatement.

A darker application of Foucault's theory of surveilling and controlling bodies within Ireland is found within Magdalene Laundries (sometimes referred to as Magdalene Asylums). Such institutions are dark stains upon Ireland's past. As the Catholic Church began to take over the operation of welfare institutions, the Magdalene Laundries became more punitive, as the newly established Irish Free State considered sexual impurity a threat to national identity.[39] With Irish society believing that morality and purity were a woman's responsibility, discussions around unmarried motherhood saw the sexuality of all women as suspect and in need of restraint.[40] Therefore, unmarried mothers became a typical inmate of Magdalene Laundries when institutionalized by family members who viewed the deviant women as shameful.[41] In recent years, survivors of the Magdalene Laundries have given accounts of the physical, psychological, and sexual abuse they experienced while institutionalized within the Laundries,[42] proving the need for an inquiry into the treatment of individuals in the care of past institutions under the State and the Catholic Church.

We are in no way comparing or equating the real lived experiences of Irish women who suffered traumatic abuse at the hands of the Irish State and Catholic Church with those of the women in the fictional Church of Night. Instead, we have explained how Foucault's theory of disciplining and controlling deviant bodies can be applied to the control of the female body within the historical contexts of the witch trials, Catholic Ireland after the establishment of the Free State, and within the Church of Night in *CAoS*. Although any expressions of sexuality outside of marriage in the Irish Free State were heavily looked down upon, at first glance, the Church of Night seems to adopt an antithetical attitude, encouraging and embracing sexuality. However, upon further analysis it becomes clear that sexuality within the Church of Night is only encouraged when it is regulated by those in power.

CONTROLLING SEXUALITY IN *CHILLING ADVENTURES OF SABRINA*

Sexuality is encouraged and embraced within *CAoS* when under the surveillance of the Church of Night. This can be seen in "Chapter One: October Country" (1:1) when Sabrina discusses her desire to postpone her Dark Baptism due to her and Harvey (Ross Lynch) "[taking] things to the next level."[43] Zelda quickly reminds Sabrina that witch law demands Sabrina remain virginal and that she is required to save herself for the Dark Lord. Sabrina expresses her shock at Zelda's comments and admits that she has reservations about saving herself for the Dark Lord, questioning, "Why does he get to decide what I do or don't do with my body?"[44] Sabrina is concerned with losing not only her free will but her bodily autonomy, as well. Zelda says it is witch law and that there is no choice in the matter. This emphasizes that although Sabrina is not shunned or shamed for engaging in physical intimacy later in life, she must wait and remain pure for the Dark Lord. Similarly, in "Chapter Sixteen: Blackwood" (2:5),[45] Zelda is visibly nervous but accepting the night before her wedding in case the Dark Lord visits her to claim her for himself, as is the Dark Lord's right with any bride-to-be, reinforcing the notion that sexuality is only embraced when under the control of an oppressive force.

Controlled sexuality, under the pretense of celebrated sexuality, is exposed once again when the Church of Night honors health and fertility, as seen during the Lupercalia festival in "Chapter Fourteen: Lupercalia" (2:3).[46] The festival coincides with mortal Valentine's Day and is comprised of three events: the first involves the matching of a witch and random warlock; the second requires that witch and warlock to begin a courtship, including spending the night in "unholy abstinence"; and the last, The Hunt, consists of a run through the woods that ends in "orgiastic carnality."[47] Here, the audience may be taken aback by how expressions of sexuality are seemingly encouraged amongst members of the coven, shedding the usual societal norms of modesty, purity, and slut shaming. However, it is still a form of heteronormativity

in the required pairing of a witch and warlock and organized by the patriarchal power structure of the Church of Night and the Academy of Unseen Arts,
both of which are headed by the domineering Father Blackwood. However, it
is not only the Church of Night that presents complicated views of sexuality
within *CAoS*. In "Chapter Twenty-Four: The Hare Moon" (3:4), a group of
Pagans create a great deal of turmoil for Sabrina and the town of Greendale.[48]
(It should also be noted that the depiction of Pagans within *CAoS* is not
reflective of contemporary Pagan practitioners.) The Pagans within *CAoS*
view sexually active women as less-than and less valuable; they search for
virgins to sacrifice to the old gods and turn those who have had sex into stone,
as seen in the case of Roz, the only non-virgin of Sabrina's friend group. This
reaction to sexually active women who threaten their plans can be read as
their need to contain unregulated female sexuality.

CAoS continues the theme of viewing unregulated female touch and those
women who control their own sexuality as deviant and a threat to the patriarchy, much like the Irish Free State and Catholic Church did. The women
in the Church of Night overcome what is expected of them (to remain within
subordinate positions within the Church) and eventually begin to take over
and operate the Church of Night under a new name, the Order of Hecate.
This decision to dedicate their worship to the Goddess of witchcraft, magic,
and the liminal crossroads between worlds is paired with a reclamation of
sexuality and power, one which calls to mind a similar recovery by Irish
feminists in recent years as they fought for the repeal of the eighth amendment of Ireland's constitution, Ireland's archaic law that prohibited abortion.
The eighth amendment saw the life of the fetus as a "constitutional person,
separate from the pregnant person to the extent that it is entitled to its own
legal representation, and with a right to life exactly equivalent to [the pregnant person]."[49] The empowered witches within the Order of Hecate who
exercised their agency over their lives is reflective of the Irish activists who
campaigned to ensure they would have control of their bodies.

Today, Irish feminists are reversing the Catholic characteristics remanent
from the intertwined relationship between the Irish Free State and Catholic
Church that surveilled and controlled female bodies. The Church and State
morally and legally confined sexual relations to the marital bed and condemned contraception, making contraception illegal in Ireland from 1935 to
1979[50] and not fully legalized until 1992.[51] If caught with contraception, one
could face a large fine, a possible jail sentence, and guaranteed social dis-
grace.[52] However, in May 1971, a group of women from the Irish Women's
Liberation Movement (IWLM) travelled from Dublin to Belfast in Northern
Ireland—which had slightly more liberal contraceptive laws, being under
British rule—to purchase contraception to highlight and protest the hypocrisy.[53] When the IWLM members entered the pharmacy in Belfast, they

requested the contraceptive pill but were denied as they did not have the relevant prescription. Thinking quickly, the IWLM members knew that the average border control worker would not know what the contraceptive pill looked like, so they purchased multiple packs of aspirin. When the activists arrived back in Dublin, they refused to hand over their contraceptive pills and were met with a group of supporters who chanted "let them through"/"let them go." This support from the wider public signified an emerging shift in social attitudes regarding how women could assert agency and regulate their own bodies. Once again, Irish women began to reclaim their lives when survivors of the Magdalene Laundries began campaigning for justice and redress. With the last Magdalene Laundry closing in 1996, the Laundries undoubtedly left emotional and physical scars, not only on the survivors but on Irish society as a collective. As survivor accounts began to surface to the public and mass graves on the premises of previous Magdalene Laundries were discovered, Ireland was forced to confront its disciplinary society and issue redress and an apology to survivors. Arguably the most publicized and well-known incident of reclamation of bodily autonomy within Ireland since the establishment of the Irish Free State happened on May 25, 2018, when the people of Ireland voted in favor to repeal Ireland's strict abortion laws. However, the repeal of the eighth amendment could not have been possible without the activism that spanned generations and those that tirelessly campaigned to ensure individuals—not the Catholic Church or the State—had control over their own bodies.

CAoS offers a similar perspective. In a powerful scene in "Chapter Ten: The Witching Hour" (1:10), Lilith (as Ms. Wardwell) tells Sabrina that "all women are taught to fear power," but that Sabrina should own her power, not passively accept it from the Dark Lord. She urges Sabrina: "Take it. Wield it [. . .] it isn't just power. It's rage. It's the desire to change the world and will to do it."[54] The unified power of women and witches is once again reinforced when Lilith gives birth in "Chapter Thirty-One: The Weird" (4:3)[55] and seeks help from Zelda and the Order of Hecate. Lilith's labor proves traumatic, and, surrounded by a circle of witches from the coven, Zelda soothes Lilith by insisting that they will share her pain through the blessing of Hecate. The witches breathe, push, and scream in unison, momentarily redistributing Lilith's suffering among them. The power of women and witches is summarized succinctly in a speech by Sabrina and Roz when they run for co-presidency of Baxter High under the campaign title "Witches United" in "Chapter Thirty-Two: The Imp of the Perverse" (4:4).[56] When their competition, Billy Marlin (Ty Wood), asks what this slogan means, Sabrina states that she and Roz are running as witches, as "powerful, disruptive women, champions of the oppressed, supporters of the othered, unapologetic feminists, allies to all those who live in the shadow of the patriarchy, reminders that the shadow has its own power. We will speak the truth, and we will fight injustice."[57]

Both *CAoS* and Irish feminists of the twentieth and twenty-first centuries exemplify how Foucault's concepts of surveilling and controlling rebel bodies has been a fundamental priority for oppressive power structures for hundreds of years, all while simultaneously showing how a group of powerful women and witches can come together to topple damaging patriarchal power structures. By veering outside the norms of society, the witches in *CAoS*, like the Irish feminist activists, overcome oppressive and damaging forces to claim their position as equals, ultimately exercising both agency and resistance.

BIBLIOGRAPHY

Beaumont, Caitriona. "Women, Citizenship and Catholicism in the Irish Free State, 1922–1948." *Women's History Review* 6, no. 4 (1997): 563–85. doi:10.1080/09612029700200154.

Briggs, Robin. *Witches & Neighbors: The Social and Cultural Context of European Witchcraft*. Hoboken, NJ: Blackwell Publishing, 2006.

Cawthorne, Nigel. *Witches: History of a Persecution*. London: Arcturus Publishing, 2004.

Chilling Adventures of Sabrina, Season 1, episode 1, "Chapter One: October Country." Directed by Lee Toland Krieger, written by Roberto Aguirre-Sacasa, featuring Kiernan Shipka, Miranda Otto, Lucy Davis, and Chance Perdomo. Released October 26, 2018, on Netflix, www.netflix.com/title/80223989.

———, Season 1, episode 2, "Chapter Two: The Dark Baptism." Directed by Lee Toland Krieger, written by Roberto Aguirre-Sacasa, featuring Kiernan Shipka, Miranda Otto, Lucy Davis, and Richard Coyle. Released October 26, 2018, on Netflix, www.netflix.com/title/80223989.

———, Season 1, episode 3, "Chapter Three: The Trial of Sabrina Spellman." Directed by Rob Seidenglanz, written by Ross Maxwell, featuring Kiernan Shipka, Miranda Otto, Lucy Davis, and Ross Lynch. Released October 26, 2018, on Netflix, www.netflix.com/title/80223989.

———, Season 1, episode 7, "Chapter Seven: Feast of Feasts." Directed by Viet Nguyen, written by Oanh Ly, featuring Kiernan Shipka, Miranda Otto, Lucy Davis, and Tati Gabrielle. Released October 26, 2018, on Netflix, www.netflix.com/title/80223989.

———, Season 1, episode 10, "Chapter Ten: The Witching Hour." Directed by Rob Seidenglanz, written by Roberto Aguirre-Sacasa and Ross Maxwell, featuring Kiernan Shipka, Miranda Otto, Lucy Davis, and Chance Perdomo. Released October 26, 2018, on Netflix, www.netflix.com/title/80223989.

———, Season 2, episode 3, "Chapter Fourteen: Lupercalia." Directed by Salli Richardson-Whitfield, written by Oanh Ly, featuring Kiernan Shipka, Miranda

Otto, Lucy Davis, and Gavin Leatherwood. Released April 5, 2019, Netflix, www .netflix.com/title/80223989.

———, Season 2, episode 5, "Chapter Sixteen: Blackwood." Directed by Alex Pillai, written by Matthew Barry, featuring Kiernan Shipka, Miranda Otto, Lucy Davis, and Richard Coyle. Released April 5, 2019, on Netflix, www.netflix.com/title /80223989.

———, Season 3, episode 4, "Chapter Twenty-Four: The Hare Moon." Directed by Viet Nguyen, written by Donna Thorland, featuring Kiernan Shipka, Miranda Otto, Lucy Davis, and Jaz Sinclair. Released January 24, 2020, on Netflix, www.netflix .com/title/80223989.

———, Season 4, episode 3, "Chapter Thirty-One: The Weird." Directed by Lisa Soper, written by Jenina Kibuka, featuring Kiernan Shipka, Miranda Otto, Lucy Davis, and Jaz Sinclair. Released December 31, 2020, on Netflix, www.netflix.com /title/80223989.

———, Season 4, episode 4, "Chapter Thirty-Two: The Imp of the Perverse." Directed by Antonio Negret, written by Christianne Hedtke, featuring Kiernan Shipka, Miranda Otto, Lucy Davis, and Chance Perdomo. Released December 31, 2020, on Netflix, www.netflix.com/title/80223989.

De Londras, Fiona and Mairead Enright. "The Case for Repealing the 8th." In *Repealing the 8th: Reforming Irish Abortion Law*, 1–14. Bristol, UK: Bristol University Press, 2018.

Dunne, Griffin, director. *Practical Magic*. Warner Bros., 1998. 1 hr. 44 min. play.hbo max.com/feature/urn:hbo:feature:GXjtShgurcY7CZgEAABBM?source=googleH BOMAX&action=play.

Federici, Silvia. *Witches, Witch-Hunting and Women*. Brooklyn, NY: Autonomedia, 2018.

Fischer, Clara. "Gender, Nation, and the Politics of Shame: Magdalen Laundries and the Institutionalization of Feminine Transgression in Modern Ireland." *Signs: Journal of Women in Culture and Society* 41, no. 4 (Summer 2016): 821–43. JSTOR.

Fleming, Andrew, director. *The Craft*. Columbia Pictures, 1996. 1 hr. 41 min. www.amazon.com/gp/video/detail/amzn1.dv.gti.d8b7ffbd-26b6-d72d-9b44 -a11f34e173b8?autoplay=0&ref_=atv_cf_strg_wb.

Foucault, Michel. *Discipline and Punish: The Birth of the Prison*. Translated by Alan Sheridan. New York: Pantheon Books, 1975.

Holland, Jack. *A Brief History of Misogyny: The World's Oldest Prejudice*. London: Robinson, 2006.

Howe, Katherine. *The Penguin Book of Witches.* New York: Penguin Group, 2014.

Hunt, Tamara L. and Micheline R. Lessard. *Women and the Colonial Gaze*. London: Palgrave Macmillan, 2002.

Inglis, Tom. "Origins and Legacies of Irish Prudery: Sexuality and Social Control in Modern Ireland." *Eire-Ireland* 40, no. 3 & 4 (May 2005): 9–37. Project MUSE.

"The Irish Women Who Fought to Legalise Contraception," BBC News, the BBC, last modified March 1, 2017, www.bbc.com/news/av/magazine-36249697.

Kelly, Laura. "The Contraceptive Pill in Ireland c.1964–79: Activism, Women, and Patient-Doctor Relationships." *Medical History* 64, no. 2 (April 2020): 195–218. doi.org/10.1017/mdh.2020.3

Luddy, Maria. "Sex and the Single Girl in 1920s and 1930s Ireland." *The Irish Review* 35, (Summer 2007): 79–91. JSTOR.

Martin, Lois. *The History of Witchcraft*. Harpenden, UK: Oldcastle Books, 2016.

McAuliffe, Mary. "Gender, History and Witchcraft in Early Modern Ireland: A Re-reading of the Florence Newton Trial." In *Gender and Power in Irish History*, edited by Maryann Gialanella Valiulis, 39–59. Dublin: Irish Academic Press, 2009.

O'Connell, Jennifer. "Witchipedia: Ireland's Most Famous Witches." *Irish Times*, October 28, 2017. www.irishtimes.com/life-and-style/people/witchipedia-ireland-s-most-famous-witches-1.3262008.

Roper, Lyndal. *Witch Craze: Terror and Fantasy in Baroque Germany*. New Haven, CT: Yale University Press, 2006.

Saxon, Martha. "Bearing the Burden? Puritan Wives." *History Today*, October 10, 1994, www.historytoday.com/archive/bearing-burden-puritan-wives.

Smith, James. *Ireland's Magdalen Laundries and the Nation's Architecture of Containment*. Chicago: University of Notre Dame Press, 2007.

Sneddon, Andrew. *Possessed by the Devil: The Real History of the Islandmagee Witches and Ireland's Only Mass Witchcraft Trial*. Dublin: The History Press Ireland, 2013.

Sneddon, Andrew. *Witchcraft and Magic in Ireland*. London: Palgrave Macmillan, 2015.

Sollee, Kristen. *Witches, Sluts and Feminists*. Los Angeles: ThreeL Media, 2017.

Zguta, Russell. "The Ordeal by Water (Swimming of Witches) in the East Slavic Word." *Slavic Review* 36, no. 2 (June 1977): 220–30. doi.org/10.2307/2495037.

Zika, Charles. "Cannibalism and Witchcraft in Early Modern Europe: Reading the Visual Images." In *Exorcising Our Demons: Magic, Witchcraft, and Visual Culture in Early Modern Europe*, 445–79. Leiden, the Netherlands: Brill, 2003.

NOTES

1. *Chilling Adventures of Sabrina*, season 1, episode 1, "Chapter One: October Country," directed by Lee Toland Krieger, written by Roberto Aguirre-Sacasa, featuring Kiernan Shipka, Miranda Otto, Lucy Davis, and Chance Perdomo, released October 26, 2018, on Netflix, www.netflix.com/title/80223989: 00:08:03.

2. Andrew Sneddon, *Possessed by the Devil* (Dublin: The History Press Ireland, 2013), 9.

3. Tom Inglis, "Origins and Legacies of Irish Prudery: Sexuality and Social Control in Modern Ireland," *Eire-Ireland* 40, no. 3 & 4 (Spring 2005): 20.

4. Michel Foucault, *Discipline and Punish: The Birth of the Prison* (New York: Pantheon Books, 1975), 176.

5. Robin Briggs, *Witches & Neighbors: The Social and Cultural Context of European Witchcraft* (Hoboken: NJ: Blackwell Publishing, 2006), 3.

6. Sneddon, *Possessed*, 38.

7. Nigel Cawthorne, *Witches: History of A Persecution* (London: Arcturus Publishing Limited, 2004), 29.

8. Jack Holland, *A Brief History of Misogyny* (London: Robinson, 2006), 113.

9. Holland, *Misogyny*, 116–22.

10. Andrew Sneddon, *Witchcraft and Magic in Ireland* (London: Palgrave Macmillan, 2015), 28.

11. Lyndal Roper, *Witch Craze: Terror and Fantasy in Baroque Germany* (New Haven, CT: Yale University Press, 2006), 15.

12. Lois Martin, *The History of Witchcraft* (Harpenden, UK: Oldcastle Books, 2016), 14.

13. Holland, *Misogyny*.

14. Kristen Sollee, *Witches, Sluts and Feminists* (Los Angeles, CA: ThreeL Media, 2017), 27.

15. Katherine Howe, *The Penguin Book of Witches* (New York: Penguin Group, 2014), 49.

16. Martha Saxon, "Bearing the Burden? Puritan Wives," *History Today*, October 10, 1994, www.historytoday.com/archive/bearing-burden-puritan-wives.

17. Howe, *Penguin Witches*, 128–29.

18. Sneddon, *Witchcraft and Magic*, 78–79.

19. Jennifer O'Connell, "Witchipedia: Ireland's Most Famous Witches," *Irish Times*, October 28, 2017, www.irishtimes.com/life-and-style/people/witchipedia-ireland-s-most-famous-witches-1.3262008.

20. Sneddon, *Witchcraft and Magic*, 78–83.

21. Sneddon, *Witchcraft and Magic*, 58.

22. Mary McAuliffe, "Gender, History and Witchcraft in Early Modern Ireland: A Re-Reading of the Florence Newton Trial," in *Gender and Power in Irish History*, ed. Maryann Gialanella Valiulis (Dublin: Irish Academic Press, 2009), 39–59.

23. *Practical Magic*, directed by Griffin Dunne (Warner Bros., 1998), 1:09:55, play.hbomax.com/feature/urn:hbo:feature:GXjtShgurcY7CZgEAABBM?source=goo gleHBOMAX&action=play.

24. *The Craft*, directed by Andrew Fleming (Columbia Pictures, 1996). www .amazon.com/gp/video/detail/amzn1.dv.gti.d8b7ffbd-26b6-d72d-9b44-a11f34e173b8 ?autoplay=0&ref_=atv_cf_strg_wb.

25. *Chilling Adventures of Sabrina*, season 1, episode 2, "Chapter Two: The Dark Baptism," directed by Lee Toland Krieger, written by Roberto Aguirre-Sacasa, featuring Kiernan Shipka, Miranda Otto, Lucy Davis, and Richard Coyle, released October 26, 2018, on Netflix, www.netflix.com/watch/80230072?trackId=200257859.

26. *Chilling Adventures of Sabrina*, season 1, episode 3, "Chapter Three: The Trial of Sabrina Spellman," directed by Rob Seidenglanz, written by Ross Maxwell, featuring Kiernan Shipka, Miranda Otto, Lucy Davis, and Ross Lynch, released October 26, 2018, on Netflix, www.netflix.com/watch/80230072?trackId=200257859.

27. Russell Zguta, "The Ordeal by Water (Swimming of Witches) in the East Slavic Word," *Slavic Review* 36, no. 2 (June 1977): 220–30.

28. Silvia Federici, *Witches, Witch-Hunting and Women* (Brooklyn: Autonomedia, 2018), 185.

29. *Chilling Adventures of Sabrina*, season 4, episode 4, "Chapter Thirty-Two: The Imp of the Perverse," directed by Antonio Negret, written by Christianne Hedtke, featuring Kiernan Shipka, Miranda Otto, Ross Lynch, and Jaz Sinclair, released December 31, 2020, on Netflix, www.netflix.com/title/80223989.00:20:19.

30. *Chilling Adventures of Sabrina*, season 1, episode 7, "Chapter Seven: Feast of Feasts," directed by Viet Nguyen, written by Oanh Ly, featuring Kiernan Shipka, Miranda Otto, Lucy Davis, and Tati Gabrielle, released October 26, 2018, on Netflix, www.netflix.com/title/80223989.2018.

31. *Chilling Adventures of Sabrina,* "Chapter Seven: Feast of Feasts," 00:03:31.

32. *Chilling Adventures of Sabrina,* "Chapter Seven: Feast of Feasts," 00:04:47.

33. *Chilling Adventures of Sabrina,* "Chapter Seven: Feast of Feasts," 00:11:06.

34. Charles Zika, "Cannibalism and Witchcraft in Early Modern Europe: Reading the Visual Images," in *Exorcising our Demons: Magic, Witchcraft, and Visual Culture in Early Modern Europe* (Leiden, the Netherlands: Brill, 2003): 445–79.

35. *Chilling Adventures of Sabrina*, "Chapter Thirty-Two: The Imp of the Perverse."

36. Howe, *Penguin Witches*, 30–31.

37. Tamara L. Hunt and Micheline R. Lessard, *Women and the Colonial Gaze* (London: Palgrave Macmillan, 2002), 49–62.

38. Caitriona Beaumont, "Women, Citizenship and Catholicism in the Irish Free State, 1922–1948," *Women's History Review* 6, no. 4 (1997): 563–85. doi:10.1080/09612029700200154.

39. Clara Fischer, "Gender, Nation, and the Politics of Shame: Magdalen Laundries and the Institutionalization of Feminine Transgression in Modern Ireland," *Journal of Women in Culture and Society* 41, no. 4 (2016): 821–43.

40. Maria Luddy, "Sex and the Single Girl in 1920s and 1930s Ireland," *The Irish Review* 35 (2007): 239.

41. Inglis, "Origins and Legacies of Irish Prudery," 27.

42. Fischer, *Politics of Shame*, 286.

43. *Chilling Adventures of Sabrina*, "Chapter One: October Country," 00:42:14.

44. *Chilling Adventures of Sabrina*, "Chapter One: October Country," 00:42:35.

45. *Chilling Adventures of Sabrina*, season 2, episode 5, "Chapter Sixteen: Blackwood," directed by Alex Pillai, written by Matthew Barry, featuring Kiernan Shipka, Miranda Otto, Lucy Davis, and Richard Coyle, released April 5, 2019, on Netflix, www.netflix.com/title/80223989.

46. *Chilling Adventures of Sabrina*, season 2, episode 3, "Chapter Fourteen: Lupercalia," directed by Salla Richardson-Whitfield, written by Ona Ly, featuring Kiernan Shipka, Miranda Otto, Lucy Davis, and Chance Perdomo, released April 5, 2019, Netflix, www.netflix.com/title/80223989.

47. *Chilling Adventures of Sabrina*, "Chapter Fourteen: Lupercalia," 00:03:54.

48. *Chilling Adventures of Sabrina,* season 3, episode 4, "The Hare Moon," directed by Viet Nguyen, written by Donna Thorland, featuring Kiernan Shipka, Miranda Otto, Lucy Davis, and Jaz Sinclair, released January 24, 2020, on Netflix, www.netflix.com/title/80223989.

49. Fiona De Londras and Mairead Enright, "The Case for Repealing the 8th," in *Repealing the 8th: Reforming Irish Abortion Law* (Bristol, UK: Bristol University Press, 2018), 1–14.

50. Laura Kelly, "The Contraceptive Pill in Ireland *c.*1964–79: Activism, Women and Patient-Doctor Relationships," *Medical History* 64, no. 2 (April 2020): 195–218. doi.org/10.1017/mdh.2020.3.

51. "The Irish Women Who Fought to Legalise Contraception," BBC News, the BBC, last modified March 1, 2017, www.bbc.com/news/av/magazine-36249697.

52. "The Irish Women Who Fought to Legalise Contraception."

53. Kelly, "The Contraceptive Pill in Ireland," 195.

54. *Chilling Adventures of Sabrina*, season 1, episode 10, "Chapter Ten: The Witching Hour," directed by Rob Seidenglanz, written by Roberto Aguirre-Sacasa and Ross Maxwell, featuring Kiernan Shipka, Miranda Otto, Lucy Davis, and Chance Perdomo, released October 26, 2018, on Netflix, www.netflix.com/title/80223989: 00:39:21.

55. *Chilling Adventures of Sabrina*, season 4, episode 3, "Chapter Thirty-One: The Weird," directed by Lisa Soper, written by Jenina Kibuka, featuring Kiernan Shipka, Miranda Otto, Lucy Davis, and Jaz Sinclair, released December 31, 2020, on Netflix, www.netflix.com/title/80223989.

56. *Chilling Adventures of Sabrina*, "Chapter Thirty-Two: The Imp of the Perverse."

57. *Chilling Adventures of Sabrina*, "Chapter Thirty-Two: The Imp of the Perverse," 00:56:29.

PART 2

"I want freedom and power"

Depictions of Feminism

Proliferating Feminisms and the Irruption of the Material in *Chilling Adventures of Sabrina*

Tp Coughlin

The popular press cannot seem to decide whether *Chilling Adventures of Sabrina* (Netflix, 2018–2020) is the new vanguard of feminist action TV in the vein of *Buffy the Vampire Slayer* (The WB/The CW, 1997–2003) or another cynical attempt to cash in on the trend of "girl boss" feminism that aestheticizes and depoliticizes the once-radical movement. Proponents of the former argument can point to the strong women living under, and fighting against, the dominion of the patriarchal Church of Night and the Dark Lord, Lucifer Morningstar (Luke Cook) himself. Proponents of the latter turn towards the muddled, often forced moments of intersectional feminism that appear in a show seemingly more concerned with individualism and personal power. What, then, are we to make of this series?

My aim is not to choose one side or the other in this debate. Instead, I chart how the ambiguous and contradictory feminism of the show is a feature rather than a defect. Drawing on Mitchum Huehls's (2016) work on the shift towards ontological literature and away from epistemological interventions and critique, I argue that feminism in *Chilling Adventures of Sabrina* (*CAoS*) is not a political project; instead, *CAoS* is an attempt to imagine a way of living in and through feminism. From this perspective, it becomes clear that the ambiguity characterizing reviews on both sides of this debate is a consequence of feminism losing its unifying epistemological focus, or the way of understanding the world through the political lens. Instead, the ontological feminism of *CAoS* becomes a diffuse project of being.

In defining the role of ontological art in Colson Whitehead's novel *Zone One,* Huehls pays special attention to the way that art in the novel is "more than mere representation," arguing that ontological art is "a transmission that alters the landscape rather than just referring to it."[1] Though Huehls is referring to a specific instance of art within the fiction of Whitehead's novel, this passage is equally applicable to what he sees as the capacity for contemporary fiction to "[introduce] a productive wrinkle into neoliberal totality by considering, not the Marxist alternative to capitalism, but ontology's alternative to standard representational forms."[2] For Huehls, neoliberalism's flexibility has rendered critique as always already incorporated. Whether one launches a critique from an objective or subjective perspective, Huehls argues, it can only effect small surface transformations, leaving the underlying power structure intact. Ontological art, in its refusal of easy legibility and express political message, ironically provides more opportunity for transformations by working within the structure of neoliberalism itself. By arguing that the feminism of *CAoS* is an ontological project, rather than an epistemological or political one, we move past the need to determine the efficacy of feminism without embracing critiques of the series as "postfeminist"—a lens that has dominated previous discussions of the series.

Before turning to the scholarly conversation on the role of feminism/postfeminism in *CAoS,* however, it is useful to contextualize the series within the various debates over neoliberalism, particularly the argument between scholars focusing on the subjective transformations of neoliberalism and those focused on material changes. This debate offers a key to understanding the limits of Sabrina's ontologizing feminism, which I will examine more in the context of one of the most jarring episodes of *CAoS,* Part Four's "Chapter Thirty: The Uninvited" (4:2).

Neoliberalism is a contested term within academic conversations. For the sake of this essay, however, it is sufficient to sketch two particular threads framing this discussion. The first traces the way subjectivity is transformed as a result of austerity measures and the rise of a hegemonic rhetoric of individual accountability, which is contrasted to calls for collective responsibility under the welfare state. According to this perspective, the shift to neoliberalism is marked by the rise of *homo economicus,* or man as governed primarily by economic discourses. There is a long history of scholars who have helped to develop this line of thinking, although one of the most influential articulations is Wendy Brown's 2017 *Undoing the Demos: Neoliberalism's Stealth Revolution.*[3] Here, Brown offers us a theory of how the demands of the neoliberal economy have slowly undermined both the philosophical and political subject. The result is the rise of entrepreneurial citizenship, one wherein each subject is called upon to treat every action and decision as an investment in the self. The consequence of this, according to Brown, is an economic imperative that dominates all modes of life. While this trend takes into account the economic transformations that occurred in the late 1970s and 1980s, it tends to use this as a springboard to broader social imaginaries and discursive systems of power.

In contrast to this, the second thread examined here attempts to trace the material transformations of neoliberalism in specific detail. Rather than attempting to understand the change in a hegemonic subjectivity, the materialist thinkers who comprise this second thread ask how the material lives of people have transformed during a period which saw a rapidly disintegrating social safety net alongside a stagnation of wages, an increase in underemployment, and a growing emphasis on financialization and speculation. While this line of inquiry is hardly new—one notable early example is Nancy Fraser's careful attention to the ways in which the decline of the family wage has led to a rise in the number of women working in the service sector and other low-paid jobs[4]—it has grown rapidly in the past decade in part as a response to, ironically enough, Brown's writing.

In perhaps the most direct response to Brown, Marxist literary scholar Annie McClanahan points to the way that Brown ultimately reinscribes a White economically privileged norm through her inattention to the material difficulty of the people living outside of the White bourgeoise. Because this critique is both vital and underrecognized, it is worth quoting McClanahan at length:

> I worry, I admit, that by characterizing neoliberalism through a *specific kind* of entrepreneurial subject—the subject who polishes her college application, who selects among schools for his kid, who improves her scholarly CV through obtaining national grants—we miss the possibility that neoliberalism is not the becoming-economic of the non-economic, but rather the introduction of economic exigencies into the lives of a group—[W]hite, educated, upper middle-class citizens of the developed world—formerly protected from them.[5]

Here McClanahan has captured the central distinction between the two threads I aim to introduce; one seeks to understand the way norms and systems of governance are newly deployed in the lives of The Subject, a category that never escapes its assumptions of Whiteness, maleness, and affluence, while the other attends to the ways that precarious lives are rendered invisible, what Grace Kyungwon Hong has termed as the "epistemological structure of disavowal" of racialized and gendered violence.[6] In this latter account, deprivation and death are occluded by the spectacle of middle-class success and the rhetoric of personal accountability.[7]

This tension, rather than being purely theoretical, animates the contemporary moment. While the emergence of the entrepreneurial subject is an important transformation of White U.S. lives, this privileged understanding of life in the contemporary United States is constantly disrupted by the irruption of visible signs of precarity, poverty, and death. It is exactly this tension that emerges so uniquely in the character of The Uninvited (Brahm Taylor). While the main aim of the series seems to be the proliferating of new feminisms, The Uninvited seems to thematize the reappearance of economic reality as the return of the repressed, the emergence of materiality into the symbolic world of ontologizing feminism.

Rather than trying to categorize *CAoS* as either good or bad representation, I seek to articulate the ways in which the series participates in a broader project of moving beyond epistemological enactments of politics and towards politicized modes of being. Once we are attuned to the ways the show eschews traditional understandings of feminism, we can understand the ways in which it both enacts and complicates its own project. By envisioning feminism as an ontological project, *CAoS* offers a vision of a new coalitional framework, one marked by flexibility and contingency. At the same time, the series exposes its own inadequacy for addressing the material realities of race and class.

In the next section, I return to the analytic of postfeminism, a concept central to existing scholarship on *CAoS*. While such an analytical tool is useful for generating a critique of the ways ostensibly feminist neoliberal media fails to meet the demands of radical politics, it also forecloses insights about the instability and proliferation of feminism within the series; while not the broad, transformative politics that feminism envisions, the series does offer its own politics grounded in coalition, contingency, and compromise. I then turn towards the figure of The Uninvited as an attempt to represent the unrepresentable in neoliberal television: class. While The Uninvited is both jarring and problematic from a political perspective, I argue that it represents a remarkable capacity for self-critique made from within the project of ontologizing feminism. Finally, I conclude the chapter by visiting the "marriage" of Sabrina and The Uninvited. I speculate what such a marriage can, or cannot, offer in terms of bridging the gap between ontologizing feminisms and material realities.

FEMINISM, POSTFEMINISM, AND THE
PROLIFERATION OF FEMINISM

In "Chapter Ten: The Witching Hour" (1:10), Sabrina Spellman (Kiernan Shipka) is tricked by Lilith (Michelle Gomez), who is posing as Sabrina's teacher Mary Wardwell, into signing away her freedom in exchange for the power to save her friends and family, answering a question which animates the series from the first episode: will Sabrina sign her name in the Dark Lord's *Book of the Beast*?[8] Given the narrative emphasis on this question, it is easy to see this moment as a foregone conclusion. But it is worth pausing to consider why the series resolves this question in this specific manner: why during a moment of crisis? Why in the name of power? And why, particularly, at the behest of Ms. Wardwell/Lilith? What follows is not an answer to these questions, per se. Rather, it is an attempt to demonstrate how the over-emphasis on the debate between good representation/bad representation forecloses certain critical questions about the way the series understands feminism.

Ostensibly, Lilith is a villain and a somewhat unwilling underling of the Dark Lord. But Lilith's development cannot be described in simple terms, either morally or narratively. At various points throughout the series, she seeks to deceive, murder, assist, rule, replace, or coexist with Sabrina and her coven. Like Sabrina, she is subjugated by the Dark Lord, forced to do his bidding without any reward or praise. Also like Sabrina, she cleverly works to subvert this domination in order to make her own life more livable. And yet, Lilith never receives a redemption arc; even in the show's final moments, she is characterized by her desire for power. This relationship with power structures her character arc throughout the show; not only is it her motivation, but it is also the tool that she uses for seduction and control.

Sabrina signing the *Book of the Beast* in "Chapter Ten: The Witching Hour" is a key example. Notably, Lilith is given the role of narrator for this episode, granting her not only diegetic power but also power over the narrative itself.[9] The episode begins with a framing device: Lilith, looking into the camera, explaining just how, exactly, she managed to convince Sabrina to sign the *Book of the Beast*. From there, the episode plays like a tragedy wherein Sabrina, perpetually overconfident and headstrong, is led to her demise. To summarize, Lilith resurrects a band of witches killed in a Salem-style witch trial. These witches seek revenge on the town by summoning the Crimson Avenger to kill every firstborn in Greendale. In order to save themselves, the characters are divided across the town, creating magical and mundane protections against the incoming threat. With Sabrina's family and friends split up, Lilith convinces Sabrina that she needs power to prevent the impending doom.

It is in this context that Sabrina acquiesces. And yet this scene suggests that it is not simply her desire to save her loved ones that convinces her. This is especially clear when Lilith deviates from her rhetorical strategy of appealing to Sabrina's desire to protect her family in order to convince Sabrina to sign the book. Tellingly, Lilith instead begins to appeal to Sabrina's ego, noting her potential for greatness. When Sabrina seems unconvinced, Lilith encourages her, saying, "I know you're scared, Sabrina. Because all women are taught to fear power. Own your power. Don't accept it from the Dark Lord.

Take it. Wield it."[10] Here Lilith is mimicking a certain hegemonic feminism that does not seek to transform existing systems of power beyond simply installing more women in upper echelons of power, a phenomenon referred to as "girl boss" feminism. This is an important moment, even if it is not ultimately the reason why Sabrina signs her name. After all, the next two seasons play out Sabrina's mixed motivations along exactly these same lines: will Sabrina succumb to power, or will she remain committed to her family? But while this dichotomy suggests a critique of "girl boss" feminism, the show seems to resist this reading.

CAoS adopts an ambivalent stance on power rather than critiquing it. Even though characters motivated by power are treated with suspicion, they are not explicitly evil in *CAoS*. In fact, Sabrina's aunt Zelda Spellman (Miranda Otto) is just as motivated by her desire for power as Lilith, despite being characterized as more-or-less good. Throughout the series, she enacts several plans to elevate herself, either through marriage or by unilaterally installing herself as High Priestess of the Church of Night, or even eventually founding her own church. And although both Lilith and Zelda experience a great deal of suffering, both ultimately succeed in their ends. In fact, *CAoS*'s equivocation on the question of power is so deep that the series can only resolve Sabrina's dilemma between power and family by creating a second Sabrina, Sabrina Morningstar, who will rule Hell while the original Sabrina, Sabrina Spellman, lives her life with her family and friends. This drive to proliferate differences rather than seek the closure of a single unified subject is central to the project of ontologizing feminism. It is in the context of this proliferation of feminism that I want to return to the earlier discussion of postfeminism as an analytic tool for understanding *CAoS*.

Unlike ontologizing feminism, the postfeminist analytic emphasizes the way that feminism shifts to a depoliticized or even aestheticized representation from the 1990s onward.[11] Offering a history of the term "postfeminism," including its uses and critiques, Rosalind Gill writes that postfeminism is at its most useful when used to understand how representations of feminism index "a patterned yet contradictory sensibility connected to other dominant ideologies (such as individualism and neoliberalism)."[12] The postfeminist analytic is used to understand the ways feminism does and does not offer a viable political project when incorporated into dominant media. Particularly, this analytic is useful for understanding the contradiction between the resurgence of feminist media and the increased hostility to both feminism and women in contemporary society.

For Gill, this analytic is vital to understanding how feminist rhetoric is not only denied in the contemporary moment but can be resignified in order to tacitly support the systems of power which feminist activism has sought to dismantle.[13] However useful, this approach seems trapped in the debate over

good/bad representation. Too often, scholars rely on the postfeminist analytic in their reflection on *CAoS*, even as they come to different conclusions.
Thinking through their work allows us to recognize the limitations of projects
predicated on assessing the political and epistemological valence of the text
that Huehls terms the neoliberal circle, or the process by which the flexible
structure of neoliberalism circumscribes critique by limiting our ability to
represent ourselves as political agents.[14]

Megan Henesy argues for a reading of Sabrina as a "reimagining of bubbly blonde Sabrina the Teenage Witch as a gothic-inspired feminist icon
for the millennial age."[15] For Henesy, *CAoS* moves beyond postfeminism
through its explicit reference to the experience of patriarchy in the show. In
order to make this argument, however, Henesy must articulate exactly what
is and is not feminist in the show. This leads her to read a degree of bad faith
into characters like Lilith. Henesy writes that "while Sabrina's fight against
patriarchal suppression drives the narrative, the older witches in the coven are
presented initially as complicit in their own subjugation. Even Madam Satan
[. . .] spends much of the time acting as a slave to the Dark Lord."[16] While
this assessment is partly true in that the characters are keenly aware of the
power of the Dark Lord as the key patriarchal antagonist, the characterization of the older witches as being defined by their complicity overlooks the
various forms of resistance that they undertake even in the earliest episodes.
Whether these small acts are a steppingstone for a more active revolution, like
when Sabrina's aunt Hilda Spellman (Lucy Davis) admits her dissatisfaction
with joining the Church of Night or advocates for Sabrina's right to maintain
her mortal relations—both of which presage a movement away from the
Dark Lord's subjugation—or a more individualist one, as in Lilith's deeply
complicit demand to share the Dark Lord's throne, they are undeniably the
foundation for a shared feminist project.

Media studies scholar Kristina Brüning argues that the postfeminist analytic offers useful insight even during the resurgence of self-consciously feminist media. Articulating her theory of the joykill, a reverse of Sara Ahmed's
killjoy, Brüning notes how feminist anger has been adopted into hegemonic
depictions of feminism in response to the #MeToo movement. Turning the
tools of the postfeminist analytic toward a new object, Brüning articulates
how emergent feminism depends on the disavowal of race as a contributing
factor in sexism and sexual violence.[17] Accordingly, a diverse cast might
offer the appearance of intersectionality without providing a grounded, intersectional account of gendered experiences. Brüning demonstrates multiple
moments in *CAoS* where Sabrina reduces difficult intersectional concerns to
the single-lens issue of gender, including the founding of the feminist activist
club WICCA[18] and attempting to end the violent hazing at the Academy of
Unseen Arts, a school for witches which Sabrina attends.[19] Brüning makes

it clear that *CAoS* fails to address the lived realities of Black women. And yet, the show demonstrates an insistent interest in trying to *represent* Black womanhood. This is nowhere clearer than in the final season, where there are three prominent Black women featured: Sabrina's childhood friend Rosalind "Roz" Walker (Jaz Sinclair), her witch frenemy Prudence Blackwood (Tati Gabrielle), and the mysterious Mambo Marie (Skye Marshall). Although each are a part of the series prior to the fourth season, it is in this season's attempt to link them together as the newly reconstituted Weird Sisters that the show comes closest to acknowledging the role of racialization in shaping the lives of Black women. And yet, this attention to race fails to move beyond the visual realm.[20]

The desire to represent race while also denying the material realities of racialization is a key contradiction in *CAoS*. Understanding it, however, requires going beyond critique and instead attending to these characters and the differences between them. It is notable that both Mambo Marie and Roz are marginal figures within the witch community; that is, neither one truly fits in with the Satan-turned-Hecate-worshiping coven. Roz is a Christian whose identity as a witch is complicated by the competing identification as a Cunning woman, a name her ancestors used to reconcile their magic and their Christianity. Mambo Marie, on the other hand, is Catholic and a Vodou practitioner. Though the Weird Sisters are intended to be a three-in-one, or a single magical force, the latter iteration is a heterogeneous assembly, one which preserves rather than assimilates the differences of those who constitute it.

Although hardly an intersectional politics, this diversity helps demonstrate the logic of proliferating feminisms in *CAoS*. Even as race is disavowed in the logic of the series, it invents new modes of difference through which characters are individuated by the ontologizing feminist project. As a result, *CAoS* cannot be said to instantiate a single, hegemonic feminism; rather, it precipitates a profusion of feminisms. Eva Cherniavsky demonstrates how this profusion of identities is a neoliberal logic that she characterizes as the rise of *serial culture*. Cherniavsky writes, "[unlike] normative culture, serial culture does not differentiate among identities (between the normal and the pathological, for example), so much as cultivate a process of differentiation that produces an ever-broader spectrum of identities."[21] In other words, serial cultures do not try to invent a hierarchy between identities, at least not officially. As such, it would be a mistake to approach the emergence of serial culture through a taxonomical lens. Rather, the project contextualizes this new variety as a feature that transforms the flow of power within society. My point is not that this movement excuses the failure to account for race as a material reality. Rather, I am arguing that in emphasizing the failures of the series' intersectional feminism as an epistemological and political project, Brüning overlooks the way the series *does* deploy racial difference.

Postfeminist readings of *CAoS* prioritize the need for legibility and a politically motivated single feminism within a text. It results in a reading practice that emphasizes uncovering and critiquing a concrete articulation of a feminist politics within the text, which, as Henesy and Brüning demonstrate, is often tied to the series' protagonist, Sabrina. *CAoS*, however, never embraces a coherent feminist position. Rather, it offers a proliferation of feminisms throughout the series, to the extent that minor characters become almost reducible to their individuated practice of being feminist. By attending to the rise of serial cultures as a foundational logic of neoliberalism, specifically as it relates to the ceaseless proliferation of mythologies, magical practices, and even the two Sabrinas themselves, we can understand how the series foregoes making a single, unified critique.

This argument takes up Huehls's call to embrace our complicity in the system of neoliberalism—at least strategically. To do this is to enter into the systems of neoliberal world-making in order to see what new flows of power and ways of being can be found. And yet, there is a certain politics within this complicity. It is only necessary to consider the various encounters between Lilith and the coven of witches to understand how an ontologizing feminism offers a potential for coalition, even assemblage, under certain conditions. The exorcism of Jesse Putnam (Jason Beaudoin), Lilith's role as Sabrina's regent, and the birth of Adam are all moments where various feminisms intertwine for a single purpose, even though they are motivated by their own ends.

For all its benefits, the ontologizing feminism of *CAoS* should not be mistaken for a perfect solution for attending to questions of gender in society. For one, Brüning has already shown the way that the series only represents race insofar as it reinforces a multiculturalist diversity that does not disturb the systems of White supremacy.[22] In the following section, I demonstrate another particular gap in the series: class. In turning to class, I will point to the way in which economic issues—unlike race, which is reduced in and through its hypervisibility in the series—are almost entirely unrepresentable. And yet, it is in the attempt to represent this disavowed knowledge that *CAoS* offers a way through ontologizing feminism and into a new mode of political being.

REPRESENTING THE REPRESSED, OR HOW TO READ THE UNINVITED

While I am interested in why class proves so uniquely impossible to represent within *CAoS*, I do not want to critique the series for its omission. In fact, the series demonstrates that it is aware of this, seemingly addressing it through the creation of the character The Uninvited.[23] The series demonstrates and even problematizes the way in which neoliberal subjectivity is always already predicated on the disavowal of class differences and the material demands of precarity. In other words, it is at the juncture of feminism and materialism that ontologizing feminism fails, where the proliferation of identities and modalities of ontological being-feminist, as opposed to epistemic feminism, are no longer producible.

The tension between identity politics and class politics is a well-worn debate within critical studies of neoliberalism. A particularly useful account comes from Grace Kyungwon Hong's careful articulation of the transformation of identity politics during the late 1970s. Writing on the emergence of the Black middle class, Hong notes that the ascendency of certain segments of marginalized communities is part of a strategy to create the appearance that race is no longer a structuring feature of society.[24] To this end, Hong describes what she terms the disavowal of death, that is to say, the sudden inability to recognize poverty, illness, or death as the result of systemic conditions. Instead, a commonsense logic of individualism and accountability is deployed, displacing the blame for these unequal conditions onto those most harmed by them. It is in the contexts of this debate and the rise in homelessness throughout the United States that The Uninvited emerges as a surprisingly important character in *CAoS*.

Introduced as the monster of the week in "Chapter Thirty: The Uninvited," the character of The Uninvited appears in the opening moments of the episode, pushing a shopping cart down the side of the road into Greendale.[25] That introduction, in addition to its knotted, dirty hair and poorly fitted clothing, makes it clear that The Uninvited is intended to evoke the specter of homelessness. The time spent introducing the character is enough to mark a significant rupture in the classless neoliberal fantasy of Greendale. While characters have been aesthetically rendered as more or less affluent, the series never otherwise addresses the material realities of class or poverty in the series. For instance, one might point to the blue-collar stylings of Harvey Kinkle (Ross Lynch) as an aesthetic coding that obfuscates the fact that his father, Mr. Kinkle (Christopher Rosamond), owns the Greendale mines and employs a large number of the town's citizens. To have the camera now tracking The Uninvited through the streets is a radical departure from the norms of the previous three parts. And yet, this is not an empathetic portrayal of The Uninvited. Even from this early moment its presence is unnerving.

Within the narrative of *CAoS,* empathy forestalls moral judgment when characters engage in selfish or dangerous behaviors. For instance, both Lilith and Zelda are given numerous occasions to demonstrate their individual plights and insecurities in order to contextualize their more questionable behavior. Meanwhile, characters such as the Dark Lord and Father Blackwell

(Richard Coyle) are rarely featured in a context that would inspire empathy. The camera pauses long enough to follow The Uninvited on its journey into town, but the way it is framed ultimately frustrates any attempt to empathize. The camera zooms in on one squeaky wheel of the shopping cart or showing The Uninvited's silhouette lit by the headlights of a passing car; we do not have much opportunity to identify with The Uninvited before we cut to the interior of a small apartment where a mother and a daughter are eating their dinner, both of whom will soon be murdered by The Uninvited. This scene offers a rich example of the way that "Chapter 30: The Uninvited" is dominated by the tension between conflicting politics; it symptomatizes the anxiety around materiality—which underlies most forms of politics, but particularly identity politics—under neoliberalism. By offering a thick description of this scene, I aim to demonstrate the value of understanding the politics embedded within the media itself rather than reading political projects into it.

The first thing we see after cutting away from The Uninvited is a mother and daughter sitting across each other, praying over their dinner. It is hard not to notice the irony of the prayer—"For what we are about to receive, may the Lord make us truly thankful"—which makes no specific reference to the dinner before them.[26] Both the mother and the daughter are dressed in collared shirts with cardigans, solidifying their status as middle class, or at least upwardly mobile. The room is decorated with a Gothic Baroque aesthetic that runs throughout the series, less a class signifier than a signifier for the classless fantasy world of Greendale. What emerges is a pleasant domestic scene that seems to gesture towards the sanctity of the home in the liberal imaginary as a site of family and privacy with all its attendant connotations of conformity and respectability.

CAoS is no stranger to subverting the safety inspired by the home, but what makes this scene so remarkable is its apparent mundanity. After all, we are not in the home of witches but rather in the home of Lucy Anderson (Evelyn Burke) and her mother, Mrs. Anderson (Kayla Deorksen), two characters who were briefly featured in "Chapter Twenty-Two: Drag Me to Hell" (3:2) and both of whom, besides having a penchant for attracting evil forces, are normal mortals.[27] The first indication that something is amiss is Lucy scrunching her nose after the prayer and complaining about the smell of garbage, which her mother quickly dismisses. However, their dinner is soon interrupted by a knock on the door, disrupting the ritual of a family meal. In the next shot, we see The Uninvited again silhouetted and obscured by the textured glass on the door. Merely positioning it in the center of the screen, seen down a long hallway, evokes a sense of dread and inevitability. This dread is confirmed when Mrs. Anderson opens the door and her expression changes from shock to disgust and finally to fear.

This is the first time the viewer sees The Uninvited in detail. The camera focuses first on a cardboard sign hanging its neck with the message "Cold. Hungry. Tired. May I Come In?" From there, the camera slowly pans upwards, past its dirty, poorly fitting clothes, revealing a face covered in sores and dry, flaking skin with long, tangled hair. The Uninvited is an exaggerated depiction of the homelessness that urban viewers, and likely those involved in the production of the series in and around Vancouver, have witnessed in daily life. Again, it is the mundanity that is striking: the horror of The Uninvited is not the cosmic terror or unfathomable weirdness of the rest of the Eldritch Terrors, the principal foes of Part Four. Rather, it is the commonplaceness that makes this character stand out amongst the various Eldritch Terrors.

What follows is a shot/reverse shot sequence that shows an increasingly frightened Mrs. Anderson refusing to help The Uninvited, first insisting and finally begging for The Uninvited to leave, all the while The Uninvited stares blankly back. The terror here seems to be overdetermined, with the fear of home invasion, sexual violence, and poverty itself all muddled in the single figure. When The Uninvited does not move, she implores it, "Please, my little girl is just inside."[28] At this, The Uninvited appears to leave. Mrs. Anderson closes the door, and the viewer hears the squeaking of the shopping cart's loose wheel. Shaken but attempting to regain her composure, Mrs. Anderson turns from the door and heads down the long hallway back to the dining room, only to be interrupted by The Uninvited, who appears from another doorway inside the apartment and plucks Mrs. Anderson's heart from her body. The scene ends with Lucy, the child, looking out into the hallway and The Uninvited moving towards her, implying she is also murdered.

As this thick description shows, this short scene is rich with political and social significance. Even a surface viewing makes evident the way The Uninvited is positioned as a threat to both private property and femininity, a point made explicit by Mrs. Anderson's apparent concern for her daughter. And certainly, both Mrs. Anderson and Lucy are the victims in this encounter, having been murdered in a manner perversely fitting their "heartless" treatment of The Uninvited. And yet, there is something so striking in how mundane a threat The Uninvited represents in the moments before the murder. If the Eldritch Terrors are meant to represent forces beyond good and evil, beyond human comprehension, why choose the figure of a homeless man?

Viewing this question from a broad social perspective might generate a critique of *CAoS* as having failed to address the lived realities of poverty and, worse, having participated in an exploitative representation that figures homelessness through the gaze of the bourgeois subject. While such a critique is certainly true, I argue that, ironically, we can learn more about the contours of neoliberalism when we approach The Uninvited as a moment of crisis within the symbolic language of the show. That is to say, rather than a failed attempt to adequately represent homelessness, The Uninvited can be read as an attempt to represent that which is unrepresentable within the series' neoliberal imaginary. In psychoanalytic terms, it is the return of the repressed, a disavowed knowledge returning in a new, uncanny form.

Rather than an external critique, one which tries to impose its own morality onto an object, the internal criticism which emerges here helps to expose the limits of ontologizing feminism. That is to say that while the series repeatedly demonstrates the potential of new coalitional formations for handling discrete issues, it fails to even imagine a form of material politics that is not rooted in a violent deprivation of individual autonomy and comfort. The presentation of The Uninvited in this scene frames the possibility of welcoming it into one's home as a profoundly dangerous act, but as we see later in the episode, when Roz and Harvey do just this, it is the only way to face the challenge at hand. The real threat emerges only in the turning away from a materialist praxis of care. Such a perspective resonates with a number of contemporary scholars who seek to enact a radical materialist praxis, such as Marquis Bey writing about the prospect of anarcho-Blackness. In their insistence that "if we must sully ourselves by hanging around a bad crowd that is bad only because the good's violent optics and ethics deem it so, then that is what is to be done," we can see a mirror for the demands of The Uninvited.[29]

While *CAoS*'s proliferation of ontologizing feminism, which opens up a myriad of ways of being for the women in the series, offers the capacity for a coalitional politics to form in resistance to patriarchy, it proves unable to imagine the needs of a materialist politics. Rather than being an external criticism, this insight is the direct result of how The Uninvited is portrayed in the series, as the irruption of the materiality's destabilizing force that penetrates directly into the heart of the bourgeois home. By drawing on the psychoanalytic concept of the return of the repressed, I argue that The Uninvited is a symptom of the way that neoliberalism disavows the material foundations of oppression. In other words, the emergence of this uniquely neoliberal subjectivity is made possible only by making neoliberalism's economic and material reality unimaginable.

In the final section of this chapter, I briefly examine the conclusion to "Chapter Thirty: The Uninvited," particularly the "marriage" of Sabrina and The Uninvited. Such a movement, I argue, demonstrates an attempt to reinstate the domestic scene disrupted by the arrival of The Uninvited in the first few minutes of the episode. This unhappy marriage mirrors the relationship between the representation of class and the ontologizing feminist project of *CAoS*.

THE UNHAPPY MARRIAGE OF MATERIALISM
AND NEOLIBERAL FEMINISMS

It does not seem like a coincidence that "Chapter Thirty: The Uninvited" is an episode that constantly orbits domestic scenes. Not only do we begin with the scene described above, but the episode features not one but two weddings—three if you count the fake marriage between Sabrina Spellman and The Uninvited. In fact, the emotional core of the episode has little to do with The Uninvited. Rather, it tracks Sabrina's own sense of alienation in relation to first her aunt Hilda's marriage and then to the marriage of Sabrina Morningstar, the second Sabrina who rules Hell while Sabrina Spellman pursues a life with her family on Earth. Rather than representing an actual threat to Sabrina and her friends, The Uninvited serves as a foil for her own loneliness and feelings of unbelonging. Despite this, however, Sabrina does not hesitate to use their shared sense of placelessness to trick The Uninvited into lowering its guard.

Having been denied entry into Hilda's wedding, The Uninvited attempts to seek its revenge during the reception. In order to prevent this, Sabrina Spellman offers to bring The Uninvited to Sabrina Morningstar's wedding as her plus one. Once there, Sabrina Spellman enacts a plan with her double and her father, the Dark Lord, to trap The Uninvited outside of space and time. This plan involves not only marrying The Uninvited but luring it into the yellow wallpaper house, an enchanted dollhouse that serves as The Uninvited's eternal prison. Trapped, The Uninvited declares that Sabrina has "broken [its] heart" before charging toward her, either to escape or to enact its revenge.[30] Beyond the obvious irony of using the trap of domesticity to vanquish The Uninvited, this resolution points to a larger issue at the core of *CAoS*'s ontologizing project. That is, as an approach to addressing the material crises of neoliberalism, the transformation of feminism into an ontology is insufficient at best. At worst, it perpetuates the disavowal of material realities and the reliance on incarceration in the name of an ever-expanding proliferation of feminism with no political valence beyond the individual act of signifying.

And yet, in its capacity for self-critique, *CAoS* demonstrates its greatest strength. In eschewing any stable political or epistemological determination of feminism, the series gains the capacity for articulating its own shortcomings, even if only in problematic fits and starts. The ability to render the invisible visible, to realize the demands of material reality alongside the neoliberal fantasy of the classless society offers a potential path forward, not through salvation or radical change, but through compromise and hard-won progress. Whether such a political venture is viable for handling the immediate crises of austerity, deregulation, and extraction is beyond the scope of this essay.

In this chapter, I have demonstrated how attending to the proliferation of feminisms within contemporary media such as *CAoS* offers a rich way of understanding representations of feminism while bypassing the cyclical debates on the status of media as "good" or "bad" feminist representation. By attending to the process of ontologizing feminism, I have demonstrated how certain forms of coalitional politics are opened up while other forms are foreclosed under this contemporary configuration of identity. In doing so, I have demonstrated the value of rich, detailed reading of contemporary media for generating insights about the political systems we inhabit.

BIBLIOGRAPHY

Bey, Marquis. *Anarcho-Blackness: Notes Toward a Black Anarchism*. Chico, CA: AK Press, 2020.

Brown, Wendy. *Undoing the Demos: Neoliberalism's Stealth Revolution*. New York: Zone Books, 2017.

Brüning, Kristina. "'I'm Neither a Slut, Nor Am I Gonna Be Shamed': Sexual Violence, Feminist Anger, and Teen TV's New Heroine." *Television & New Media* 23, no. 7 (May 2021): 1–16. doi.org/10.1177/15274764211015307.

Cherniavsky, Eva. "Neocitizenship and Critique." *Social Text* 27, no. 2 (2009): 1–23. doi.org/10.1215/01642472-2008-020.

Chilling Adventures of Sabrina, Season 1, episode 10, "Chapter Ten: The Witching Hour." Directed by Rob Seidenglanz, written by Roberto Aguirre-Sacasa and Ross Maxwell, featuring Kiernan Shipka, Miranda Otto, Lucy Davis, and Chance Perdomo. Released October 26, 2018, Netflix, www.netflix.com/watch/80230080?trackId=200257859.

———, Season 3, episode 2, "Chapter Twenty-Two: Drag Me to Hell." Directed by Alex Pillai, written by Ross Maxwell, featuring Kiernan Shipka, Miranda Otto, Lucy Davis, and Chance Perdomo. Released December 31, 2020, Netflix, www.netflix.com/watch/81062653?trackId=14277283.

———, Season 4, episode 2, "Chapter Thirty: The Uninvited." Directed by Alex Pillai, written by Katie Avery, featuring Kiernan Shipka, Miranda Otto, Lucy Davis, and Sam Corlett. Released December 31, 2020, Netflix, www.netflix.com/watch/81062661?trackId=200257859.

Fraser, Nancy. "Feminism, Capitalism and the Cunning of History." *New Left Review* 56 (March/April 2009): 97–117.

Gill, Rosalind. "Post-Postfeminism?: New Feminist Visibilities in Postfeminist Times." *Feminist Media Studies* 16, no. 4 (2016): 610–630. doi.org/10.1080/14680777.2016.1193293.

Henesy, Megan. "'Leaving my girlhood behind': Woke Witches and Feminist Liminality in *Chilling Adventures of Sabrina*." *Feminist Media Studies* 21, no. 7 (2021): 1143–1157. doi.org/10.1080/14680777.2020.1791929.

Hong, Grace Kyungwon. *Death Beyond Disavowal: The Impossible Politics of Difference*. Minneapolis: University of Minnesota Press, 2015.

Huehls, Mitchum. *After Critique: Twenty-First-Century Fiction in a Neoliberal Age*. New York: Oxford University Press, 2016.

Konings, Martijn. *Capital and Time: For a New Critique of Neoliberal Reason*. Redwood City: Stanford University Press, 2018.

Lotz, Amanda D. "Postfeminist Television Criticism: Rehabilitating Critical Terms and Identifying Postfeminist Attributes." *Feminist Media Studies* 1, no. 1 (2001): 105–121. doi.org/10.1080/14680770120042891.

McClanahan, Annie J. "Becoming Non-Economic: Human Capital Theory and Wendy Brown's *Undoing the Demos*." *Theory & Event* 20, no. 2 (2017): 510–519. muse.jhu.edu/article/655783.

McRobbie, Angela. "Post-Feminism and Popular Culture." *Feminist Media Studies* 4, no. 3 (2004): 255–264. doi.org/10.1080/1468077042000309937.

Murphy, Michelle. *The Economization of Life*. Durham: Duke University Press, 2017.

NOTES

1. Mitchum Huehls, *After Critique: Twenty-First-Century Fiction in a Neoliberal Age* (New York: Oxford University Press, 2016): 27.

2. Huehls, *After Critique*, 28.

3. Wendy Brown, *Undoing the Demos: Neoliberalism's Stealth Revolution* (New York: Zone Books, 2017): 32–33.

4. Nancy Fraser, "Feminism, Capitalism and the Cunning of History," in *New Left Review*, no. 56 (2009): 110.

5. Annie J. McClanahan, "Becoming Non-Economic: Human Capital Theory and Wendy Brown's *Undoing the Demos*." *Theory & Event* 20, no. 2 (2017): 512. muse.jhu.edu/article/655783.

6. Grace Kyungwon Hong, *Death Beyond Disavowal: The Impossible Politics of Difference*, (Minneapolis: University of Minnesota Press, 2015): 7.

7. Huehls's (2016) theorization tends towards the former perspective, although he extensively critiques Brown, who he accuses of misreading Foucault's work on neoliberalism as an epistemological project rather than one detailing a new ontological mode. I tend towards the latter thread, emphasizing economic and material realities over subjectivity. My engagement with Huehls's work is an attempt to work through this impasse, as will be clear in the discussion of The Uninvited.

8. *Chilling Adventures of Sabrina*, season 1, episode 10, "Chapter Ten: The Witching Hour," directed by Rob Seidenglanz, written by Roberto Aguirre-Sacasa and Ross Maxwell, featuring Kiernan Shipka, Miranda Otto, Lucy Davis, and Chance Perdomo, released October 26, 2018, on Netflix, www.netflix.com/watch/80230080?trackId=200257859.

9. *Chilling Adventures of Sabrina*, season 1, episode 10, "Chapter Ten: The Witching Hour."

10. *Chilling Adventures of Sabrina,* season 1, episode 10, "Chapter Ten: The Witching Hour," 00:39:18.

11. Both Amanda Lotz (2001) and Angela McRobbie (2004) offer rich accounts of the ways postfeminism has shifted in its meaning over the past three decades.

12. Rosalind Gill, "Post-Postfeminism?: New Feminist Visibilities in Postfeminist Times," *Feminist Media Studies* 16, no. 4 (2016): 621. doi.org/10.1080/14680777.2016.1193293.

13. Gill, "Post-Postfeminism," 621.

14. Huehls, *After Critique*, 11.

15. Megan Henesy, "'Leaving My Girlhood Behind': Woke Witches and Feminist Liminality in *Chilling Adventures of Sabrina,*" *Feminist Media Studies* 21, no. 7 (2021): 1145. doi.org/10.1080/14680777.2020.1791929.

16. Henesy, "Leaving My Girlhood Behind," 1148.

17. Kristina Brüning, "'I'm Neither a Slut, Nor Am I Gonna Be Shamed': Sexual Violence, Feminist Anger, and Teen TV's New Heroine," *Television & New Media* 23, no. 7 (May 2021): 13. doi.org/10.1177/15274764211015307.

18. Brüning, "I'm Neither a Slut, Nor Am I Gonna Be Shamed," 8–9.

19. Brüning, "I'm Neither a Slut, Nor Am I Gonna Be Shamed," 13.

20. Although it is beyond the scope of this essay, it is worth noting the way that the reconstitution of the Weird Sisters indexes the shift from a neoliberal multiculturalist paradigm, where the sisterhood is formed across racial lines, to the new sisterhood of Black or Black-coded women. In this moment we see the emergence of a Black feminism, though one that is distinctly post-racial. A critical approach might view this as a commodification of "Black girl magic" and the renewed fetishization of Black women as icons of wokeness. However, as the discussion of the proliferation of feminism in the following passage demonstrates, there is no clear unity between any version of feminism which appears in the show. In this way, *CAoS* indexes the hazards of appropriating Black feminism for a White audience while still remaining implicated in this criticism.

21. Eva Cherniavsky, "Neocitizenship and Critique," *Social Text* 27, no. 2 (2009): 20. doi.org/10.1215/01642472-2008-020.

22. Kristina Brüning, "I'm Neither a Slut, Nor Am I Gonna Be Shamed," 12.

23. *Chilling Adventures of Sabrina*, season 4, episode 2, "Chapter Thirty: The Uninvited," Directed by Alex Pillai, written by Katie Avery, featuring Kiernan Shipka, Miranda Otto, Lucy Davis, and Sam Corlett, released December 31, 2020, on Netflix, www.netflix.com/watch/81062661?trackId=200257859.

24. Grace Kyungwon Hong, *Death Beyond Disavowal,* 7–8.

25. *Chilling Adventures of Sabrina*, season 4, episode 2, "Chapter Thirty: The Uninvited," 00:01:50.

26. *Chilling Adventures of Sabrina*, season 4, episode 2, "Chapter Thirty, The Uninvited," 00:02:13.

27. *Chilling Adventures of Sabrina*, season 3, episode 2, "Chapter Twenty-Two: Drag Me to Hell," by Alex Pillai, written by Ross Maxwell, featuring Kiernan Shipka, Miranda Otto, Lucy Davis, and Chance Perdomo, released December 31, 2020, on Netflix, www.netflix.com/watch/81062653?trackId=14277283.

28. *Chilling Adventures of Sabrina*, season 4, episode 2, "Chapter Thirty, The Uninvited," 00:03:02.

29. Marquis Bey, *Anarcho-Blackness: Notes Toward a Black Anarchism* (Chico, CA: AK Press, 2020), 30–31.

30. *Chilling Adventures of Sabrina*, season 4, episode 2, "Chapter Thirty, The Uninvited," 00:51:23.

Chapter 5

The Devil You Know?

Feminism and Postmodern Pastiche of Satanism and the Infernal in Chilling Adventures of Sabrina

Alice Capstick

Based on the comics written by Roberto Aguirre-Sacasa and illustrated by Robert Hack, Netflix's *Chilling Adventures of Sabrina* (2018–20) features many recognizable infernal, horror, and Gothic figures from literary and cultural history as part of its worldbuilding. Judeo-Christian mythology and some of the most prominent literary cornerstones of Western culture, including the works of Dante Alighieri, William Shakespeare, and John Milton influence many of the characters in *Chilling Adventures of Sabrina* (*CAoS*). The show's reliance on references to cultural icons for worldbuilding is a common postmodernist technique evident in many other popular television shows with Gothic and infernal themes, such as *Supernatural* (The WB, 2005–06/The CW, 2006–20), *The Vampire Diaries* (The CW, 2009–17), *Lucifer* (FOX, 2016–18/Netflix, 2019–21), *Once Upon a Time* (ABC, 2011–18), *Teen Wolf* (MTV, 2011–17), and more. The specific device of indirect referencing used by these shows and by *CAoS* is known as "pastiche." Fredric Jameson defines pastiche as "the imitation of a peculiar or unique style, the wearing of a stylistic mask, speech in a dead language."[1] Jameson further clarifies that pastiche is usually a neutral device, without the mimicry or satire normally associated with parody. Rather than participating in an existing tradition associated with the source, pastiche usually acts as a means of provoking nostalgia or establishing a certain style, aesthetic, or commentary, without necessarily commenting on or developing the significance of the reference.[2] In *CAoS*, pastiche acts as an important device for characterizing Lucifer

(Luke Cook), Faustus Blackwood (Richard Coyle), Caliban (Sam Corlett), and Hell itself—the most infernal aspects and main antagonists of the show. Pastiche is an essential part of *CAoS*'s world building, but rather than producing nostalgia, it creates the conditions for the show's most important underlying messages. *CAoS*'s use of pastiche defamiliarizes these cultural icons from their original source to re-identify them in accordance with the show's main theme—feminist rebellion. Pastiche empowers *CAoS* to reject the traditional meaning of these figures by refusing to sincerely replicate them or contribute to their cultural significance.

Influential feminist scholars Sandra Gilbert and Susan Gubar's premise for *The Madwoman in the Attic* (1979) is that women writers have overcome what they view to be pervasive patriarchal tradition and influence in the literary sphere through radical revisionist mythmaking. While the works that Gilbert and Gubar examine often achieve their mythmaking through a feminist re-imagination of the source text, *CAoS*'s use of pastiche decentralizes the source and prioritizes the feminist re-identification of the figure. The show therefore acts as a more radical postmodern version of the revisionist mythmaking Gilbert and Gubar discuss. This essay will identify the combination of various cultural and literary traditions that characterize *CAoS*'s infernal antagonists. It will also examine the extent to which the significance of the original source is both essential for establishing the show's engagement with important traditions and is displaced or abstracted in favor of feminist commentary.

The subjugation of important cultural traditions and references to the show's own narrative is most apparent in *CAoS*'s characterization of the main antagonists. The significance of the cultural tradition and significance of Lucifer, Faustus, and Caliban cannot be understated. Faustus has been an important figure in German folklore since the Middle Ages and would become a famous English cultural emblem after Christopher Marlowe's *The Tragical History of Doctor Faustus* (1604) and, later, Johann Wolfgang Goethe's *Faust* (1790). Similarly, Caliban and Lucifer have been the subject of two of the most important writers in English history—William Shakespeare and John Milton—in *The Tempest* (1611) and *Paradise Lost* (1667), respectively. These authors established the archetypal characters that have since become the subject of cultural experimentation. Rather than experimenting with these figures, *CAoS* reduces their mode of characterization to pastiche. The show's depiction of Hell is the most significant example of pastiche, and the combination of references has a similarly reductive effect because no recognizable version of Hell becomes apparent, meaning that Sabrina (Kiernan Shipka) and Lilith's (Michelle Gomez, who also plays Miss Wardwell) "restoration" of Hell becomes a feminist revisionist mythmaking exercise in and of itself. Although the series often directly references many of the significant sources for these figures, no one source dominates. The result is that their characters lose much of the significance traditionally associated with them, often to the point that they become unrecognizable, not only displacing but often erasing the importance of the original source. In *CAoS*, pastiche returns many of these infernal concepts back to abstraction by subverting the implications and significance of their literary precedents and subjecting them to postmodernist commentary.

Jameson argues that pastiche is parody that "has lost its sense of humor,"[3] but contemporary forms of pastiche can often be more accurately described as parody that denies a connection with the original source. Using pastiche also means that it is not essential for audiences to understand the relevance of the original source because it does not inform the narrative directly. In the case of *CAoS*, which draws from so many sources, pastiche informs the themes and aesthetic of the show. Because the show's references are distinct from their sources, *CAoS* is often a direct example of the type of pastiche Jameson describes. Even if viewers understand the significance of the reference, it usually does not act as a form of allusion. In the first few minutes of "Chapter One: October Country" (1:1) Ambrose (Chance Perdomo) asks Sabrina, "penny dreadful for your thoughts?" and refers to Zelda (Miranda Otto) and Hilda (Lucy Davis) as "madams Jekyll and Hyde."[4] Neither of these references are explained, nor are they relevant to the narrative, but they establish the mood of the show's contemporary Gothic themes and aesthetic and demonstrate its self-aware and nostalgic connection with Gothic tradition. Another obvious example of pastiche occurs when Ambrose produces a compass in Part Three to help them find King Herod's crown. He so quickly explains that the compass's previous owners include the Flying Dutchman, Aleister Crowley, and the Ancient Mariner that the names could be easily missed.[5] Again, the references do not inform the narrative directly but instead establish nostalgia and inform the aesthetic.

Throughout its four seasons *CAoS* draws on a plethora of "high" and "low" literary and cultural sources, including Oscar Wilde's *The Picture of Dorian Gray* (1890), various plays by William Shakespeare, *Edward Scissorhands* (Tim Burton, 1990), The Bible, the tradition of Robin Goodfellow, the myth of Daniel Webster, the Pagan gods, Hieronymus Bosch—and, of course, witches from various cultures and traditions, including Lilith, Salome, Sycorax, Grýla, Hecate, and the Weird Sisters, just to name a few.[6] "Chapter Sixteen: Blackwood" (2:5) is dedicated to a revision of Shakespeare's *Hamlet* (1603), depicting Sabrina meeting her father's ghost, who asks her to avenge his death. Characters utter famous lines—such as Zelda asking, "Am I my sister's keeper?,"[7] a variation of Cain's famous question to God in Genesis 1:5. Pastiche establishes the mythological landscape of *CAoS*'s world and creates a nostalgic connection with the cultural traditions that inspired the show. Yet, there are simply too many references and traditions operating at once for any one of them to become the primary source of reference or to develop into a meaningful allusion. Instead, the references all become subject to the over-arching storyline of the protagonist's development.

CAoS's characterization of Lucifer—the main antagonist—is a combination of every major cultural interpretation of the Devil in Western history, and yet those versions of the Devil are ultimately inconsequential and displaced in favor of Sabrina's triumph over Satan. As Neil Forsyth explains, Satan is often considered to be the great "adversary" of epic myth, appearing in various forms in the classical period and in Genesis. The Bible features a version of Satan in The Book of Job (1:6–12) and Revelation (12:7–10) as the great tempter of humanity, but it was largely medieval superstition and fear which inspired the horrific three-headed version of the Devil that features at the end of Dante Alighieri's *Inferno* (1472) and dominated cultural interpretation of Satan in the Middle Ages.

CAoS's Lucifer has much in common with the traditional Christian Devil, yet John Milton's *Paradise Lost* (1667) is the primary influence on *CAoS's* Devil. Milton's epic marked a turning point in Satanic tradition by directly associating Satan with the heroes of Classical epics and fully characterizing him as a recognizable cultural figure—Milton took the Devil out of abstraction. Milton's sympathetic portrayal of the Devil inspired the Romantics' own fascination with Satan. Milton established a heroic version of Satan who championed autonomy and argued that it is "better to reign in Hell, than serve in heaven."[8] In the Romantic period, Milton's Satan is notoriously synonymous with his belief in free will, exemplified in some of his most famous lines, where he argues in favor of:

> A mind not to be changed by place or time.
> The mind is its own place, and in itself
> Can make a heaven of hell, a hell of heaven.[9]

The Romantics viewed Satan as a multi-faceted figure and interpreted the empowering qualities of Satan's pride as akin to Prometheus' own defiance of tyranny. Satan's "pride / Had cast him out from heaven" because he aspired to "set himself in glory" and "trusted to have equaled the most high" by opposing the "throne and monarchy of God."[10] Pride, independence, and resistance to tyranny became a virtue rather than a sin for the Romantics. Neil Forsyth argues that Satan became a source of "poetic energy and imagination, indeed the one *real* source, and his opponents represent the repressive."[11] After Milton, Romantic writers such as William Blake, Lord Byron, Percy Bysshe Shelley, Mary Shelley, and others continued to develop sympathetic versions of the Devil. Peter Schock argues that "Blake, Shelley, and Byron turned Milton's fallen angel into a different kind of mythic anchor for ideological identification."[12] He further suggests that "Milton's Satan assumes in the Romantic era a prominence [. . .] nearly rivalling Prometheus as the most characteristic mythic figure of the age [. . .] the reimagined figure of Milton's Satan embodied [. . .] the apotheosis of human desire and power."[13] Schock asserts that during the Romantic period a "cultural matrix of Satanism" was developed, which viewed the Devil as a misunderstood hero.[14] Essentially, the Romantic "assault on the Christian Mythology changed the way people wrote about Satan," because it "defamiliarized the figure of Satan," making it possible to reconceive Satan's character.[15] Because of the cultural influence of Milton and the Romantics, the medieval Devil has not been a common figure in popular culture, whereas the Romanticized Satan has thrived.

CAoS first uses the Romantic understanding of Satan as an introduction to Lucifer. Father Faustus Blackwood's explanation of the Dark Lord describes Lucifer as the "embodiment of free will," and he assures Sabrina that "free choice" is the "bedrock on which this church is built."[16] He almost directly invokes Milton's Satan when explaining that the Devil "preferred the loss of Heaven to his pride."[17] Blackwood espouses a Romantic view of the Devil as the heroic rebel who resists God's tyrannical expectations, insisting that "good and evil are words for the false god."[18] However, the show's use of pastiche means that the Romantic view of the Devil is soon combined with a more medieval understanding of him and a return to the belief that the Devil is the ultimate adversary. The series reveals that Faustus's worship of Lucifer is propaganda designed to trick Sabrina, as Blackwood himself is under pressure from Lucifer to convince her to sign her name in the *Book of the Beast*. Although Blackwood describes the recognizably ideologically heroic figure of Romantic writers, the reality of Lucifer's character has more in common with the medieval Satan. Lucifer's possession of Sabrina's school principal, George Hawthorne (Bronson Pinchot), acts as the Devil's introduction. Principal Hawthorne drools, his neck twists, and his eyes bulge and bleed as he threatens Sabrina in a horrific form.[19] The first time viewers see Lucifer himself, he manifests as a giant evil goat with clawed feet and horns, advancing threateningly on its hind legs and snorting maliciously.[20] He resembles the monstrous and horrifying medieval Devil depicted by Dante as well as Fra Angelico in *The Last Judgment* (1431), and Michael Pacher's *The Devil Presenting St. Augustine with the Book of Vices* (c. 1455–98), which all undermine the Miltonic and Romantic idea of Satan that Blackwood previously presented.

The allusions and references usually invoked to contribute to the "cultural matrix of Satanism" are in *CAoS* revealed to be a form of propaganda. The reality is that Satan is another substitute for God in a patriarchal and misogynistic institution which is clearly an antithetical version of the Catholic

Church. In a kind of mass Faustian pact, Lucifer requires that all witches and wizards sign their name in the *Book of the Beast* at the age of sixteen; in return, Lucifer allows them to keep their powers, which grow stronger under his blessing. Although Blackwood assures Sabrina that the Church of Night values free will, it becomes apparent that Lucifer requires complete allegiance from his "flock" as he tells Sabrina, "When I call on you, girl, you must answer."[21] Though the Romantic and medieval version of the Devil are both present in *CAoS*'s first season, it is this horrifying, patriarchal version that dominates. Lucifer threatens Sabrina's family and friends, murders Lilith's Adam, and appears to witch-brides on their wedding nights to "claim" them.[22] Viewers later learn that he extended his Faustian pacts with some people in return for an innocent heart—requiring the murder of a child. *CAoS*'s Lucifer is a conflation of every major Western Satanic tradition rather than a recognizable continuation of any distinct idea.

Lucifer's character is further complicated when he returns to "walk the earth in his true form."[23] The Satan of Romantic poetry and art, with chiseled muscles, delicate facial features, and sympathetic scarred gashes on his shoulders—indicating where his wings were torn from him—is the primary influence on Lucifer. Lilith relates the story of his Fall and their love, explaining that he "lifted [her] up" as his "handmaiden" before he grew "dark" and insisted upon her service rather than her love.[24] Lilith's version of Satan again has much in common with the sublime Satan of *Paradise Lost* who:

> In shape and gesture proudly eminent
> Stood like a tower; his form had yet not lost
> All her original brightness, nor appeared
> Less than archangel ruined, and the excess
> Of glory obscured: as when the sun new ris'n
> Looks through the horizontal misty air
> Shorn of his beams[25]

Like Milton's Satan, Lucifer loses his "original brightness" and becomes a cruel and vindictive alternative to the God he originally opposed. *CAoS*'s Lucifer undermines the obsession with free will that empowered his anti-heroic forebears, telling Sabrina that "there is no such thing as choice, only my desire."[26] Lilith confirms that "he's not a god [and] never has been," that his claim to be equal to one is "one of the Devil's greatest lies," and that his "arrogance, pride, [and] ego" are his greatest weaknesses.[27] Initially, *CAoS* relies on pastiche to establish expectations about who Lucifer is in the tradition of Miltonic and Romantic ideology, but the series undermines these references through the reality of his monstrous form. Later, the series utilizes pastiche as Lucifer adopts a more Romantic version of Satan, but the reality of his cruel and misogynistic characterization subverts his character. The Christian, medieval, Miltonic, Romantic, and popular culture Devil are all included, but the symbolic sum of the meaning of these references working simultaneously defamiliarizes the figure of Satan and returns him to abstraction. They also undermine the "cultural matrix of Satanism," which in *CAoS* is invoked to reveal him as the patriarchal antagonist of the show to re-imagine the dominant Miltonic and Romantic myths. Gilbert and Gubar argue that "the story that Milton [. . .] most notably tells to women is of course the story of woman's secondness, her otherness, and how that otherness leads inexorably to her demonic anger, her sin, her fall, and her exclusion from that garden of the gods which is also, for her, the garden of poetry."[28]

Regardless of the extent to which one might agree with their statement, Gilbert and Gubar also observe that "in an effort to come to terms with the institutionalized and often elaborately metaphorical misogyny Milton's epic expresses, many of these women devised their own revisionary myths and metaphors."[29] Because none of the traditional versions of the Devil in *CAoS* prevail as the dominant mythological or cultural point of reference and are instead all blended into the one misogynistic character, the Devil eventually becomes a farcical figure with limited power—in Hell or otherwise. *CAoS*'s treatment of the cultural tradition of the Devil criticizes the patriarchy and undermines the notion of women's "secondness," as Sabrina and her coven overpower and eventually replace the Devil on his own throne. *CAoS* uses pastiche to destabilize patriarchal Satanic tradition in favor of a feminist revisionist critique to establish a postmodern feminist version of Satanic myth.

Chilling Adventures of Sabrina also uses pastiche to revise the tradition associated with the other main male antagonists. The eloquent, intelligent, and Machiavellian Beelzebub of *Paradise Lost* who desires Satan's place on the throne is replaced by an ugly, sniveling figure who briefly haunts Sabrina but is defeated by a single spell from a teenage girl. The other demons and kings of Hell, also from Judeo-Christian tradition, are not fearsome devils, but enemies who the teenage witch and her friends repeatedly and easily dispatch. After Lucifer, Faustus Blackwood is the most troublesome villain of the show and the primary antagonist to the female characters. Not only does he attempt to undermine the Church of Night's legacy and traditions, but he also stages a coup by assassinating the Anti-Pope, plans to sacrifice his own children to the Eldritch Terrors, and wages patriarchal tyranny on the witches. During his time as head of the coven, he attempts to limit the freedoms of witches, subjects them to bigoted dogma, reinstates anachronistic traditions—such as the cannibalistic "Feast of Feasts"—and turns Zelda into a subservient Stepford wife.

Faustus's character has little in common with his namesake. Before Marlowe, Faust was the subject of German folklore, and there were versions of him ranging from a buffoonish caricature in popular chapbooks, to ballet-pantomimes, to puppet plays.[30] Generally, he epitomizes humanity's insatiable quest for knowledge and is a cautionary tale about the consequences of pride. Marlowe's *Doctor Faustus*, the most established Faust narrative, is a combination between an Elizabethan tragedy and a morality play. Marlowe canonizes Faust as an accomplished academic with aspirations to gain more knowledge through dark magic. Faust makes a deal with Mephistopheles—the Devil's servant—to exchange forbidden knowledge for his soul. *CAoS*'s Faustus is a powerful and well-educated mage with a similarly unquenchable thirst for knowledge, but when attempting to convince Sabrina to sign the *Book of the Beast* he is more representative of the tempter Mephistopheles. Faustus does eventually make a deal with Lilith to receive the Mark of Cain, but the deal does not seem to be a direct allusion—there is no time limit, he does not promise his soul or otherwise in return, and the mark acts as a kind of blessing from Lilith.

The Faustian tradition of the overreaching mage implicitly influences Blackwood's characterization, yet the complexity of his character is entirely abandoned in favor of feminist revision and has more in common with the tradition of the Gothic villain. Although the Gothic villain is now often a sympathetic figure, Faustus represents the original version who first appeared in Horace Walpole's *The Castle of Otranto* (1761). Ann Radcliffe and Matthew Lewis's later contributions further developed the Gothic villain into an archetypal fixture in Gothic fiction who is almost synonymous with patriarchal oppression. According to Peter Thorslev, the Gothic villain is

> always striking, and frequently handsome. Of about middle age or somewhat younger, he has a tall, manly, stalwart physique, with dark hair and brows frequently set off by a pale and ascetic complexion [. . .] By birth the Gothic Villain was always of the aristocracy, partly for the sense of power which his nobility confers, and partly for the air of the fallen angel, the air of Satanic greatness perverted.[31]

These qualities are all present in Faustus's character, associating him with the archetype of the Gothic villain rather than the Faustian mage and rendering his name an insignificant example of pastiche. Thorslev also acknowledges that "they are misogynists all. They take great delight in persecuting women . . . but they go much further in this persecution than would be necessary to further their particular ends."[32] Faustus's constant attempts to subjugate and control the witches of the coven further identify him with the tradition of the Gothic villain and distance him from the Faustian archetype. Faustus is reduced to pastiche because his name invokes nostalgia by referring to popular tradition and is synonymous with powerful magic, but the tradition has no recognizable bearing or influence on the show itself. His alignment with the Gothic villain again destabilizes an established tradition by prioritizing the show's narrative over an important literary figure and re-identifying Faustian tradition with Gothic tradition. The re-identification symbolically prioritizes the story of Faustus's long-suffering illegitimate child Prudence's empowerment over her cruel father and Sabrina's own consistent thwarting of Faustus's tyrannical plans. Rather than revise these traditions as Gilbert and Gubar suggest female authors have done in the past, Sabrina and Prudence re-mythologize them. Their efforts symbolize the feminist destruction of the archetype of the Gothic villain and the de-centralization of existing literary traditions, such as Faust, in favor of feminist empowerment.

Introduced at the beginning of season two, Caliban initially seems like another villain whose name signifies the show's engagement with cultural icons associated with devils and witchcraft. Although Caliban serves the same purpose as the other male antagonists in the sense that Sabrina triumphs over him and the tradition he represents, the trajectory of his characterization in the show establishes him as more of a direct allusion than pastiche because Caliban has more in common with his namesake than Faustus does. William Shakespeare's Caliban from *The Tempest* is the son of the witch Sycorax who created the island he lives on. Prospero is a powerful wizard who is shipwrecked and claims authority over the island, enslaves Caliban, and denies his claim to the island. In Alden and Virginia Vaughan's *Shakespeare's Caliban: A Cultural History*, they explain that although Caliban has been variously interpreted and reimagined, many argue that he embodies Shakespeare's own criticism of European representations of the Indigenous inhabitants of the lands they colonized—representations popularized by works such as Michel de Montaigne's essay "Of Cannibals" (1580).[33] Caliban may also have been a version of a "woodwose," the uncivilized and intemperate "salvage men" of the forest in English tradition.[34]

Although Shakespeare's Caliban initially appears as a grotesque and off-putting character who harasses Prospero's daughter Miranda and is "a born Devil, on whose nature / Nurture can never stick,"[35] he challenges European expectations because of his often-sympathetic characterization and because he is preoccupied with questions of authority and ownership relevant to sixteenth-century issues of colonialism. For instance, Caliban argues that:

> All the charms
> Of Sycorax—toads, beetles, bats—light on you,
> For I am all the subjects that you have,
> Which was first mine own king. And here you sty me
> In this hard rock, whiles you do keep from me
> The rest o' the island.[36]

He believes that, as the son of the creator of the island, it is his by right and Prospero is a tyrannical imposter. He curses his mother and Prospero for their autocratic efforts to control him. The attractive and smooth-talking Caliban of *CAoS* is very different from the often ugly, malformed, and babbling figure of Shakespeare's play, and his genteel manners and accent characterize him as a far cry from representations of the "woodwose," though his concerns are very similar to the original Caliban's. *CAoS*'s Caliban is the "prince of Hell [. . .] molded from the clay of the pit itself" and challenges Sabrina for the throne of Hell.[37] Sabrina's claim is strong because she is Lucifer's daughter, but Caliban argues that because he was created out of Hell, his claim is stronger and insists that it is "basic cosmology" that he should be king.[38] He is also initially confused when Sabrina refuses his challenge, asking "have you no pride, girl?"[39] Caliban's interest in legitimacy in relation to Hell is an allusion to the representation of the same theme in *The Tempest*, but it is strange in the context of Hell as the place Satan was damned to spend eternity after his own attempt to challenge God, and which is often symbolic of resistance to ideas such as "divine rights"[40] in favor of a deranged form of meritocracy. The power struggle reproduces ideas from *The Tempest*, but it also allows the narrative to follow Sabrina's triumph over yet another male antagonist.

Although *CAoS*'s Caliban is similar to Shakespeare's version, important aspects of his character are misrepresented to re-identify him. In *CAoS*, Caliban makes a similar mistake as his namesake. Shakespeare's Caliban pledges his loyalty to Stephano, vowing that:

> I'll show thee the best springs. I'll pluck thee berries.
> I'll fish for thee and get thee wood enough.
> A plague upon the tyrant that I serve!
> I'll bear him no more sticks, but follow thee,
> Thou wondrous man.[41]

Caliban naïvely repeats the mistake he made with Prospero and undermines his own ideals and well-being, giving his allegiance to the next figure who inspires him rather than establishing his independence. Similarly, *CAoS*'s Caliban loses the competition for the throne of Hell, then falls in love with the Sabrina Morningstar—who is the result of a time paradox and who becomes Queen of Hell in Sabrina Spellman's place—and marries her, subjecting himself to her rule and will as Queen. He even castrates himself in "Chapter Thirty: The Uninvited" (4:2) when the original Sabrina is unconvinced of his commitment to her twin, presenting her with his clay testicles in a box as a symbol of his devotion. Like Shakespeare's Caliban, *CAoS*'s Caliban substitutes one ruler for another; however, the show does not represent his subjugation sympathetically as Shakespeare's play does, and Caliban has more in common with the smooth-talking Byronic hero than he does with the arche-typal "salvage man." Instead, *CAoS* depicts Sabrina as triumphant in love and in power as the revisionist mythmaking of the series undermines Caliban's original narrative. Although Caliban's inclusion in the show develops beyond the basic pastiche of Faustus' character to develop meaningful allusions, the original significance and purpose of his character is again repurposed as a means of empowering the heroine. The trade-off of the postmodernist revision of Caliban's character is that it diminishes the issues of autonomy and free will associated with him and represents him as part of the patriarchal tradition, rather than a victim of it.

The most prominent example of pastiche in *CAoS* is the show's version of Hell. It begins as an abstract place where Lilith takes Nick Scratch (Gavin Leatherwood) at the end of season two after he sacrifices himself by becoming a vessel that holds Lucifer captive. Typical understandings of Hell would indicate that Nick is in a place of suffering and torture, but the specifics of Hell are vague, which is a challenge Sabrina must overcome when she decides she will rescue him. Various literary and cultural representations of Hell inspire *CAoS*'s version of Hell. Sabrina and her friends enter Hell through a Hieronymus Bosch painting of the same name, which acts as a portal. Dorian Gray himself tells them that Bosch's works were considered to be "windows overlooking the fields of Hell."[42] Gray helps them on the condition they procure a "*fleur du mal*," which he explains is "the original flower of evil that inspired the poet Baudelaire."[43] References to Bosch, Wilde, and Baudelaire act only as cultural signifiers and are not further explained but unceremoniously combined to allow the heroine passage to the infernal world.

Among other examples of pastiche, the most significant influence on *CAoS*'s Hell is Dante's *Inferno* (1472). *CAoS* reduces Dante's complex theological world to culturally recognizable concepts which become meaningless and eventually entirely displaced by the heroine's story of empowerment. At the beginning of season three, the circles of Dante's Hell appear on the blackboard of Miss Wardwell's classroom. Sabrina also quotes from Dante's famous inscription above the gate of Hell[44] in the spell that propels them through the portal: "Through me, pass into the unholy kingdom. Through me, pass into the city of fear. I am the gate for the lost and forsaken. Abandon all hope, ye who enter here."[45] A pithy spell demonstrating Sabrina's magical power diminishes Dante's dreadful warning about the consequences of lack of faith; the reference is recognizable to a popular audience but disassociated from its original meaning. When they arrive in Hell, they find themselves on the "Shores of Sorrow," which has something in common with Dante's own landing on the Shores of Acheron.[46] They encounter crucified people in the "Fields of Wetness" before proceeding into the "Forest of Torment," but neither of these are references to Dante, and other than the distinct landscapes the friends encounter, Hell itself has little in common with Dante's *Inferno*.[47] There are no specific punishments or areas of Hell that correlate to crimes of certain severity in accordance with Dante's *contrapasso* ("suffer the opposite")—the idea that the punishment in Hell will be the ironic fulfillment of the sin they committed. Most famously, the lustful in the first circle of Hell who abandoned themselves to incontinence on Earth are doomed to blow relentlessly in "the swirling winds of Hell."[48] The friends encounter people they know who have died, including Theo's (Lachlan Watson) uncle Jesse Putnam (Jason Beaudoin) and Harvey's (Ross Lynch) brother Tommy (Justin Dobies), but their presence in Hell is not justified by any sins or crimes they committed, and their suffering is part of no moral scheme.

Unexpectedly, another major influence on Hell comes from American popular culture with no ostensible infernal content, L. Frank Baum's *The Wonderful Wizard of Oz* (1900). Caliban warns Sabrina and her friends not to step off "the blood-red road" and tells them that all "blood flows to Pandemonium," recalling the "yellow brick road" that Dorothy and her friends must follow.[49] Tommy chases them in the form of a "woodsman" who is dressed similarly to the Tin Man.[50] Later, in the nightmare scenario the friends experience in Hell, Principal Hawthorne is a deranged version of Edward Scissorhands who tortures them in their classroom. The distinct version of Hell depicted on Wardwell's blackboard is a far cry from the chaotic and absurdist madness the friends encounter as the various allusions challenge each other for precedence. The world building of *CAoS*'s Hell is distinctly postmodern because it is without the moral and spiritual order that defines Dante's Hell or Baum's world. The epic mythology of Dante's Hell is diminished to vague references and aesthetics, and it acts as another layer of Hell's pastiche rather than an overarching cosmology. What does prevail repeatedly is Sabrina; the protagonist overcomes, outsmarts, and outruns every danger in Hell as the meanings of various allusions are displaced, becoming simple narrative obstacles for her to overcome in increasingly impressive episodes of feminist empowerment.

The friends' initial entrance into Hell is the last time they will encounter the so-called "nine realms," as their later visits all take place in its throne room. A more distinct version of Hell is made apparent upon their entrance. The room is referred to as "Pandemonium,"[51] signifying a transition from Dante's Hell to Milton's, as the name is taken from the city the demons build in Hell in book two of *Paradise Lost*. Although *CAoS*'s budget presumably prevented it from being a throne room similar in scale to the one in *Paradise Lost*, Milton's representation of Satan's throne is a clear main influence on the one Lilith is seated on:

> High on a throne of royal state, which far

Outshone the wealth of Ormus and of Ind,
Or where the gorgeous East with richest hand
Showers on her kings barbaric pearl and gold,
Satan exalted sat, by merit raised.[52]

With its skeletal decorations and stairs leading up to the chair, the throne is regal, exalted, and invokes the sublime magnificence of Milton's Hell on a smaller scale. There are no other obvious references to Milton or Dante in *CAoS*'s Hell; however, Lilith's minions are very similar to the minions in *The Wonderful Wizard of Oz*, suggesting that Lilith is in some way analogous to the Wicked Witch of the West. Rather than characterizing a specific version of Hell, *CAoS* represents Hell as a place defined by pastiche—many allusions and versions that are distinguishable when distinct from each other but, when combined, are overwhelmingly unintelligible. Unlike Dante's Hell or Milton's Hell, *CAoS*'s Hell has no discernible order or structure; the show's use of postmodern pastiche achieves the chaos that becomes its defining feature. The landscape, cosmology, and mythology of Hell all become secondary to the protagonist who triumphs over it.

Although no distinguishable version of Hell prevails in *CAoS*, what dominates the infernal world is the protagonist's victory. Caliban and his concerns regarding succession and legitimacy become even more relevant in the play itself and to compare with the series, given that Shakespeare was likely considering the question of Elizabeth I's authority and Mary, Queen of Scots's attempt to challenge her for the English throne, and because Sabrina herself becomes an analogue of Queen Elizabeth I. Those who sympathize with Caliban in *The Tempest* must come to terms with the uncomfortable realization that Caliban makes his claim on the same basis as Mary's and supporting it means supporting treason in the context of Elizabethan England. *CAoS* represents Caliban as an illegitimate challenge to Sabrina rather than a sympathetic figure, removing complicated issues of legitimacy originally associated with his character to further ennoble Sabrina. By depicting Sabrina as a version of Queen Elizabeth I, the show represents her as the rightful queen who overcame those who challenged her, rather than the real Queen Elizabeth I, who out-matched her cousin in a struggle for power. The focus on a particular version of Elizabeth and omission of significant aspects of Caliban's character removes any question of Sabrina's legitimacy and focuses the narrative on her feminist empowerment. As Lilith prepares Sabrina Morningstar—who will stand in for Sabrina Spellman in Hell—for her coronation, she applies white makeup and a distinctly Elizabethan outfit complete with collared ruff and wig. Lilith also counsels Sabrina to adopt a similar leadership style to the "Virgin Queen": "gird your loins, let nothing touch you, let no man hold power over you."[53] Although Sabrina later marries

Caliban and undermines the importance of the scene, the symbolism is still significant. Like Dorothy, Sabrina unmasks her own wizards—her patriarchal antagonists, Lucifer, Faustus, and Caliban—and takes their place in her own version of Hell though they all believe her unworthy, as Elizabeth I did on the throne of England. In every instance, Sabrina's narrative prevails over her adversaries and the allusions they represent. By reducing the various infernal references to abstraction and absurdism and depicting the success of the female protagonist over these references, *CAoS* joins the feminist revisionist mythmaking of male dominated narratives and cultural traditions.

The postmodernist technique of pastiche allows *CAoS*'s creators to develop a twenty-first century version of the revisionist feminist mythmaking that Gilbert and Gubar recognize in the works of Mary Shelley, Charlotte and Anne Brontë, Jane Austen, George Eliot, and Emily Dickinson. Pastiche allows the show to develop nostalgic references to the cultural history of the Gothic, witches and witchcraft, horror, and Satanic tradition. Sabrina's use of pastiche challenges the tradition of the Satanic "cultural matrix" associated with these infernal icons, instead using them to produce culturally relevant meaning and significance in a rebellious rejection of tradition. In some cases, pastiche has the basic effect Jameson associates with it, because it acts as a nostalgic point of reference. In other cases, *CAoS* uses pastiche more purposefully. The series creates Lucifer's character by combining various literary and cultural interpretations of the Devil. The references are reductive rather than summative, as no one version of the Devil prevails and he becomes an inconsistent and contradictory figure, effectively defamiliarizing the "cultural matrix of Satanism" and the other various traditions that comprise his character. Caliban is similarly defamiliarized because although direct allusion to his original source is relevant to the narrative, the significance of his character becomes subject to feminist critique. *CAoS*'s representation of Hell is also a combination of the most famous imagined versions of it. Because the style of pastiche means that no single version is dominant, these famous landscapes also become victims of postmodernism as the allusions become culturally insignificant. Although the examples of pastiche in *CAoS* often return the subject to cultural abstraction, they also provide the opportunity for revision, which the series takes advantage of. In each instance, Sabrina triumphs over the infernal tradition or character in a symbolic victory of feminism over cultural tradition. In some ways, this version of feminist revisionism is more successful than those previous because rather than rewriting the myth or subjecting it to feminist commentary, pastiche has a unique effect in that it returns many of the references to abstraction. By refusing to develop significant connections between the show and the source, the allusions become a kind of aesthetic rather than an intelligible frame of narrative reference. From a literary perspective, the sterilization of these important cultural and literary influences is a disservice. From a feminist perspective, though, *CAoS* is a feminist revisionist triumph over the stories that have dominated Western thought for hundreds of years.

BIBLIOGRAPHY

Alighieri, Dante. *The Divine Comedy.* Edited by Clive James. London: Picador, 2013.

Chilling Adventures of Sabrina. Season 1, episode 1, "Chapter One: October Country." Directed by Lee Toland Krieger, written by Roberto Aguirre-Sacasa, featuring Kiernan Shipka, Miranda Otto, Lucy Davis, and Chance Perdomo. Released October 26, 2018, Netflix, www.netflix.com/watch/80230071?trackId =200257859.

———, Season 1, episode 2, "Chapter Two: The Dark Baptism." Directed by Lee Toland Krieger, written by Roberto Aguirre-Sacasa, featuring Kiernan Shipka, Miranda Otto, Lucy Davis, and Richard Coyle. Released October 26, 2018, Netflix, www.netflix.com/watch/80230072?trackId=200257859.

———, Season 1, episode 5, "Chapter Five: Dreams in a Witch House." Directed by Maggie Kiley, written by Matthew Barry, featuring Kiernan Shipka, Miranda Otto, Lucy Davis, and Chance Perdomo. Released October 26, 2018, Netflix, www .netflix.com/watch/80230075?trackId=200257859.

———, Season 1, episode 10, "Chapter Ten: The Witching Hour." Directed by Rob Seidenglanz, written by Roberto Aguirre-Sacasa and Ross Maxwell, featuring Kiernan Shipka, Miranda Otto, Lucy Davis, and Chance Perdomo. Released October 26, 2018, Netflix, www.netflix.com/watch/80230080?trackId=200257859.

———, Season 2, episode 5, "Chapter Sixteen: Blackwood." Directed by Alex Pillai, written by Matthew Barry, featuring Kiernan Shipka, Miranda Otto, Lucy Davis, and Richard Coyle. Released April 5, 2019, Netflix, www.netflix.com/watch /80230086?trackId=14170289.

———, Season 2, episode 8, "Chapter Nineteen: The Mandrake." Directed by Kevin Sullivan, written by Joshua Conkel, featuring Kiernan Shipka, Miranda Otto, Lucy Davis, and Chance Perdomo. Released April 5, 2019, Netflix, www.netflix.com/ watch/80230089?trackId=14277283.

———, Season 2, episode 9, "Chapter Twenty: The Mephisto Waltz." Directed by Rob Seidenglanz, directed by Roberto Aguirre-Sacasa, featuring Kiernan Shipka, Miranda Otto, Lucy Davis, Luke Cook, and Gavin Leatherwood. Released April 5, 2019, Netflix, www.netflix.com/watch/80230090?trackId=200257859.

———, Season 3, episode 1, "Chapter Twenty-One: The Hellbound Heart." Directed by Rob Seidenglanz, written by Roberto Aguirre-Sacasa, featuring Kiernan Shipka, Chance Perdomo, Tati Gabrielle, and Michelle Gomez. Released December 31, 2020, Netflix, www.netflix.com/watch/81062652?trackId=200257859.

———, Season 3, episode 3, "Chapter Twenty-Three: Heavy Is the Crown." Directed by Rob Seidenglanz, written by Oanh Ly, featuring Kiernan Shipka, Miranda Otto,

Lucy Davis, and Chance Perdomo. Released January 24, 2020, Netflix, www .netflix.com/watch/81062654?trackId=200257859.

———, Season 3, episode 8. "Chapter Twenty-Eight: Sabrina Is Legend." Directed by Rob Seidenglanz, written by Roberto Aguirre-Sacasa and Daniel King, featuring Kiernan Shipka, Miranda Otto, Lucy Davis, and Sam Corlett. Released January 24, 2020, Netflix, www.netflix.com/watch/81062659?trackId=200257859.

Forsyth, Neil. *The Satanic Epic.* Princeton: Princeton University Press, 2008.

Gilbert, Sandra, and Susan Gubar. *The Madwoman in the Attic: The Woman Writer and the Nineteenth-Century Literary Imagination.* 2nd ed. New Haven: Yale University Press, 2000.

Jameson, Fredric. *The Cultural Turn: Selected Writings on the Postmodern.* London: Verso, 1998.

Milton, John. *Paradise Lost.* Edited by Alastair Fowler. New York: Routledge, 2013.

Pagels, Elaine. *The Origins of Satan.* New York: Random House, 1996.

Schock, Peter. *Romantic Satanism.* New York: Palgrave Macmillan, 2003.

Shakespeare, William. *The Norton Shakespeare.* Edited by Stephen Greenblatt. New York: W. W. Norton & Company, 2016.

Thorslev, Peter L. *The Byronic Hero.* Minneapolis: University of Minnesota Press, 1965.

Vaughan, Alden T. and Virginia Mason Vaughan. *Shakespeare's Caliban: A Cultural History.* Cambridge: Cambridge University Press, 1991.

NOTES

1. Fredric Jameson, *The Cultural Turn: Selected Writings on the Postmodern* (London: Verso, 1998), 5.

2. Jameson, *The Cultural Turn*, 7.

3. Jameson, *The Cultural Turn*, 5.

4. *Chilling Adventures of Sabrina*, season 1, episode 1, "Chapter One: October Country," by Lee Toland Krieger, written by Roberto Aguirre-Sacasa, featuring Kiernan Shipka, Miranda Otto, Lucy Davis, and Chance Perdomo, released October 26, 2018, on Netflix, www.netflix.com/watch/80230071?trackId=200257859: 00:13:57–00:14:20.

5. *Chilling Adventures of Sabrina*, season 3, episode 3, "Chapter Twenty-Three: Heavy is the Crown," directed by Rob Seidenglanz, written by Oanh Ly, featuring Kiernan Shipka, Miranda Otto, Lucy Davis, and Chance Perdomo, released January 24, 2020, on Netflix, www.netflix.com/watch/81062654?trackId=200257859: 00:26:57.

6. These examples of witches come from a wide range of traditions. Lilith is a demonic character from Jewish folklore who is perhaps most commonly known for being Adam's first wife and the mother of demons. Salome is most famously known as the daughter of Herodias in the Gospel of Mark, who, when given the opportunity to have any wish granted, asked for John the Baptist's head on a platter (6:21–28). She has become a common figure in popular culture, featuring in plays, novels, ballet,

and music and is commonly associated with the *femme fatale*. Sycorax from Shakespeare's *The Tempest* (1611) is often considered to be a variation of Medea or Circe. She is the witch who was banished to the island because of her powerful magic and is the mother of Caliban; little is known regarding Shakespeare's source, but she is often identified as a comparison to Prospero's powerful magic and colonialist presence. Grýla is a figure from Norse mythology, originally mentioned in *Prose Edda* from the thirteenth century; she is a giantess and mother of the Yule Lads, known for being a menace to children. Hecate features in numerous myths and stories but she is usually represented as the most powerful aspect of the tripartite figure of the Maiden, Mother, and Crone, of which she is the latter. She is also often identified with the Weird Sisters, who feature most famously in Shakespeare's *Macbeth* (1606) but also represent the tradition of the "Wyrd" sisters who are identified with the fates.

7. *Chilling Adventures of Sabrina*, season 1, episode 5, "Chapter Five: Dreams in a Witch House," directed by Maggie Kiley, written by Matthew Barry, featuring Kiernan Shipka, Miranda Otto, Lucy Davis, and Chance Perdomo, released October 26, 2018, on Netflix, www.netflix.com/watch/80230075?trackId=200257859: 00:35:19.

8. John Milton, *Paradise Lost*, ed. Alastair Fowler (New York: Routledge, 2013), I.263.

9. Milton, *Paradise Lost*, I.253–55.

10. Milton, *Paradise Lost*, I.36–42.

11. Neil Forsyth, *The Satanic Epic* (Princeton: Princeton University Press, 2008), 65.

12. Peter Schock, *Romantic Satanism* (New York: Palgrave Macmillan, 2003), 3.

13. Schock, *Romantic Satanism,* 3.

14. Schock, *Romantic Satanism,* 5.

15. Schock, *Romantic Satanism,* 16.

16. *Chilling Adventures of Sabrina*, season 1, episode 2, "Chapter Two: The Dark Baptism," directed by Lee Toland Krieger, written by Roberto Aguirre-Sacasa, featuring Kiernan Shipka, Miranda Otto, Lucy Davis, and Richard Coyle, released October 26, 2018, on Netflix, www.netflix.com/watch/80230072?trackId=200257859: 00:03:16–00:05:40.

17. *Chilling Adventures of Sabrina*, "Chapter Two: The Dark Baptism," 00:43:35.

18. *Chilling Adventures of Sabrina*, "Chapter Two: The Dark Baptism," 00:03:23.

19. *Chilling Adventures of Sabrina*, "Chapter Two: The Dark Baptism," 00:54:10.

20. *Chilling Adventures of Sabrina*, "Chapter One: October Country," 00:57:12.

21. *Chilling Adventures of Sabrina*, season 1, episode 10, "Chapter Ten: The Witching Hour," directed by Rob Seidenglanz, written by Roberto Aguirre-Sacasa and Ross Maxwell, featuring Kiernan Shipka, Miranda Otto, Lucy Davis, and Chance Perdomo, released October 26, 2018, on Netflix, www.netflix.com/watch/80230080?trackId=200257859: 00:40:44.

22. *Chilling Adventures of Sabrina*, season 2, episode 5, "Chapter Sixteen: Blackwood," directed by Alex Pillai, written by Matthew Barry, featuring Kiernan Shipka, Miranda Otto, Lucy Davis, and Richard Coyle, released April 5, 2019, on Netflix, www.netflix.com/watch/80230086?trackId=14170289: 00:23:20.

23. *Chilling Adventures of Sabrina*, season 2, episode 8, "Chapter Nineteen: The Mandrake," directed by Kevin Sullivan, written by Joshua Conkel, featuring Kiernan Shipka, Miranda Otto, Lucy Davis, and Chance Perdomo, released April 5, 2019, on Netflix, www.netflix.com/watch/80230089?trackId=14277283: 00:51:50.

24. *Chilling Adventures of Sabrina*, season 2, episode 9, "Chapter Twenty: The Mephisto Waltz," directed by Rob Seidenglanz, directed by Roberto Aguirre-Sacasa, featuring Kiernan Shipka, Miranda Otto, Lucy Davis, Luke Cook, and Gavin Leatherwood, released April 5, 2019, on Netflix, www.netflix.com/watch/80230090?trackId=200257859.00:02:29.

25. Milton, *Paradise Lost*, 1.590–99.

26. *Chilling Adventures of Sabrina*, "Chapter Twenty: The Mephisto Waltz," 00:23:00.

27. *Chilling Adventures of Sabrina*, "Chapter Twenty: The Mephisto Waltz," 00:31:36–00:33:19.

28. Sandra Gilbert and Susan Gubar, *The Madwoman in the Attic: The Woman Writer and the Nineteenth-Century Literary Imagination*, 2nd ed. (New Haven: Yale University Press, 2000), 191.

29. Gilbert and Gubar, *The Madwoman in the Attic*, 189.

30. Peter L. Thorslev, *The Byronic Hero* (Minneapolis: University of Minnesota Press, 1965), 84–87.

31. Thorslev, *The Byronic Hero*, 53–54.

32. Thorslev, *The Byronic Hero*, 55.

33. Alden T. Vaughan and Virginia Mason Vaughan, *Shakespeare's Caliban: A Cultural History* (Cambridge: Cambridge University Press, 1991), 24.

34. Vaughan and Vaughan, *Shakespeare's Caliban: A Cultural History*, 72, 246.

35. William Shakespeare, "The Tempest," *The Norton Shakespeare*, ed. Stephen Greenblatt (New York: W. W. Norton & Company, 2016), IV.i.188–89.

36. Shakespeare, *The Tempest*, I.ii.344–49.

37. *Chilling Adventures of Sabrina*, season 3, episode 1, "Chapter Twenty-One: The Hellbound Heart," directed by Rob Seidenglanz, written by Roberto Aguirre-Sacasa, featuring Kiernan Shipka, Chance Perdomo, Tati Gabrielle, and Michelle Gomez, released December 31, 2020, on Netflix, www.netflix.com/watch/81062652?trackId=200257859: 00:48:20.

38. *Chilling Adventures of Sabrina*, "Chapter Twenty-One: The Hellbound Heart," 00:50:03.

39. *Chilling Adventures of Sabrina*, "Chapter Twenty-One: The Hellbound Heart," 00:49:45.

40. *Chilling Adventures of Sabrina*, "Chapter Twenty-One: The Hellbound Heart," 00:52:56.

41. Shakespeare, *The Tempest*, II.ii.71–75.

42. *Chilling Adventures of Sabrina*, "Chapter Twenty-One: The Hellbound Heart," 00:12:08.

43. *Chilling Adventures of Sabrina*, "Chapter Twenty-One: The Hellbound Heart," 00:13:47.

44. Dante Alighieri, *The Divine Comedy*, ed. Clive James (London: Picador, 2013), *Inf.*3.1–9.

45. *Chilling Adventures of Sabrina*, season 3, episode 1, "Chapter Twenty-One: The Hellbound Heart," 00:18:16.

46. Alighieri, *The Divine Comedy*, *Inf.*3.78.

47. *Chilling Adventures of Sabrina*, "Chapter Twenty-One: The Hellbound Heart," 00:24:51.

48. Alighieri, *The Divine Comedy*, *Inf.*5.31.

49. *Chilling Adventures of Sabrina*, "Chapter Twenty-One: The Hellbound Heart," 00:19:36–00:19:42.

50. *Chilling Adventures of Sabrina*, "Chapter Twenty-One: The Hellbound Heart," 00:30:28.

51. *Chilling Adventures of Sabrina*, "Chapter Twenty-One: The Hellbound Heart," 00:47:37.

52. Milton, *Paradise Lost*, II.1–5.

53. *Chilling Adventures of Sabrina*, season 3, episode 8, "Chapter Twenty-Eight: Sabrina Is Legend," directed by Rob Seidenglanz, written by Roberto Aguirre-Sacasa and Daniel King, featuring Kiernan Shipka, Miranda Otto, Lucy Davis, and Sam Corlett, released January 24, 2020, on Netflix, www.netflix.com/watch/81062659 ?trackId=200257859: 00:48:38.

Chapter 6

Giving Satanic and Divine Patriarchy a Run for Their Money

Hybridity, Liminality, and Female Empowerment in Chilling Adventures of Sabrina

Luisa Fernanda Grijalva-Maza

After being expelled from the Academy of Unseen Arts in "Chapter Seventeen: The Missionaries" (2:6) for attempting to uncover Faustus Blackwood's (Richard Coyle) criminal behavior, Sabrina Spellman (Kiernan Shipka) runs to her mortal friends, Harvey Kinkle (Ross Lynch) and Rosalind "Roz" Walker (Jaz Sinclair), to gain some certainty and support. When Harvey and Roz, who have become increasingly distrustful of witches, reject her, Sabrina then goes looking for her warlock boyfriend, Nicholas "Nick" Scratch (Gavin Leatherwood), who also turns her down, but because of her mortal background. Sabrina is now experiencing life in-between space and place, a life of belonging nowhere, and yet, it is at this point she gains such power that she is able to resurrect herself and others and slaughter the angels that threaten her Coven.

How is it that life in-between, of not belonging, empowers Sabrina? What source of power is she hacking into even though her two worlds have just rejected her? Megan Henesy argues that the Gothic nature of Sabrina's character, as well as her progressive empowerment through the series, derives from her liminality,[1] that is, a state of transition that is located in-between states.[2] Sabrina's liminality, therefore, allows her to move both in the mortal and witch worlds; she is a teenager going through the changes and drama of development, and she is also a woman, which sets her in a liminal stage.[3] As

Sara K. Day, Miranda A. Green-Barteet, and Amy L. Montz posit, liminality, the movement in-between defined positions or states, is "a path to empowerment."[4] By moving in-between planes, Sabrina escapes the boundaries of defined positions and identities, becoming disturbing and monstrous as she tends to upset the social order.[5] The transgressions enacted by liminal movement allow the re-evaluation of norms which can potentially lead to deep social transformations, empowering the liminal person politically, a process that Sabrina experiences.[6]

Indeed, female empowerment in *Chilling Adventures of Sabrina* (*CAoS*) is directly related to liminality in the witch and mortal worlds.[7] And yet, Sabrina's friends do not garner the amount of power she does. There seems to be something else working in concert with liminality—the Dark Lord (Luke Cook) knows it and exploits it—that engenders extraordinary powers in Sabrina. As I argue here, Sabrina's empowerment is not only due to her liminality but to the fact that she is also a hybrid—a result of the sexual encounter between her mortal mother, Diana (Annette Reilly) and the Dark Lord (Lucifer Morningstar). Although hybridity commonly implies liminality, they are not necessarily the same thing. While liminality refers to in-between states of transition, hybridity is related to the mixing of different identities into one. Identifying the difference and understanding the way hybridity is played out in the series provides an interesting opportunity to draw out the empowering potentiality of hybrids that are also liminal, both in fiction and in practice. To comply with the argument, the first part of this chapter presents a theoretical discussion of identity, hybridity, and liminality and the identification of these processes in parts 1 and 2 of the series. In particular, I focus on the ways Sabrina uses her witch and mortal abilities to solve particular problems, leading eventually to a full state of liminality in "Chapter Seventeen: The Missionaries" (2:6). Her movement is, from this moment on, in-between place and space, in liminality, where the result is the production of a particular knowledge that severs the dichotomous logic between space and place, transgresses the limits of place, and begins moving her coven and her human friends closer together without the need of a homogenized identity of inclusion or assimilation.

The second part of this chapter deals precisely with this liminal hybrid movement and the different actions that explode the dichotomies and identities she is forced to take, such as the destruction of the Order of the Innocents and her split into two Sabrinas in parts 3 and 4. I also explore the resistance on the part of patriarchal structures and their need for Sabrina to choose between identity or death. Given that Sabrina's first death pushes her further into liminality instead of a fixed identity, in the third part of the chapter, I look at the consequences of ultimate liminality and the relationship between The Void and the two Sabrinas—a relationship that is destroyed by the final death of Sabrina Spellman, understood as a move towards immanence, from where movement is forever unlimited.

"I KNEEL BEFORE NO ONE": PATRIARCHAL
IDENTITIES AND LIMINAL HYBRIDITY

From "Chapter One: October Country" (1:1) of *Chilling Adventures of Sabrina*, the protagonist is commonly identified as a "half-breed." Sabrina is constantly confronted by and rejected because of the fact that her mother was a mortal and her father was a warlock[8] and therefore she is not a full witch, making her, as she points out in "Chapter Eighteen: The Miracles of Sabrina Spellman" (2:7), "less than [a witch], in some way"—that is, she is a hybrid.[9] This is further emphasized by the fact that she has been brought up in an openly magical household by her paternal witch aunts, Zelda Spellman (Miranda Otto) and Hilda Spellman (Lucy Davis), and her warlock cousin, Ambrose Spellman (Chance Perdomo), while at the same time attending mortal school and having meaningful relationships with the mortals Harvey, Roz, and Susie/Theo. Despite the constant bullying at the hands of the Weird Sisters—a powerful trio of orphaned witches at the Academy of Unseen Arts who despise mortals—Sabrina relishes having magical powers and mortal friends. It provides a sense of freedom in her movement—she is not completely constricted by the limits of either identity because she can move from one to the other and back, adhering to either one depending on the context in which she is located and her personal needs and interests at the time.

An important example of the allowances provided by hybridity is developed in "Chapter Eight: The Burial" (1:8) and "Chapter Nine: The Returned Man" (1:9) where Sabrina uses her magical powers and knowledge to resurrect Harvey's brother, Tommy Kinkle (Justin Dobies). Unfortunately, he comes back without a soul, pushing Sabrina to correct the failed resurrection by going to Limbo to retrieve his soul. Aunt Hilda warns Sabrina that witches cannot go to mortal Limbo, yet, given that Sabrina is half-mortal, she can, in fact, go into that mortal realm. She is unsuccessful in getting Tommy's soul back, but what is relevant in these two episodes is the way she adheres to one of her two identities depending on her needs—she uses her witch powers for resurrection and her mortal nature to go into mortal Limbo. As a hybrid, Sabrina has both natures—and, therefore, both sets of powers—and she uses them often to solve different parts of the same problem that exist in different realms. Hybridity plays a fundamental role in the narrative; therefore, it is important to take a serious look at it to begin to understand the role it plays in Sabrina's empowerment.

Sayyed Rahim Moosavinia and Sayyede Maryam Hosseini explain that hybridity, as the mix of identities, can be experienced as either frightening or liberating and sometimes even subversive.[10] The negative presentation of hybridity is easily identified in figures such as the werewolf, the vampire, and the zombie, which are socially categorized as confusions that must be abominated because they transgress the limits of normality and order in society.[11] These figures' narration elicits a frightening and dehumanizing response from society legitimizing their elimination. In *CAoS*, the negative or terrifying characterization of the hybrid is shadowed by alluding to its empowering potentiality. When the Weird Sisters bully Sabrina it is due to her hybrid nature; she is a "half-breed" and therefore does not deserve to go to the prestigious Academy of Unseen Arts. At the same time, Sabrina positively uses the powers afforded by hybridity as she sees fit, overpowering the Weird Sisters, for example, when they are harrowing her.

This double presentation of hybridity is becoming more common in cultural productions. For example, it can also be identified in the character of Hermione Granger in the *Harry Potter* books, where it takes a fundamental place in the narrative. However, and in contradistinction to Sabrina, Hermione's actions in the progression of the story suggest that in the dichotomous distinction between the Muggle and wizarding worlds there is an inherent hierarchy where the magical realm is superior, which explains why she ends up fully assimilating to one of her two identities and discarding the least desirable one—the Muggle world—sustaining a Western liberal discourse of inclusion based on discriminatory practices and categories.[12]

Unlike Hermione, *CAoS* posits a different experience and understanding of hybridity, one that engenders empowerment by *not* abandoning either identity. While in Hermione's case her Muggle nature only functions to motivate her to prove herself as a worthy witch while relinquishing her Muggle background, with Sabrina, hybridization affords her more power as she is able to draw from both worlds while not prioritizing either. For example, in "Chapter 3: The Trial of Sabrina Spellman" (1:3), during her trial in the Satanic court, her hybridity—and, in this case, her mortal background—allows her to pursue her defense against the Dark Lord with the help of a tormented mortal lawyer, Daniel Webster (John Rubinstein). When her aunt Hilda confesses to having witnessed Sabrina's Catholic baptism her defense is strengthened, and she wins the case, permitting her to stay in both worlds. In the mortal world Sabrina uses her witch abilities to gain more power as well. For example, in "Chapter One: October Country" (1:1), Sabrina curses the principal of her mortal school to keep him away for a few days while she and Roz create the Women's Intersectional Cultural and Creative Association (WICCA) to, as Roz notes, "topple the White patriarchy."[13] Although Sabrina is White and privileged, the fact that Roz and Sabrina specifically name intersectionality in forming their group is revealing: Kimberlé Crenshaw designed the concept to identify the multiple structures of oppression and the way they intersect in discriminatory practices towards a particular subject, especially in terms of gender and race, which implies that Roz and Sabrina are conscious of both— something that will serve Sabrina in identifying the patriarchal structures that dominate both the mortal and magical worlds.

The experience of hybridity that is narrated in the series, therefore, is related to empowerment. This is, of course, deliberate. As we are led to believe towards the end of Part 2, the Dark Lord purposefully had inter- course with Diana,[14] Sabrina's mortal mother, to create a "half-shadow girl" that could help him initiate the Apocalypse and enslave the witch and mortal worlds, precisely because that hybrid girl would be able to draw power from both her witch and mortal identities.[15] She would be what Ernesto Laclau calls the leader "primus inter pares," one that comes from within the group, being both leader and brother.[16] Its function is to produce a new identity that can serve as a point of identification and articulation of the members of a heterogeneous group, thereby homogenizing identities and creating a strong political unity. The Dark Lord's plan is for Sabrina to become this "leader inter pares" for both sides, creating identities that could create strong libidi- nal bonds that make it easier to enslave the witches and the mortals—a plan that she is inadvertently carrying out when she begins preaching her adoptive father's gospel, which asserts that witches can intermingle with mortals.

The Dark Lord's master design was for Sabrina's hybridity to serve practi- cal matters, such as being able to relate to mortals and witches alike, as well as having abilities from both worlds. The point was for her to have more power and to finally choose the dark path through her Dark Baptism. What the Dark Lord did not foresee was that Sabrina's hybridity would propel her to a permanent liminality. She is not only a hybrid—she is a liminal hybrid.[17] As several scholars including Megan Henesy, Sara K. Day, Miranda A. Green-Barteet, and Amy L. Montz note, liminality, originally taken from Victor Turner's work, relates to rites of passage.[18] The liminal is the transition stage from one defined identity to another.[19] However, in the case of women in Gothic texts—including terror and horror, as in this series—liminality appears as a permanent stage because of their gender condition and the rela- tionship to chaos within a patriarchal structure. Elisabeth Bronfen argues that death and women are systematically related in Western cultural productions for two reasons: their untamed, chaotic/destructive natures and their liminal- ity.[20] In this sense, liminality is both a site of exclusion (the subject does not belong to a defined identity) and of emancipation/empowerment because, as Sayyed Rahim Moosavinia and Sayyede Maryam Hosseini note in reference to Bessie Head's *A Question of Power*, the liminal "presents a new picture in which a lonely woman can build her identity."[21]

Although Sabrina is constantly attempting to construct a new identity for herself, the development of her character problematizes this notion of "new identity." Every time she attempts to be autonomous in her decisions, it is eventually revealed she has been manipulated in some way or another by her aunt Zelda, Miss Wardwell/Lilith (Michelle Gomez), the Dark Lord, and even Nick, very much in the sense of what Jacques Lacan terms "the drama of the subject" in "Position of the Unconscious." In Lacan's words, "[T]his secondary subordination not only closes the effect of the first by projecting the topology of the subject into the instant of fantasy; it seals it, refusing to allow the subject of desire to realize that he is an effect of speech, to realize, in other words, what he is in being but the Other's desire."[22] Following Lacan's argument, Sabrina discovers that whenever she tries to make an autonomous decision to determine her identity, the decision is always already determined by the structures of power—structures that have the fundamental objective of producing subjectivity and identity and are, for Gilles Deleuze and Félix Guattari, Oedipal and therefore patriarchal.[23] Unfortunately for her, the decision is not optional within reality.[24] In order to become a full-fledged subject that can live in society in a meaningful way, the decision is demanded, even if it is an act of madness.[25] Yet, Sabrina will take the less traveled path and will avoid the decision to produce an identity in "Chapter Seventeen: The Missionaries" (2:6), where, without adhering to one identity, she draws from both to overpower the angels that are threatening the coven.

This avoidance has important implications for the way we think about liminality. Drawing from geographer Yi-Fu Tuan and his theory about the difference between space and place, Robert Tally, Jr. explains that liminality is the in-between place (location of limits and security but also of imprisonment) and space (freedom but also anxiety and uncertainty).[26] Although the limits between these two locations might seem set in stone, in reality the production of strict limits is never fully totalized because limits are discursively produced, as Jacques Derrida points out in *Writing and Difference*.[27] Furthermore, the idea of natural or essential limits dwindles between what Tally, Jr. explains as the difference between "limes" and "limen." While "limes" relates to limits or boundaries that demarcate the borders of place and that allow the identification of that which is beyond (space), "limen" translates to "threshold," or the point of entry to place. "Limen" implies not the space nor the place, but the in-between and the possibility of touching the sacrality of place.[28] When the limits of place are touched or transgressed, they are revealed as having been produced by relations of power and become thresholds.[29]

Tally Jr. explains that, in a similar way to the Deleuzian nomad—the subject that transgresses the limits of the hegemonic order by moving in and out of the system—the political program of liminality is to transgress and to transform into thresholds that which is guarded, policed, and secured as untouchable limits. Given that limits of space and place are subject to human experience and therefore can never be fully totalized, the political program of the limen is not only to transform but to reveal the entry points, the points where the limits are touched by the hand of the in-between—that is, the liminal subject that has no defined identity, that dwindles in-between identities without adhering permanently to any. Here we can identify the difference between hybridity and liminality, particularly if we consider the case of Prudence Night/Blackwood, a full witch given both her parents were magical. She is also Black and a supposed orphan under the care of Father Blackwood. In "Chapter Seven: Feast of Feasts" (1:7) it is revealed that Prudence is the illegitimate child of Father Blackwood, who is White, making Prudence a hybrid, as well. The difference between Sabrina and Prudence is that Prudence is not liminal; she is completely adhered to her identity as a full witch, and even after learning the truth about her father and of her hybridity, she completely identifies with the Blackwood name. Although this identification with the Blackwood lineage changes at the end of Part 2, hybridity in Prudence's case does not lead her automatically to liminal movement until she rejects the identity provided by her father—it is at that point that liminal hybridity motivates Prudence to transgress the limits of her coven by moving in-between Satanic witchcraft and Vodou. In both Sabrina and Prudence's cases, the political program of liminal hybridity is to identify the entry points of the mortal and witch patriarchal worlds by transgressing their limits. As we observe all through the series, Sabrina constantly transgresses the limits of her family's and friends' values and beliefs, very much to the frustration of the Dark Lord.

SABRINA'S MIRACLES: "TOPPLING THE WHITE PATRIARCHY" OF HEAVEN AND HELL

In the final chapter of Part 1, Sabrina is forced to sign the *Book of the Beast* to save her mortal and witch friends, and by the beginning of Part 2, she is under the impression that she cannot go back fully to the mortal world. She has been coerced to make a final decision about her identity, putting a stop to the freedom of movement provided by hybridity. However, Sabrina is not fully liminal until Part 2, when she is rejected by both worlds in "Chapter Seventeen: The Missionaries" (2:6). Despite Sabrina's frustration and disappointment in her friends' reaction, rejection and the experience of liminality mark the point when she finally realizes that she is a liminal hybrid, after which she accepts and takes advantage of her position, one which provides her an enormous amount of power.

In "Chapter Seventeen: The Missionaries" (2:6), after Sabrina and Nick are expelled from the Academy of Unseen Arts and her cousin, Ambrose, is arrested for allegedly killing the Anti-Pope, Enoch of Antioch (Ray Wise), and attempting to murder Father Blackwood, Sabrina feels the need to look for her mortal friends, thinking they will provide support at a time of uncertainty. However, Roz and Harvey have now a strong distrust of witches because they cursed the women in Roz's family and Sabrina only made things worse after Harvey's brother died. They accuse Sabrina of making Roz go blind, and she flees the school. Sabrina then goes in search of her warlock boyfriend, Nick, who would not reject her for being a witch; however, he has fallen into a deep depression after being expelled, and in a drunken outburst, also rejects her for being half-mortal. In the past, Sabrina was not liminal; she could always adhere to either identity as she saw fit and always found support from her family and friends. As her friends' rejection makes clear, this is no longer the case. Sabrina finally realizes that her hybridity has led her to liminality, and she is alone in-between space and place.

Although Nick, Roz, and Harvey change their minds and return to support Sabrina, the effects of liminality are already evident in her. To save her coven from the Order of the Innocents, a group of angels that attempts to redeem (and kill) all the witches in Greendale, Sabrina draws from her two sets of abilities at the same time. After Sabrina finds out that the angels have reconsecrated the witches' deconsecrated church and taken Sabrina's entire coven there to kill them, she decides to go in and save them. However, Quentin (Liam Hughes), the ghost child, warns her that witches cannot enter a reconsecrated church. Sabrina reminds Nick and Harvey that she is half-mortal and was baptized in a Catholic ritual as a baby, so she, unlike Nick, can cross the doors of the church. She goes alone and is immediately shot with an arrow by Jerathmiel (Spencer Treat Clark). Sabrina manages to continue walking as she begins uttering a spell to save the coven, but the other angel, Mehitable (Bayley Corman), puts a crown of thorns on her head—alluding to the crown put on Jesus Christ while he was being crucified—to prevent the effect of witchcraft. Sabrina is shot twice more and dies. A moment later, she resurrects and levitates, her eyes turning white, and she calls forth hellfire. In contradistinction to the angels that were unable to convert the witches in the church, Sabrina is quickly able to make the angels say the Dark Lord's prayer, after which she burns them in hellfire.

Sabrina is drawing from the two sets of powers awarded by hybridity at the same time. She enters the church thanks to her mortal side and begins using witchcraft against the angels. Mehitable's use of the crown of thorns has a double objective: to stop Sabrina from using witchcraft and to ensure that her death leads to a full rejection of her feminine body and sexuality, both liminal and therefore polluting and dangerous, as well as a rebirth that guarantees the preservation of order and therefore the social world of traditional authority based on the figure of the father.[30] However, as Elisabeth Bronfen argues, in order for death to actually achieve this rebirth of women into the normative social order, a second burial is required, that is, the "replacement [of the decomposed feminine body] by the eternal forms of a tomb or burial mound, which serve as a signifier for a place of permanence, stability and non-differentiation [which] assures the continuity of the social world of the fathers."[31] In Sabrina's case this does not happen. Without the patriarchal burial, Sabrina experiences the liminality of death—she has not yet putrefied, thus becoming a biological and a social subject that has died but is not buried yet.[32] It is in this process that her hybridity begins to work in concert with liminality, allowing her to resurrect and to pull from all available sources of power without adhering to a specific identity, leading to the angels' slaughter. With this death, Sabrina now moves as a truly liminal hybrid, and from that point on, she begins performing "miracles"—healing Ambrose, controlling the weather, restoring Roz's sight, resurrecting the dead witches and the familiar, Leviathan, etc.

Towards the end of Part 2, in "Chapter Nineteen: The Mandrake" (2:8), viewers find out that this miraculous power of Sabrina's was part of the Dark Lord's plan all along to eventually crown Sabrina as Queen of Hell. To do this, however, Sabrina would have to leave liminality and strictly determine her path. As mentioned before, what the Dark Lord did not anticipate was for Sabrina to be liminal and therefore to deny the decision of her identity, "toppling White patriarchy" both in Heaven and in Hell, as is presented when Lilith finally ascends to the throne of Hell.[33] Nothing will be the same after this.

FROM VOID TO IMMANENCE: DOUBLES AND HAUNTINGS FROM THE "SWEET HEREAFTER"

There is no doubt that Sabrina's liminal hybridity starts to impact the limits of the defined identities of mortals and witches, to the extent that the Church of Night transfers their allegiance to Lilith and then Hecate (the Three-in-One) with Aunt Zelda as their High Priestess, allowing them to tap into new powers as well as gain new allies like the marginalized witches of the Church of Night and Mambo Marie LeFleur/Baron Samedi (Skye Marshall). At the same time in the mortal realm, Harvey reflects on his rejection of witches in relation to his own perception of his weakness—a statement of toxic masculinity—and finally accepts Roz as a witch. All of these transgressions and transformations do not imply that there is a fusion of identities to create a new hegemonic one; instead, the limits of each realm are transgressed to the point of opening dialogues, debates, reflections, alliances, and the sharing of powers and knowledges.

In the transgression of limits, Sabrina's liminal hybridity progressively transforms those limits into thresholds that are much easier to cross and disrupt by those marginalized and positioned as Other. The interruption of limits reaches such depth in *CAoS* that even the order of time is disjointed by Sabrina's actions. By the end of Part 3, after Sabrina goes back in time to save Greendale, she encounters the Sabrina from the past and decides not to keep the time loop going in order to allow both Sabrinas to exist in two realities—in Greendale and as the full Queen of Hell. A first look at this might suggest that the demands of identity have won and that Sabrina has finally submitted to the patriarchal structures of identity formation. Yet, the fact that there are two Sabrinas existing in different realms, both as liminal hybrids,[34] further exacerbates the effects of liminality—Sabrina is now existing everywhere and nowhere. Deleuze's immanence is coming forth, which will not only disrupt the social structures but threatens to dissolve everything so that only movement of bodies without form or essence is possible.[35]

As viewers find out in Part 4 of the series, not only are the Eldritch Terrors[36] coming to Greendale after being summoned by Father Blackwood—a potentiality opened by the impacts of liminality—but the disruption of time produced by the existence of two Sabrinas is accelerating the resultant fusion of the realms of Heaven, Hell, and Earth, eliminating the limits between them. At the same time, an alternate universe has been propelled into existence by the continued presence of the two Sabrinas, attracting the Cosmos (the fifth Eldritch terror), which will also crash with the present realms. The angel Metatron (Pollyanna McIntosh) proposes a solution: one Sabrina can die, or they can again become one being. However, the angel's true plan is soon revealed: Metatron firmly states in "Chapter Thirty-Three: Deus Ex Machina" (4:5) that "there will be order at all costs,"[37] and Ambrose realizes that Metatron intends the death of both Sabrinas—the point being again the death of the polluting liminal-hybrid feminine body to restore the limits of the patriarchal structures. The Dark Lord—with the help of Caliban, Zelda, Hilda, Ambrose, and Nick—kills Metatron. Afterward, they decide to send Sabrina Morningstar to the alternate universe as a sacrifice to stop the crash. However, as we learn in "Chapter Thirty-Five: The Endless" (4:7), Sabrina Morningstar dies in her attempt to warn Sabrina Spellman that the Void (the last Eldritch Terror) is coming to suck in her universe. While Sabrina Spellman tries to capture the Void in Pandora's Box, her family calls back her soul to insert it into Sabrina Morningstar's body. One Sabrina has died, and although one might assume that Metatron's plan is moving ahead, Sabrina's liminal hybridity continues to move towards immanence because Spellman's soul is in Morningstar's body—they are still everywhere and nowhere, so some of the Void stays in Sabrina.

Although the Void presents itself as the existence of nothing, Sabrina Spellman realizes that its purpose is to kill, as it did with Sabrina Morningstar. Immanence is a plane without essence or form, but it is still a plane of movement, while the Void is a plane that stops movement—it is the plane of death. For authors such as Laclau, Jacques Lacan, and Martin Heidegger there is a void where the true origin of society should be. To close it and inaugurate social structures, identities have to be determined and norms have to be established. The equivalence of the Void with Sabrina is a warning tale of patriarchy for what happens when determined identities are refused—the result is inevitable death, as happens with Sabrina in the finale of Part 4. Unfortunately for the normative structures of patriarchy, not even the death of the liminal hybrid can stop the ontological transformations it has engendered. Order is restored, but a different kind, one with limits that could not have been imagined before.

Additionally, the masculine burial of the feminine body does not consider the implications of the death of liminal hybridity. In *CAoS*'s finale, Sabrina dies, and the episode's ending shows her reading peacefully in the "Sweet Hereafter." What is this place? Is it Heaven? Hell? Limbo? It is not Heaven, because Nick joins her after dying by suicide, which would automatically ban him from Heaven according to traditional Christian beliefs and norms. Because Sabrina sacrificed herself to save others, it cannot be Hell, as that action guarantees entrance to Heaven. It is not Limbo, because no soul-eater is hunting them, as with the case of Tommy's soul when he goes to Limbo. So, what is it? If we analyze this in terms of temporality, we can assume it is not the *after*life—it clearly states it is an articulation of the *here* and the *after*. That is, it is immanence, a plane of life that is here because it is the ultimate condition of potentiality for the actualization of reality.[38] Sabrina's death is the ultimate emancipation from social structures; she is now in immanence, in the plane of absolute movement and affect. How will this materialize in reality? How will her hauntings look in the mortal realm? It is reasonable to assume that her ghost would appear in Greendale to continue haunting patriarchal structures.

There is no denying that *Chilling Adventures of Sabrina* has its issues—a poor representation of race, the romanticization of suicide, etc. Yet, the narrative approaches a very important topic—the female empowerment that can derive from liminal hybridity. In a present time where the limits of identity are again being reinforced to the detriment of difference and heterogeneity, Sabrina's narrative pushes against these current trends through the figure of the liminal hybrid.

Furthermore, the approach that is presented in relation to hybridity distinguishes Sabrina's narrative from traditional texts in which the hybrid is othered and subjected to a legitimized ultimate destruction. By the end of *CAoS*, viewers mourn the liminal hybrid maybe because Sabrina continues to be White and privileged. Although the series is not necessarily concerned with racial or ethnicity issues, particularly from the Latinx community (there is not one Latinx character in the series), the figure of the hybrid is one that has been very important for this community. As Antonio Alcalá and Ilse Bussing posit, the figures of hybrids and doubles are particularly relevant in Gothic productions of the Global South because of the legacy of colonization and slavery that led to a "violent mixing of indigenous cultures and European conquerors [and] produced hybrid (mestizo) cultures that gave rise to doubles and other transformations reflected in Gothic fictions from the area."[39] Sabrina is not located in the Global South and is White and privileged, yet she is narrated as hybrid which is a common trope in the Latinx community. This begs the question: is the narrative saying something about this community, especially since its creator, Roberto Aguirre-Sacasa, is Nicaraguan-American? It is important to continue discussing this particular issue of how Latinx tropes are being inserted and interpreted in a narrative where the Latinx community does not appear.

Finally, it is important to stress that liminal hybridity is presented in the series as attached to a female body. Sabrina is killed several times because of the demands of patriarchal identity—of both Heaven and Hell—and continues to survive because of hybridity and liminality until she becomes the ontological potentiality of Life. In the end, not only is Heaven disrupted by the newly established norms within Greendale, but Lilith makes Lucifer human and returns him to the mortal realm, after which she finally takes over Hell. It would be interesting to see what kind of Hell is created by the first witch, the one that would not submit to God. The effect of Sabrina's disruptions because of her liminal hybridity certainly gives Satanic and Divine patriarchy a run for their money.

BIBLIOGRAPHY

Alcalá González, Antonio, and Ilse Bussing López. "Introduction." In *Doubles and Hybrids in Latin American Gothic*, 1–16. New York and London: Routledge, 2020.

Bronfen, Elisabeth. *Over Her Dead Body: Death, Femininity, and the Aesthetic.* Manchester, UK: Manchester University Press, 1992.

Chilling Adventures of Sabrina, Season 1, episode 1, "Chapter One: October Country." Directed by Lee Toland Krieger, written by Roberto Aguirre-Sacasa, featuring Kiernan Shipka, Miranda Otto, Lucy Davis, and Chance Perdomo.

Released October 26, 2018, Netflix, www.netflix.com/watch/80230071?trackId =200257859.

———, Season 1, episode 3, "Chapter Three: The Trial of Sabrina Spellman." Directed by Rob Seidenglanz, written by Ross Maxwell, featuring Kiernan Shipka, Miranda Otto, Lucy Davis, and Ross Lynch. Released October 26, 2018, Netflix, www.netflix.com/watch/80230073?trackId=200257859.

———, Season 1, episode 7, "Chapter Seven: Feasts of Feasts." Directed by Nguyen Viet, written by Oanh Ly, featuring Kiernan Shipka, Miranda Otto, Lucy Davis, and Tati Gabrielle. Released October 26, 2018, Netflix, www.netflix.com/watch /80230077?trackId=200257859.

———, Season 1, episode 8, "Chapter Eight: The Burial." Directed by Maggie Kiley, written by Christianne Hedtke and Lindsey Calhoon Bring, featuring Kiernan Shipka, Ross Lynch, Jaz Sinclair, and Tati Gabrielle. Released October 26, 2018, Netflix, www.netflix.com/watch/80230078?trackId=200257859.

———, Season 1, episode 9, "Chapter Nine: The Returned Man." Directed by Craig William Macneill, written by Axelle Carolyn and Christina Ham, featuring Kiernan Shipka, Miranda Otto, Ross Lynch, and Jazz Sinclair. Released October 26, 2018, Netflix, www.netflix.com/watch/80230079?trackId=200257859.

———, Season 2, episode 6, "Chapter Seventeen: The Missionaries." Directed by Rob Seidenglanz, written by Donna Thorland, featuring Kiernan Shipka, Miranda Otto, and Lucy Davis, and Spencer Treat Clark. Released April 5, 2019, Netflix, www.netflix.com/watch/80230087?trackId=14277283.

———, Season 2, episode 7, "Chapter Eighteen: The Miracles of Sabrina Spellman." Directed by Antonio Negret, written by Christianne Hedtke and Lindsay Calhoon Bring, featuring Kiernan Shipka, Miranda Otto, Lucy Davis, and Chance Perdomo. Released April 5, 2019, Netflix, www.netflix.com/watch/80230088 ?trackId=200257859.

———, Season 2, episode 8, "Chapter Nineteen: The Mandrake." Directed by Kevin Sullivan, written by Joshua Conkel, featuring Kiernan Shipka, Miranda Otto, Lucy Davis, and Chance Perdomo. Released April 5, 2019, Netflix, www.netflix.com/ watch/80230089?trackId=14277283.

———, Season 4, episode 5, "Chapter Thirty-Three: Deus Ex Machina." Directed by Amanda Tapping, written by Eleanor Jean, featuring Kiernan Shipka, Miranda Otto, Lucy Davis, and Lachlan Watson. Released December 31, 2020, Netflix, www.netflix.com/watch/81062664?trackId=200257859.

———, Season 4, episode 7, "Chapter Thirty-Five: The Endless." Directed by Kevin Sullivan, written by Donna Thorland and Matthew Barry, featuring Kiernan Shipka, Miranda Ott, Lachlan Watson, Richard Coyle, Ross Lynch, Lucy Davis, Chance Perdomo, and Michelle Gomez. Released December 31, 2020, Netflix, www.netflix.com/watch/81062666?trackId=200257859.

Day, Sara K., Miranda A. Green-Barteet, and Amy L. Montz. "Introduction: From 'New Woman' to 'Future Girl': The Roots and the Rise of the Female Protagonist in Contemporary Young Adult Dystopias." In *Female Rebellion in Young Adult Dystopian Fiction*, 1–14. Surrey, England: Ashgate Publishing Limited, 2014.

Deleuze, Gilles. *Spinoza: Practical Philosophy*. Translated by Robert Hurley. San Francisco: City Lights Books, 1988.

Deleuze, Gilles, and Félix Guattari. *Anti-Oedipus: Capitalism and Schizophrenia*. New York: Penguin Group, 1977.

Deleuze, Gilles, and Félix Guattari. *Kafka: Toward a Minor Literature*. Translated by Dana Polan. Minneapolis and London: University of Minnesota Press, 1986.

Derrida, Jacques. "Force of Law: The 'Mystical Foundation of Authority.'" In *Deconstruction and the Possibility of Justice*, edited by Drucilla Cornell, Michael Rosenfeld, and David Gray Carlson, 3–67. New York and London: Routledge, 1992.

Derrida, Jacques. *Writing and Difference*. London: Routledge, Taylor and Francis Group, 1978.

Douglas, Mary. *Purity and Danger: An Analysis of Concepts of Pollution and Taboo*. London and New York: Routledge, 1984.

Grijalva-Maza, Luisa Fernanda. "Deconstructing the Grand Narrative in Harry Potter: Inclusion/ Exclusion and Discriminatory Policies in Fiction and Practice." *Politics and Policy* 40, no. 3 (2012): 424–43.

Henesy, Megan. "'Leaving My Girlhood Behind': Woke Witches and Feminist Liminality in *Chilling Adventures of Sabrina*." *Feminist Media Studies* 21, no. 7 (2020): 1–15. doi.org/10.1080/14680777.2020.1791929.

Lacan, Jacques. "Position of the Unconscious." In *Écrits*, translated by Bruce Fink, 703–21. New York and London: W.W. Norton and Company, Inc., 2002.

Laclau, Ernesto. *On Populist Reason*. London and New York: Verso, 2007.

Madden, Victoria. "'We Found the Witch, May We Burn Her?': Suburban Gothic, Witch-Hunting, and Anxiety-Induced Conformity in Stephen King's *Carrie*." *The Journal of American Culture* 40, no. 1 (March 2017): 7–20.

Manning, Erin. *The Minor Gesture*. United States of America: Duke University Press, 2016.

Moosavinia, Sayyed Rahim and Sayyede Maryam Hosseini. "Liminality, Hybridity and 'Third Space': Bessie Head's *A Question of Power*." *Neohelicon* 45 (2018): 333–49. doi.org/10.1007/s11059-017-0387-8.

Oleszkiewics-Peralba, Matgorzata. *Fierce Feminine Divinities of Eurasia and Latin America: Baba Yaga, Kālī, Pombagira, and Santa Muerte*. London: Palgrave MacMillan, 2015.

Tally Jr., Robert T. "Forward: 'A Utopia of the In-Between,' or, Limning the Liminal." In *Landscapes of Liminality: Between Space and Place*, ix–xv. London and New York: Rowman & Littlefield, 2016.

NOTES

1. Megan Henesy, "Leaving My Girlhood 'Behind': Woke Witches and Feminist Liminality in Chilling Adventures of Sabrina," *Feminist Media Studies* 21, no. 7 (2020): 2, doi.org/10.1080/14680777.2020.1791929.

2. Sara K. Day, Miranda A. Green-Barteet, and Amy L. Montz, "Introduction: From 'New Woman' to 'Future Girl': The Roots and the Rise of the Female Protagonist in

Contemporary Young Adult Dystopias," in *Female Rebellion in Young Adult Dystopian Fiction* (Surrey, England: Ashgate Publishing Limited, 2014), 3.

3. Elisabeth Bronfen, *Over Her Dead Body: Death, Femininity, and the Aesthetic* (Manchester, UK: Manchester University Press, 1992), 198.

4. Sara K. Day et al., "Introduction," in *Female*, 2.

5. Victoria Madden, "We Found the Witch, May We Burn Her?": Suburban Gothic, Witch-Hunting, and Anxiety-Induced Conformity in Stephen King's *Carrie*," *The Journal of American Culture* 40, no. 1 (March 2017): 11.

6. Bronfen, *Over Her Dead Body*, 198.

7. Roz begins moving towards her witch nature; Susie/Theo Putnam (Lachlan Watson) is transitioning from girl to boy; and Prudence Blackwood (Tati Gabrielle) is an orphan in search of her identity.

8. At least until it is revealed that her true father is not the warlock Edward Spellman (Georgie Daburas) but the Dark Lord himself.

9. *Chilling Adventures of Sabrina*, season 2, episode 7, "Chapter Eighteen: The Miracles of Sabrina Spellman," by Antonio Negret, written by Christianne Hedtke & Lindsay Calhoon Bring, featuring Kiernan Shipka, Miranda Otto, Lucy Davis, and Chance Perdomo, released April 5, 2019, on Netflix, www.netflix.com/watch /80230088?trackId=200257859: 00:18:40.

10. Sayyed Rahim Moosavinia and Sayyede Maryam Hosseini, "Liminality, Hybridity and 'Third Space': Bessie Head's *A Question of Power*," *Neohelicon* 45 (2018): 333. doi.org/10.1007/s11059-017-0387-8.

11. Mary Douglas, *Purity and Danger: An Analysis of Concepts of Pollution and Taboo* (London and New York: Routledge, 1984), 54.

12. Luisa Fernanda Grijalva-Maza, "Deconstructing the Grand Narrative in *Harry Potter*: Inclusion/Exclusion and Discriminatory Policies in Fiction and Practice," *Politics and Policy* 40, no. 3 (2012): 431.

13. *Chilling Adventures of Sabrina*, season 1, episode 1, "Chapter One: October Country," directed by Lee Toland Krieger, written by Roberto Aguirre-Sacasa, featuring Kiernan Shipka, Miranda Otto, Lucy Davis, and Chance Perdomo, released October 26, 2018, on Netflix, www.netflix.com/watch/80230071?trackId=20025785900: 22:56.

14. Given that Diana was not fully conscious of the act, it is accurate to state that the Dark Lord raped her.

15. *Chilling Adventures of Sabrina*, season 2, episode 8, "Chapter Nineteen: The Mandrake," directed by Kevin Sullivan, written by Joshua Conkel, featuring Kiernan Shipka, Miranda Otto, Lucy Davis, and Chance Perdomo, released April 5, 2019, on Netflix, www.netflix.com/watch/80230089?trackId=14277283.: 00:46:19.

16. Ernesto Laclau, *On Populist Reason* (London and New York: Verso, 2007), 59.

17. I elaborate on this concept in "'Entre la Santa y la Muerte': Liminality, Hybridity, and Empowerment in Mexico's Santa Muerte" that will appear in the book *Monsters & Saints: Latindigenous Landscapes and Spectral Storytelling* edited by Shantel Martínez and Kelly Medina-López (forthcoming 2023).

18. Sara K. Day et al., "Introduction," in *Female*, 3.

19. Matgorzata Oleszkiewics-Peralba, *Fierce Feminine Divinities of Eurasia and Latin America: Baba Yaga, Kālī, Pombagira, and Santa Muerte* (Palgrave MacMillan, 2015), 3–4.

20. Bronfen, *Over Her Dead Body*, 197–98.

21. Moosavinia and Maryam Hosseini, "Liminality, Hybridity and 'Third Space,'" 337.

22. Jacques Lacan, "Position of the Unconscious," in *Écrits*, trans. Bruce Fink (New York and London: W.W. Norton and Company, Inc., 2002), 709 [836].

23. Gilles Deleuze and Félix Guattari, *Anti-Oedipus: Capitalism and Schizophrenia* (New York: Penguin Group, 1977), 52.

24. The decision is an important concept in Jacques Derrida's thought. It relates to the moment in which a potential subject makes a decision about what they will identify with—the limits of their identity. This political moment marks the rise of the full subject.

25. Jacques Derrida, "Force of Law: The 'Mystical Foundation of Authority,'" in *Deconstruction and the Possibility of Justice*, ed. Drucilla Cornell, Michael Rosenfeld, and David Gray Carlson (New York and London: Routledge, 1992), 26.

26. Robert T. Tally, Jr., "Forward: 'A Utopia of the In-Between,' or, Limning the Liminal," in *Landscapes of Liminality: Between Space and Place* (London and New York: Rowman & Littlefield, 2016), x.

27. Jacques Derrida, *Writing and Difference* (London: Routledge, Taylor and Francis Group, 1978), 351–52.

28. Tally Jr., "Forward," xi.

29. Tally Jr., "Forward," xi.

30. Bronfen, *Over Her Dead Body*, 199.

31. Bronfen, *Over Her Dead Body*, 199.

32. Bronfen, *Over Her Dead Body*, 198.

33. *Chilling Adventures of Sabrina*, "Chapter One: October Country," 00:22:56.

34. Let us remember that Sabrina Morningstar visits Sabrina Spellman in the mortal realm and vice versa. Also, they will join forces to defeat the Eldritch Terrors.

35. The plane of immanence is without form. It is constant movement, composition and recomposition. Gilles Deleuze, *Spinoza: Practical Philosophy*, trans. Robert Hurley (San Francisco: City Lights Books, 1988), 128.

36. Terrors that predate the social production of time and space.

37. *Chilling Adventures of Sabrina*, season 4, episode 5, "Chapter Thirty-Three: Deux Ex Machina," directed by Amanda Tapping, written by Eleanor Jean, featuring Kiernan Shipka, Miranda Otto, Lucy Davis, and Lachlan Watson, released December 31, 2020, on Netflix, www.netflix.com/watch/81062664?trackId=200257859: 00:42:01.

38. Deleuze and Guattari, *Anti-Oedipus*, 1–2.

39. Antonio Alcalá González and Ilse Bussing López, "Introduction," in *Doubles and Hybrids in Latin American Gothic* (New York and London: Routledge, 2020), 2–3.

PART 3

"I feel more myself in boys' clothes"

Identity and Intersectionality

Chapter 7

From Having to Choose to Being Chosen

Analyzing Sabrina as a Mixed (Race) Being

*Lisa Delacruz Combs, Nicole Neifert,
and Marc P. Johnston-Guerrero*

Racial representations in popular culture have been shown to matter in shaping identity development.[1] Despite expanding scholarship on racial representation across various media, more examinations are needed of multiracial characters; for example, scholars across different disciplines have conducted studies focused on multiracial Disney Channel characters.[2] Yet, these same scholars also argue that more attention is needed to understand mixed race representation more accurately on television. In this chapter, we expand upon this work by exploring the complexities of race, multiraciality, and the connections between critical mixed race studies and supernatural hybridity in Netflix's *Chilling Adventures of Sabrina* (*CAoS*, Netflix, 2018- –20). Though *CAoS*'s protagonist, Sabrina Spellman (Kiernan Shipka), is not racially mixed, her portrayal reveals nuances related to racial liminality[3] imposed by a societal dependence on monoracialism, the social force and preference for single racial categorizations.[4] By centering the complexities of race, multiraciality, and the connections between mixedness and supernatural hybridity, we highlight how Sabrina's characterization connects to common themes or tropes found in multiracial studies and argue for more nuanced portrayals of mixed or hybrid characters given their potential to shape identity development.

First, we want to acknowledge and elevate the important work of others arguing how *CAoS* writers and producers are cruel to Black characters by centering whiteness, for instance, by giving characters of color secondary plot-lines or using them to fulfill supernatural tropes like "the human sacrifice."[5] Though our analysis focuses on Sabrina, who we argue benefits strongly from her white privilege, our goal is not to re-center whiteness and pull away important attention from the characters of color, so we urge readers to seek out that work. Our initial goal of analyzing *CAoS* was to try to compare Sabrina's witch/human hybridity to the other mixed characters of color in the series. However, so much happens with Sabrina on her own that we wanted to be able to dive more deeply into the symbolism of her character and connections to mixedness. It became evident to us that Sabrina being half-witch and half-mortal was a central thread of the show, and we wanted to trace the tensions as she navigates in-between worlds—first the witch world and human world, and later the human/witch world and Hell. Sabrina struggles to find her place and is ultimately expected to be a savior in the final season, illuminating a white savior complex and a potential connection between supernatural hybridity, cultural mixedness, and multiraciality.

FRAMING ANALYSIS THROUGH LIMINALITY AND MONOCENTRICITY

The emerging interdisciplinary field of critical mixed-race studies[6] has helped coalesce the sometimes-disparate theories and constructs connected to multiraciality. For our analysis, we utilize liminality[7] and monocentricity[8] in tandem to frame our understanding of Sabrina as a hybrid or mixed being. Victor Turner (1979) coined the term "liminality" to describe a threshold existence or in-between space in anthropological and religious studies. Turner developed liminality in response to Arnold Van Gennep's[9] conceptualization of religious rites of passage—the transitory stages associated with rituals and pivotal life events—and built upon the concept to expand the experience beyond religious contexts and emphasize fluidity across one's life. We apply liminality to *CAoS* because of Sabrina's liminal existence between multiple worlds. Other scholars such as Megan Henesy also use liminality as a frame to analyze *CAoS*, explicitly calling attention to the liminality of the teen feminist experience, making the argument that many women characters are outsiders throughout the storyline because of their liminality.[10] Similar to Henesy's employment of liminality as a frame to examine gender, we call attention to liminality and race within *CAoS*.

Moreover, we focus on monocentricity to complement liminality in our analysis. Monocentricity is the preference for single identity categories within society.[11] Similar to monoracialism, or the preference imposed onto individuals to identify with only one race,[12] monocentricity focuses on the predisposition for single, discrete, and concrete categories including and beyond race. In other words, monoracialism focuses on singular *racial* categories, while monocentricity is a preference for single categories more broadly. We chose monocentricity as a piece of our conceptual framing because of the innate preference for single categorization throughout the series and the ability for monocentricity to transcend racial categories in our application to supernatural hybridity. Ultimately, we frame Sabrina's duality as both witch and mortal as a liminal experience that pushes against the intense monocentricity featured in the series.

SABRINA AS A MIXED BEING THROUGH CHAOTIC RACIAL SYMBOLISM

Analyzing *CAoS* through the lenses of mixedness and liminality allowed us to see clear connections to prominent themes or tropes related to multiracial identities, even though Sabrina is not multiracial herself. Her mixed or hybrid nature across the supernatural and mundane connects closely to being mixed race, yet with some key distinctions. Here, our thematic analysis centers ideas of choice or being forced to choose, consequences of choices, and being the "chosen one." These themes of choice evolve throughout the series. In season one, choice is a major focus and clearly symbolizes mixedness (e.g., the repeated use of "half-breed"[13]). In later seasons, the idea of choice becomes less central, yet Sabrina eventually becomes "chosen" due to her uniqueness, bringing the idea of choice full circle and establishing its connection to mixedness.

Theme 1: Being Forced to Choose

Circumstances surrounding Sabrina continually pressure her to choose between two monocentric paths. The first time Sabrina is pressured into denying one of her identities occurs during the first several chapters of season one. The very first line in the entire series, "Chapter One: October Country" (1:1), explains this ultimatum: "In the town of Greendale . . . there lived a girl who was half-witch, half-mortal, who, on her sixteenth birthday, would have to choose between two worlds: the witch world of her family, and the human world of her friends."[14] This opening sequence sets the tone for the first season and classically symbolizes the trope of mixed race individuals being forced to choose one of their component identities, families, and/or worlds.

Sabrina is pressured to choose between the Path of Night and the Path of Light, culminating in the Dark Baptism on her sixteenth birthday. She receives pressure from her family and the Church of Night to let go of all things mortal, and her aunts remind her in the first episode that witch law states she must choose "The Path of Night or the Path of Light, but not both."[15] In "Chapter One: October Country" (1:1), Sabrina expresses reservations about choosing life as a witch, saying it entails having to "say goodbye to half your life, your friends, your boyfriend."[16] Choosing a mortal life would also place monocentric limitations on Sabrina, though, because as a mortal, she would not be able to develop her witch powers. Additionally, her boyfriend in season one, Harvey Kinkle (Ross Lynch), turns out to be descended from witch-hunters, further pitting her mortal and witch sides against each other. These circumstances show that Sabrina needs to give up her duality and choose only a monocentric path.

These themes of choice in *CAoS* have been written about previously, but mostly around women's bodily choice and autonomy from a feminist perspective.[17] Here, we highlight how certain scenes and dialogue also connect closely to racial choices. In the first episode of the series, Sabrina talks to her aunts about wanting to make "an educated choice" and also wanting to understand her parents' wishes.[18] Across many different cultures, various rules of racial determination have made distinctions between how one should identify depending on who their mother or father is. In the U.S., laws of hypodescent—the so-called "one-drop rule"—were somewhat tied to the mother's race, due to slavery and white enslavers who raped enslaved women.[19] As Nikki Khanna explains, biracial "children of enslaved mothers were classified as black and remained slaves, which provided an economic asset to white slave owners."[20] Consider also matrilineal rules of descent held by some Conservative and Orthodox sects of Judaism, which dictate that one must be born to a Jewish mother in order to claim being Jewish. If Sabrina follows her father in choosing the Path of Night and embracing her witch nature fully, she would be going against common rules that would have her follow her mother's identity.

This sense of a mother's womb dictating one's true nature is fully portrayed in the third episode of the series. In "Chapter Three: The Trial of Sabrina Spellman" (1:3), when Sabrina is tried before the Infernal Court for breach of promise to the Dark Lord, her lawyer, Daniel Webster (John Rubinstein) argues that Sabrina is "born of a mortal womb, making her half-witch and half-mortal and therefore only half subject to the laws of this [witch] court."[21] The explicit attention to the mother's womb being mortal highlights this essentialist notion that one follows the path of the mother's identity over the father. Though the court ultimately rejects this argument, the rebuttal by prosecutor Father Faustus Blackwood (Richard Coyle) is that

Sabrina indeed has a dominant nature, one that could be determined through tests. This idea of testing to figure out who or what one truly is also connects to themes in multiracial literature highlighting the common experience of authenticity or legitimacy "tests" by others to demonstrate one's cultural knowledge.[22] Throughout the series, Sabrina is tested by others to validate her identity choices and desire to embrace her duality, such as the Harrowing from Prudence Blackwood (Tati Gabrielle) and the Weird Sisters, and the competition with Caliban (Sam Corlett) for Hell's throne. If she wants the crown, "she's going to have to prove herself worthy."[23] This authenticity testing is a way in which monocentricity manifests to police identity borders and push people who do not fit into single categories into a liminal existence.

The consistent use of "half" to describe Sabrina throughout the series calls in tropes related to biracial identity, but rather being than a mere descriptor, it is often used to demean or denigrate Sabrina for not being fully one identity. In "Chapter Twelve: The Epiphany" (2:1), the three higher demons manifest and exclaim "we wish death upon the half-spawn witch and the chaos she engenders! She must be stopped!" and assert the "half-witch must not ascend."[24] These negative "half" terms applied to Sabrina are juxtaposed with the persistent kinds of "what are you?" questions so common within multiracial scholarship.[25] For example, in "Chapter Seventeen: The Missionaries" (2:6), an Innocent explicitly says to Sabrina: "You're not a witch. What are you?"[26] In the following episode, "Chapter Eighteen: The Miracles of Sabrina Spellman" (2:7), Prudence even explicitly asks Ambrose Spellman (Chance Perdomo) about Sabrina: "What is she, really?" Ambrose responds, "Why don't you ask her for yourself?"[27] These lines of questioning signal the pressure and social forces working on Sabrina to define herself in monocentric ways, to choose one of her dual identities and thereby define herself as legible to others. Yet, she continues to fight against monocentricity, which ultimately has consequences.

Theme 2: Duality as Chaos and Consequences of Choices Resisting Categorization

Central throughout *CAoS* is the idea of duality, as well as the inevitable negative consequences that follow each time Sabrina makes a choice that resists monocentric categorization. When pressured to choose between two options, Sabrina often finds a way to choose both, and this duality allows her to exist in a space beyond categories. However, her victories are often short-lived; since Sabrina's duality is so different from the carefully maintained norms of her world, her actions and choices stemming from duality are often followed by painful punishment—even death.

When Sabrina is forced to choose between the witch and mortal worlds, despite the two apparent choices in front of her, Sabrina chooses her own option: duality. She flees her Dark Baptism in "Chapter Two: The Dark Baptism" (1:2), stating, "And so the girl who had to decide between being a witch and being mortal chose neither path. Or, if you look at it another way, chose both. She was half-witch, but with two covens."[28] Here, Sabrina demonstrates her first major choice where she rejects the traditional, monocentric rules and pressures of the world around her and instead forms a new space of her own. Her dual identities appear to gain acceptance in the following episode, after the trial, when Sabrina is granted permission to study witchcraft without leaving her mortal friends behind. Lawyer Daniel Webster tells her to consider this verdict "a dual citizenship."[29]

For a short time, Sabrina achieves validation of both of her identities, and the forces that try to make her choose one side are tempered. However, because forces in the background continue to pit her existences against each other, she occupies a space similar to the "marginal man" or "tragic mulatto" archetypes[30] where she is still pressured to choose or face tragic consequences. Because she must keep her witch side secret for much of the first season, she feels the stress of potential rejection and withholding her true identity from friends. In "Chapter Ten: The Witching Hour" (1:10), when Sabrina's friends Rosalind "Roz" Walker (Jaz Sinclair) and Theo Putnam (Lachlan Watson) ask if she is a witch, Sabrina cries, "I wanted to tell you so many times, but how could I?"[31] This emotional stress parallels the identity conflict and inner turmoil "tragic" archetypes might experience around dilemmas of "passing" and authenticity.

External pressures and physical dangers also continue to make Sabrina's dual existence difficult to sustain. In "Chapter Five: Dreams in a Witch House" (1:5), when Sabrina's mortal insights and witch skills allow her to open the Acheron Configuration, she releases a demon that wants to kill her family and spread terror throughout the world via dreams. Her Aunt Zelda Spellman (Miranda Otto) pithily summarizes this danger, "Sabrina's duality almost got us killed."[32] This sequence of events illustrates how even a duality-related achievement leads to eventual negative consequences, and how the choices stemming from her mixedness could lead to a tragic ending. Sabrina's dreams in this episode further illustrate this central conflict. Sabrina dreams that Harvey and her mortal friends try to kill her after finding out her true witch identity, illustrating Sabrina's fear that she would be harmed if the mortal world found out about her duality. In this dream, Zelda encapsulates Sabrina's conflicting identities, stating, "Your attempts to conciliate your duality will only bring you pain and suffering,"[33] echoing the "tragic mulatto" archetype. As the series continues, this prophetic statement becomes one of its recurring themes. The sleep demon plays on Sabrina's real fears, demonstrating that both external figures and internal anxieties remind Sabrina that her dual nature is unusual and perilous. Importantly, however, Sabrina does not make any changes after this dream; she continues to choose duality and reject monocentricity.

Throughout the series, Sabrina's dual nature is rejected by the mortal world, Lucifer Morningstar's (Luke Cook) world, and eventually the entire universe, with it being finally snuffed out in the end. This rejection relates to the idea that supernaturally mixed people may suffer until they eventually choose one monocentric identity or another. Season three of the series highlights a different duality for Sabrina: Hell and Earth. Nick Scratch (Gavin Leatherwood) recognizes Caliban as a new suitor for Sabrina, with Caliban representing Hell and Nick Earth. Even when the central conflict of *CAoS* shifts from the human versus witch worlds toward the witch/mortal world versus Hell, the push for monocentricity remains.

Sabrina's duality manifests most intensely with the creation of two Sabrinas, a past one that current/future Sabrina saves through a time loop and who eventually reigns as Queen of Hell (also known as "Sabrina Morningstar") while the other (referred to as "Sabrina Spellman") lives on Earth. In "Chapter Twenty-Nine: The Eldritch Dark" (4:1), Sabrina Spellman questions her choices, even asking Ambrose if she could visit Sabrina Morningstar in Hell. Ambrose is adamant that they do not visit each other. Despite Ambrose's warning, the two Sabrinas do visit each other and are eventually killed by the end of the series as their two worlds collide,[34] which is the manifestation of Zelda's warning that having duality will only lead to suffering, or from a mixed perspective, a tragic ending. Sabrina's dual nature is so far outside of what is accepted in the rules of this universe that she must be terminated.

Like many multiracial people who fight to maintain their mixed identities against external forces pressuring them to choose a monoracial identity, Sabrina struggles to maintain dual identities when others try to force her to choose a monocentric one. Sabrina's liminal position, wherein she bends the rules of her worlds to maintain her duality, is punished with pain and suffering. Similarly, in the real world, Roger Herring claims that mixed race youths are often pressured to choose a "singular ethnic identity," or they will risk "combating societal forces in the expression of biracialism."[35] Through Sabrina's death, the series suggests there may never be a time when she can embrace her duality; we argue this parallels the fact that multiracial people are not allowed to embrace their mixed identities without receiving pressure to change. Despite the painful consequences, Sabrina consistently chooses duality anyway, and never succumbs to a monocentric path. Her choices indicate that the pain and suffering linked to duality are sacrifices she is willing to make.

Theme 3: Uniqueness and Being Used as a "Chosen One" Pawn

Another theme that emerged from our analysis is the emphasis on Sabrina's uniqueness, specifically termed "special" multiple times throughout the series. This uniqueness is tied explicitly to her duality as a mortal and witch, allowing her to traverse multiple contexts in the *CAoS* universe. For instance, in "Chapter Eight: The Burial," during Tommy's botched resurrection, Ambrose has a rare moment of anger, scolding Sabrina and saying, "Why must you always insist that the universe grant you special privileges? You've upset the natural order . . . there are rules. There is no cheating fate." Sabrina responds, "What's the point of being a witch if I can't help the ones I love?" Ambrose answers, "You've crossed a line this time. No, no, no, you've completely erased it."[36] This exchange demonstrates the severity of the consequences of Sabrina having both a place among her mortal friends and witches. She makes a decision that no other witch would make because she is special. Moreover, other characters attempt to utilize Sabrina, specifically her supernatural hybridity, as a pawn in their strategic plays that ultimately support their desired endgame. As we outline below, Sabrina becomes "chosen" in different ways and by different characters, and by her embracing this unique position, she ultimately symbolizes a kind of white saviorism.

One example of the prominence of her uniqueness throughout the show is when Nick, her love interest, describes their relationship in "Chapter Fourteen: Lupercalia" (2:3) when he mentions that he has never been with a mortal before—not even a half-mortal—and explicitly states, "You're pretty special, Spellman."[37] Here, Nick spotlights Sabrina's supernatural hybridity as half-human and half-witch in the context of a romantic relationship. This example aligns with previous literature on multiracial women experiencing exoticization related to appearance and attractiveness.[38] This is not the last time the series distinctly marks Sabrina as special. In "Chapter Nineteen: The Mandrake" (2:8), Sabrina has a conversation with Lilith, also known as Madam Satan, who—despite ulterior motives—ultimately serves as Sabrina's frequent mentor in the series. At this point in the series, Sabrina is working to prevent an apocalypse, and Lilith recommends a mandrake spell that will render Sabrina powerless and mortal, leading Sabrina to question her:

Sabrina: Why me?

Lilith: You're special, aren't you? Half-witch, half-mortal, representing the two tribes to be tyrannized.

Nick: You can't ask Sabrina to stop being a witch. It's who she is.

Lilith: Don't you mean it's half of who she is?[39]

Nick is compellingly defensive when Sabrina chooses to relinquish her witch side as she performs the mandrake spell to save the realms from an apocalypse. Moreover, Lilith repeats the sentiment that Sabrina is special, and both mortals and witches depend on and try to utilize Sabrina as a pawn to prevent disaster. However, we know from her frequent choices to go against norms that Sabrina still has agency, despite others trying to control her for their own agendas.

There are other points throughout the series where other characters utilize Sabrina's supernatural hybridity for their own gain. One example is when Lilith controls the narrative around Uncle Jesse's death in "Chapter Six: An Exorcism in Greendale" (1:6). Theo's uncle Jesse Putnam (Jason Beaudoin) has been possessed and is exorcised in this episode.[40] Lilith controls the situation to convince Sabrina to perform an exorcism, drawing her closer to the Dark Lord and the Path of Night. Lilith uses Sabrina's liminal existence and emotional connection to the mortal world—in this case, Theo and Uncle Jesse—for her ultimate endgame to impress the Dark Lord. This concept of Sabrina as a pawn and Lilith's manipulative ownership over Sabrina is also illustrated in "Chapter Sixteen: Blackwood" (2:5), when Lilith states, "It is time to push our little half-breed further toward the Dark Lord's prophecy."[41] The use of the word "our" implies Lilith's ownership of Sabrina as a pawn in fulfilling the prophecy. Similar to the last example, Lilith pulls the strings to control and manipulate the situation for her own gain.

Sabrina's abilities as a witch also contribute to the argument and the storyline that she is unique and special (see the Acheron Configuration puzzle example described earlier). In "Chapter Five: Dreams in a Witch House" (1:5), Sabrina's Aunt Hilda (Lucy Davis) emphasizes her uniqueness in a conversation about solving the Acheron puzzle when she says, "Witches couldn't solve it, but a half-witch could,"[42] explicitly highlighting her special location and liminal existence through her ability to solve the puzzle.

The emphasis on Sabrina as "special" and the continued attempts to control her supernatural hybridity contribute to the larger trope of Sabrina as the "chosen one."[43] Though this trope is connected to our larger findings surrounding choice, this theme focuses on Sabrina being chosen rather than on the duality of the choices that she makes. Throughout the entire series, Sabrina is expected to use her hybrid existence as mortal and witch to save others leading to the ultimate sacrifice, her death in the show's conclusion. As the storyline develops and becomes more complicated, the consequences of one's choices culminates in the multiple Sabrinas mentioned earlier. In "Chapter Thirty-Three: Deus Ex Machina" (4:5), a character called Metatron (Pollyanna McIntosh) appears intending to eliminate one or both Sabrinas. Metatron explicitly calls attention to order and states, "For the order to be restored, one Sabrina must die. There will be order at all costs."[44] Sabrina is also the "chosen one" because her death ultimately saves both the mortal and witch worlds from the final Eldritch Terror, the Void. Sabrina's complexity and liminal existence are ultimately destroyed in order to maintain monocentric order.

Taken together, and in connection to our theoretical frames of mixedness and liminality, we offer some broader discussion points regarding the themes. In taking up an analysis of *CAoS* from a critical mixed race lens, the series offers some potential areas for better understanding how monocentricity gets represented and how the construct might need further updating.

MONOCENTRICITY IS A HELL OF A FORCE

Throughout the series, Sabrina constantly chooses to embrace her dualistic or mixed nature, as she straddles multiple worlds that both have inherent preferences for the singular nature of being *either* a mortal *or* a witch, and eventually to *either* be on Earth *or* in Hell. However, chaos ensues when Sabrina exudes a liminal existence that operates beyond this known either/or binary, and the characters must work to restore order. Her liminality works in direct opposition to the monocentricity embedded in the *CAoS* universe. Monocentricity and the preference for rigid distinct categories, in this case related to the supernatural, may reveal larger themes related to race and racial categories within society. From the series, we eventually see that pressure for Sabrina to be one or the other is not just a preference, but a threat to nature and the universe as a whole. We argue that mixedness is portrayed as such an inherent threat to monocentricity that it must be killed to maintain order even in fictional worlds and the supernatural.

In one sense, we can read Sabrina's constant embrace of her liminal existence and choice of duality as a form of resistance. Similar to Henesy's[45] argument that "liminality can be manipulated to fight for choice if the person in question is strong enough," perhaps Sabrina is fighting to change society from a liminal standpoint, rather than what mostly seems to be a sense of self-interest. We see this most clearly in "Chapter Eighteen: The Miracles of Sabrina Spellman" (2:7) when Nick and Sabrina discuss the uniqueness of her new powers. Sabrina ponders:

> Maybe it's because I'm not a normal witch. I mean, I've assumed being half-mortal made me less than, in some way. But maybe being half-mortal is what's allowing me to tap into these other mystical energies. And maybe I was given these gifts so that I could make the world a better place. That could be why my father's vision for the future of the Church of Night hinged on the union between witches and mortals. Because it would produce—

Nick cuts her off with "—you. Witches 2.0."[46] This dialogue signals that Sabrina and other half-witch/half-mortals would constitute a newly-produced type of witch, one more powerful than either of their component identities. So instead of Sabrina's mixedness and duality representing chaos that must be stopped, the forces of monocentricity want to prevent a new hybrid species— one more powerful than the single category groups that already exist—from becoming a reality. Power will be maintained at all costs, no matter what one chooses.

The fact that choice is threaded throughout our analysis causes us to question if there is something dangerous about this portrayal—of the mixed character being both the "chosen one" and expected to be the savior. Throughout the show, other characters view Sabrina's supernatural mixedness and duality as a potential threat, often calling to create order and eliminate her dualistic existence. However, Sabrina resists monocentricity and categorization as she continues to choose duality, creating tensions and consequences throughout the plotline. In season one, the showrunners emphasize this idea of Sabrina's choice; however, this particular plot point becomes diminished as the focus shifts from Sabrina making a choice to her becoming the "chosen one." In the beginning of the show, others insult her dualistic nature, but by the end of the series, they depend upon her supernatural mixedness to save both the mortal and witch worlds. This tension of choosing versus being chosen parallels common tropes and experiences related to multiracial people navigating monoracism and the complexity of choice while simultaneously being tokenized or utilized as a bridge between communities.[47] We argue that this portrayal of supernatural mixedness in *CAoS* perpetuates this larger narrative of mixed people and those with liminal identities as the answers to saving society from its past ills.

This idea is symbolized explicitly in *CAoS* when the "chosen one" of supernatural mixedness has to sacrifice themselves for the good of others. Although Sabrina dies by the end of *CAoS,* she comes back through *Riverdale*'s (The CW, 2017–present) "Rivervale" storyline in episode "Chapter Ninety-Nine: The Witching Hour(s)" (6:4), where an alternate reality exists and dead characters from *Riverdale* are back as well.[48] Although Sabrina is not necessarily alive, she once again occupies dual spaces; she is both dead and alive, existing in this alternate reality that bends the rules of the universe, allowing her to exist in a liminal space between life and death. Although Sabrina's death in the *CAoS* finale implies that mixedness is always killed in the end, Sabrina's introduction to *Riverdale* indicates that it can also continue to survive in various ways and her liminal existence between the worlds of living and dead demonstrate that mixedness cannot be completely destroyed no matter how hard monocentric forces try.

MIXED CHARACTERS WILL NOT SAVE THE WORLD

In a paper focused on whiteness and mixedness, Orkideh Mohajeri interrogated the commonly used phrasing "mixed kids are gonna save the world!" Despite the labor placed on mixed folk to serve as bridges across groups toward racial reconciliation or already being idealized as the racial future, the truth is that mixed people have always existed, and no matter how much their numbers grow or how much more representation they get in the media, their mere existence will not save the world. Portraying mixed characters, racial or supernatural, as saviors perpetuates this dangerous stereotype and lets others, particularly white people, off the hook for doing the work toward actual change. Rather than providing audiences with a nuanced portrayal of a mixed protagonist with agency who resists monocentric norms to change society, the series ultimately buys into age-old tropes about mixed race people presented in new packaging in the form of the supernatural. We urge future producers and show writers to construct more nuanced mixed and liminal characters who are not always forced to choose nor have to sacrifice themselves to save the world. Given how racial representations in media can influence identity development, mixed young people need these portrayals to show them the possibilities of choosing their own identities and paths without chaotic or tragic consequences.

BIBLIOGRAPHY

Anderson, Celia Rousseau. "What Are You? A CRT Perspective on the Experiences of Mixed Race Persons in 'Post-Racial' America." *Race Ethnicity and Education* 18, no. 1 (2015): 1–19. doi.org/10.1080/13613324.2014.911160.

Besana, Tiffany, Dalal Katsiaficas, and Aerika Brittian Loyd. "Asian American Media Representation: A Film Analysis and Implications for Identity Development." *Research in Human Development* 16, no. 3–4 (2019): 201–25. doi.org/10.1080/15 427609.2020.1711680.

Brüning, Kristina. "'I'm Neither a Slut, Nor Am I Gonna Be Shamed': Sexual Violence, Feminist Anger, and Teen TV's New Heroine." *Television & New Media* 23, no. 7 (May 2021): 1–16. doi.org/10.1177/15274764211015307.

Burton, Nylah. "'The *Chilling Adventures of Sabrina* Treats Black Characters as Sacrifices." *Wear Your Voice* (blog), February 4, 2020. wearyourvoicemag.com/the-chilling-adventures-of-sabrina-treats-black-characters-as-sacrifices/.

Cheng, Simon, and Kathryn J. Lively. "Multiracial Self-Identification and Adolescent Outcomes: A Social Psychological Approach to the Marginal Man Theory." *Social Forces* 88, no. 1 (2009): 61–98. doi.org/10.1353/sof.0.0243.

Chilling Adventures of Sabrina, Season 1, episode 1, "Chapter One: October Country." Directed by Lee Toland Krieger, written by Roberto Aguirre-Sacasa, featuring Kiernan Shipka, Miranda Otto, Lucy Davis, and Chance Perdomo. Released October 26, 2018, Netflix, www.netflix.com/watch/80230071?trackId =200257859.

———, Season 1, episode 2, "Chapter Two: The Dark Baptism." Directed by Lee Toland Krieger, written by Roberto Aguirre-Sacasa, featuring Kiernan Shipka, Miranda Otto, Lucy Davis, and Richard Coyle. Released October 26, 2018, Netflix, www.netflix.com/watch/80230072?trackId=200257859.

———, Season 1, episode 3, "Chapter Three: The Trial of Sabrina Spellman." Directed by Rob Seidenglanz, written by Ross Maxwell, featuring Kiernan Shipka, Miranda Otto, Lucy Davis, and Ross Lynch. Released October 26, 2018, Netflix, www.netflix.com/watch/80230073?trackId=200257859.

———, Season 1, episode 5, "Chapter Five: Dreams in a Witch House." Directed by Maggie Kiley, written by Matthew Barry, featuring Kiernan Shipka, Miranda Otto, Lucy Davis, and Chance Perdomo. Released October 26, 2018, www .netflix.com/watch/80230075?trackId=200257859.

———, Season 1, episode 6, "Chapter Six: An Exorcism in Greendale." Directed by Rachel Talalay, written by Joshua Conkel and MJ Kaufman, featuring Kiernan Shipka, Miranda Otto, Lucy Davis, and Michelle Gomez. Released October 26, 2018, Netflix, www.netflix.com/watch/80230072?trackId=200257859.

———, Season 1, episode 8, "Chapter Eight: The Burial." Directed by Maggie Kiley, written by Christianne Hedtke and Lindsey Calhoon Bring, featuring Kiernan Shipka, Ross Lynch, Jaz Sinclair, and Tati Gabrielle. Released October 26, 2018, Netflix, www.netflix.com/watch/80230078?trackId=200257859.

———, Season 1, episode 10, "Chapter Ten: The Witching Hour." Directed by Rob Seidenglanz, written by Roberto Aguirre-Sacasa and Ross Maxwell, featuring Kiernan Shipka, Miranda Otto, Lucy Davis, and Chance Perdomo. Released October 26, 2018, Netflix, www.netflix.com/watch/80230080?trackId=200257859.

———, Season 2, episode 1, "Chapter Twelve: The Epiphany." Directed by Kevin Rodney Sullivan, written by Roberto Aguirre-Sacasa, featuring Kiernan Shipka, Miranda Otto, Lucy Davis, and Lachlan Watson. Released April 5, 2019, Netflix, www.netflix.com/watch/80230082?trackId=200257859.

———, Season 2, episode 3. "Chapter Fourteen: Lupercalia." Directed by Salli Richardson-Whitfield, written by Oanh Ly, featuring Kiernan Shipka, Miranda Otto, Lucy Davis, and Chance Perdomo. Released April 5, 2019, Netflix, www .netflix.com/watch/80230084?trackId=200257859.

———, Season 2, episode 5, "Chapter Sixteen: Blackwood." Directed by Alex Pillai, written by Matthew Barry, featuring Kiernan Shipka, Miranda Otto, Lucy Davis, and Richard Coyle. Released April 5, 2019, Netflix, www.netflix.com/watch /80230086?trackId=14170289.

———, Season 2, episode 6, "Chapter Seventeen: The Missionaries." Directed by Rob Seidenglanz, written by Donna Thorland, featuring Kiernan Shipka, Miranda Otto, and Lucy Davis, and Spencer Treat Clark. Released April 5, 2019, Netflix, www.netflix.com/watch/80230087?trackId=14277283.

———, Season 2, episode 7, "Chapter Eighteen: The Miracles of Sabrina Spellman." Directed by Antonio Negret, written by Christianne Hedtke and Lindsay Calhoon

Bring, featuring Kiernan Shipka, Miranda Otto, Lucy Davis, and Chance Perdomo. Released April 5, 2019, Netflix, www.netflix.com/watch/80230088 ?trackId=200257859.

———, Season 2, episode 8, "Chapter Nineteen: The Mandrake." Directed by Kevin Sullivan, written by Joshua Conkel, featuring Kiernan Shipka, Miranda Otto, Lucy Davis, and Chance Perdomo. Released April 5, 2019, Netflix, www.netflix.com/watch/80230089?trackId=14277283.

———, Season 3, episode 1, "Chapter Twenty-One: The Hellbound Heart." Directed by Rob Seidenglanz, written by Roberto Aguirre-Sacasa, featuring Kiernan Shipka, Chance Perdomo, Tati Gabrielle, and Michelle Gomez. Released December 31, 2020, Netflix, www.netflix.com/watch/81062652?trackId=200257859.

———, Season 4, episode 1, "Chapter Twenty-Nine: The Eldritch Dark." Directed by Jeff Woolnough, written by Roberto Aguirre-Sacasa and Gigi Swift, featuring Kiernan Shipka, Miranda Otto, Lucy Davis, and Chance Perdomo. Released December 31, 2020, Netflix, www.netflix.com/watch/81062660?trackId =200257859.

———, Season 4, episode 5, "Chapter Thirty-Three: Deus Ex Machina." Directed by Amanda Tapping, written by Eleanor Jean, featuring Kiernan Shipka, Miranda Otto, Lucy Davis, and Lachlan Watson. Released December 31, 2020, Netflix, www.netflix.com/watch/81062664?trackId=200257859.

———, Season 4, episode 8, "Chapter Thirty-Six: At the Mountains of Madness." Directed by Rob Seidenglanz, written by Roberto Aguirre-Sacasa, featuring Kiernan Shipka, Miranda Otto, Lucy Davis, and Gavin Leatherwood. Released December 31, 2020, Netflix, www.netflix.com/watch/81062667?trackId=200257859.

DaCosta, Kimberly McClain. *Making Multiracials: State, Family, and Market in the Redrawing of the Color Line*. Redwood City, CA: Stanford University Press, 2007.

Daniel, G. Reginald. *More than Black: Multiracial Identity and the New Racial Order*. Philadelphia, PA: Temple University Press, 2001.

Daniel, G. Reginald, Laura Kina, Wei Ming Dariotis, and Camilla Fojas. "Emerging Paradigms in Critical Mixed Race Studies." *Journal of Critical Mixed Race Studies* 1, no. 1 (2014): 6–65. doi.org/10.5070/C811013868.

Gabe & Kat. "Chilling Adventures of Sabrina." *Ghouls Next Door*. Aired October 13, 2020, anchor.fm/the-ghouls-next-door/episodes/Chilling-Adventures-of-Sabrina-ekv8i2/a-a767q1f.

Harris, Jessica C. "Multiracial Campus Professionals' Experiences with Racial Authenticity." *Equity & Excellence in Education* 52, no. 1 (2019): 93–107. doi.org /10.1080/10665684.2019.1631232.

———, "Whiteness as Structuring Property: Multiracial Women Students' Social Interactions at a Historically White Institution." *The Review of Higher Education* 42, no. 3 (April 4, 2019): 1023–50. doi.org/10.1353/rhe.2019.0028.

Henesy, Megan. "'Leaving My Girlhood Behind': Woke Witches and Feminist Liminality in *Chilling Adventures of Sabrina*." *Feminist Media Studies* 21, no. 7 (July 2020): 1143–57. doi.org/10.1080/14680777.2020.1791929.

Herring, Roger D. "Developing Biracial Ethnic Identity: A Review of the Increasing Dilemma." *Journal of Multicultural Counseling and Development* 23, no. 1 (1995): 29–38. doi.org/10.1002/j.2161-1912.1995.tb00264.x.

Jackson, Kelly Faye, and Gina Miranda Samuels. *Multiracial Cultural Attunement*. New York: NASW Press, 2019.

Johnston, Marc P., and Kevin L. Nadal. "Multiracial Microaggressions: Exposing Monoracism in Everyday Life and Clinical Practice." In *Microaggressions and Marginality: Manifestation, Dynamics and Impact*, edited by Derald Wing Sue, 123–44. New York: Wiley & Sons, 2010.

Johnston-Guerrero, Marc P., and Kristen A. Renn. "Multiracial Americans in College." In *Race Policy and Multiracial Americans*, edited by Kathleen O. Korgen, 139–54. Bristol, UK: Policy Press, 2016.

Joseph, Ralina L. *Transcending Blackness: From the New Millennium Mulatta to the Exceptional Multiracial*. Durham, NC: Duke University Press, 2013.

Khanna, Nikki. "'If You're Half Black, You're Just Black': Reflected Appraisals and the Persistence of the One-Drop Rule." *Sociological Quarterly* 51, no. 1 (January 2010): 96–121. doi.org/10.1111/j.1533-8525.2009.01162.x.

Larson, Paloma Miya. "The Mixed Race Mouse: Discovering Mixed Race Identity in Disney Channel Programs from High School Musical to K.C. Undercover." *Berkeley Undergraduate Journal* 29, no. 2 (2016): 1–38.

Mohajeri, Orkideh. "'Mixed Kids Are Gonna Save the World!': Mixed and Multiracial Students Push Back against Directives of Racialized Healing Labor." Portland, OR: Association for the Study of Higher Education 44th Annual Conference, 2019.

Paragg, Jillian. "'What Are You?': Mixed Race Responses to the Racial Gaze." *Ethnicities* 17, no. 3 (June 1, 2017): 277–98. doi.org/10.1177/1468796815621938.

Renn, Kristen A. *Mixed Race Students in College: The Ecology of Race, Identity, and Community on Campus*. Albany, NY: SUNY Press, 2004.

Riverdale, Season 6, episode 4, "Chapter Ninety-Nine: Witching Hour(s)." Directed by James DeWille, written by Roberto Aguirre-Sacasa, Arabella Anderson, and Chrissy Maroon, featuring K.J. Apa, Lili Reinhart, Cole Sprouse, Camila Mendes, and Madelaine Petsch. Aired December 7, 2021, The CW, www.netflix.com/watch/81487576?trackId=200257859.

Root, Maria P. P. "Resolving 'Other' Status: Identity Development of Biracial Individuals." *Women & Therapy* 9, no. 1–2 (May 25, 1990): 185–205. doi.org/10.1300/J015v09n01_11.

Turner, Victor W. "Betwixt and Between: The Liminal Period in Rites de Passage." In *Reader in Comparative Religion: An Anthropological Approach*, edited by William A. Lessa and Evon Z. Vogt, 4th edition, 234–43. New York: Harper & Row, 1979.

Ureña-Ravelo, Briana L. "How 'Chilling Adventures of Sabrina' Is Cruel to Its Black Characters." *The Black Youth Project* (blog), November 13, 2018. blackyouthproject.com/how-chilling-adventures-of-sabrina-is-cruel-to-its-black-characters/.

Van Gennep, Arnold. *The Rites of Passage*. Chicago: University of Chicago Press, 1960.

NOTES

1. Tiffany Besana, Dalal Katsiaficas, and Aerika Brittian Loyd, "Asian American Media Representation: A Film Analysis and Implications for Identity Development," *Research in Human Development* 16, no. 3–4 (October 2, 2019): 201–25. doi.org/10.1080/15427609.2020.1711680.

2. Kimberly McClain DaCosta, *Making Multiracials: State, Family, and Market in the Redrawing of the Color Line* (Stanford University Press, 2007); Paloma Miya Larson, "The Mixed Race Mouse: Discovering Mixed Race Identity in Disney Channel Programs from *High School Musical* to *K.C. Undercover*," *Berkeley Undergraduate Journal* 29, no. 2 (2016): 1–38.

3. Victor W. Turner, "Betwixt and Between: The Liminal Period in Rites de Passage," in *Reader in Comparative Religion: An Anthropological Approach*, ed. William A. Lessa and Evon Z. Vogt, 4th edition (New York: Harper & Row, 1979), 234–43.

4. Marc P. Johnston-Guerrero and Kristen A. Renn, "Multiracial Americans in College," in *Race Policy and Multiracial Americans*, ed. Kathleen O. Korgen (Bristol, UK: Policy Press, 2016), 139–54.

5. Briana L. Ureña-Ravelo, "How 'Chilling Adventures of Sabrina' Is Cruel to Its Black Characters," *The Black Youth Project* (blog), November 13, 2018, blackyouthproject.com/how-chilling-adventures-of-sabrina-is-cruel-to-its-black-characters/; Nylah Burton, "'The Chilling Adventures of Sabrina' Treats Black Characters as Sacrifices," *Wear Your Voice* (blog), February 4, 2020, wearyourvoicemag.com/the-chilling-adventures-of-sabrina-treats-black-characters-as-sacrifices/.

6. See G. Reginald Daniel et al., "Emerging Paradigms in Critical Mixed Race Studies," *Journal of Critical Mixed Race Studies* 1, no. 1 (2014): 6–65. doi.org/10.5070/C811013868.

7. Turner, "Betwixt and between: The Liminal Period in Rites de Passage."

8. Kelly Faye Jackson and Gina Miranda Samuels, *Multiracial Cultural Attunement* (New York: NASW Press, 2019).

9. Arnold Van Gennep, *The Rites of Passage* (Chicago: University of Chicago Press, 1960).

10. Megan Henesy, "'Leaving my girlhood behind': Woke Witches and Feminist Liminality in Chilling Adventures of Sabrina," *Feminist Media Studies* 21, no. 7 (July 2020): 1–15. doi.org/10.1080/14680777.2020.1791929.

11. Jackson and Samuels, *Multiracial Cultural Attunement*.

12. Johnston-Guerrero and Renn, "Multiracial Americans in College."

13. As authors, we do not encourage or approve the use of the term "half-breed" but directly quote the text to accurately portray the dialogue in the series. This is also our approach to other derogatory terms such as "mulatto" that appear.

14. *Chilling Adventures of Sabrina*, season 1, episode 1, "Chapter One: October Country," by Lee Toland Krieger, written by Roberto Aguirre-Sacasa, featuring Kiernan Shipka, Miranda Otto, Lucy Davis, and Chance Perdomo, released October 26, 2018, on Netflix, www.netflix.com/watch/80230071?trackId=200257859: 00:01:51.

15. *Chilling Adventures of Sabrina*, "Chapter One: October Country," 00:43:27.

16. *Chilling Adventures of Sabrina*, "Chapter One: October Country," 00:15:01.

17. In addition to Henesy's work referenced earlier, see also: Kristina Brüning, "'I'm Neither a Slut, Nor Am I Gonna Be Shamed': Sexual Violence, Feminist Anger, and Teen TV's New Heroine," *Television & New Media* 23 no.7 (May 2021): 1–16. doi.org/10.1177/15274764211015307.

18. *Chilling Adventures of Sabrina,* "Chapter One: October Country," 00:42:42.

19. G. Reginald Daniel, *More than Black: Multiracial Identity and the New Racial Order* (Philadelphia, PA: Temple University Press, 2001); Nikki Khanna, "'If You're Half Black, You're Just Black': Reflected Appraisals and the Persistence of the One-Drop Rule," *Sociological Quarterly* 51, no. 1 (January 2010): 96–121. doi.org/10.1111/j.1533-8525.2009.01162.x.

20. Khanna, "If You're Half Black, You're Just Black," 98.

21. *Chilling Adventures of Sabrina,* season 1, episode 3, "Chapter Three: The Trial of Sabrina Spellman," directed by Rob Seidenglanz, written by Ross Maxwell, featuring Kiernan Shipka, Miranda Otto, Lucy Davis, and Ross Lynch, released October 26, 2018, on Netflix, www.netflix.com/watch/80230073?trackId=200257859: 00:33:07.

22. Kristen A. Renn, *Mixed Race Students in College: The Ecology of Race, Identity, and Community on Campus* (Albany, NY: SUNY Press, 2004); Jessica C. Harris, "Multiracial Campus Professionals' Experiences with Racial Authenticity," *Equity & Excellence in Education* 52, no. 1 (January 2, 2019): 93–107. doi.org/10.1080/1066 5684.2019.1631232.

23. *Chilling Adventures of Sabrina,* season 3, episode 1, "Chapter Twenty-One: The Hellbound Heart," directed by Rob Seidenglanz, written by Roberto Aguirre-Sacasa, featuring Kiernan Shipka, Chance Perdomo, Tati Gabrielle, and Michelle Gomez, released December 31, 2020, on Netflix, www.netflix.com/watch/81062652?trackId =200257859: 00:52:58.

24. *Chilling Adventures of Sabrina,* season 2, episode 1, "Chapter Twelve: The Epiphany," directed by Kevin Rodney Sullivan, written by Roberto Aguirre-Sacasa, featuring Kiernan Shipka, Miranda Otto, Lucy Davis, and Lachlan Watson, released April 5, 2019, on Netflix, www.netflix.com/watch/80230082?trackId=200257859: 00:46:02.

25. Celia Rousseau Anderson, "What Are You? A CRT Perspective on the Experiences of Mixed Race Persons in 'Post-Racial' America," *Race Ethnicity and Education* 18, no. 1 (2015): 1–19. doi.org/10.1080/13613324.2014.911160; Jillian Paragg, "'What Are You?': Mixed Race Responses to the Racial Gaze," *Ethnicities* 17, no. 3 (June 1, 2017): 277–98, doi.org/10.1177/1468796815621938.

26. *Chilling Adventures of Sabrina,* season 2, episode 6, "Chapter Seventeen: The Missionaries," directed by Rob Seidenglanz, written by Donna Thorland, featuring Kiernan Shipka, Miranda Otto, and Lucy Davis, and Spencer Treat Clark, released April 5, 2019, on Netflix, www.netflix.com/watch/80230087?trackId=14277283: 0:50:55.

27. *Chilling Adventures of Sabrina,* season 2, episode 7, "Chapter Eighteen: The Miracles of Sabrina Spellman," directed by Antonio Negret, written by Christianne Hedtke and Lindsay Calhoon Bring, featuring Kiernan Shipka, Miranda Otto, Lucy Davis, and Chance Perdomo, released April 5, 2019, on Netflix, www.netflix.com/watch/80230088?trackId=200257859: 00:38:52.

28. *Chilling Adventures of Sabrina*, season 1, episode 2, "Chapter Two: The Dark Baptism," directed by Lee Toland Krieger, written by Roberto Aguirre-Sacasa, featuring Kiernan Shipka, Miranda Otto, Lucy Davis, and Richard Coyle, released October 26, 2018, on Netflix, www.netflix.com/watch/80230072?trackId=200257859: 00:52:04.

29. *Chilling Adventures of Sabrina,* "Chapter Three: The Trial of Sabrina Spellman," 00:50:49.

30. Simon Cheng and Kathryn J Lively, "Multiracial Self-Identification and Adolescent Outcomes: A Social Psychological Approach to the Marginal Man Theory," *Social Forces* 88, no. 1 (September 1, 2009): 61–98, doi.org/10.1353/sof.0.0243; Ralina L. Joseph, *Transcending Blackness: From the New Millennium Mulatta to the Exceptional Multiracial* (Duke University Press, 2013); Khanna, "If You're Half Black, You're Just Black"; Marc P. Johnston and Kevin L. Nadal, "Multiracial Microaggressions: Exposing Monoracism in Everyday Life and Clinical Practice," in *Microaggressions and Marginality: Manifestation, Dynamics and Impact*, ed. Derald Wing Sue (New York: Wiley & Sons, 2010), 123–44.

31. *Chilling Adventures of Sabrina* season 1, episode 10, "Chapter Ten: The Witching Hour," directed by Rob Seidenglanz, written by Roberto Aguirre-Sacasa and Ross Maxwell, featuring Kiernan Shipka, Miranda Otto, Lucy Davis, and Chance Perdomo, released October 26, 2018, on Netflix, www.netflix.com/watch/80230080 ?trackId=200257859: 00:08:49.

32. *Chilling Adventures of Sabrina*, season 1, episode 5, "Chapter Five: Dreams in a Witch House," directed by Maggie Kiley, written by Matthew Barry, featuring Kiernan Shipka, Miranda Otto, Lucy Davis, and Chance Perdomo, released October 26, 2018, on Netflix, www.netflix.com/watch/80230075?trackId=200257859: 00:07:23.

33. *Chilling Adventures of Sabrina*, "Chapter Five: Dreams in a Witch House," 00:12:12.

34. *Chilling Adventures of Sabrina*, season 4, episode 8,"Chapter Thirty-Six: At the Mountains of Madness," directed by Rob Seidenglanz, written by Roberto Aguirre-Sacasa, featuring Kiernan Shipka, Miranda Otto, Lucy Davis, and Gavin Leatherwood, released December 31, 2020, on Netflix, www.netflix.com/watch/81062667 ?trackId=200257859.

35. Roger D. Herring, "Developing Biracial Ethnic Identity: A Review of the Increasing Dilemma," *Journal of Multicultural Counseling and Development* 23, no. 1 (1995): 31, doi.org/10.1002/j.2161-1912.1995.tb00264.x.

36. *Chilling Adventures of Sabrina*, season 1, episode 8, "Chapter Eight: The Burial," directed by Maggie Kiley, written by Christianne Hedtke and Lindsey Calhoon Bring, featuring Kiernan Shipka, Ross Lynch, Jaz Sinclair, and Tati Gabrielle, released October 26, 2018, on Netflix, www.netflix.com/watch/80230078?trackId =200257859: 00:11:36.

37. *Chilling Adventures of Sabrina*, season 2, episode 3, "Chapter Fourteen: Lupercalia," directed by Salli Richardson-Whitfield, written by Oanh Ly, featuring Kiernan Shipka, Miranda Otto, Lucy Davis, and Chance Perdomo, released April 5, 2019, on Netflix, www.netflix.com/watch/80230084?trackId=200257859: 00:19:36.

38. Jessica C. Harris, "Whiteness as Structuring Property: Multiracial Women Students' Social Interactions at a Historically White Institution," *The Review of Higher Education* 42, no. 3 (April 4, 2019): 1023–50, doi.org/10.1353/rhe.2019.0028; Maria P. P. Root, "Resolving 'Other' Status: Identity Development of Biracial Individuals," *Women & Therapy* 9, no. 1–2 (May 25, 1990): 185–205, doi.org/10.1300/J015v09n01_11.

39. *Chilling Adventures of Sabrina*, season 2, episode 8, "Chapter Nineteen: The Mandrake," directed by Kevin Sullivan, written by Joshua Conkel, featuring Kiernan Shipka, Miranda Otto, Lucy Davis, and Chance Perdomo, released April 5, 2019, on Netflix, www.netflix.com/watch/80230089?trackId=14277283: 00:06:26–00:07:39.

40. *Chilling Adventures of Sabrina*, season 1, episode 6, "Chapter Six: An Exorcism in Greendale," directed by Rachel Talalay, written by Joshua Conkel and MJ Kaufman, featuring Kiernan Shipka, Miranda Otto, Lucy Davis, and Michelle Gomez, released October 26, 2018, on Netflix, www.netflix.com/watch/80230072?trackId=200257859.

41. *Chilling Adventures of Sabrina*, season 2, episode 5, "Chapter Sixteen: Blackwood," directed by Alex Pillai, written by Matthew Barry, featuring Kiernan Shipka, Miranda Otto, Lucy Davis, and Richard Coyle. Released April 5, 2019, Netflix, www.netflix.com/watch/80230086?trackId=14170289: 00:03:44.

42. *Chilling Adventures of Sabrina*, "Chapter Five: Dreams in a Witch House," 00:07:20.

43. Gabe and Kat, "Chilling Adventures of Sabrina," *Ghouls Next Door*, October 13, 2020, anchor.fm/the-ghouls-next-door/episodes/Chilling-Adventures-of-Sabrina-ekv8i2/a-a767q1f.

44. *Chilling Adventures of Sabrina*, season 4, episode 5, "Chapter Thirty-Three: Deus Ex Machina," by Amanda Tapping, written by Eleanor Jean, featuring Kiernan Shipka, Miranda Otto, Lucy Davis, and Lachlan Watson. Released December 31, 2020, Netflix, www.netflix.com/watch/81062664?trackId=200257859: 00:42:03.

45. "Leaving My Girlhood Behind," 9.

46. *Chilling Adventures of Sabrina*, "Chapter Eighteen: The Miracles of Sabrina Spellman," 00:18:30–00:19:20.

47. Johnston and Nadal, "Multiracial Microaggressions"; Harris, "Multiracial Campus Professionals' Experiences with Racial Authenticity."

48. *Riverdale*, season 6, episode 4, "Chapter Ninety-Nine: The Witching Hour(s)," directed by James DeWille, written by Roberto Aguirre-Sacasa, Arabella Anderson, and Chrissy Maroon, featuring K.J. Apa, Lili Reinhart, Cole Sprouse, Camila Mendes, and Madelaine Petsch, aired December 7, 2021, on The CW, www.netflix.com/watch/81487576?trackId=200257859.

Chapter 8

"I want freedom and power"

The Allegory of Queer Rhetorics in Chilling Adventures of Sabrina

Stephanie A. Graves

LIMINALITY AND HYBRIDITY

"In the town of Greendale, where it always feels like Halloween, there lived a girl who was half-witch, half-mortal who, on her sixteenth birthday, would have to choose between two worlds: the witch world of her family, and the human world of her friends."[1] This opening voiceover in "Chapter One: October Country" (1:1)—named for the Ray Bradbury short story collection—is our introduction to Netflix's *Chilling Adventures of Sabrina* (2018–20), which centers on the exploits of the titular Sabrina Spellman (Kiernan Shipka) and her aforementioned family and friends in the strange, temporally-displaced town of Greendale. Based on the classic 1962 *Archie* spinoff comic series *Sabrina the Teenage Witch* and adapted and produced by *Riverdale* creator and showrunner Roberto Aguirre-Sacasa, the show is a patent departure from the 1996 ABC adaptation of *Sabrina the Teenage Witch* that starred Melissa Joan Hart alongside an animatronic talking cat; whereas the network version of Sabrina was a rather conservative, lighthearted, campy comedy, *Chilling Adventures of Sabrina* (hereafter *CAoS*) is primarily situated within the horror genre. Despite its many horror bona fides, however, *CAoS* is perhaps most notably marked by an aesthetic *and* thematic generic hybridity; horror may be its primary aesthetic marker, but the show features both camp sensibilities and comedic moments, as well as being shaped significantly by the Gothic, teen drama, and *bildungsroman* tropes that situate *CAoS* within liminal and transgressive spaces. Through the show's repeated

139

centering and normalizing of these transgressive themes, motifs, and relation-ships, *Chilling Adventures of Sabrina* is a curious queer rhetorical object that allegorically encodes multiple narratives of queer resistance.

As defined by Jonathan Alexander and Jacqueline Rhodes, *queer rhetoric* is the discursive practice of resistance to hetero- (and often homo-) norms, the "self-conscious and critical engagement with normative discourses of sexuality."[2] The presence or deployment of queer rhetoric(s)—for they are, after all, multiple—indicates space held for identificatory differences; stated more simply, queer rhetorics refuse to uncritically render cultural scripts of normativity. This is often visible in narratives that reproduce cultural atti-tudes toward nonnormative sexualities or gender nonconforming behaviors; in "Rhetorics of Gay Future and Queer Futurity: Strategies of Disruption," Dustin Bradley Goltz points out that "[h]appiness has been oriented within a heteronormative framework in discourse and popular culture, while queer future (unmarried, without children, nonbiological family/community focus, sexually active, gender queer, nonnormative maturation) is traditionally ori-ented with isolation, loneliness, selfishness, sexual promiscuity, predation, and failure."[3] *CAoS,* however—despite its sometimes inconsistent rendering of progressive or feminist values (discussed in greater detail elsewhere in this collection)—steadfastly refuses to reify heteronormativity as the singular acceptable cultural structure, instead creating an expansive narrative in which queer possibilities are not only allowed to manifest, but in which such queer disruptions to normative cultural strictures are not, by necessity, narratively punished or eliminated. Refreshingly, in the world of *CAoS,* the queer is not inherently monstrous, and the show resists the tired—and harmful—"bury your gays" tropes that have marked queer inclusion in horror since its inception.

Across four seasons, the generic and aesthetic slippage that sets the stage for the show's allegorical queer disruption permeates *CAoS* at all registers: visual, discursive, aural, and even temporal. The composition of the *mise en scène,* the use of language, the musical inclusions, and the overall asyn-chronicity of Sabrina's world evokes the notion of queer temporalities in which time is perceived as nonlinear, relative, occasionally stuttering or recursive, but, ultimately, not structured in the context of heteronormative milestones centered on futurity. The show's visual style dislocates the setting from a fixed and defined time by juxtaposing objects and styles of differ-ent eras. In Greendale, vehicles are primarily 1950s models, the fashion is heavily influenced by the 1960s, the diegetic literary inclusions are mostly from the 1970s—and yet we also get glimpses of iPhones and MacBooks. The characters also experience what Sara Jaffe terms a "liberatory relation-ship to time,"[4] as evidenced by the greatly prolonged life span and slow aging process of witches and warlocks. As this relationship with time dilates and contracts within the diegesis, the relationship to time itself—and to our ability as an audience to orient ourselves within it—is queered as well. In fact, throughout its narrative, *CAoS* radically incorporates queerness—both diegetically and extradiegetically—as not only subjectivity but also as practice. The diverse representations of both gender and sexuality—and, although prioritized less, their intersections with race and class—are thoughtful, natural, and thorough; although main character Sabrina is a cisgender White woman who we only see in opposite-sex relationships, her paramour Nicholas Scratch (Gavin Leatherwood) is polyamorous and either bi- or pansexual, her cousin Ambrose Spellman (Chase Perdomo) is a Black British pansexual, her aunt Zelda Spellman (Miranda Otto) is shown in intimate relationships with both a man and a woman, Prudence Night (Tati Gabrielle) is a sexually-fluid Black woman, and Suzie Putnam (Lachlan Watson) is (in Part One) a nonbinary character who (in Part Two) comes out as transgender and takes the name Theo. Within the landscape of contemporary TV, *CAoS* offers a remarkable variety of subject positions within its central cast. In her essay "Punks, Bulldaggers, and Welfare Queens: The Radical Potential of Queer Politics," Cathy J. Cohen suggests that "if any truly radical potential is to be found in the idea of queerness and the practice of queer politics, it would seem to be located in its ability to create a space in opposition to dominant norms, a space where transformational political work can begin."[5] The world of *CAoS* is explicitly created in opposition to such dominant norms, frustrating discrete compartmentalizing of identities, repudiating heteronormative hegemony, and rejecting *de rigueur* acceptance of patriarchal control.

DISCURSIVE DETERRITORIALIZATION

A central conceit throughout *Chilling Adventures of Sabrina* is the discursive inversion of modern American Christian values and social constructs in such a way that even the rhetorical markers within the text read as subversive. Throughout its four seasons, the narrative fairly consistently centers on Sabrina's ambivalence between her mortal half and her witch half, and thus between her life at Baxter High with her mortal friends, and her life at the Academy of Unseen Arts amongst members of the Church of Night, the coven to which her family belongs. Zelda Spellman and Hilda Spellman (Lucy Davis), Sabrina's aunts, raised Sabrina after the death of her parents in a plane crash when she was an infant; along with her cousin Ambrose, Zelda and Hilda are both devout members of the Church of Night, an amalgam of Satanic, Wiccan, and Pagan elements that is devoted to the Dark Lord (Luke Cook)—Lucifer himself. The Church of Night—one denomination of the larger Church of Darkness over which the Anti-Pope presides—is positioned as the antithesis of Christianity, a wholly opposite entity. As such, within domestic spaces as well as within the Church and its attendant institutions, *CAoS* discursively replaces references to Christian tradition with dialogic allusions to an opposite philosophy—Sabrina prepares for her "Dark Baptism," phrases such as "Praise the Lord!" are replaced with "Praise Satan!" and the like, helpful figures are "Hell sent" instead of "Heaven sent," and other linguistic phrasing is likewise transposed to privilege the path of darkness rather than light. This readily—and occasionally jarringly—fore-grounds how deeply entrenched the rhetorical markers of Christianity are within American culture by virtue of replacing such references with those of the Dark Lord, Satan, Hell, etc. Through such repeated textual disavowal of western Christian paradigms, *CAoS* similarly subverts the moral panic that arises out of such conservative religious tradition as described by Gayle Rubin in "Thinking Sex: Notes for a Radical Theory of the Politics of Sexuality;" the show is instead centered around feminist sex positivity, gender fluidity, and "benign sexual variation," which all seek to destigmatize pleasure and self-expression.[6] Enacted at the discursive register, this deterritorialization of language also opens queer spaces within the narrative.

DEPATHOLOGIZED SEX POSITIVITY

One significant site of subversion and transgression in *Chilling Adventures of Sabrina* is the show's take-it-or-leave-it attitude toward the practice of monogamy; in *CAoS,* witches and warlocks are often nonmonogamous and routinely value sexual pleasure without conflating it with love. This refusal to reproduce heteronormative structures directly contradicts our cultural scripts regarding the use of and attitude toward sex. Of the six "ideological forma-tions" she identifies, Rubin argues that "the most important is sex negativity. Western cultures generally consider sex to be a dangerous, destructive, nega-tive force."[7] She calls attention to how Christian tradition frames sex as the marker of original sin, and how only procreative sex—wherein "pleasurable aspects are not enjoyed too much"—is redeemable. Further, Rubin points out that these attitudes have become so inculcated in our culture that they "no longer depend solely on religion for their perseverance."[8] Given the show's fundamental resistance to dominant paradigms of Christian morality, *CAoS* embraces a refreshing sex positive approach that is seldom found in contemporary television. Breanne Fahs offers a history of and context for sex-positive feminism, arguing that "sex positivity has laid the groundwork to depathologize sexuality, particularly for women, sexual minorities, people of color, and sex workers"[9]—categories that all appear within the diegetic world of *CAoS*. As such, this depathologizing is evident in the narrative, which renders the show as grounded in a rejection of social constructs that value only monogamy—but also importantly resists those which would forbid it.

In terms of Rubin's chart of "sex hierarchy," while Sabrina herself may be inexperienced at the outset of the narrative, the Church of Night and the society she inhabits exhibits and embraces the sexual expressions located in the "outer limits" (homosexual, unmarried, promiscuous, nonprocreative, casual, in public, sadomasochistic, etc.)—but, importantly, those behaviors located within what Rubin terms the "charmed circle" (heterosexual, married, monogamous, procreative, in private, vanilla, etc.) are not forbidden or even shunned.[10] Instead, an entire range of social and sexual arrangements are treated with equal validity: Zelda (at least initially) has a casual but monogamous relationship with Father Faustus Blackwood (Richard Coyle), and later with Mambo Marie LeFleur (Skye Marshall); Hilda exclusively dates Dr. Cerberus (Alessandro Juliani); open nudity and assorted sex acts occur in the woods during the celebration of Lupercalia; Nicholas (Nick) Scratch tells Sabrina that he used to date Prudence, Agatha (Adeline Rudolph), and Dorcas (Abigail Cowen) simultaneously; and Sabrina walks in on an instance of group sex involving Prudence, Dorcas, Agatha, Nicholas, Ambrose, and Ambrose's boyfriend, Luke (Darren Mann)—which also renders Ambrose and Luke's relationship as ostensibly open. Further illustrating the show's attitude to such poly encounters, Sabrina amusedly chats rather casually to the group as they all carry on with what they were doing before her arrival.

Yet, despite this sexually open and expressive environment that seems in many ways to privilege nonmonogamous relationship structures, when Sabrina is considering having sex for the first time—which she discusses openly with her aunts and her best friend Roz (Jaz Sinclair), as well as with her boyfriend and potential bedmate, Nick—her concerns and hesitation are neither dismissed or ridiculed, nor is her monogamous relationship with Nick. In "Chapter Fourteen: Lupercalia" (2:3), Sabrina gets well-rounded counsel; Zelda tells her that sex is a "symphony of sensation and pleasure, not shame and regret, as the false god and your Aunt Hilda would have you believe,"[11] while Hilda tells her that, ultimately, it is up to Sabrina to decide when she feels ready—advice that emphasizes Sabrina's agency in her own sexual choices. When Sabrina then seeks advice from Roz (who lost her virginity at Bible camp—a fact related to the audience with neither judgment nor shame), Roz offers her a solid checklist to consider when making the decision whether or not to relinquish her virginity to Nick Scratch: "You like this Nick guy, huh?"; "Do you trust him?"; and "He's not pressuring you?"[12] In an age of disappearing sex education for adolescents, and given contemporary social scripts that simultaneously both fetishize *and* shame virginity while also both expecting *and* demonizing young women's sexual agency, *CAoS*'s attitude toward sexuality feels revolutionary. In "Mobilizing Metaphor: Considering

Complexities, Contradictions, and Contexts in Adolescent Girls' and Young Women's Sexual Agency," Donna Tolman et al. contextualize how the spectrum of adolescent sexual experience is typically portrayed:

> The slut/virgin/prude continuum remains pervasive as the constant, perennial reference for girls' sexuality; even as girls, groups or institutions refuse it, the slut/prude/virgin paradigm is always a touchstone for labeling and judging girls' and young adult women's sexuality and for how girls navigate their sexual experiences, however they are doing so. It is, literally, ever-present and inescapable as a part of adolescent girls' lives.[13]

Notably, however, this is not the attitude toward sex within either Sabrina's mortal *or* witch spheres. Although Prudence does express disbelief that one of her fellow male students is sexually inexperienced—"Can you imagine? A virgin at his age?"[14]—this seems attributable to Prudence's character rather than an expression of the show's attitude toward virginity. The world of *CAoS* trusts its young adults to govern their own sexuality. "You'll know if you're ready,"[15] Roz tells Sabrina; she has the space and the agency to make the decision, to choose to—or choose *not* to—have sex for herself. This is a marked departure from normative cultural scripts. In *The Cultural Politics of Emotion,* Sara Ahmed asks, "Do queer moments happen when this failure to reproduce norms as forms of life is embraced or affirmed as a political and ethical alternative? Such affirmation would not be about the conversion of shame into pride, but the enjoyment of the negativity of shame, an enjoyment of that which has been designated shameful by normative culture."[16] This redrafting of typical Christian-based cultural shame into a site and source of joy imbues *CAoS* with such "queer moments."

DIVERSE QUEER INCLUSION

One particular aspect of *CAoS* that resists more typical rhetorical depictions of queerness is the way in which it embraces both the *freedom from* and *freedom to* model. Ahmed points out that when "queer" is defined only as *opposite of* or *in resistance to* heterosexuality, and in the conflation of queerness and movement (in which fluidity is fetishized), there is a kind of "negative model of freedom" at work—if *queer* can only be located in concepts of movement, then this necessarily excludes the relationship models and lived experiences of queer people who may nonetheless be outside of yet are not read as *actively* resisting heteronorms.[17] She argues that "the idealization of movement depends upon a prior model of what counts as queer life, which may exclude others, those who have had attachments that are not readable as queer, or indeed those who may lack the (cultural as well as economic) capital to support the 'risk' of maintaining anti-normativity as a permanent orientation."[18] In Fahs's survey of the history of rhetorics of "positive and negative liberty" in feminist movements, she argues explicitly that "one cannot have true freedom without *both* the *freedom to* and the *freedom from*" (emphasis in original).[19] The world of *CAoS* is one in which no single model of relationship, desire, or embodiment is privileged over another—and also one in which none are castigated, either. Fahs warns that "definitive and universal claims about freedom and choice for all women must be met with caution or even downright suspicion."[20] *CAoS* is fundamentally rooted in a refusal to privilege monolithic totalizing ideologies. This links back to Cohen's interest in "examining the concept of 'queer' in order to think about how we might construct a new political identity that is truly liberating, transformative, and inclusive of all who stand on the outside of the dominant constructed norm of state-sanctioned White middle- and upper-class heterosexuality."[21]

This "new political identity" is precisely what *CAoS* offers, played out at the level of the personal. Sexualities outside of heteronorms are diegetically included, particularly in the case of Ambrose, Zelda, Nick, and Prudence, all of whom are central to the narrative. Yet these representations are, unfortunately, rather novel within the contemporary televisual landscape; Ambrose, Zelda, Nick, and Prudence are all characters who are located on the LGBTQ+ spectrum, rather than LGBTQ+ characters—that is, their sexuality is *part of* their characters, rather than the fundamental defining aspect *of* their characters. The "liberating, transformative, and inclusive" elements of *CAoS* are also evident throughout the storyline of another central character, Suzie/Theo Putnam—played by nonbinary actor Lachlan Watson—who transitions as part of the diegesis. Unlike many other mainstream depictions of trans issues and characters, *CAoS*'s thoughtful and respectful handling of Theo's journey takes place in the real time of the narrative; while both *sense8* (2015–18) and *Orange is the New Black* (2013–19)—interestingly, like *CAoS*, both also Netflix productions—as well as HBO's *Euphoria* (2018–present) include complex and nuanced trans characters, we only encounter them post-transition. By contrast, we watch Theo's character transition from female to male onscreen, and issues bound up in the process of transitioning are explicitly included within the narrative.

In Part One, Suzie is clearly gender-nonconforming, and although she does not correct anyone's use of female pronouns to refer to her, she does get bullied and at one point physically assaulted by a group of boys at Baxter High for her refusal to disambiguate her gender expression. Her friends all immediately support her, however—forming a club to protect one another, taking up the matter with the school administration to demand change, and, in the case of Sabrina, doling out some witchy payback to the boys who hurt Suzie.

In Part Two, however, in a moving scene with her father, Suzie comes out as transgender; when he suggests she get a new dress for the Valentine's Dance, Suzie tells him, "Dad . . . I'm not a girl. Even though I look like a girl, even though I have a girl's name, even though you've always thought of me as a girl—I'm a boy."[22] When his dad offers a stunned protest, he says, "I can't keep going on as a girl, Dad, I just *can't,*" and then tells his father that he will go by Theo from now on.[23] This is a pivotal moment in the narrative, but Theo makes himself unambiguously clear about his gender identity, no matter the discrimination he may encounter. In "Are Transgender Rights *In*human Rights?," Kendall Thomas notes that it is "distressingly clear that trans activists must contend with a social order and a legal regime of 'infrahumanity' under which transgendered people are viewed as 'non-persons, with no right to marry, to work, to use a public bathroom, or even to walk down the street in safety.'"[24] This may be the initial state in *CAoS,* but once Theo comes out, is accepted and supported by his friends, and makes the boys' basketball team, the world of Baxter High and of Greendale eventually make space for his "new political identity"[25]; by the end of the season, Theo asserts his comfort in his own body and helps save Greendale from annihilation by the hordes of Hell, becoming a hero in the process. Critics have suggested that *CAoS* depicts an unrealistic acceptance of Theo's gender identity, but the show's rhetorical stance toward Theo's trans identity is no different than its stance toward the sexual fluidity of Ambrose, Zelda, Nick, or Prudence; *CAoS* is not bound up in depicting realism, but instead creates a liberatory queer fantasy that shows us not *what is,* but rather *what could be.* Thomas argues that "the success of the transgender movement will depend on its ability to create a culture in which trans people are not just a curiosity or a perversion of nature."[26] In this regard, *CAoS* shows us what that culture could look like—even if it might be aspirational.

ALLEGORICAL RESISTANCE

Alongside these radically diegetic queer inclusions, *Chilling Adventures of Sabrina* centers on Sabrina's resistance to the Dark Lord, to whose doctrine she has been exposed her entire life. She initially refuses to follow family tradition and sign her name in the *Book of the Beast* and, after finally giving in to Lilith's (Michelle Gomez) machinations and doing so in order to save a friend's life, she continues to struggle against the Dark Lord's path and the Church of Night's rule—both of which she sees as the loss of agency and control that they are. In "Chapter Two: The Dark Baptism" (2:2), when discussing her doubts about her impending Dark Baptism with the Weird Sisters, Sabrina tells Prudence, "It still feels wrong to me—signing my name in the *Book of the Beast*, knowing that, on some level, I—I'm giving up my freedom." "You are," Prudence replies derisively, "in exchange for power. An *even* exchange." Shaking her head, Sabrina replies almost pleadingly, "But I want both—I want freedom *and* power." At this, the Weird Sisters all laugh, and Prudence replies with condescension: "He'll *never* give you that. The Dark Lord? The thought of you, of *any* of us, having both . . . terrifies him." "Why is that?" Sabrina asks, brow furrowed, and as Prudence saunters away, she calls over her shoulder, "He's a man, isn't he?"[27]

This exchange distills *CAoS*'s critique and attendant repudiation of dominant structures of patriarchy, which is itself a pillar of heteronormativity. Sabrina's constant struggle against submitting to the Dark Lord's will and against the institution of the Church of Night as led by Father Blackwood easily reads as a metaphor for resistance to not only religious doctrines but also to the controlling mechanisms of the State, subjugation by patriarchal family structures, dichotomous identity positions, and reified heteronormative frameworks. This resistance is evident throughout the narrative, but is particularly focused in Part Two; as Sabrina transitions to full-time study at the Academy of Unseen Arts (also presided over by Father Blackwood), *CAoS* also aggressively interrogates and confronts the patriarchal practices within the Church of Night, thus metaphorically exploring how Judeo-Christian tradition is not the only locus of patriarchal control, as well as disentangling these two loci of repression—or, perhaps, critiquing *all* hierarchical religious systems as fundamentally repressive. In the second half of the narrative, Sabrina directly confronts patriarchal structures. In "Chapter Twelve: The Epiphany" (2:1), she defies Father Blackwood by insisting she be allowed to compete for Top Boy against Nick; "The top boy is traditionally a male student," Father Blackwood tells Sabrina, to which she retorts, "But is that an actual rule in a rulebook?"[28] This establishes the tone for the back half of the season, and sets in motion Sabrina's growing resistance to Father Blackwood's increasingly misogynistic, draconian rule over the Church of Night and his conscription of members into what he calls the "Five Facets of Judas," which include the tenets that "As Lilith served Satan, so must witches serve warlocks," and "Warlocks shall claim dominion in the Church of Night just as their Father rules over Hell."[29]

There is an attendant irony at work in Blackwood's doctrine; not only do his tenets directly contradict the manifesto of Edward Spellman—Sabrina's deceased father who served as High Priest before Blackwood—but given Lilith's narrative presence as one of the most influential figures in Sabrina's life (albeit disguised as Baxter High teacher and later principal Ms. Wardwell) and the *mise-en-abyme* play about Lilith's subjugation within the diegesis, Blackwood's ego-fueled machinations toward power are anathema to Sabrina, and, eventually, to those around her. In "Chapter Eighteen: The Miracles of Sabrina Spellman" (2:7), she directly confronts Blackwood—in front of the High Council, no less—when he questions her about her growing powers:

> You know the story of Pandora, don't you, Father Blackwood? It's almost a parable—a cautionary tale. The gods gave Pandora a jar containing all the sorrows of the world—toil, famine, pestilence, death. They armed her for vengeance, Father Blackwood. For destruction. So when you ask me to explain these "miracles," as you call them, I feel I must warn you: do you *really* want to open that lid?[30]

Blackwood becomes a metonymic representation of the patriarchy, one that Sabrina—who declares to Blackwood early in Part Two that she will be the first High Priestess of the Church of Night—tirelessly works to dismantle. *CAoS* situates Blackwood and his misogyny as repugnant, but his attitude clearly does reflect the toxicity and trauma with which the history of anti-feminist, patriarchal structures of control have left us. As Rubin argues, the cultural opprobrium of women shapes our reality: "the consequences of these great nineteenth-century moral paroxysms are still with us. They have left a deep imprint on attitudes about sex, medical practice, child-rearing, parental anxieties, police conduct, and sex law."[31] As Blackwood rises in power, he negates the sex-positive feminism previously visible within the Church of Night, yet his abdication of leadership of the Church due to Sabrina's ascension to power creates an avenue for feminist control of the church that is taken up by Zelda, who enlists the members of the Church to call first upon Lilith and then upon Hecate—both loci of feminine power.

THE QUEER IMAGINARY

Ultimately, *Chilling Adventures of Sabrina* offers us a fantasy of liberatory success in the fight against dominant structures of power obsessed with maintaining their own primacy to the exclusion of others. Cohen argues, "at the intersection of oppression and resistance lies the radical potential of queerness to challenge and bring together all those deemed marginal and all those committed to liberatory politics."[32] Yet she also frames this potential as an idealism that practice has not been capable of living up to. In *CAoS*, we see these liberatory politics both imagined and enacted, giving us a sense of what a world in which queerness were not bound up with an essential rhetorical opprobrium might look like. The show's embrace of feminist ideals of equity, the complex representation of queer characters with unique intersecting identities, and its challenge to patriarchal domination *intentionally* create a vision of a potentially optimistic future—a radical queer project in and of itself. Queer rhetoric, Alexander and Rhodes argue, is constituted through two significant avenues: first, through "a recognition of the dense and complicated ways in which sexuality, à la Foucault, constitutes a nexus of power, a conduit through which identities are created, categorized, and rendered as subjects constituted by and subject to power," and secondly, through "a reworking of those identifications to disrupt and reroute the flows of power, particularly discursive power."[33] By focusing on a young woman discovering her own power and the diverse queer community to which she belongs, the primary project of *CAoS* is arguably disrupting flows of power. In horror, we repeatedly see how repression manifests by turning people into monsters or rendering them monstrous in some essential way. In *CAoS*, however, repression is not centrally located in Sabrina and her accomplices—such repression—and therefore monstrousness—is instead the purview of those seeking to uphold heteronormativity, patriarchal structures, or other forms of exploitative power that deny people agency. One of the central tenets of *CAoS* is that power should be shared rather than hoarded, which is itself a queer rhetorical notion. At a fundamental level, *Chilling Adventures of Sabrina* acts as an allegory of the transformative power of queer resistance—a crucial factor in fueling a queer imaginary that has the potential to inspire us to enact real change in our own world.

BIBLIOGRAPHY

Ahmed, Sara. *The Cultural Politics of Emotion.* London: Routledge, 2014.

Alexander, Jonathan and Jacqueline Rhodes. "Queer Rhetoric and the Pleasures of the Archive," *Enculturation* (2012): www.enculturation.net/files/QueerRhetoric/queerarchive/Home.html.

Chilling Adventures of Sabrina. Season 1, episode 1, "Chapter One: October Country." Directed by Lee Toland Krieger, written by Roberto Aguirre-Sacasa, featuring Kiernan Shipka, Miranda Otto, Lucy Davis, and Chance Perdomo. Released October 26, 2018, Netflix, www.netflix.com/watch/80230071?trackId=200257859.

———, Season 1, episode 2, "Chapter Two: The Dark Baptism." Directed by Lee Toland Krieger, written by Roberto Aguirre-Sacasa, featuring Kiernan Shipka, Miranda Otto, Lucy Davis, and Richard Coyle. Released October 26, 2018, Netflix, www.netflix.com/watch/80230072?trackId=200257859.

———, Season 2, episode 1, "Chapter Twelve: The Epiphany." Directed by Kevin Rodney Sullivan, written by Roberto Aguirre-Sacasa, featuring Kiernan Shipka, Miranda Otto, Lucy Davis, and Lachlan Watson. Released April 5, 2019, Netflix, www.netflix.com/watch/80230082?trackId=200257859.

————, Season 2, episode 3. "Chapter Fourteen: Lupercalia." Directed by Salli Richardson-Whitfield, written by Oanh Ly, featuring Kiernan Shipka, Miranda Otto, Lucy Davis, and Chance Perdomo. Released April 5, 2019, Netflix, www.netflix.com/watch/80230084?trackId=200257859.

————, Season 2, episode 5, "Chapter Sixteen: Blackwood." Directed by Alex Pillai, written by Matthew Barry, featuring Kiernan Shipka, Miranda Otto, Lucy Davis, and Richard Coyle. Released April 5, 2019, Netflix, www.netflix.com/watch/80230086?trackId=14170289.

————, Season 2, episode 7, "Chapter Eighteen: The Miracles of Sabrina Spellman." Directed by Antonio Negret, written by Christianne Hedtke & Lindsay Calhoon Bring, featuring Kiernan Shipka, Miranda Otto, Lucy Davis, and Chance Perdomo. Released April 5, 2019, Netflix, www.netflix.com/watch/80230088?trackId=200257859.

Cohen, Cathy J. "Punks, Bulldaggers, and Welfare Queens: The Radical Potential of Queer Politics." In *Black Queer Studies: A Critical Anthology,* edited by E. Patrick Johnson and Mae Henderson, 21–50. Durham, NC: Duke UP, 2005.

Fahs, Breanne. "'Freedom to' and 'Freedom from': A New Vision for Sex-Positive Politics." *Sexualities* 17, no. 3 (2014): 267–290. doi: 10.1177/1363460713516334.

Goltz, Dustin Bradley. "Rhetorics of Gay Future and Queer Futurity: Strategies of Disruption." In *The Routledge Handbook of Queer Rhetoric*, edited by Jacqueline Rhodes and Jonathan Alexander, 413–420. London: Routledge, 2022.

Jaffe, Sara. "Queer Time: The Alternative to 'Adulting.'" *JSTOR Daily* (2018): daily.jstor.org/queer-time-the-alternative-to-adulting/.

Rubin, Gayle. "Thinking Sex: Notes for a Radical Theory of the Politics of Sexuality." In *Pleasure and Danger: Exploring Female Sexuality,* edited by Carole S. Vance, 267–319. Kitchener, ON: Pandora, 1992.

Thomas, Kendall. "Afterword: Are Transgender Rights *In*human Rights?" In *Transgender Rights,* edited by Paisley Currah et. al., 310–325. Minneapolis: U of Minnesota Press, 2006.

Tolman, Deborah L., et al. "Mobilizing Metaphor: Considering Complexities, Contradictions, and Contexts in Adolescent Girls' and Young Women's Sexual Agency." *Sex Roles* 73 (2015): 298–310. doi: 10.1007/s11199-015-0510-0.

NOTES

1. *Chilling Adventures of Sabrina*, season 1, episode 1, "Chapter One: October Country," directed by Lee Toland Krieger, written by Roberto Aguirre-Sacasa, featuring Kiernan Shipka, Miranda Otto, Lucy Davis, and Chance Perdomo, released October 26, 2018, on Netflix, www.netflix.com/watch/80230071?trackId=20025785900: 01:53-00:02:09.

2. Jonathan Alexander and Jacqueline Rhodes, "Queer Rhetoric and the Pleasures of the Archive," *Enculturation* (2012), www.enculturation.net/files/QueerRhetoric/queerarchive/Home.html.

3. Dustin Bradley Goltz, "Rhetorics of Gay Future and Queer Futurity: Strategies of Disruption," in *The Routledge Handbook of Queer Rhetoric*, edited by Jacqueline Rhodes and Jonathan Alexander (Milton: Routledge, 2022), 415.

4. Sara Jaffe, "Queer Time: The Alternative to 'Adulting,'" *JSTOR Daily* (2018): daily.jstor.org/queer-time-the-alternative-to-adulting/.

5. Cathy J. Cohen, "Punks, Bulldaggers, and Welfare Queens: The Radical Potential of Queer Politics," in *Black Queer Studies: A Critical Anthology,* edited by E. Patrick Johnson and Mae Henderson (Durham, NC: Duke UP, 2005), 22.

6. Gayle Rubin, "Thinking Sex: Notes for a Radical Theory of the Politics of Sexuality," in *Pleasure and Danger: Exploring Female Sexuality,* edited by Carole S. Vance (Kitchener, ON: Pandora, 1992), 278.

7. Rubin, "Thinking Sex," 278.

8. Rubin, "Thinking Sex," 278.

9. Breanne Fahs, "'Freedom to' and 'Freedom from': A New Vision for Sex-Positive Politics," *Sexualities* 17, no. 3 (2014): 268.

10. Rubin, "Thinking Sex," 281.

11. *Chilling Adventures of Sabrina*, season 2, episode 3, "Chapter Fourteen: Lupercalia," directed by Salli Richardson-Whitfield, written by Oanh Ly, featuring Kiernan Shipka, Miranda Otto, Lucy Davis, and Chance Perdomo, released April 5, 2019, on Netflix, www.netflix.com/watch/80230084?trackId=200257859: 00:04:31–00:04:47.

12. *Chilling Adventures of Sabrina*, "Chapter Fourteen: Lupercalia," 00:51:27–00:52:03.

13. Deborah L. Tolman, et al. "Mobilizing Metaphor: Considering Complexities, Contradictions, and Contexts in Adolescent Girls' and Young Women's Sexual Agency," *Sex Roles* 73 (2015): 302.

14. *Chilling Adventures of Sabrina*, "Chapter Fourteen: Lupercalia," 00:49:41.

15. *Chilling Adventures of Sabrina*, "Chapter Fourteen: Lupercalia," 00:52:01.

16. Sara Ahmed, *The Cultural Politics of Emotion* (London: Routledge, 2014): 146.

17. Ahmed, *Cultural Politics,* 151–52.

18. Ahmed, *Cultural Politics,* 152.

19. Fahs, "'Freedom to' and 'Freedom from,'" 275.

20. Fahs, "'Freedom to' and 'Freedom from,'" 282.

21. Cohen, "Punks, Bulldaggers, and Welfare Queens," 25.

22. *Chilling Adventures of Sabrina*, "Chapter Fourteen: Lupercalia," 00:15:12–00:15:48.

23. *Chilling Adventures of Sabrina*, "Chapter Fourteen: Lupercalia," 00:16:10–00:16:32.

24. Kendall Thomas, "Afterword: Are Transgender Rights *In*human Rights?," *Transgender Rights,* edited by Paisley Currah et. al. (Minneapolis: U of Minnesota Press, 2006): 311.

25. Thomas, "Afterword," 312.

26. Thomas, "Afterword," 312.

27. *Chilling Adventures of Sabrina*, season 1, episode 2, "Chapter Two: The Dark Baptism," by Lee Toland Krieger, written by Roberto Aguirre-Sacasa, featuring

Kiernan Shipka, Miranda Otto, Lucy Davis, and Richard Coyle, released October 26, 2018, on Netflix, www.netflix.com/watch/80230072?trackId=200257859: 00:25:57–00:26:19.

28. *Chilling Adventures of Sabrina*, season 2, episode 1, "Chapter Twelve: The Epiphany," directed by Kevin Rodney Sullivan, written by Roberto Aguirre-Sacasa, featuring Kiernan Shipka, Miranda Otto, Lucy Davis, and Lachlan Watson, released April 5, 2019, on Netflix, www.netflix.com/watch/80230082?trackId=200257859: 00:08:50–00:08:57.

29. *Chilling Adventures of Sabrina*, season 2, episode 5, "Chapter Sixteen: Blackwood," directed by Alex Pillai, written by Matthew Barry, featuring Kiernan Shipka, Miranda Otto, Lucy Davis, and Richard Coyle, released April 5, 2019, on Netflix, www.netflix.com/watch/80230086?trackId=14170289: 00:20:15–00:21:06.

30. *Chilling Adventures of Sabrina*, season 2, episode 7, "Chapter Eighteen: The Miracles of Sabrina Spellman," directed by Antonio Negret, written by Christianne Hedtke and Lindsay Calhoon Bring, featuring Kiernan Shipka, Miranda Otto, Lucy Davis, and Chance Perdomo, released April 5, 2019, on Netflix, www.netflix.com/watch/80230088?trackId=200257859: 00:15:35–00:16:15.

31. Rubin, "Thinking Sex," 268.

32. Cohen, "Punks, Bulldaggers, and Welfare Queens," 24.

33. Alexander and Rhodes, "Queer Rhetoric," www.enculturation.net/files/QueerRhetoric/queerarchive/intro.html.

Chapter 9

Empowering Liminality in *Chilling Adventures of Sabrina*

Laura Davidel

Sabrina Spellman (Kiernan Shipka), the protagonist in Netflix's *Chilling Adventures of Sabrina* (2018–20), is characterized by her liminal position between the human world and the supernatural one of her witch family and coven. The first episode opens with Sabrina's voice-over confession of her hybridity: she is half-witch, half-mortal. On her sixteenth birthday, Sabrina must choose "between the witch world of her family, and the human world of her friends."[1] Sabrina's transition towards her witch identity is scripted by her aunts and especially by her dead parents' desire that she be a full-fledged member of their coven, the Church of Night. What this entails is that Sabrina must complete the rite of passage by accepting her Dark Baptism and by signing her name in the *Book of the Beast*. The Dark Baptism is constructed as a traditional ritual through which the novice's identity is confirmed, magical powers are enhanced, and incorporation in the witch community is achieved. According to her aunt Zelda (Miranda Otto), Sabrina's transition would define her as "not the young woman but the young witch she is becoming."[2] As the series progresses, Sabrina is faced with the conundrum of having to give up her freedom and her human life for the "delicious things about being a witch"[3] together with the power and limitations that this aspect of her identity involves.

Sabrina's period of ambivalence and her approaching Dark Baptism correspond to what Victor Turner defines as the liminal period. Drawing on Arnold Van Gennep's *The Rites of Passage* (1909), Turner focuses on the spatial, temporal, and cultural implications of the three phases of initiation rites. The first one is "separation" from the previous cultural system or social group. This is followed by the "liminal phase" characterized by ambiguity.[4] Finally, by means of "reaggregation" into what Turner calls a "relatively stable state once more,"[5] the novice acquires a new place within the social structure. Turner's studies focused on the condition of the liminal subjects within the rites specific to the Ndembu tribe from Zambia. However, he extended the idea of in-betweenness to modern societies, as individuals pass from a certain structural status to another. From this perspective, Sabrina illustrates the Gothic liminality of the teenager who undergoes a complex transition: from child to adult but also from human to witch, a process that is not without ambiguity and fear.

Liminality is inherently paradoxical. It implies danger and anxiety[6] yet it can lead to creativity, functioning as "a realm of pure possibility whence novel configurations of ideas and relations may arise,"[7] to borrow Turner's formulation. Furthermore, the liminal is not restricted to a stage in which novices simply follow the prescribed rules pertaining to their reaggregation; if anything, it is the unpredictable part of ritual passing. In a postmodern context where master narratives are questioned, the liminal offers the potential of destabilizing traditional roles and norms. As Athena Bellas notes, Turner's theories on liminality were not specifically concerned with feminist issues, yet his work "provides a foundation for feminists to theorize how ruptures in dominant representational systems and narratives may occur."[8] For feminist theorists, the liminal state, and especially the period of adolescence, is important because it suggests that the person undergoing the ritual transition is momentarily situated in a space of ambiguity, of metaphorical "gaps or fissures"[9] from where the patriarchal system can be troubled and contested. Jill Morawaski underlines that liminal phases can lead to "momentary inversion, or reversal, of mundane social reality," with the possibility of bringing about "substantive change in existing social arrangements."[10] What these feminist perspectives on liminality bring to the following reading of Sabrina's journey is the articulation of her transition and her fight against the patriarchal inequalities ingrained in the coven from the position of the liminal voice belonging to the non-assimilated Other.

Building upon the spatial dimension of liminality as a state of in-betweenness with regards to two opposing worlds, this chapter examines other aspects of Sabrina's liminality in terms of ritual passing, oscillation, and the experience of being socially "unstructured."[11] Considering the ceremonial quality of Sabrina's Dark Baptism, these aspects emphasize her identity-formation, as well as her "critical powers"[12] when questioning the beliefs and traditions of the witch coven. I argue that Sabrina's empowerment stems from her liminal state as a novice who has not yet been incorporated in the hierarchical order of the coven. Sabrina's inquisitive stance and her critical view of the witch laws and antiquated traditions is not only feminist but also characteristic of the liminal novice who struggles to make sense of their identity and their place in the social construction of the coven. It is from this liminal position with regards to the coven's power structures—both within and somewhat not fully integrated—that Sabrina develops her agency, her sensitivity to feminist issues, and her critical stance regarding the limiting categories of the coven. Sabrina illustrates the figure of the Gothic teenager who does not simply accept the conventions imposed by society but rather takes control of her own destiny[13] because her liminality offers empowering possibilities of disrupting patriarchal order.

By combining theories on liminality and feminist perspectives, this chapter focuses on key moments from the first season of the TV series to demonstrate that Sabrina is empowered by her liminality in her fight against injustice and strict social norms. The notion of female empowerment will be used in relation to individualism, choice, and "agency as resistance"[14] while acknowledging that the teenage witch is imbricated in a power structure that is both "constraining and constituting"[15] her agency. Firstly, Sabrina's Dark Baptism will be considered as a ritual passage that overlaps the separation stage and the liminal one. The Gothic imagery used to construct the scenes of the Dark Baptism will be discussed as markers of Sabrina's crossing from the human world towards the supernatural one. Secondly, Sabrina's trial illustrates how her in-betweenness cannot be easily assimilated within the Church of Night. She is eventually allowed to retain her mortal life but is required to attend the Academy of Unseen Arts. The Feast of Feasts is another tradition that Sabrina challenges. While the rite is presented as a great honor conferred to a witch who is briefly declared Queen, Sabrina criticizes the monstrosity of this cannibalistic tradition. Furthermore, Sabrina's empowerment as a half-witch is emphasized by her crossing the threshold into Limbo. As a liminal entity, Sabrina fights patriarchy on two grounds: the mortal one through the club WICCA, and the magical one through her unsettling of the coven's status quo, by refusing to submit to the Dark Lord (Luke Cook) and his emissary, Father Blackwood (Richard Coyle). Before looking at Sabrina's liminality and how it empowers her and shapes her identity, it is important to discuss the series' American cultural context, and more specifically the feminist movement that has metaphorically summoned and reappropriated the figure of the witch.

"GENERATION WITCH"

While a growing number of Americans are renouncing organized religion[16] with a large proportion of these questioning religious teachings or/and disagreeing with churches' positions on social and political issues,[17] interest in the occult has continued to grow. According to Shutterstock, there was an increased interest in Occulture in 2020, with 525 percent more searches for "magic" and more than 289 percent searches for "spiritual."[18] Rebekah King's discussion of WitchTok demonstrates how social media has led to an abundance of magic-related content. Users do tarot readings or offer spell tutorials displaying their witchy paraphernalia in videos no longer than sixty seconds.[19] The commodification of the occult has gone beyond the selling of candles, sage, and crystals. Objects associated with Pagan practices have been appropriated by the mainstream through products such as Sephora's "Starter Witch Kit," which contains sage, a rose quartz, a tarot deck, and several vials of perfume. Just as teenagers are tempted by magic to influence their own lives, adult feminists may find that "exploring alternative avenues for liberation often goes hand in hand with exploring alternative philosophies and spirituality."[20] Since our reality is bombarded by fake news and a technologically-induced virtual world, it is perhaps not surprising that women feel empowered by spiritual practice.

Despite the stereotypical association with evil and persecution, the figure of the witch is both feared and admired for her magical powers and knowledge. The witch has been reclaimed by second-wave feminist groups, especially the Women's International Terrorist Conspiracy from Hell (W.I.T.C.H.). As Natalie Wilson points out, this organization "used the witch figure and related iconography to stage theatrical, attention-grabbing protests" and to fight against all forms of oppression.[21] The revival of the witch aesthetic resurged after Donald J. Trump's election, with activists dressing up as witches and holding banners that read, "Hex the Patriarchy." This coincides with the concurrent rise of fourth-wave feminism, whose activism was mainly carried out online through "technological mobilization," which enabled women to denounce "everyday forms of sexism and misogyny."[22] In this highly digital context that helped the voices of the marginalized to be heard, the election of Trump as the president of the United States and Hillary Clinton's loss was considered a rollback of women's rights and a blow to feminism.[23] What is more, Trump's supporters used "witch" as a slur to denigrate Clinton, thus perpetuating the misogynistic idea that highly qualified and powerful women are evil.

The #MeToo movement that exploded on social media in 2017 revealed numerous individual stories of women being sexually harassed or abused, thus becoming "the largest cultural reckoning with sexual violence since women began to enter the workforce en masse in the 1980s."[24] Adding to this online revolution, the movement #MagicResistance developed on social media after Trump's election. It brought together magic practitioners, inviting them to engage in a monthly ritual for binding Trump and preventing him from causing harm.[25] Practitioners taking part in "anti-Trump magical activism" through spellcasting described their experience as cathartic and empowering.[26] While not all Pagans and magic practitioners identify as witches, the complex relation between the feminist movement and the witch figure has developed as an empowering duality. After all, the witch is an agent of healing but also one capable of unsettling the patriarchal status quo. As Miranda Corcoran argues, "the fourth-wave teen witch" is not "a victim of oppressive patriarchal power, instead inhabiting a field of power which encompasses points of resistance and possibilities of subversion."[27]

When *CAoS* premiered on October 26, 2018, it attracted not only Gothic and horror enthusiasts but also an audience that had already been exposed to the political imbrication of the witch figure and her incarnation of women's agency and empowerment. Furthermore, depictions of the occult were already popular, considering the success of TV series such as *Charmed* (The WB, 1998–2006), *The Vampire Diaries* (The CW, 2009–17), *The Originals* (The CW, 2013–18), *Salem* (WGN America, 2014–17), and *American Horror Story: Coven* (FX, 2013–14), which depict witches learning to control their powers to fight evil, accessing ancestral energies, or undermining patriarchy from within to further their own ends. Sabrina's "political 'wokeness'"[28] and her coming-of-age story in the context of patriarchal structures both in the human and the witch world speaks to issues of feminism, otherness, and to the desire to improve one's life either individually or by forming (online) communities.

SABRINA'S DARK BAPTISM

Rituals are initiated by the removal of the novitiates from their previous status in the community. However, from the perspective of ritual passing, Sabrina experiences an overlap between the separation stage and the liminal one. For example, she confesses to her boyfriend, Harvey Kinkle (Ross Lynch), that she is a witch, but when he does not accept her, she spellbinds him to forget her confession.[29] What this suggests is that Sabrina's otherness as a witch cannot be easily incorporated in the human world, which ultimately marks her as a liminal persona. In fact, the human and the witch worlds are continuously intertwined for Sabrina as she uses her powers to protect her friends from the inequalities of the patriarchal system ingrained in their high school. With her cousin Ambrose's (Chance Perdomo) help, Sabrina casts a spell to scare Principal Hawthorne (Bronson Pinchot) so that during his absence the creation of a support group for young women is accepted. The group's name, WICCA: Women's Intersectional Cultural and Creative Association, alludes both to witchcraft and feminism. It echoes organized feminist activism and the spiritual movement Wicca, which reconstructs "pre-Christian traditions originating in Ireland, Scotland, and Wales" and promotes "free thought and will of the individual and encourages learning and an understanding of the earth and nature, thereby affirming the divinity in all living things."[30] Sabrina bewitches the patriarchal power of Principal Hawthorne—a reference to the Salem Witch Trials, in which John Hathorne was one of the judges—in order to help her friends defend women's rights and their access to literature. However, as her birthday and Dark Baptism approach, she becomes more and more aware that, to fully enter the witch world, she will have to sever her ties to the human world: her friendship with Roz (Jaz Sinclair) and Susie (later Theo; Lachlan Watson), and her love for Harvey.

The importance of Sabrina's separation from the human world is further emphasized through her argument with Zelda and her discussion with Ambrose. Sabrina's feminist principles in terms of individuality and control over her life and body are highlighted when she asks her aunts: "Why does [the Dark Lord] get to decide what I do or don't do with my body?"[31] Sabrina's question rightly criticizes the supernatural patriarchal power to which novices are forced to submit even before they take their baptism and sign the *Book of the Beast*. Zelda stresses that signing is by no means a choice as Sabrina would naively believe: "It is our sacred duty and honor to serve the Dark Lord. The extraordinary, delicious gifts he bestows on us in return for signing his book."[32] The implication here is that witches' powers stem from the symbolic signing of their name, an act that confirms their submission to the Dark Lord. Furthermore, signing the Dark Lord's book is presented as an intergenerational duty that precedes Sabrina and will be followed by her descendants. Contrary to the *Book of Shadows* in *Charmed* and Ashmole 782 in *A Discovery of Witches*—both constituting sources of knowledge and power for the Halliwell Sisters and Diana Bishop, respectively—for the witches in *CAoS*, the Dark Lord's book records the pact of submission for the novices. Nevertheless, as Ambrose explains to Sabrina, her magical powers will fade if she does not accept the Dark Baptism. He enumerates the advantages of being a witch as opposed to being human: longer life, developing one's magical abilities, and most importantly, the promise that "[she] will belong."[33] Ambrose suggests that the separation from meaningful connections with the human world is inevitable: "It's as though a veil drops . . . between you and the mortal world, and eventually, quite quickly, you're . . . weaned from it. [. . .] The pain is too much to bear. [. . .] Time slows down, and they'll grow old and you won't."[34] Sabrina's witch side defines her as a being outside of time, thus, liminality only deepens the difference she embodies. Furthermore, Sabrina's temporal liminality in relation to human temporality would inevitably lead to a social desynchronization from her mortal friends and finally to a painful separation.

As a master of ceremonies who will conduct the ritual of the Dark Baptism, Father Blackwood is invited to answer Sabrina's questions. Interestingly, he dismisses Sabrina's fears of pledging her soul to Satan once she signs her name in the book: "That's one interpretation, but it's largely a symbolic gesture, as rituals in most religions are."[35] Father Blackwood emphasizes the formal dimension and the pre-scripted sequences of action which ensure that the ritual is correctly executed.[36] In other words, he privileges the performance dimension of the ritual in terms of the gestures accomplished while concealing the performative one[37] that refers precisely to the symbolic new identity Sabrina would receive as a witch and, simultaneously, as a subject of the Dark Lord. Moreover, Blackwood's approach of minimizing the implications of the ritual and emphasizing the sense of belonging to the witch community and to the Academy of Unseen Arts corresponds to what Gavin Brown refers to as the institutional connotation of the ritual—"an institutional project for ordering and sustaining patterns of belief and conduct in it."[38] From this perspective, the ritual of baptism works on the novice just as much as it strengthens the witch coven, their religious beliefs, and the submission to patriarchal power that it perpetuates. This scene illustrates the extent to which Sabrina is imbricated in the power structures of the coven even before her baptism. On the one hand, Blackwood symbolizes the patriarchal force that intends to "normalize"[39] Sabrina and harness her power. He even offers her an illusion of choice by suggesting that after she takes her baptism she could leave the coven, an idea that is highly misleading. On the other hand, the young witch is influenced by her aunts to accept the baptism, especially through Zelda's nudges: "She'll be there, Your Excellency. With bells on, won't you, Sabrina?"[40] Although Sabrina's baptism is framed as an act of free will, it is not a choice but an obligation that she must fulfill to retain her magical powers, escape Hell, and be recognized as a member of the coven.

Sabrina's position as "betwixt and between"[41] the human and the magical worlds corresponds to the duality that Miguel Aguirre identifies as a specificity of Gothic texts. On this interpretation, liminality juxtaposes "two ontological zones or dimensions. One is the human cosmos, a domain of rationality and relative order. The other is the realm of the Numinous (whether or not supernatural), characterized by its incognoscibility."[42] Sabrina's oscillation between these two zones is further emphasized through her reluctance to renounce her human friends. Although Sabrina chooses to spend her birthday with them, she later runs from the party to the dark woods where the ritual of her Dark Baptism is meant to take place. This scene abounds in Gothic imagery, such as the dark passage made of branches, its three occult and Satanic symbols, and the ominous Blood Moon.[43] Sabrina pauses in the in-between and observes how this site of liminality acts upon her through the symbolic change of her dress's color from white to black, in accordance with her choice of following the Path of Night. The Gothic atmosphere of mystery and

supernatural follows Sabrina's crossing of the second threshold: the portal of
blue flames that takes her to the numinous realm of the witch coven.

Sabrina's baptism is framed as a ceremonial pact with Satan, but it also
alludes to a sexual initiation. The ritual of the Dark Baptism consists of a
system of elaborated rites, such as the symbolic disrobing of the initiand, the
blood anointing, as well as a set of questions that suggest Sabrina would be
granted freedom and power in exchange for her devotion to the Dark Lord.
During the ritual, Sabrina is stripped of identity and property[44] only to be
later infused with the coven's cultural values about belief in Lucifer that
would be rewarded with freedom to pursue one's own feelings and sense
of self. However, while she is being guided to sign her name in the *Book of
the Beast*, the ritualistic speech acts uttered by Father Blackwood confer to
Sabrina the status of a servant with no agency: "In signing his book, the *Book
of the Beast*, you swear to give your mind, body, and soul unreservedly to the
furtherance of the designs of our Lord Satan."[45] Accordingly, Sabrina is not
granted power and free will, as Father Blackwood had promised, but power
to obey Satan's orders.

When Sabrina's blood touches the pages of the book for her to sign as part
of her symbolic allegiance to Satan and while she is being coerced to sign
her name, she experiences a series of visions that frighten her. One depicts
the hanged witches of the past, another presents the horrific image of Satan
as a horned god, and the third consists of her dead parents and herself as an
infant. These visions can be interpreted in relation to Monica Greco and Paul
Stenner's concept of "liminal hotspots," which refer to "the uncertain, ambiguous, and undecidable experience of suspension in transitional limbo to an
encounter with paradox."[46] Greco and Stenner associate liminal hotspots with
"ontological indeterminacy"[47] and with a paralyzing paradox that hinders
one's actions and experience.[48] From this perspective, Sabrina's baptism is a
ritual that places her in a liminal hotspot whereby the unsettling glimpses into
witches' dark past, the horror of Satan's approaching, and the ghostly apparition of her parents are omens that the teenage witch tries to interpret in relation
to what signing the book entails. The ceremonial words uttered by Blackwood
and the supernatural that manifests through these visions correspond to what
Brown calls "the indeterminacy of meaning" inherent in ritual performances
whereby "ritual participants read and appropriate ritual symbols and actions
differently."[49] In Sabrina's case the indeterminacy and the contradictions she
observes in the ritual of baptism suggest that signing her name equates with
a future just as dark as that of the hanged witches, to submission to the Dark
Lord and to her assimilation into the patriarchal power structure of the coven.
In her liminal position, literally standing before Satan's book with the bone
quill in hand under Blackwood's pressure, Sabrina refuses to sign and runs
away from the forest without completing the ritual. Rather than accepting the

ritual to act upon her and categorize her, Sabrina demonstrates her agentic power in rejecting her baptism.

Sabrina's interrupted rite of passage marks her as a liminal persona characterized by oscillation, yet it simultaneously enables her to assert her identity. If the "crossing of the threshold is perhaps the prototypical deed in Gothic fiction,"[50] as Manuel Aguirre argues, it should be noted that in Sabrina's case there is a double crossing. One is towards the numinous realm of the witches, a realm governed by the Dark Lord, while the other crossing takes her back towards to the ancestral house and to the mortal world. In a horror-infused scene, Sabrina escapes the numinous and its eerie magical vines that try to prevent her from crossing back. From her family grounds, she announces to the coven that she chooses "a third way."[51] Sabrina's agentic power that stems from her emotions, her sense of self, and her ability "to act independently of social structural constraints"[52] manifests in her assertion that she would not "sign away"[53] her name thereby retaining the duality of her identity. It is telling that Sabrina feels more at home in liminality than in the coven that wishes to incorporate her. The teenage witch's liminality is emphasized as Sabrina informs the viewer via voice-over that "the girl who had to decide between being a witch and being mortal chose neither path. Or, if you look at it another way, chose both. She was half-witch but with two covens."[54] However, as Sabrina's story unfolds, she realizes that her in-betweenness does not necessarily imply balance but rather a constant oscillation.

SABRINA'S TRIAL

An event that further emphasizes Sabrina's dual nature and the power she derives from it is her trial for breaking the promise given by her father to the Dark Lord. Father Blackwood's charges against Sabrina suggest that her baptism is analogous to a wedding where her refusal to sign the book equates with her fleeing "at the moment of consummation."[55] Sabrina's hybridity as half-witch and half-mortal is used as a line of defense by her lawyer, Daniel Webster (John Rubinstein), to demand a jury of mortals, while Blackwood invokes human law and gruesome ways of determining Sabrina's dominant nature by drowning or by examination of her body for a witch's mark. Although Sabrina's liminality as a mark of impurity can be read as "a monstrous birth,"[56] as Henesy suggests, it is important to note how in the legal system of the trial, this liminality may very well be Sabrina's winning card. It is not a coincidence that Blackwood, acting as an emissary of Satan, offers Sabrina a bargain: she can visit her human friends and her punishment will be lifted if she signs the book and transfers from the human high school to the Academy of Unseen Arts. In other words, this bargain requires Sabrina to go through the stages of separation and reincorporation of her baptism. As a result, Sabrina's liminality, both as hybridity and in terms of ritual in-betweenness, would no longer have the potential to disrupt the dominant order and hierarchies of the witch coven. If ritual passing is constituted by "powerful mechanisms for constructions of the self and the other, of personal and collective identities,"[57] Sabrina's incorporation in the witch academy represents a means of reinforcing the status quo of the coven and an attempt at "educating" the wayward teenage witch by assigning her to a fixed position. Not surprisingly, Sabrina demonstrates her resistance to the tricks of the evil forces and refuses the bargain Blackwood offers.

Sabrina's duality can be traced back to secrets regarding her parents just as it pertains to her hybrid nature. Zelda reveals that Sabrina's father promised her soul to Satan, in exchange for permission to marry Diana, Sabrina's mortal mother; however, Hilda (Lucy Davis) produces Sabrina's Christian baptism certificate during the trial. The document is dated one day before her name was inscribed in the *Book of the Beast*. This turn of events is characteristically Gothic as Sabrina's liminal identity is influenced by her parents' past actions: her father pledged her to the Path of Night, while her mother ensured that Sabrina received a Christian baptism, thus setting her on the Path of Light. Like Deborah Harkness's Diana in *A Discovery of Witches*, whose parents spellbind her to suppress her magical powers and protect her in her childhood, and Alexis Henderson's Imanuelle in *The Year of the Witching*, whose identity is affected by her mother's connection to the three witches in the woods, Sabrina's liminality is a family issue dating back to her parents' choices.

Sabrina is imbricated in a system of contrasting power relations through her father's pledge of her soul to Satan and through the protective Christian baptism. As such, she embodies an "interstructural liminality"[58] that is finally recognized by the legal court of the witches. Since Sabrina constitutes the excess that cannot be assimilated within the hierarchy of the Church of Night, she is granted what her lawyer calls "dual citizenship to both worlds"[59]: she is allowed to retain her mortal life but is required to attend the Academy of Unseen Arts. Sabrina's access to both the human school and the magic one is consistent with Sandor Klapcsik's understanding of liminality as "*a constant oscillation, crossing back and forth between social and cultural positions.*"[60] In this reading, Sabrina is grounded in the social structure of her human ties to her friends and to Harvey, but she is also empowered by the knowledge she gains at the Academy. This idea is further emphasized by Sabrina's agenda of gaining knowledge to fight the Dark Lord: "I'm going to learn how to conjure him, bind him, banish him."[61] Sabrina's pledge to fight the patriarchal power of Satan resonates with feminist activists' agendas while simultaneously echoing the witches who set out to hex Trump and Brett Kavanaugh.

FEAST OF FEASTS

In episode seven, we are presented with the Feast of Feasts, a cannibalistic ritual that involves the self-sacrifice of a witch whose flesh is to be consumed by the coven members. Meant to honor the memory of Freya, a young witch who offered her body as sustenance to other witches in a dreadful winter of famine, the coven recreates the feast as "an annual demonstration of [their] devotion to the Dark Lord."[62] The celebration involves fourteen women as tributes from the witch families, with one of them declared queen and worshipped for three days, only to be devoured by the coven members. The rite is perceived by most of the witches as a great honor worth the self-sacrifice of one's body. Not surprisingly, Sabrina assumes the role of the activist in that she criticizes the monstrosity of the tradition for its exploitation and manipulation of women.

Despite her liminal position, Sabrina is requested to "obey and participate"[63] in the tradition. She offers to take Zelda's place in the drawing of the next queen to challenge her aunt's beliefs in the feast. Sabrina's strong objections to the relevance of the rite corresponds to Turner's contention that "during the liminal period, neophytes are alternately forced and encouraged to think about their society, their cosmos, and the powers that generate and sustain them. Liminality may be partly described as a stage of reflection."[64] Sabrina's liminality grants her a critical stance which enables her to challenge and fight against a cannibalistic tradition that she considers immoral and irrelevant, since "no one's starving."[65] Sabrina and her aunts go to great extents to influence Father Blackwood in canceling the feast. Together, they demonstrate an agency of resistance that has a dual function: they fulfill their roles in the social structure of the coven (especially as Sabrina is elected to be shepherd and pamper the future queen-to-be-sacrificed), while they also create a moment of opposition to the patriarch who reinstated the feast. Hilda's truth cake served to the Blackwoods and the Weird Sisters reveals that Prudence's (Tati Gabrielle) election as a queen was orchestrated by Lady Blackwood (Alvina August). Following the events at the dinner, Blackwood is forced to annul the Feast of Feasts. Although Sabrina's challenge and successful subversion of the cannibalism ritual prevents Prudence from being sacrificed, she had not foreseen the fanaticism of the coven. One of the witches sacrifices herself just as Father Blackwood announces the cancelation of the feast. Sabrina's critical position regarding the cannibalistic tradition succeeds in opening her aunts' eyes to the monstrosity under which a female member of the coven would be sacrificed for the ideal of becoming a source of power for the whole coven.

SABRINA'S CROSSING INTO LIMBO

In *CAoS*, life and death are continuously intertwined: Hilda and Zelda use their house as a mortuary, are midwives, and possess a magical plot in their graveyard that contains earth from Cain's garden and revives the person buried in it. Therefore, it is not surprising that Sabrina would cross the boundaries between life and death in order to bring Harvey's brother, Tommy (Justin Dobies) back to life. In "Chapter Eight: The Burial" (1:8), she disrupts the balance through a ritual meant to revive Tommy, but cheats Death by putting Agatha (Adeline Rudolph)—the witch responsible for the accident at the mines—in the magical grave. Despite Sabrina's success in resurrecting Tommy, she only brings back his body and not his soul. Sabrina decides to rectify her error through an even more extreme action: that of going to Limbo to retrieve Tommy's soul. To do so, she relies on her human side, which would grant her access to Limbo, a realm that witches cannot enter. Limbo is depicted as a horrific dimension with a distinctive Gothic atmosphere. It is a realm of darkness, where the screams of those trapped echo in a chorus of terrible sounds.

The act of crossing the threshold into Limbo is a crucial event that underlines Sabrina's empowerment as a half-mortal. When Sabrina enters Limbo, the camera shifts between shots of Sabrina's hand tied with the red thread that connects her to the living world and shots of what she sees: the misty realm, dark figures, her mother, and finally Tommy. Interestingly, when the thread is cut and the Soul Eater approaches, Sabrina invokes the spirits of the dead to reveal the portal to her and Tommy. Despite Sabrina's efforts, Tommy's soul is caught by the Soul Eater and she is forced to confess to Harvey that the Tommy brought back from the dead is a dangerous creature. Through her refusal of rigid cultural constructs and boundaries between life and death or those between the realm of the living and Purgatory, Sabrina illustrates the adolescent's struggle with the cycle of life and death that is perhaps best left undisturbed. As Glennis Byron and Sharon Deans argue, the Gothic empowers teenagers who do not accept the place they are ascribed to in the power structure, but challenge categories and assert their autonomy.[66] Sabrina bends rules, crosses thresholds, and takes advantage of her duality in order to fight for what she feels to be right, even if her perspective is distorted by her rebellious attitude.

In examining essential moments of Sabrina's liminality, this chapter has emphasized the idea that the teenage witch's duality and in-betweenness are neither negative characteristics nor a rebellious period that she is expected to grow out of. Sabrina's liminality, agency, and critical spirit enable her to fight against injustice, even though this implies crossing boundaries and challenging traditions. Sabrina's agency resonates with the protagonists of teen Gothic texts, who, as Byron and Deans argue, "are generally shown to take control of their own destinies, and, in due course, change their environment."[67] In asking questions and challenging the status quo, Sabrina changes not only her environment, but also power relations and hierarchies in both the mortal and the witch world. For Dara Downey, Ian Kinane, and Elizabeth Parker, liminality or "the *entre-deux* arises in-between two or more categorical definitions, but its spatial (physical and/or conceptual) position implies both integration of and resistance to whatever is either side of or outside of the in-between."[68] Through a resistance to fixed categories and through the acceptance of her duality, Sabrina affects both the human world and the witch one. In addition to the community for women at her high school, Sabrina enlists the Weird Sisters to help her in contacting the spirit of her mother, and even convinces her aunts and Lilith/Ms.Wardwell (Michelle Gomez) to help her in the first exorcism ever to be performed by witches.

Although Sabrina demonstrates a constant rejection of rigid social and cultural structures pertaining to both humans and the witch coven, she is finally tricked into accepting her subordination to the Dark Lord. In "Chapter Ten: The Witching Hour" (1:10), Lilith/Ms. Wardwell's scheming leads Sabrina to willingly sign the *Book of the Beast*. She only agrees to do so in order to access the power of being a full-fledged witch and defend the mortal world from the thirteen resurrected witches who were haunting the streets of Greendale. This return to the point where the ritual of baptism was interrupted coincides with Ute Hüsketi and Donna L. Seamone's notion of the ritual as returning or persisting after its denial by participants.[69] It is telling that Lilith, a figure associated with feminist ideals of equality and with the postfeminist stance of the woman who "uses her femininity to gain power,"[70] brings Sabrina back to the moment of signing which was suspended in the ritual of baptism. While Sabrina receives power, and more precisely the power of invoking hellfire, she also assumes her place in the witches' coven. Sabrina may accept her reaggregation into the coven as a witch and as a servant of the Dark Lord, yet her identity has developed in relation to complex aspects of liminality in terms of her hybridity, spatial oscillation, and through her critical stance regarding the validity of witches' law and traditions. Sabrina's empowerment is made evident through her agency and individual choice to act according to her beliefs, even though her perspective can sometimes be skewed and trouble boundaries between life and death.

BIBLIOGRAPHY

Aguirre, Manuel. "A Grammar of Gothic: Report on a Research Project on the Forms of the Gothic Genre." *Textualities: Literature and Print Culture, 1780–1840* 21 (2013): 124–34.

Austin, J. L. *How to Do Things with Words*. Oxford: Clarendon Press, 1962.

Bellas, Athena. *Fairy Tales on the Teen Screen*. Cham: Palgrave Macmillan, 2017.

Boland, Tom. *The Spectacle of Critique: From Philosophy to Cacophony.* *Contemporary Liminality Series*. London and New York: Routledge, Taylor & Francis Group, 2019.

Brown, Gavin. "Theorizing Ritual as Performance: Explorations of Ritual Indeterminacy." *Journal of Ritual Studies* 17, no. 1 (2003): 3–18.

Butler, Judith. *Gender Trouble: Feminism and the Subversion of Identity*. Routledge Classics. New York and London: Routledge, 2006.

Byron, Glennis, and Sharon Deans. "Teen Gothic." In *The Cambridge Companion to the Modern Gothic*, edited by Jerrold E. Hogle, 87–104. Cambridge Companions to Literature. Cambridge: Cambridge University Press, 2014.

Campbell, Colin. "Distinguishing the Power of Agency from Agentic Power: A Note on Weber and the 'Black Box' of Personal Agency," *Sociological Theory* 27, no. 4 (2009): 407–18.

Celtic Connection. "What Is Wicca?" wicca.com/wicca/what-is-wicca.html.

Chilling Adventures of Sabrina, Season 1, episode 1, "Chapter One: October Country." Directed by Lee Toland Krieger, written by Roberto Aguirre-Sacasa, featuring Kiernan Shipka, Miranda Otto, Lucy Davis, and Chance Perdomo. Released October 26, 2018, Netflix, www.netflix.com/watch/80230071?trackId=200257859.

———, Season 1, episode 2, "Chapter Two: The Dark Baptism." Directed by Lee Toland Krieger, written by Roberto Aguirre-Sacasa, featuring Kiernan Shipka, Miranda Otto, Lucy Davis, and Richard Coyle. Released October 26, 2018, Netflix, www.netflix.com/watch/80230072?trackId=200257859.

———, Season 1, episode 3, "Chapter Three: The Trial of Sabrina Spellman." Directed by Rob Seidenglanz, written by Ross Maxwell, featuring Kiernan Shipka, Miranda Otto, Lucy Davis, and Ross Lynch. Released October 26, 2018, Netflix, www.netflix.com/watch/80230073?trackId=200257859.

———, Season 1, episode 4, "Chapter Four: Witch Academy." Directed by Rob Seidenglanz, written by Diana Thorland, featuring Kiernan Shipka, Miranda Otto, Lucy Davis, and Richard Coyle. Released October 26, 2018, Netflix, www.netflix.com/watch/80230074?trackId=200257859.

———, Season 1, episode 7. "Chapter Seven: Feasts of Feasts." Directed by Nguyen Viet, written by Oanh Ly, featuring Kiernan Shipka, Miranda Otto, Lucy Davis, and Tati Gabrielle. Released October 26, 2018, Netflix, www.netflix.com/watch/80230077?trackId=200257859.

Corcoran, Miranda. "The Monstrous Girl: Teen Witches, Power and Fourth-Wave Feminism." In *Women and the Abuse of Power: Interdisciplinary Perspectives*, edited by Helen Gavin, 61–78. Bingley: Emerald Publishing, 2022. doi. org/10.1108/978-1-80043-334-220221006.

Crockett, Emily. "Why Feminism Didn't Lose in 2016," *Vox*, 2017, www.vox.com/ identities/2016/12/30/14053516/2016-year-in-feminism-trump-clinton.

Downey, Dara, Ian Kinane, and Elizabeth Parker. "Introduction Locating Liminality: Space, Place, and the In-Between." In *Landscapes of Liminality: Between Space and Place*, 1–25. London and New York: Rowman & Littlefield, 2016.

Drury, Nevill. "The Modern Magical Revival." In *Handbook of Contemporary Paganism*, edited by James R. Lewis and Murphy Pizza, 13–80. Leiden, Netherlands: Brill, 2009.

Fine, Julia C. "#MagicResistance: Anti-Trump Witchcraft as Register Circulation." *Journal of Linguistic Anthropology* 30, no. 1 (May 26, 2020): 68–85. doi. org/10.1111/jola.12249.

Fuselli, Grace. "Astrology and Alchemy and Palmistry, Oh My! See How Younger Generations' Interest in The Occult Is Shaping One of 2020's Major Creative Trends," 2020. www.shutterstock.com/blog/occulture-mystical-design-trend.

Greco, Monica, and Paul Stenner. "From Paradox to Pattern Shift: Conceptualizing Liminal Hotspots and Their Affective Dynamics." *Theory & Psychology* 27, no. 2 (April 5, 2017): 147–66. doi.org/10.1177/0959354317693120.

Henesy, Megan. "'Leaving my girlhood behind': Woke Witches and Feminist Liminality in *Chilling Adventures of Sabrina*." *Feminist Media Studies* 21, no. 7 (2021): 1143–1157. doi.org/10.1080/14680777.2020.1791929.

Hüsken, Ute, and Donna Lynne Seamone. "The Denial of Ritual and Its Return—An Introduction." *Journal of Ritual Studies* 27, no. 1 (2013): 1–9.

Hughes, Michael. "A Spell to Bind Donald J. Trump and All Those Who Abet Him." February 16, 2017. extranewsfeed.com/a-spell-to-bind-donald-trump-and-all-those-who-abet-him-february-24th-mass-ritual-51f3d94f62f4.

King, Rebekah. "WitchTok: The Rise of The Occult on Social Media Has Eerie Parallels with the 16th Century," *The Conversation*, 2021. theconversation.com/witchtok-the-rise-of-the-occult-on-social-media-has-eerie-parallels-with-the-16th-century-168322.

Klapcsik, Sandor. *Liminality in Fantastic Fiction: A Poststructuralist Approach.* Jefferson,

North Carolina, and London: McFarland & Company, Inc., Publishers, 2012.

Kreinath, Jens, Jan Snoek, and Michael Stausberg. "Preliminary Material." In *Theorizing Rituals: Issues, Topics, Approaches, Concepts*, edited by Jens Kreinath, Jan Snoek, and Michael Stausberg, 114/1:i–xxv. Leiden, Netherlands: Brill, 2006. doi.org/10.1163/9789047410775_001.

McNay, Lois. "Agency." In *The Oxford Handbook of Feminist Theory*, edited by Lisa Disch and Mary Hawkesworth, 39–60. Oxford: Oxford University Press, 2015. doi. org/10.1093/oxfordhb/9780199328581.001.0001.

Morawski, Jill. *Practicing Feminisms, Reconstructing Psychology: Notes on a Liminal Science*. Ann Arbor: The University of Michigan Press, 1994.

Parry, Diana C., Corey W. Johnson, and Faith-Anne Wagler. "Fourth Wave Feminism: Theoretical Underpinnings and Future for Leisure Research." In *Feminisms in*

Leisure Studies Advancing a Fourth Wave, edited by Diana C. Parry, 1–12. London: Routledge, 2019.

Pew Research Center. "Modeling the Future of Religion in America," 2022. www .pewresearch.org/religion/2022/09/13/modeling-the-future-of-religion-in-america /#fn-38123-2.

———. "Why America's 'Nones' Don't Identify with a Religion," 2018. www .pewresearch.org/fact-tank/2018/08/08/why-americas-nones-dont-identify-with-a -religion/.

Sollée, Kristen J. *Witches, Sluts, Feminists: Conjuring the Sex Positive*. Berkeley: ThreeL Media, 2017.

Soucie, Stephen, Diana C. Parry, and Luc S. Cousineau. "The Fourth Wave #MeToo Can Teach Us About Millennial Mobilization, Intersectionality, and Men's Accountability." In *Feminisms in Leisure Studies*, 2018.

Szakolczai, Arpad. "Liminality and Experience: Structuring Transitory Situations and Transformative Events." *International Political Anthropology*, 2009, 141–72.

Tambiah, S. J. "A Performative Approach to Ritual." In *Proceedings of the British Academy*, 1980. archive.org/details/aperformativeapproachtoritualtambiahstanley/ mode/2up?q=performative.

Thomassen, Bjørn. *Liminality and the Modern: Living Through the In-Between*. Farnham, Surrey and Burlington, VT: Ashgate, 2014.

Tink, Courtney, and Jenni Lauwrens. "'A Face Like This Is Hard to Beat': Negotiating Lilith in the Postfeminist Media Economy." *Communicatio*, July 25, 2022, 1–20. doi.org/10.1080/02500167.2022.2086893.

Turner, Victor. *The Forest of Symbols: Aspects of Ndembu Ritual*. Ithaca and London: Cornell University Press, 1970.

———. *The Ritual Process: Structure and Anti-Structure*. London: Routledge, 1969.

Wilson, Natalie. *Willful Monstrosity: Gender and Race in 21st Century Horror*. Jefferson, North Carolina: McFarland, 2020.

NOTES

1. *Chilling Adventures of Sabrina,* season 1, episode 1," Chapter One: October Country," directed by Lee Toland Krieger, written by Roberto Aguirre-Sacasa, featuring Kiernan Shipka, Miranda Otto, Lucy Davis, and Chance Perdomo, released October 26, 2018, on Netflix, www.netflix.com/watch/80230071?trackId=200257859: 00:01:58.

2. *Chilling Adventures of Sabrina,* "Chapter One: October Country," 00:13:35.

3. *Chilling Adventures of Sabrina,* "Chapter One: October Country," 00:31:03.

4. Victor Turner, *The Ritual Process: Structure and Anti-Structure* (London: Routledge, 1969), 94.

5. Turner, *The Ritual Process,* 95.

6. Bjørn Thomassen, *Liminality and the Modern: Living Through the In-Between* (Farnham, Surrey and Burlington, VT: Ashgate, 2014), 83; Arpad Szakolczai,

"Liminality and Experience: Structuring Transitory Situations and Transformative Events," *International Political Anthropology*, 2009, 166.

7. Victor Turner, *The Forest of Symbols: Aspects of Ndembu Ritual* (Ithaca and London: Cornell University Press, 1970), 97.

8. Athena Bellas, *Fairy Tales on the Teen Screen* (Cham: Palgrave Macmillan, 2017), 19.

9. Bellas, *Fairy Tales,* 18.

10. Jill Morawski, *Practicing Feminisms, Reconstructing Psychology: Notes on a Liminal Science* (Ann Arbor: The University of Michigan Press, 1994), 54.

11. Turner, *The Forest of Symbols*, 98.

12. Tom Boland, *The Spectacle of Critique: From Philosophy to Cacophony*, Contemporary Liminality Series (London and New York: Routledge, Taylor & Francis Group, 2019), 41.

13. Glennis Byron and Sharon Deans, "Teen Gothic," in *The Cambridge Companion to the Modern Gothic*, ed. Jerrold E Hogle, Cambridge Companions to Literature (Cambridge: Cambridge University Press, 2014), 102.

14. Lois McNay, "Agency," in *The Oxford Handbook of Feminist Theory*, ed. Lisa Disch and Mary Hawkesworth (Oxford: Oxford University Press, 2015), 45.

15. Judith Butler, *Gender Trouble: Feminism and the Subversion of Identity*, Routledge Classics (New York and London: Routledge, 2006), 169.

16. According to the Pew Research Center, in 2020, approximately 30 percent of Americans were "religiously unaffiliated." The Center's projections estimate that by 2070, this proportion will rise somewhere "between 34 percent and 52 percent of the U.S. population." Pew Research Center, "Modeling the Future of Religion in America," 2022, www.pewresearch.org/religion/2022/09/13/modeling-the-future-of -religion-in-america/#fn-38123-2.

17. "Why America's 'nones' don't identify with a religion," 2018, www.pewresearch .org/fact-tank/2018/08/08/why-americas-nones-dont-identify-with-a-religion/.

18. Grace Fuselli, "Astrology and Alchemy and Palmistry, Oh My! See How Younger Generations' Interest in the Occult Is Shaping One of 2020's Major Creative Trends," 2020, www.shutterstock.com/blog/occulture-mystical-design-trend.

19. Rebekah King, "WitchTok: The Rise of the Occult on Social Media Has Eerie Parallels With the 16th Century," *The Conversation*, 2021, theconversation.com/ witchtok-the-rise-of-the-occult-on-social-media-has-eerie-parallels-with-the-16th-century-168322; Since the writing of this article, TikTok has increased the time limit twice so that videos can be three and, more recently, ten minutes long.

20. Kristen J. Sollée, *Witches, Sluts, Feminists: Conjuring the Sex Positive* (Berkeley: ThreeL Media, 2017).

21. Natalie Wilson, *Willful Monstrosity: Gender and Race in 21st Century* Horror (Jefferson, North Carolina: McFarland, 2020), 132

22. Diana C. Parry, Corey W. Johnson, and Faith-Anne Wagler, "Fourth Wave Feminism: Theoretical Underpinnings and Future for Leisure Research," in *Feminisms in Leisure Studies Advancing a Fourth Wave*, ed. Diana C. Parry (London: Routledge, 2019), 6.

23. Emily Crockett, "Why Feminism Didn't Lose in 2016," *Vox*, 2017, www.vox .com/identities/2016/12/30/14053516/2016-year-in-feminism-trump-clinton.

24. Stephen Soucie, Diana C. Parry, and Luc S. Cousineau, "The Fourth Wave #MeToo Can Teach Us About Millennial Mobilization, Intersectionality, and Men's Accountability," in *Leisure Studies Advancing a Fourth Wave*, ed. Diana C. Parry (London: Routledge, 2019), 151, emphasis added.

25. Michael Hughes's ritual text "A Spell to Bind Donald J. Trump and All Those Who Abet Him," extranewsfeed.com/a-spell-to-bind-donald-trump-and-all-those-who-abet-him-february-24th-mass-ritual-51f3d94f62f4. Allegedly, around 13,000 practitioners joined and used Hughes' spell to bind Trump.

26. Julia C. Fine, "#MagicResistance: Anti-Trump Witchcraft as Register Circula-tion," *Journal of Linguistic Anthropology* 30, no. 1 (May 26, 2020): 71, 82. Fine notes feminist indexicalities in the texts of spells composed to bind Trump and Brett Kavanaugh.

27. Miranda Corcoran, "The Monstrous Girl: Teen Witches, Power and Fourth-Wave Feminism," in *Women and the Abuse of Power: Interdisciplinary Perspectives*, ed. Helen Gavin (Bingley: Emerald Publishing, 2022), 62.

28. Megan Henesy, "'Leaving My Girlhood Behind': Woke Witches and Feminist Liminality in Chilling Adventures of Sabrina," *Feminist Media Studies* 21, no. 7 (2021): 1155.

29. *Chilling Adventures of Sabrina*, "Chapter One: October Country," 00:31:43.

30. Celtic Connection, "What Is Wicca?" wicca.com/wicca/what-is-wicca.html.

31. *Chilling Adventures of Sabrina*, "Chapter One: October Country," 00:42:35.

32. *Chilling Adventures of Sabrina*, "Chapter One: October Country," 00:42:56.

33. *Chilling Adventures of Sabrina*, "Chapter One: October Country," 00:15:14.

34. *Chilling Adventures of Sabrina*, season 1, episode 2, "Chapter Two: The Dark Baptism," directed by Lee Toland Krieger, written by Roberto Aguirre-Sacasa, featur-ing Kiernan Shipka, Miranda Otto, Lucy Davis, and Richard Coyle, released Octo-ber 26, 2018, on Netflix, www.netflix.com/watch/80230072?trackId=200257859: 00:33:16.

35. *Chilling Adventures of Sabrina*, "Chapter Two: The Dark Baptism," 00:02:30.

36. Gavin Brown opposes the scripted dimension of the ritual performance to the more "creative and dynamic" conceptualization that stems from the indeterminacy inherent in the performance as the participants can introduce changes based on their own interpretation of symbols. Gavin Brown, "Theorizing Ritual as Performance: Explorations of Ritual Indeterminacy," *Journal of Ritual Studies* 17, no. 1 (2003): 7–12.

37. This differentiation between performance and performativity is informed by J.L. Austin's theories of performative speech acts in which "the issuing of the utterance is the performing of an action," in a conventional and formal procedure. J.L. Austin, *How to Do Things with Words* (Oxford: Clarendon Press, 1962), 6. Furthermore, S.J. Tambiah also distinguishes between the performativity of speech acts in rituals and the performance of rituals as staged patterns of action. S.J. Tambiah, "A Performative Approach to Ritual," in *Proceedings of the British Academy*, 1980, 119. archive.org/ details/aperformativeapproachtoritualtambiahstanley/mode/2up.

38. Brown, "Theorizing Ritual," 7.

39. Henesy, "'Leaving My Girlhood Behind,'" 1144.

40. *Chilling Adventures of Sabrina,* "Chapter Two: The Dark Baptism," 00:05:54.

41. Turner, *The Forest of Symbols,* 97.

42. Manuel Aguirre, "A Grammar of Gothic: Report on a Research Project on the Forms of the Gothic Genre," *Textualities: Literature and Print Culture, 1780–1840* 21 (2013): 127–28.

43. The eerie Blood Moon is a symbol of new beginning and regeneration for Wiccans, yet it has also been regarded with superstition as an apocalyptic symbol. For Wiccans, the Blood Moon corresponds to the first esbat (monthly meetings which are held when there is a full-moon phase) according to the lunar calendar, which consists of thirteen months. As Nevill Drury explains, the Blood Moon is "traditionally associated with the slaughter of animals for food prior to the onset of winter and is therefore represented by the colour red." Nevill Drury, "The Modern Magical Revival," in *Handbook of Contemporary Paganism*, ed. James R. Lewis and Murphy Pizza (Leiden, Netherlands: Brill, 2009), N209. P64.

44. Turner, *The Forest of Symbols*, 97–98.

45. *Chilling Adventures of Sabrina,* "Chapter Two: The Dark Baptism," 00:45:19.

46. Monica Greco and Paul Stenner, "From Paradox to Pattern Shift: Conceptualising Liminal Hotspots and Their Affective Dynamics," *Theory & Psychology* 27, no. 2 (April 5, 2017): 155.

47. Greco and Stenner, "From Paradox to Pattern Shift," 160.

48. Greco and Stenner, "From Paradox to Pattern Shift," 160.

49. Brown, "Theorizing Ritual as Performance," 12.

50. Aguirre, "A Grammar of Gothic," 127.

51. *Chilling Adventures of Sabrina,* "Chapter Two: The Dark Baptism," 00:47:50.

52. Colin Campbell, "Distinguishing the Power of Agency from Agentic Power: A Note on Weber and the 'Black Box' of Personal Agency," *Sociological Theory* 27, no. 4 (2009): 416.

53. *Chilling Adventures of Sabrina,* "Chapter Two: The Dark Baptism," 00:47:54.

54. *Chilling Adventures of Sabrina,* "Chapter Two: The Dark Baptism," 00:52:03.

55. *Chilling Adventures of Sabrina,* season 1, episode 3, "Chapter Three: The Trial of Sabrina Spellman," directed by Rob Seidenglanz, written by Ross Maxwell, featuring Kiernan Shipka, Miranda Otto, Lucy Davis, and Ross Lynch, released October 26, 2018, on Netflix, www.netflix.com/watch/80230073?trackId=200257859: 00:19:10.

56. Henesy, "'Leaving My Girlhood Behind,'" 1144.

57. Jens Kreinath, Jan Snoek, and Michael Stausberg, "Preliminary Material," in *Theorizing Rituals: Issues, Topics, Approaches, Concepts*, vol. 114/1 (Leiden, Netherlands: Brill, 2006), xv.

58. Turner, *The Forest of Symbols*, 101.

59. *Chilling Adventures of Sabrina,* "Chapter Three: The Trial of Sabrina Spellman," 00:50:48.

60. Sandor Klapcsik, *Liminality in Fantastic Fiction: A Poststructuralist Approach* (Jefferson, North Carolina, and London: McFarland, 2012), 14. Emphasis in original.

61. *Chilling Adventures of Sabrina,* season 1, episode 4, "Chapter Four: Witch Academy," directed by Rob Seidenglanz, written by Diana Thorland, featuring Kiernan Shipka, Miranda Otto, Lucy Davis, and Richard Coyle, released October 26, 2018, on Netflix, www.netflix.com/watch/80230074?trackId=200257859: 00:03:33.

62. *Chilling Adventures of Sabrina,* season 1, episode 7, "Chapter Seven: Feast of Feasts," by Nguyen Viet, written by Oanh Ly, featuring Kiernan Shipka, Miranda Otto, Lucy Davis, and Tati Gabrielle, released October 26, 2018, on Netflix, www .netflix.com/watch/80230077?trackId=200257859: 00:04:30.

63. *Chilling Adventures of Sabrina,* "Chapter Seven: Feast of Feasts," 00:05:07.

64. Turner, *The Forest of Symbols*, 105.

65. *Chilling Adventures of Sabrina,* "Chapter Seven: Feast of Feasts," 00:05:12.

66. Byron and Deans, "Teen Gothic," 97.

67. Byron and Deans, "Teen Gothic," 102.

68. Dara Downey, Ian Kinane, and Elizabeth Parker, "Introduction Locating Liminality: Space, Place, and the In-Between," in *Landscapes of Liminality: Between Space and Place* (London and New York: Rowman & Littlefield International, 2016), 6, emphasis added.

69. Ute Hüsken and Donna Lynne Seamone, "The Denial of Ritual and Its Return—An Introduction," *Journal of Ritual Studies* 27, no. 1 (2013): 2.

70. Courtney Tink and Jenni Lauwrens, "'A Face Like This Is Hard to Beat': Negotiating Lilith in the Postfeminist Media Economy," *Communicatio*, July 25, 2022, 10.

PART 4

"Top Boy, Sabrina?": Gender and Gender Performance

Chapter 10

"I'm sick of being the afterthought, the joke"

Hilda Spellman's Empowering Domesticity in Netflix's Chilling Adventures of Sabrina

Katie E. Cline

Netflix's series *Chilling Adventures of Sabrina* (2018–20)—an adaptation of the Archie Comics series of the same name (2014–present)—features an array of diverse, complex female characters, but scholars do not typically consider Aunt Hilda (Lucy Davis) among them, likely because of socially constructed ideas that define feminine strength by traits associated with masculinity rather than femininity. Hilda and her career-savvy sister Zelda (Miranda Otto) raise their half-witch, half-mortal niece Sabrina (Kiernan Shipka) after the deaths of their brother and sister-in-law, with Zelda serving as the strict disciplinarian and Hilda as the caring homemaker. This family dynamic immediately acknowledges the feminist and matriarchal undercurrents of *Chilling Adventures of Sabrina* (*CAoS*), which are amplified by supporting female characters like Rosalind "Roz" Walker (Jaz Sinclair), a mortal friend of Sabrina's with a powerful sense of self, keen intuition, and the ability to literally see the future; Prudence Blackwood (Tati Gabrielle), the mean girl-turned-vigilante who wields longswords valiantly; and Madam Satan/Lilith (Michelle Gomez), Adam's first wife and the mother of demons.[1] Because of the stereotype that a "strong" female character is one that possesses tradition-ally masculine qualities and forsakes that which is conventionally feminine, the audience is likely tempted to disregard Hilda as a feminist role model, but her stereotypically feminine skills—like healing, cooking, and knitting—are an integral part of keeping the family safe and helping them overcome the show's antagonists.

Hilda is the bubbly, kind-hearted—and occasionally overwhelmed and bumbling—caretaker aunt, whereas her sister Zelda is the smart, straightforward, de facto leader of the family, but Hilda's domestic skills prove to be as critical to the plot as Zelda's drive to become Directrix of the Academy of Unseen Arts. While Zelda's independent, proud, and assertive nature is usually expected of female leads, Hilda proves to be equally competent despite having the opposite skillset; she is able to heal Sabrina and her friends from potentially fatal curses and injuries, and she takes pride in domestic hobbies like reading romance novels and watching sitcoms. While many supporting female characters on television shows are written as one-dimensional plot devices, Aunt Hilda embodies two personas that rarely co-exist in a single character—the homemaker and the badass—emphasizing the power in feminine duality.

Rather than hindering her, Hilda's feminine skills are used to showcase her strength as a witch. In "'Leaving my girlhood behind': Woke Witches and Feminist Liminality in *Chilling Adventures of Sabrina*," Megan Henesy argues that *CAoS* "represents the politics of feminism in its reimagining of bubbly blonde Sabrina the Teenage Witch as a gothic-inspired feminist icon for the millennial age,"[2] but I argue that Hilda is as valid a feminist role model as her titular niece because she represents an overlooked and underexplored faction of feminist characters on television—the homemaker. Western society valorizes, idealizes, and centralizes youth and conventional beauty—represented in *CAoS* by the young female characters like Sabrina, Roz, and Prudence—but Hilda broadens the definition of what it means to be a strong female character in contemporary entertainment. Though consumers of media might assume that a woman must be thin, assertive, and traditionally masculine to be a strong character—because of that archetype's frequent, prevalent depiction in twenty-first century media—Hilda invites audiences to view a fat, middle-aged woman with penchants for baking and knitting as another embodiment of feminist ideals. This chapter draws on work from Sarah Ward and Laurel Zwissler to first identify how current interpretations of strong female characters are a direct legacy of the New Woman movement. Then, it establishes the longstanding symbolism and cultural connotations between witches and feminism in popular culture, followed by an examination of the persistent connections between witchcraft, feminism, and sexuality, paying special attention to how women who abstain from sexual intercourse are treated. Finally, it analyzes how *CAoS*'s multifaceted characterization of Hilda redefines feminist role models by encouraging young female audiences to see themselves as strong, valuable women, regardless of their domestic interests or skill sets.

HILDA SPELLMAN, A NEW NEW WOMAN

The "strong female leads" popularized in twenty-first century media are the latest iteration of the New Woman legacy. The New Woman was a popular social movement among White, middle-and-upper class women in England and, later, the United States that bled into the works of many Victorian-era authors. The term "New Woman" referred to "women who exercised control over their own lives be it personal, social, or economic," and the movement "eschewed the traditional path of marriage and motherhood favored by most of American and English society."³ Though the phrase itself was not coined until approximately 1894 by Sarah Grand and Maria Louise Ramé (under the pseudonym Ouida), the idea of women seeking freedom from restrictive Victorian gender roles permeated earlier works. A New Woman in society was "a feminist and a social reformer [or] a poet or a playwright who addressed female suffrage," and in literature, she sometimes appeared as a woman "whose excellent education [left] her intellectually isolated from her family and friends," like Grace Melbury in Thomas Hardy's *The Woodlanders* (1887).⁴ For Victorian women, being a New Woman meant claiming for their own that which had been reserved exclusively for men—be it additional education, better jobs, higher income, or more social independence—a sentiment echoed by later waves of feminism. In *CAoS*, Zelda's aspirations to climb the Church of Night's political ladder, Sabrina's campaign for the position of Top Boy at the Academy of Unseen Arts, Prudence's proclivity with weapons, and the Walker family's maternal lineage of the Cunning align more with the Victorians' definition of a New Woman, as each woman's story attempts to reclaim aspects of her society that have traditionally been held by men. Hilda, conversely, seems to conform to the meek and passive attitude of a "proper" Victorian woman, and the full potential of her domestic power is only revealed incrementally throughout the series.

Hilda Spellman embraces that which the New Woman of Victorian England rejected. In "Chapter Twenty-Nine: The Eldritch Dark" (4:1), the coven names Hilda "the Mother" as a tribute to the goddess Hecate, who embodies the Maiden, Mother, and Crone.⁵ The direct correlation between Hilda and motherhood seems to contradict the goals of the New Woman movement, and, when added to her expressive emotional personality, most viewers will have been conditioned to dismiss her. However, I argue that Hilda is an example of twenty-first century entertainment redefining the parameters of feminine empowerment. Hilda does not reject all New Woman ideals, though; rather, she shows that domesticity and independence are not mutually exclusive. She still pursues an education at the Academy of Unseen Arts when she is young; she holds multiple jobs, including a barista at Cerberus Books, a romance novelist, and the co-owner of Spellman Sisters Mortuary; she remains unmarried for the first several hundred years of her life, and chooses to be childless until Sabrina is left in her and Zelda's care. Domestic skills are only part of Hilda's character, and by allowing her to be a multifaceted woman who does not completely conform to either the "traditional" or the "New Woman" label, *CAoS* enables audiences, especially women, to view domesticity as a form of power. In a pivotal confrontation scene in "Chapter Twenty-Three: Heavy Is the Crown" (3:3), Hilda stands up to Zelda's condescending comments about her career, culminating in an exchange that articulates Hilda's willpower and bravery:

> Zelda: Now is not the time to reinvent yourself as a pulp novelist. We are in a moment of grave crisis. Your responsibility is to the Academy, and only the Academy.
>
> Hilda: No, it's not. It's not. I care, of course I care. I'll do what I can to help protect these little lambs. But the Academy, it's your calling, it's not mine. You wanted to be Directrix. You wanted to be high priestess, not me.
>
> Zelda: You are a Spellman. You have a duty—
>
> Hilda: I have a duty to myself to be happy.
>
> Zelda: We'll talk about this tonight.
>
> Hilda: No, we won't, because I'm going to the carnival tonight with Dr. Cee. So you cook your own dinner.[6]

Hilda's primary goal, to care for the "little lambs" (the ill students at the school), is domestic in nature, but she does not depict this goal as less worthy than her sister's administrative goals. As the scene ends, Hilda maintains control of the conversation, telling Zelda to "cook [her] own dinner," implying that it is a task Zelda is not comfortable with or even capable of. Viewers are prompted to see Hilda's defense of the domestic as a moment of self-empowerment and freedom, while Zelda's lofty career goals have left her, ironically, dependent on Hilda for basic tasks.

Historically, the New Woman movement "initiated the process of redefining what it means to be a young woman in the modern world,"[7] and Hilda's characterization in *CAoS* works to achieve similar ends in the twenty-first century. By elevating Hilda's domesticity, *CAoS* reflects a shift in the social constructs surrounding women's roles. Like a pendulum, social expectations once swung toward the domestic, emphasizing that a "good woman" should be a meek and motherly angel in the house[8]; feeling trapped, many women pushed back by encouraging others to embrace that which had once been denied them, from masculine clothing to masculine careers and mannerisms.

To embrace traditional femininity was to embrace the old and oppressive status quo. But the danger of a pendulum metaphor is that it attempts to dictate femininity as an "either/or" decision, and further examination of Hilda's character shows that women do not have to be physically powerful to be empowered and that domesticity should also be considered a valid marker of a woman's strength. To fully understand why Hilda's domestic empowerment is significant, this essay will first untangle the history of women, witchcraft, and feminine expectations.

IT'S NOT A PHASE: WITCHES, WOMEN, AND POPULAR CULTURE OVER TIME

Entertainment centering around witches is anything but novel, as society's fascination with magic, witchcraft, and femininity has persisted for generations. For example, Americans have long been presented with stories across media platforms that feature women who utilize witchcraft and magic for both good and ill. On stage, Abigail Williams in Arthur Miller's *The Crucible* (1957) uses her town's fear of witchcraft to incite mass hysteria, and Carol S. Lashof's play *Witch Hunt* (2019) follows the character Tituba—who is accused of witchcraft in Miller's play—and restructures her story. On television, witches have appeared as the central character—such as *Bewitched*'s Samantha Stephens (ABC, 1964–72) or *Sabrina the Teenage Witch*'s Sabrina Spellman (ABC, 1996–2000/The WB, 2000–03)—or primary storyline— *American Horror Story: Coven* (FX, 2013–14)—as well as featured characters in many supernatural series, including *Buffy the Vampire Slayer*'s Willow Rosenberg (The WB, 1997–2001/UPN, 2002–03), *Supernatural*'s Rowena MacLeod (The WB, 2005–06/The CW, 2006–20), and *The Vampire Diaries*' Bonnie Bennett (The CW, 2009–17). Several cult films of the 1990s centered around witches, such as *Hocus Pocus* (1993), *The Craft* (1996), and *Practical Magic* (1998)—even Disney Channel Original Movies such as the *Halloweentown* (1998–2006) and *Twitches* series (2005–07). Addressing the "perennial popularity" of witchcraft in entertainment, film critic Sarah Ward notes in the article "All of Them Witches: Individuality, Conformity, and the Occult On Screen" that the term witchcraft "has become shorthand for preternatural opposition to or deviance from normality,"[9] arguing that the near-cultural obsession with it is rooted in "societal needs to both fit in and stand out."[10] Witches thus mark a tense intersection between individuality and conformity, an intersection explored explicitly and implicitly in popular culture.

Another contributing factor to witchcraft's popularity in media is its historical integration with feminism, a topic that is oft dissected in literature, television, and film. It could be argued that witchcraft and accusations of witchcraft have always been feminist issues, but there is clear evidence that politicizes witchcraft as a tool of feminist movements over the last 130 years. The suffragists of the first-wave feminist movement—generally considered to be from 1880–1920—advocated that women and witches both experience what Laurel Zwissler, a professor of religion at Central Michigan University, calls "victimization by patriarchy,"[11] comparing early modern witch hunts to the relegation of women to the domestic sphere.[12] The first wave of feminism focused on shared gender identity, but by the second-wave movement of the 1960s and 1970s, activists began to embrace the possibility of genuine magic in the historical witchcraft accusations, believing that feminists, like witches, *were* doing something different, powerful, and special.[13] Second-wave feminists believed that it was these women's "natural knowledge"[14] or "skilled abilities" in healing and midwifery, their agricultural knowledge, and their financial, social, and sexual independence that frightened men.[15] Retroactively, witches began to be considered "the original feminist[s]" because they were "political rebel[s]" who were "not properly subservient to patriarchy."[16] During the third wave of feminism in the 1990s and continuing into the present-day fourth wave, the witch became colloquially synonymous with feminism. Even more so than second-wave feminists, third- and fourth-wave feminists embraced the qualities of witchcraft that first-wave feminists skirted, specifically sexuality. Along with infanticide and cannibalism, "indiscriminate sex" was considered one of the "three heresies" of early modern witchcraft,[17] so in order to reclaim witchcraft as an empowering identity, witches and sexuality became closely linked in the public eye and in entertainment. (This chapter will go into more detail about sexuality in *CAoS* in the next section.)

Feminism and witchcraft also emphasize community, dating back to first-wave feminists who drew parallels between historically persecuted witches and the women of the late nineteenth and early twentieth centuries. When faced with discrimination, popular culture's witches band together for protection and camaraderie, usually in a biological family or a family-like group such as a coven. One example of a family-based coven is the Russo family in *Wizards of Waverly Place* (Disney, 2007–12). All members, save for the mother, have magical abilities, allowing the three siblings, including only daughter Alex (Selena Gomez), to learn magic together. Isabel Sterling's young adult novel *These Witches Don't Burn* (2019), however, uses a larger, more diverse coven to explore the complicated emotions that arise when protagonist Hannah's ex-girlfriend is also part of her magical community. When a lone witch is prominently featured, finding community becomes an essential part of her storyline, such as in *Harry Potter and the Sorcerer's Stone* (1997) when Hermione Granger learns she is a witch and must leave the Muggle world for the wizarding world, or in the graphic novel *Witches of Brooklyn* (2020), when Effie moves in with her witch aunts following her mother's death. In each of the aforementioned cases, the young witches are provided with "a place to belong, rather than a force to be afraid of," which Ward defines as a coven.[18] Ward further shows how covens can be grounded in community, reading the coven formed by Nancy, Bonnie, Rochelle, and Sarah in *The Craft* as "an act of reclamation" that allows its members to "find their identities, unleash their preferred selves on their peers, try to conquer rather than cower through their adolescence, and learn the consequences of using their difference for selfish means."[19] However, covens can also become microcosms of oppression that discourage change and repress its individual members who do not conform to the group's dominant ideology, as happens to Hilda.

The Spellmans' coven, the Church of Night, emphasizes the tension between individuality and conformity. To Hilda, her coven is a source of anxiety and resentment, as exemplified by an exchange with Sabrina in "Chapter Two: The Dark Baptism" (1:2):

> Sabrina: Aunt Hilda, did you ever have any doubts about your Dark Baptism?
>
> Hilda: When I was your age, I signed my name in the *Book of the Beast*. I mean . . . us girls didn't have any options back then. It's just simply what was done. Do I have regrets? You mustn't tell your aunt Zelda this, but . . . some days, some nights . . . I dream that I am walking into the Greendale woods, in the peak of dry season, with a lit torch in each hand, so that I'd watch the whole forest burn, like so much kindling.[20]

Beginning early in the series, showrunner Roberto Aguirre-Sacasa emphasizes Hilda's feelings of powerlessness and inferiority to Zelda, and the insecurities revealed in her conversation with Sabrina provide a foil for her later character development. In an interview with *Variety*, Aguirre-Sacasa acknowledges the connotation of witches in the twenty-first century, saying, "when you're dealing with witchcraft, you're dealing with themes of female sexuality and female empowerment—to be a witch is to have powers and be empowered."[21] As this reading of Hilda shows, there is no longer a single, overriding definition of what it means for a female character to be "empowered," and the word should now include anything a woman takes joy or finds purpose in.

For Hilda, empowerment comes when she embraces that which differentiates her from Zelda: her domesticity. Rather than trying to deny her identity, she finds happiness with a partner who shares her values. Even though that happiness comes in the traditional form of heterosexual marriage, Dr. Cerberus's (Alessandro Juliani) proposal in "Chapter Twenty-Three: Heavy is the Crown" (3:3) centers on accepting Hilda, not exalting the ideal housewife:

Hilda: I didn't exactly expect [Zelda] to like what I'd written in my book.

Dr. Cerberus: She'll get over it, Hilda.

Hilda: Well, I don't know that she will, Dr. Cee.[22] I mean, she has never yet accepted that we're just different witches, and we just want different things and different lives. I just want to grow old in a little cottage with a fire and my spiders and a dog. Not a stuffed one! And I just, I don't know, I wanna knit and read and watch reruns of *The Munsters* on T.V.

Dr. Cerberus: I want that, too, Hilda.

Hilda: Aww.

Dr. Cerberus: I've wanted it for a while now. Hilda?

Hilda: Yeah? [Dr. Cee gets down on one knee] You all right? What are you doing? No. Dr. Cee.

Dr. Cerberus: I've been waiting for the right moment to ask. Hildegarde Antoinette Spellman, will you marry me?

Hilda: Yeah. Yeah, absolutely.[23]

Hilda's relationship with Dr. Cerberus contrasts the third and fourth-wave feminist ideals described in the previous section; it is not hypersexual, but, rather, it is distinctly monogamous and domestic. While Hilda's role in their relationship echoes the patriarchal gender divide that first-wave feminists initially used witches to push back against, Zwissler's idea that "depictions of witches within entertainment media have evolved to the point where almost any witch character can default to feminist archetype"[24] informs audiences' understanding of Hilda as an empowered female character. Her unique combination of traditional gender roles in the wake of feminist self-identification with witches suggests that Hilda's characterization in *CAoS* is a new iteration of the feminist witch, one that embraces the complex histories of feminism and witchcraft and integrates them into one multifaceted woman.

DAMNED IF YOU DO, DAMNED IF YOU DON'T: SEXUALITY & WITCHES

One underlying connection between women and witches continues to be sexuality. Ward uses Robert Eggers's 2015 film *The Witch* to illustrate how "simply existing in witchcraft-fearing times [was] a dangerous act"; the female protagonist, Thomasin (Anya Taylor-Joy), "is singled out because she stands out, and, in one of the strongest manifestations of the fear of femininity, particularly of the blossoming, pubescent kind, she stands out because she's a teenage girl on the cusp of womanhood."[25] Magic often presents itself in adolescence—as is the case in the *Harry Potter* series, where children receive their Hogwarts letters at age eleven, and in *Halloweentown*, where Marnie begins her witch training at age thirteen—rendering it a supernatural manifestation of puberty. Just as puberty—and menstruation for girls—has been perceived as shameful in the public sphere, witches are often tasked with hiding their magic from mortals, lest they be shunned or killed for that which makes them different. This physical marker of coming-of-age often leads to an exultation of sexual exploits for boys and a suppression of those same actions for girls, but more and more contemporary media, like *CAoS*, are showing the nuanced nature of sex for women and teenage girls.

Before looking at *CAoS*'s treatment of sex, it is necessary to look at the long intertwining history of witches, female sexuality, shame, and misogyny. Zwissler notes that early modern society viewed witchcraft as a "pact which enslaved women sexually to the Devil"[26] and argues that "the [contemporary] feminist Witch image is deliberately constructed in opposition to the historical stereotype of the diabolical witch."[27] To completely deconstruct the negative connotations of the diabolical witch—an early modern term that refers to a woman whose magic derives from the worship of Satan[28]—feminist witches need to have sex-positive attitudes. Such attitudes purposefully push back against the historical belief that a woman's feelings of sexual attraction were laid on her by the Devil and help to untangle the preconception that a woman's sexuality should be regulated. Perhaps because of this deep association of witchcraft with sex and the recent cultural push to reclaim female sexuality, witch-centric stories suit young adult media, where sexual escapades are already common. Depending on the subgenre, the sex itself can be portrayed as casual and funny or serious and momentous, and *CAoS* chooses to approach the topic of sexuality with gravity and respect.

Roberto Aguirre-Sacasa, the *CAoS* showrunner, is also the showrunner of *Riverdale* (The CW, 2017–present), and while both shows are adapted from Archie Comics characters and are canonically set in the neighboring towns of Riverdale and Greendale, Aguirre-Sacasa admits that the two series have different tones, calling *CAoS* "more innocent." In a move of simultaneously contemporary and archaic ideology, Aguirre-Sacasa acknowledges that young people are sexually active while mistakenly conflating maturity with sexual experience, saying that *CAoS* has "a core innocence that is [different] from *Riverdale*" because "the *Riverdale* kids are always having sex" and "acting a lot more like grownups," whereas Sabrina is "really a sixteen-year-old girl who has not had sex and Harvey is a boy, sixteen, who hasn't had sex."[29] Aguirre-Sacasa's suggestion that sexual activity constitutes the *Riverdale* teens' "grownup" behavior is concerning given the coming-of-age nature of *CAoS*, because it prompts audiences to assume that Sabrina must have sex in order to "grow" like her *Riverdale* contemporaries, and it is not a stretch to assume that virginal characters, in general, are less valued in this universe.

Sixteen-year-old Sabrina is not the only female virgin when the series begins. Hilda has also never had sex—another example of her traditional femininity—and, true to stigmas surrounding adult virgins, she has a deep anxiety about people's reactions to her virginity. In "Chapter Five: Dreams in a Witch House" (1:5), a sleep demon is set upon the Spellman house, lulling each family member into a nightmare-fueled sleep. Hilda's nightmare centers around Zelda mocking her about her virginity:

> Zelda: You do realize you're going to have to put out [on your date]. That's the only way you'll ever hold his interest.
>
> Hilda: Please just . . . help me pick [an outfit] out because I want to look my best.
>
> Zelda: Good luck. You know what they say: "You can't polish a turd."
>
> Hilda: Devil's Hooves, Zelda, be supportive for once!
>
> Zelda: Don't you take that tone with me.
>
> Hilda: You never want me to be happy, do you? You've never wanted me to live me [*sic*] life. I'm sick to death of it! I'm sick to death of being the put upon one. I'm sick of being treated like dirt by my own flesh and blood. I'm sick of being the afterthought, the joke.
>
> Zelda: You'll never be happy, Hilda. Because who could love you?[30]

Hilda does not harbor shame or uncertainty about her abstinence; rather, her anxiety stems from her sister's response to her decisions. In this nightmare, Zelda takes on the perspective of an extreme sect that holds frequent, indiscriminate sex as a pillar of feminism. While Zelda gives voice to a particular line of thought, *CAoS* collectively leaves sex as a personal decision for each of its characters and does not let sexual experience determine a character's power.

Because Hilda is not ashamed of her virginity, she supports others' right to choose to be sexually active or not. In a conversation with Sabrina in "Chapter Fourteen: Lupercalia" (2:3) about the Lupercalia festival, Hilda and Zelda advocate for opposing but equally important positions on the Academy of Unseen Arts' tradition. Originally a fertility festival, Zelda describes the current Lupercalia celebration as "a frenzy of orgiastic carnality" and "a symphony of sensuality and pleasure, not shame and regret."[31] Hilda is more hesitant about Lupercalia, making sure that Sabrina is not pressured into having sex during the festival and assuring her that participation is voluntary. Both adults verbalize key factors of fourth-wave feminism. While Zelda's position emphasizes female sexual pleasure, which patriarchal society and popular culture has conventionally ignored in favor of more visible results like impregnation or the male orgasm, Hilda's position highlights a vital part of all that her character stands for: choice. Just as Hilda reminds Sabrina that she has the choice to engage in sexual activity or not, her existence as an adult virgin who is loved by herself and others reminds viewers that the most constructive form of feminism is one that is inclusive and respects each person's choices for their individual lives and bodies.

CAoS characters explore different approaches to female sexuality, but the language used to describe sex leaves audiences with the message that the decision of when or if to have sex does not affect one's identity as a witch. For example, after talking to her aunts about the sexual overtones of the Lupercalia festival, Sabrina seeks out her best friend Roz's advice about having sex for the first time. Roz frames the conversation around Sabrina's comfort, emphasizing that she should trust her potential partner and that he should not be pressuring her.[32] But one word with heavy sexual connotation that does not appear in any discussion of sex in the series is "slut." According to the *Oxford English Dictionary,* the derogatory term has been used since the early fifteenth century and refers to "a sexually promiscuous or lascivious woman," "a female prostitute," or "a vulgar, impudent, or disreputable woman,"[33] but this perspective is not voiced in *CAoS* by any of the characters. Sabrina and Hilda do not criticize those who are sexually active, and Sabrina is not shamed for changing her mind when she has sex with Nick Scratch (Gavin Leatherwood) in "Chapter Thirty-Three: Deus Ex Machina" (4:5).[34] This sex-positive message aligns with *CAoS*'s "witch-positive" message, as the show recasts much of what was historically condemnable about witches as something to be proud of. When Sabrina announces her and Roz's student council campaign, she says that they are "running as witches," which means they are "powerful, disruptive women, champions of the oppressed, supporters of the othered, unapologetic feminists, allies to all those who live in the shadows of the patriarchy, reminders that the shadow has its own power."[35] Nothing in Sabrina's definition of "witch" calls for any of the traditional markers of strength typically associated with men and "strong" female characters like physicality, aggression, or emotional stoicism. If witches are synonymous with feminism as Zwissler notes, then, by Sabrina's own words, Hilda's gentle power should be acknowledged in those ranks, too.

GOOD WITCH, BAD BITCH, OR BOTH: DOMESTICITY AS POWER

Thus far, I have discussed Hilda's domesticity in terms of its adherence to the mercurial social guidelines of femininity but have yet to examine how Hilda wields her domesticity as a weapon in the show. Despite Aguirre-Sacasa's description of the show as "more innocent," *CAoS* is riddled with violence—murder, mutilation, and sadomasochistic sex demons abound in the series—and Hilda's subtle approach to violence is quietly dangerous in contrast to characters like Prudence who battle with physical weapons.

In "Chapter Sixteen: Blackwood" (2:5), Hilda commits her first on-screen murder by disguising cyanide in almond cookies and inviting her mark over for tea. The victim, Shirley Jackson (Rochelle Greenwood), is a minor antagonist in Part Two and a former classmate of Hilda and Zelda's. Shirley harasses Zelda as she transitions to her new job as a teacher at the Academy of Unseen Arts, and Hilda takes it upon herself to defend her sister:

> Hilda: Oh, Shirley, Shirley. So . . . so folks . . . folks tend to get the wrong impression of me. They always think I'm meek and mild. You know, always the bridesmaid, never the bride. Story of my life. And, oh, for sure, I mean, here I am, playing Zelda's maid of dishonor. But I'm gonna . . . I'm gonna tell you a little tiny secret about me. [. . .] If you hurt my family, there will be Heaven to pay.
>
> Shirley Jackson: Threatening me, Hilda?
>
> Hilda: Oh!
>
> Shirley Jackson: You should know. Ever since Zelda put that earworm in my head, I've been wearing a protection that guards me against all magical attacks.
>
> Hilda: I . . . I would assume nothing less, my love. That's why you're eating those almond cookies. 'Cause almond hides the taste of cyanide, you know.
>
> Shirley Jackson: [chokes, dies, head hits table]
>
> Hilda: Oops. That'll bruise.[36]

The flippant way that Hilda acknowledges Shirley's death is equal parts humorous and unsettling. There is an emotional catharsis that viewers get from seeing Hilda outsmart her sister's tormentor, but they also see a new side of the sweet, maternal aunt—one that is ruthless and calculating. In this scene, Hilda's weapon of choice is her baking; her method recalls a study conducted by the FBI and reported on by *The Washington Post* that shows that women are seven times as likely as men to poison their victims.[37] Because most poisons need to be ingested, poisoning has long been considered a feminine weapon, as women have traditionally handled food preparation and house-hold care.[383940] Hilda, then, is a perfect candidate for "death by domesticity," mixing a soft, feminine activity like baking with the violent act of murder.

Shirley is not the only character to die at Hilda's hand; she is also responsible for the death of Circe the Pagan witch (Lucie Guest) in the Part Three finale, "Chapter Twenty-Eight: Sabrina Is Legend" (3:8):

> Hilda: You going somewhere? It's just that I was remembering the day that we first met. You were so complimentary about my talents as, um, well . . . What do you call it? Oh, yeah . . . a weaver. [shows voodoo doll to Circe as she approaches her] Uh! Before you toddle off, I just wanted to show you some of my other talents. All right, my love?
>
> Circe: [shakes head no]
>
> Hilda: [uses voodoo doll to break Circe's arms and legs before snapping her neck][41]

Hilda's domestic talents of baking and knitting enable her to kill without suspicion from those around her, making "weaver" an apt description of the woman who effortlessly combines the identities of delicate femininity and forceful masculinity. Emma E. Fridel and James Alan Fox's article "Gender Differences in Patterns and Trends in U.S. Homicide, 1976–2017" indicates that women are more likely to kill in self-defense or to protect the "emotional well-being of themselves or their children" but that men "use violence as an offensive move to establish superiority."[42] For Hilda, Circe's murder is both revenge and protection, as Circe and the other Pagan witches were attempting to destroy the Church of Night and sacrifice Sabrina's friends to their newly-resurrected god. In killing Shirley and Circe, Hilda protects her family without sacrificing her traditional femininity. Whereas some female characters on the show are given a level of physicality on par with hyper-masculine characters, Hilda creates similar death and damage using skills that are traditionally feminine.

Hilda's feminized acts of violence are an intentional choice, because other prominent female characters in the show use more traditionally masculine weapons, particularly Prudence Blackwood and Zelda. Prudence's weapons of choice are two swords she uses to slice, stab, and decapitate various enemies. The proximity required to strike her victims makes Prudence's murders significantly messier than Hilda's preferred method of poisoning. Additionally, the elongated, phallic shape of the swords and the connotations of these weapons with medieval knights, all of whom were men, code these murders as distinctly masculine in nature. Zelda, too, uses masculine-preferred methods when she kills—and specifically when she kills Hilda. Zelda kills and resurrects Hilda twice, once by bludgeoning her with a hammer in "Chapter Two: The Dark Baptism" (1:2)[43] and once by shooting her in "Chapter Twenty-Six: All of Them Witches" (3:6).[44] While *The Post* notes that 90 percent of all murderers are men[45]—meaning there are significantly more male murderers than female ones—men favor bludgeoning more than women do, bludgeoning their victims approximately 21 percent of the time compared to women who do so 19 percent of the time.[46] Gun violence is also distinctly masculine in the United States, where guns are used in two-thirds of all murders committed by men compared to less than half of all murders committed by women.[47] Fridel and Fox note that between 1976 and 2017, women were far more likely to suffer gun violence at the hands of men than vice versa—men shoot women 14.5 percent of the time, whereas women shoot men 5.3 percent of the time[48]—so Zelda using a gun to kill Hilda reinforces the established depiction of Zelda as the more active, masculine sister and Hilda as the more passive, feminine sister.

Just as we have seen Hilda's femininity encompass characteristics of Victorian idealization as well as contemporary fourth-wave feminism, her domesticity, too, is used in multiple ways: for violence, as seen in her murders, and for deliverance. In the episode "Chapter Thirty-Two: The Imp of the Perverse" (4:4), the characters are stripped of their memories and trapped in an alternate reality where Reverend Blackwood (Richard Coyle) has taken control of the Church of Night and the city of Greendale, forcing anyone who opposes him underground. Hilda leads the faction of resistance and houses the rebels in a secret room in the back of the bookstore where she works, evoking images of classic works of literature that correlate books to intellectual resistance, such as *The Diary of a Young Girl* (1952) by Anne Frank and *Fahrenheit 451* (1953) by Ray Bradbury. When Ambrose's (Chance Perdomo) memory is overtaken by the magic of the alternate world, Hilda devises how to unlock the powers of the Stone of Omphalos (4:4): "Well, I mean, he said it was obvious, didn't he? Well, all right then, why don't we do what Cronus did and eat the stone? . . . I could make it into a stone soup."[49] After drinking the soup, the characters have their memories restored, defeat Blackwood, and return to their own timeline, acts that are spurred forward by Hilda's domesticity. Hilda retains no memories of Sabrina as her niece or the impending threat of the Eldritch Terrors in the alternate universe, but she still relies on her cooking skills, cementing domesticity as an integral part of her personhood. In this way, the series subtly separates the idea of domesticity from maternal caregiving and elevates the former as an empowering, specialized skillset.

Duality—be it the use of domestic life skills for both murder and rescue or the existence of violence and compassion within one woman—is a recurring quality in the scholarly conversation surrounding witches. Ward identifies a similar "war" between individuality and conformity and argues that contemporary media about witches offers "multifaceted interpretations of daring to defy convention—or the consequences of simply being suspected of such—that tunnel to the heart of societal needs to both fit in and stand out."[50] Whereas societies once damned witches for their differences from the prototypical woman, popular culture has begun to reclaim the witch, aligning witches with feminist movements that embrace female sexuality and women in positions of authority. *CAoS* places Hilda somewhere in the middle of this spectrum of conformity and individuality, as she is both traditionally feminine and undeniably powerful. Domesticity—as it is equated to femininity and, in some views, weakness—is not the opposite of strength, but, rather, the former should be viewed as a subset of the latter.

While this chapter has explored a close reading of Hilda Spellman as she is portrayed in Netflix's *Chilling Adventures of Sabrina*, the context of the series' production should also be considered, particularly the presence of women in the *CAoS* writers' room. Of the sixteen different writers credited on the series, nine are women, and a woman wrote or co-wrote twenty-one of the thirty-six episodes in the series. Calls for intersectional feminism have increasingly come from all feminists in the last decade—not just academics and activists—and its application will create a more authentic viewing experience for rapidly diversifying audiences. Perhaps as creative spaces become more open to women—specifically, queer women and women of color—and as they occupy more executive roles, the women on-screen will reflect a similar diversity of character, ideology, and experience.

Far from relegating Hilda to the supporting role of sidekick, *CAoS* does not promote one form of "strong woman" over another and celebrates an array of women, each with their own strengths and weaknesses. These women are all flawed in some way—Sabrina is rash; Prudence is proud; Roz is insecure; Lilith is selfish; Zelda is narrow-minded; Hilda is timid—but they are all multifaceted women, making *CAoS* a refreshing series about the power—magical or otherwise—inherent in all women, regardless of their pursuits. In a pushback against a dominant strain of thinking that "strong" equates to "masculine," Hilda Spellman encourages audiences, especially young women, to embrace the strength of the domestic.

BIBLIOGRAPHY

Buzell, Greg. "Daughters of Decadence: The New Woman in the Victorian *Fin de Siècle*," *The British Library*, 2014. bl.uk/romantics-and-victorians/articles/daughters-of-decadence-the-new-woman-in-the-victorian-fin-de-siecle.

Chilling Adventures of Sabrina, Season 1, episode 1, "Chapter One: October Country." Directed by Lee Toland Krieger, written by Roberto Aguirre-Sacasa, featuring Kiernan Shipka, Miranda Otto, Lucy Davis, and Chance Perdomo.

Released October 26, 2018, Netflix, www.netflix.com/watch/80230071?trackId=200257859.

———, Season 1, episode 5, "Chapter Five: Dreams in a Witch House." Directed by Maggie Kiley, written by Matthew Barry, featuring Kiernan Shipka, Miranda Otto, Lucy Davis, and Chance Perdomo. Released October 26, 2018, Netflix, www.netflix.com/watch/80230075?trackId=200257859.

———, Season 2, episode 1, "Chapter Twelve: The Epiphany." Directed by Kevin Rodney Sullivan, written by Roberto Aguirre-Sacasa, featuring Kiernan Shipka, Miranda Otto, Lucy Davis, and Lachlan Watson. Released April 5, 2019, Netflix, www.netflix.com/watch/80230082?trackId=200257859.

———, Season 2, episode 3. "Chapter Fourteen: Lupercalia." Directed by Salli Richardson-Whitfield, written by Oanh Ly, featuring Kiernan Shipka, Miranda Otto, Lucy Davis, and Chance Perdomo. Released April 5, 2019, Netflix, www.netflix.com/watch/80230084?trackId=200257859.

———, Season 2, episode 5, "Chapter Sixteen: Blackwood." Directed by Alex Pillai, written by Matthew Barry, featuring Kiernan Shipka, Miranda Otto, Lucy Davis, and Richard Coyle. Released April 5, 2019, Netflix, www.netflix.com/watch/80230086?trackId=14170289.

———, Season 3, episode 3, "Chapter Twenty-Three: Heavy Is the Crown." Directed by Rob Seidenglanz, written by Oanh Ly, featuring Kiernan Shipka, Miranda Otto, Lucy Davis, and Chance Perdomo. Released January 24, 2020, Netflix, www.netflix.com/watch/81062654?trackId=200257859.

———, Season 3, episode 6, "Chapter Twenty-Six: All of Them Witches." Directed by Michael Goi, written by Joshua Conkel, featuring Kiernan Shipka, Miranda Otto, Lucy Davis, and Sam Corlett. Released January 24, 2020, Netflix, www.netflix.com/watch/81062660?trackId=200257859.

———, Season 3, episode 8. "Chapter Twenty-Eight: Sabrina Is Legend." Directed by Rob Seidenglanz, written by Roberto Aguirre-Sacasa and Daniel King, featuring Kiernan Shipka, Miranda Otto, Lucy Davis, and Sam Corlett. Released January 24, 2020, Netflix, www.netflix.com/watch/81062659?trackId=200257859.

———, Season 4, episode 1, "Chapter Twenty-Nine: The Eldritch Dark." Directed by Jeff Woolnough, written by Roberto Aguirre-Sacasa and Gigi Swift, featuring Kiernan Shipka, Miranda Otto, Lucy Davis, and Chance Perdomo. Released December 31, 2020, Netflix, www.netflix.com/watch/81062660?trackId=200257859.

———, Season 4, episode 4, "Chapter Thirty-Two: The Imp of the Perverse." Directed by Antonio Negret, written by Christianne Hedtke, featuring Kiernan Shipka, Miranda Otto, Ross Lynch, and Jaz Sinclair. Released December 31, 2020, Netflix, www.netflix.com/watch/81062663?trackId=200257859.

———, Season 4, episode 5, "Chapter Thirty-Three: Deus Ex Machina." Directed by Amanda Tapping, written by Eleanor Jean, featuring Kiernan Shipka, Miranda Otto, Lucy Davis, and Lachlan Watson. Released December 31, 2020, Netflix, www.netflix.com/watch/81062664?trackId=200257859.

Day, Sara K., Miranda A. Green-Barteet, and Amy L. Montz, "Introduction: From 'New Woman' to 'Future Girl': The Roots and the Rise of the Female Protagonist in Contemporary Young Adult Dystopias," *Female Rebellion in Young Adult Dystopian Fiction*, (New York: Routledge, 2016): 1–14.

Fridel Emma F. and James Alan Fox. "Gender Differences in Patterns and Trends in U.S. Homicide, 1976–2017," *Violence and Gender* 6, no. 1 (2019): 27–36.

Henesy, Megan. "'Leaving my girlhood behind': Woke Witches and Feminist Liminality in *Chilling Adventures of Sabrina*." *Feminist Media Studies* 21, no. 7 (2021): 1143–1157. doi.org/10.1080/14680777.2020.1791929.

Keating, Dan. "The Weapons Men and Women Most Often Use to Kill," *The Washington Post*, 2015. www.washingtonpost.com/news/wonk/wp/2015/05/07/poison-is-a-womans-weapon/.

Neill, Roy William, dir. *Pursuit to Algiers*. 1945 Universal City, CA: Universal Pictures, youtu.be/1rS2RAtkAgc

"slut, n.." OED Online. March 2022. Oxford University Press. www-oed-com.er.lib.k-state.edu/view/Entry/182346?rskey=EAfVek&result=1&isAdvanced=false.

The Swaddle. "Why Was Poison Stereotyped as the 'Woman's Weapon'?," YouTube video, 00:02:41. April 19, 2022, youtu.be/XfMoiMVXqhY.

Turchiano, Danielle. "Roberto Aguirre-Sacasa on the 'Paradox' of *Chilling Adventures of Sabrina*," *Variety*, 2018. variety.com/2018/tv/features/riverdale-chilling-adventures-of-sabrina-roberto-aguirre-sacasa-interview-paradox-innocence-witchcraft-bughead-1202962129/.

Ward, Sarah. "All of Them Witches: Individuality, Conformity, and the Occult On Screen," *Screen Education* 83 (2016): 34–41.

Zwissler, Laurel. "'I Am That Very Witch': On The Witch, Feminism, and Not Surviving Patriarchy," *Journal of Religion & Film* 22, no. 3 (2018): 1–14.

NOTES

1. *CAoS* does not always adhere to Judeo-Christian mythology in its depiction of characters. In the show, Madam Satan/Lilith is canonically Adam's first wife, as she is in the Jewish belief system, but the show does not explicitly name her the mother of demons. There are nods to this phrase, especially in "Chapter Thirty-One: The Weird" (4:3), where she gives birth to a son sired by Lucifer, but the show is not consistent in its religious replication.

2. Megan Henesy, "'Leaving my girlhood behind': Woke Witches and Feminist Liminality in *Chilling Adventures of Sabrina*," *Feminist Media Studies* 21, no. 7 (2021): 1146, DOI: 10.1080/14680777.2020.1791929.

3. Sara K. Day, Miranda A. Green-Barteet, and Amy L. Montz, "Introduction: From 'New Woman' to 'Future Girl': The Roots and the Rise of the Female Protagonist in Contemporary Young Adult Dystopias," *Female Rebellion in Young Adult Dystopian Fiction* (New York: Routledge, 2016), 2.

4. Greg Buzell, "Daughters of Decadence: The New Woman in the Victorian *Fin de Siècle*," *The British Library* (2014): bl.uk/romantics-and-victorians/articles/daughters-of-decadence-the-new-woman-in-the-victorian-fin-de-siecle.

5. *Chilling Adventures of Sabrina*, part 4, episode 1, "Chapter Twenty-Nine: The Eldritch Dark," directed by Jeff Woolnough, written by Roberto Aguirre-Sacasa and Gigi Swift, featuring Kiernan Shipka, Miranda Otto, Lucy Davis, and Chance Perdomo, released December 31, 2020, on Netflix, www.netflix.com/watch/81062660?trackId=200257859: 00:10:24.

6. *Chilling Adventures of Sabrina*, part 3, episode 3, "Chapter Twenty-Three: Heavy Is the Crown," directed by Rob Seidenglanz, written by Oanh Ly, featuring Kiernan Shipka, Miranda Otto, Lucy Davis, and Chance Perdomo, released January 24, 2020, on Netflix, www.netflix.com/watch/81062654?trackId=200257859: 00:21:05.

7. Day, Green-Barteet, and Montz, "Introduction," 2.

8. The term "angel in the house" comes from Coventry Patmore's four-part narrative poem of the same name that was published between 1854 and 1862. The poem detailed the ideal wife, one who was selfless to her family and submissive to her husband and who was happy to serve as domestic caretaker and mother, deferring to her husband on issues of business, finance, and politics. The phrase has since been used to described women, both real and fictional, who embody those ideals.

9. Sarah Ward, "All of Them Witches: Individuality, Conformity, and the Occult On Screen," *Screen Education* 83 (2016): 35.

10. Ward, "All of Them Witches," 41.

11. Laurel Zwissler, "'I Am That Very Witch': On The Witch, Feminism, and Not Surviving Patriarchy," *Journal of Religion & Film* 22, no. 3 (2018): 11.

12. Zwissler, "I Am That Very Witch," 10.

13. Zwissler, "I Am That Very Witch," 12.

14. Zwissler, "I Am That Very Witch," 13.

15. Zwissler, "I Am That Very Witch," 14.

16. Zwissler, "I Am That Very Witch," 14.

17. Zwissler, "I Am That Very Witch," 2.

18. Ward, "All of Them Witches," 39.

19. Ward, "All of Them Witches," 39.

20. *Chilling Adventures of Sabrina*, part 1, episode 2, "Chapter Two: The Dark Baptism," directed by Lee Toland Krieger, written by Roberto Aguirre-Sacasa, featuring Kiernan Shipka, Miranda Otto, Lucy Davis, and Richard Coyle, released October 26, 2018, on Netflix, www.netflix.com/watch/80230072?trackId=200257859: 00:07:55.

21. Danielle Turchiano, "Roberto Aguirre-Sacasa on the 'Paradox' of *Chilling Adventures of Sabrina*," *Variety* (2018), par. 6, variety.com/2018/tv/features/riverdale-chilling-adventures-of-sabrina-roberto-aguirre-sacasa-interview-paradox-innocence-witchcraft-bughead-1202962129/.

22. Hilda referring to Dr. Cee (short for Cerberus) as such as opposed to his given name, Kenny Kosgrove, could be a reference to how Victorian wives would refer to their husbands by their honorific as a sign of respect and deference. In a twist fitting with Hilda's character, she turns this Victorian housewife practice into a more contemporary term of endearment, showing, again that she is not the "proper" Victorian woman she appears to be on first glance.

23. *Chilling Adventures of Sabrina*, part 3, episode 3, "Chapter Twenty-Three: Heavy is the Crown," 00:37:20.

24. Zwissler, "I Am That Very Witch," 15.

25. Ward, "All of Them Witches," 40.

26. Zwissler, "I Am That Very Witch," 10.

27. Zwissler, "I Am That Very Witch," 3.

28. Zwissler, "I Am That Very Witch," 2.

29. Turchiano, "Roberto Aguirre-Sacasa on the 'Paradox' of *Chilling Adventures of Sabrina*," par. 4.

30. *Chilling Adventures of Sabrina*, part 1, episode 5, "Chapter Five: Dreams in a Witch House," directed by Maggie Kiley, written by Matthew Barry, featuring Kiernan Shipka, Miranda Otto, Lucy Davis, and Chance Perdomo, released October 26, 2018, on Netflix, www.netflix.com/watch/80230075?trackId=200257859:00:25:00.

31. *Chilling Adventures of Sabrina*, part 2, episode 3, "Chapter Fourteen: Lupercalia," directed by Salli Richardson-Whitfield, written by Oanh Ly, featuring Kiernan Shipka, Miranda Otto, Lucy Davis, and Chance Perdomo, released April 5, 2019, on Netflix, www.netflix.com/watch/80230084?trackId=200257859.: 00:04:01.

32. *Chilling Adventures of Sabrina*, part 2, episode 3, "Chapter Fourteen: Lupercalia," 00: 51:44.

33. "slut, n.." OED Online. March 2022. Oxford University Press. www-oed-com.er.lib.k-state.edu/view/Entry/182346?rskey=EAfVek&result=1&isAdvanced=false.

34. *Chilling Adventures of Sabrina*, part 4, episode 5, "Chapter Thirty-Three: Deus Ex Machina," directed by Amanda Tapping, written by Eleanor Jean, featuring Kiernan Shipka, Miranda Otto, Lucy Davis, and Lachlan Watson, released December 31, 2020, on Netflix, www.netflix.com/watch/81062664?trackId=200257859: 00:35:07.

35. *Chilling Adventures of Sabrina*, part 4, episode 4, "Chapter Thirty-Two: The Imp of the Perverse," directed by Antonio Negret, written by Christianne Hedtke, featuring Kiernan Shipka, Miranda Otto, Ross Lynch, and Jaz Sinclair, released December 31, 2020, on Netflix, www.netflix.com/watch/81062663?trackId=200257859: 00:56:25.

36. *Chilling Adventures of Sabrina*, part 2, episode 5, "Chapter Sixteen: Blackwood," directed by Alex Pillai, written by Matthew Barry, featuring Kiernan Shipka, Miranda Otto, Lucy Davis, and Richard Coyle, released April 5, 2019, on Netflix, www.netflix.com/watch/80230086?trackId=14170289: 00:29:22.

37. Dan Keating, "The Weapons Men and Women Most Often Use To Kill," *The Washington Post* (2015), par. 8, www.washingtonpost.com/news/wonk/wp/2015/05/07/poison-is-a-womans-weapon/.

38. There is no one reason for the association of poison as a woman's weapon. Author Agatha Christie frequently used poison as a murder weapon in her novels, and though it was not specifically limited to female killers, women did use it, and the 1945 Sherlock Holmes film *Pursuit to Algiers* features the line "Possibly, poison is a woman's weapon." There is also a long cultural history of poison as a feminine weapon, dating back to Medea in Greek mythology. Legal historians propose that this has to do with a morbid fascination of the woman, who was usually the nurturer, becoming a killer.

39. *Pursuit to Algiers*, directed by Roy William Neill (1945, Universal City, CA: Universal Pictures, 37:30), youtu.be/1rS2RAtkAgc.

40. The Swaddle. "Why Was Poison Stereotyped as the 'Woman's Weapon'?," YouTube video, 00:02:41, April 19, 2022, youtu.be/XfMoiMVXqhY.

41. *Chilling Adventures of Sabrina*, part 3, episode 8, "Chapter Twenty-Eight: Sabrina Is Legend," directed by Rob Seidenglanz, written by Roberto Aguirre-Sacasa and Daniel King, featuring Kiernan Shipka, Miranda Otto, Lucy Davis, and Sam Corlett, released January 24, 2020, on Netflix, www.netflix.com/watch/81062659?trackId=200257859: 00:37:52.

42. Emma E. Fridel and James Alan Fox, "Gender Differences in Patterns and Trends in U.S. Homicide, 1976–2017," *Violence and Gender* 6, no. 1 (2019): 28, DOI: 10.1089/vio.2019.0005.

43. *Chilling Adventures of Sabrina*, part 1, episode 2, "Chapter Two: The Dark Baptism," 00:07:55.

44. *Chilling Adventures of Sabrina*, part 3, episode 6, "Chapter Twenty-Six: All of Them Witches," directed by Michael Goi, written by Joshua Conkel, featuring Kiernan Shipka, Miranda Otto, Lucy Davis, and Sam Corlett. Released January 24, 2020, Netflix, www.netflix.com/watch/81062660?trackId=200257859.

45. Keating, "The Weapons Men and Women Most Often Use to Kill," par. 3.

46. Keating, "The Weapons Men and Women Most Often Use to Kill," par. 11.

47. Keating, "The Weapons Men and Women Most Often Use to Kill," par. 3–4.

48. Fridel and Fox, "Gender Differences in Patterns and Trends in U.S. Homicide, 1976–2017," 29.

49. *Chilling Adventures of Sabrina*, part 4, episode 4, "Chapter Thirty-Two: The Imp of the Perverse," 00:42:02.

50. Ward, "All of Them Witches," 41.

Chapter 11

The Gothic Mother and Daughter in *Chilling Adventures of Sabrina*

Melissa Tyndall

Chilling Adventures of Sabrina (Netflix, 2018–20), based on the Archie Horror comic series from showrunner Roberto Aguirre-Sacasa, is a darker take on Sabrina Spellman, a character who originated in the *Archie* comics and has appeared in numerous television projects, perhaps most recognizably as the heroine of a teen sitcom (ABC, 1996–2000/The WB, 2000–03). The visual aesthetics of *Chilling Adventures of Sabrina (CAoS)* reflect the new perspective on Sabrina's world, but the effects of the genre switch from comedy to horror is especially apparent in the themes of this reprisal. Specifically, moving Sabrina Spellman (Kiernan Shipka) into a spookier version of Greendale allows the series to explore maternal representation in Gothic horror. Often, in teen drama series, parents are missing, dead, neglectful, or working long hours as a plot device that allows their children to participate in teenage shenanigans. In *CAoS*, biological mothers are almost entirely absent from the series, which may seem odd at first considering it is a show about a teenage witch, but while the term "witch" may spark the image of a woman in the collective consciousness, this series navigates covens oppressed by patriarchal leaders. Considering the makeup of the Church of Night's (male) hierarchy alone, it is not a coincidence that the mothers are often dead, absent, or abhorrent people. In Gothic narratives, it is implied that "good" mothers threaten the established society and act as a buffer between children and abusive fathers and/or undermine male authority. Similarly, the lack of knowledge a mother could have provided makes it more difficult for Sabrina and her friends to traverse the horrors the men in power have established. When mothers do persist, they are monstrous, surrogates, focused on their individual pursuit of power within the established system, or are some combination

195

of these archetypes. The surviving monstrous women sometimes even cause the death of the children in her charge or are used as anecdotal evidence by men as to why there is no need for mothers. The male characters in the series seem to believe in a Jacques Lacan-like philosophy[1] akin to "symbolic order," which states that patriarchies dictate culture, and that children need to be separated from their mothers so the children begin to identify with and obey the rules of fathers or father-like figures and develop in his, or his system's, image. In *CAoS,* any witch who deviates from the roles set by the Church of Night poses a threat that may have to be eliminated. Should the "Gothic daughter" follow suit, with or without her mother's influence, those in power see her, too, as a danger unless she can break the Gothic cycle.

THE GOTHIC FEMININE

Before delving into the mothers—or lack thereof—in Greendale, it is impor- tant to establish *Chilling Adventures of Sabrina* as part of the horror genre, as well as how women are historically depicted in the Gothic space. While viewers may often depend on a sense of dread, the supernatural, or even Victorian-style architecture (like the Spellman Mortuary) to categorize a narrative as Gothic, the genre is also defined by its treatment of women— especially mothers. The term "Female Gothic" was coined by Ellen Moers in *Literary Women* (1976), as she examined how women novelists like Mary Wollstonecraft Shelley approached dark motifs.[2] As Ellen Ledoux points out, "Women-authored texts that do not feature 'Female Gothic' tropes—a distressed heroine, domestic incarceration, threats of sexual violence, anxiety about monstrous or absent mothers—are often given little critical attention,"[3] perhaps because the narratives by women authors examine the supernatural and everyday anxieties about subjugation within patriarchal societies. The distinction between authors is important, as scholars find that texts from the Male Gothic perspective rely on tropes that "other" women, placing them on the border between good and bad at all times. Because of the two gazes within the Gothic, Avril Horner and Sue Zlosnik find that the genre is an examination of anxieties and angers experienced by women due to their lack of agency but also still contains mixed messages about what defines a woman as saint versus sinner—categories that seem to change only when women fail to conform to patriarchal expectations."[4] The problem with the presence of mothers in Gothic narratives, as Ruth Bienstock Anolik explains, is that she subverts the pre-established roles of her society; she is neither saint nor sin- ner. One of the Gothic anxieties explored in *Chilling Adventures of Sabrina* is the distinction between a good mother versus a bad mother. In Gothic literature, the absence of a good mother is typical. That is no coincidence, as her absence coincides with her lack of voice, making her "an emblem for women to create and to sustain a female tradition within the patriarchy."[5] The division between the Male and Female Gothic in *CAoS* may be best depicted when Ambrose suggests Sabrina find and bite a *malum malus* in the pilot. When Sabrina asks her cousin what a *malum malus* is, he says, "It depends on who's translating. If it's a man, it's the apple of evil. If it's a woman, it's the fruit of knowledge."[6] This pursuit of truth for Sabrina mimics the original sin committed in the Garden of Eden, but also insinuates that men associate women gaining knowledge with evil. Knowledge, in this genre, is demonized because it leads to women challenging the power structure and uncovering dark truths about their society. The absence of mother figures able to pass down knowledge prevents women from having a foothold in the community. However, that knowledge is most threatening to men when it comes to good mothers; the monstrous women or surrogate mothers—so long as they abide by societal norms—can stay.

THE GOOD MOTHERS OF GREENDALE

In *Chilling Adventures of Sabrina*, it seems that not a single biological mother is present or closely connected to the group of teenagers. Considering women pose a potential problem for men in power, especially as it relates to how children are raised, as Bienstock Anolik asserts, "no woman is in greater peril in the world of the Gothic than is the mother. The typical Gothic mother is absent: dead, imprisoned or somehow abjected [. . .] [t]he mothers of most Gothic heroines are dead long before the readers meet the daughters."[7] This is especially true in Greendale, where mothers are nearly extinct. The names of their mothers, save for Diana Spellman (Annette Reilly), are never mentioned. Where is Theo[8] Putnam's (Lachlan Watson) mother? Harvey Kinkle (Ross Lynch) never talks about his other than the morning he's disgusted to find a gorgon wearing his mother's robe. Rosalind "Roz" Walker (Jaz Sinclair) says her parents are out of town at church retreats in the first few episodes—but we never see her mother a single time or even hear much about her again. When Father Faustus Blackwood (Richard Coyle) would not marry the mother of his illegitimate child, Prudence Night (Tati Gabrielle), the woman supposedly leapt to her death. After Lady Constance Blackwood (Alvina August) dies bringing her children into the world, her husband does not even react to the news of her death; even while his daughter Prudence is present, Blackwood solely focuses on his "only begotten son . . . and heir."[9] Similarly, Mrs. Anderson is still targeted after her daughter, Lucy, is saved. The seemingly single mother is snuffed out when the herald of the Void snatches out her heart and eats it, simply because she would not invite a strange man into her home (to protect her child).[10] Biological mothers of daughters, it seems, come to violent ends.

Good mothers pose a problem, because as Mary Beth Spore, Marsha Dianne Harrison, and Nelson L. Haggerson explain, she is present, she protects, and she encourages, but she also gives children freedom as they move toward adulthood.[11] It is well-established in the series that giving children freedom is not an option. In "Chapter Two: The Dark Baptism" (1:2), when Sabrina says she wants both freedom and power, Prudence laughs and responds, "He'll never give you that. The Dark Lord. The thought of you, of any of us, having both terrifies him."[12] This commentary is not only consistent with how women are often depicted in Gothic narratives, but illustrates what Victoria L. Godwin explains about witches specifically—"media representations frequently depict witches' magical abilities as coming from demons, spell books, or other (usually patriarchal) sources. Witches' power is borrowed, again casting these women in normative roles defined by their relationship to more powerful sources."[13] Should a woman violate those norms, any sense of power or agency she has must go.

One example of women being punished for violating the rules is in "Chapter Two: The Dark Baptism" (1:2), when Sabrina asks her aunt Hilda Spellman (Lucy Davis) if she had any doubts or regrets about her own Dark Baptism. Hilda replies, "When I was your age, I signed my name in the *Book of the Beast*. I mean . . . us girls didn't have any options back then. It simply what was done," before expressing a fantasy about burning down the Greendale woods.[14] This fantasy hints at a deep-seated rage or regret that could sway Sabrina's choice to sign the *Book of the Beast*. Her sister, Zelda Spellman (Miranda Otto), who was spying on this interaction, kills Hilda (albeit temporarily) for her "transgression" and buries her in the Cain Pit, which allows whoever is buried there to come back to life. When Hilda resurrects, Zelda chastises her, claiming that if Sabrina did not sign the *Book of the Beast*, it would mean they failed both Edward Spellman (Sabrina's father) and the Dark Lord. She adds, "The simple truth is Sabrina has no choice in this matter. To pretend otherwise is reckless."[15] While the viewer might classify Hilda's behavior as that of an open, honest surrogate mother who is undeserving of being murdered—even for a short time—her society perceives her as a threat to the Church of Night. In "The Social Construction of Maternal Absence," Diana Gustafson notes that a good mother is defined as an ordinary woman representing the accepted values deemed appropriate by the ruling class.[16] Throughout the series, Hilda displays traditionally maternal and feminine qualities, such as cooking, cleaning, and knitting and being more likely to provide comfort to Sabrina, the Fright Club, and students at the Academy of Unseen Arts than Zelda. However, Hilda proves to be problematic because she offers Sabrina retrospection that conflicts with their patriarchal traditions by suggesting Sabrina has a choice and could violate their coven's traditions.

Similarly, the Church of Night would also consider Diana Spellman a problematic mother to the Church of Night. Because Diana is mortal, the series suggests her presence—outside of the occasional séance—would have made Sabrina "purer" and protected her from the Path of Night. This is visually suggested when Sabrina wears her mother's white wedding dress—a symbol of purity—to her Dark Baptism, but then the dress turns an inky black the moment she arrives in the woods to sign her name in the *Book of the Beast*. The Weird Sisters also suggest several times throughout the series that Edward and Diana did not simply perish in an accidental plane crash but were murdered for their attempts to introduce new philosophies to the Church of Night that included more interaction between mortals and witches. Even before Sabrina's birthday, Zelda blames any waffling of Sabrina's feelings on her mother's influence. Diana's identity is solely that of Sabrina's mother and a representative of the mortal half of Sabrina that the Church of Night wants her to leave behind. However, while a missing mother is problematic for a young woman and a necessary part of exploring Gothic themes, it is also for audience entertainment. Envisioning the protagonist as a Ravenette with a helicopter mom does not make for good storytelling. Instead, like in *Buffy the Vampire Slayer* (The WB, 1997–2001/UPN 2001–03), we want our cheerleaders to kick ass and save the world. We want a "cheerleader by day . . . Queen of Hell by night."[17] It just comes at the cost of their biological mothers or any good mother who might buck the system.

THE PERSISTENCE OF MONSTROUS MOTHERS

The fact that good mothers are often in peril in Gothic texts should not suggest that no mothers are present in *CAoS*. When a biological mother does persist in the narrative, she is monstrous and often the mother of a male child. Gryla (Heather Doerksen), a hedge witch born in the Dark Ages, collects ghostly children and argues that Zelda is a midwife but no mother. Gryla, though a surrogate mother to the ghostly Yule Lads herself, seems to devalue Zelda's role as a surrogate mother to Sabrina and Baby Leticia/Judith Blackwood (daughter of Faustus Blackwood and the late Constance Blackwood). While some may argue that Gryla is pointing out that Zelda stole the baby from Blackwood in "Chapter Ten: The Witching Hour," Zelda took and hid the baby at the behest of a dying Constance Blackwood to keep the child safe from her misogynistic husband, Faustus.[18] Gryla, however, seems to have persisted because she is a monstrous mother who once ate her own child during a famine. She was also willing to pull Baby Leticia/Judith in half like a wishbone to claim ownership of that baby from Zelda in "Chapter Eleven: A Midwinter's Tale" (1:11), indicating she valued possession over true motherhood. Gryla seems to pose no threat to the men in power in the series as an outcast, but even the men with the most power seem to loathe mothers with any potential influence.

Even male-presenting, supernatural characters in *CAoS* struggle with whether mothers should persist. The Dark Lord (Luke Cook) confirms a dead mother is better than a woman who challenges his authority or tricks him.[19] He tells Lilith (Michelle Gomez), "I promised you death should you betray me. I should kill you now. But I won't make you a martyr to our son."[20] Lucifer not only believes women should follow his commands, but that a dead mother is placed on a pedestal she is unworthy of. When he scoffs at the idea that baby Adam needs a mother and says that a hellhound could just as easily suckle him, it seems he believes Lilith is of less use than an animal. Perhaps he wishes he would have killed Lilith, for while a good mother could potentially thwart his agenda for his children, an infernal, "bad" mother like Lilith would rather slaughter their son with a meat cleaver than have Adam raised in Lucifer Morningstar's image. Though she begs for death, the Dark Lord lets Lilith live, furthering the idea that bad mothers in horror find a way to persist.

Like the good mother, sometimes the bad mother can also claw her way back from death. Perhaps because we expect compassion from mortal women, or liken them to Diana Spellman, the most disturbing mother is Elaine Kosgrove (Christine Willes), Dr. Cerberus's (Alessandro Juliani) mother, who died a decade before the events of the series begin. However, when she is resurrected in "Chapter Thirty-Four: The Returned" (4:6), she refers to women as "whores her son sniffs out" and "witches, all of you."[21] She claims to have killed Dr. Cee's previous girlfriends, but it is unclear how much he knew about his mother's activities because he laughs when she mentions his old flames. However, the audience is led to believe she murdered these women because they, like Hilda, tried "to steal [her] little boy."[22] Through this, viewers understand that Dr. Cerberus could have been at risk for more than being possessed by a sex-crazed incubus had his mother lived longer. Instead, he might have been more reminiscent of Norman Bates—a man isolated and abused by his mother.[23] While her behavior is scary enough, Mrs. Kosgrove is subtly painted as a monster with visuals on the set. As Dr. Cee keeps his mother trapped in a closet, he sits under a movie poster for *Mummy's Vengeance* (1975) and tells Hilda, "I'd really like her to be dead again, I think."[24] The message seems to be that some mothers should be dead and stay dead; however, a good mother returning from the dead does not evoke the Gothic fear the way bad mothers do. A ghostly apparition like Diana Spellman has nothing on murderers and cannibals.

THE SURROGATE OR OTHER MOTHER

The presence of cannibalistic mothers, murderous mothers, and the mother of demons (Lilith) should not suggest that no older women exist in *CAoS* that fulfill mother-like roles. However, the relationships these witches—specifically Zelda and Hilda—have with their non-biological children, as well as how they adhere to or rebel against the patriarchy, places them in a liminal space; they are not always good mothers, but they are not monstrous either. Susan Douglas and Meredith Michaels write that there is a prevailing notion that motherhood is supposed to be the primary function of a woman. They argue there is a:

> feminist insistence that women have choices, that they are active agents in control of their own destiny, that they have autonomy. But here's where the distortion of feminism occurs. The only truly enlightened choice to make as a woman, the one that proves, first, that you are a "real" woman, and second, that you are a decent, worthy one, is to become a "mom" and to bring to child-rearing a combination of selflessness and professionalism.[25]

A "bad" mother, alternatively, may be neglectful, self-serving, or do nothing to break themselves and their children out of cycles of oppression. There is a reason that surrogates, sometimes called "other mothers,"[26] are depicted as flawed or lesser than the "good" mother. Lindsey Rock argues that the prevailing rules or discourse in society about how mothers should behave, dress, parent, work, etc., "are weapons meant to divide and conquer women and mothers. These tenants are polarizing tactics used by a system bound to patriarchy that oppresses not only mothers but all women. Any resistance to these disciplinary mechanisms works as a binary showing all the ways the 'Other' is deviant."[27] While the modern, feminist notion is that a woman can occupy more than one role or space, in the Church of Night, that duality is unacceptable. "Chapter One: October Country" (1:1) immediately addresses the idea that Sabrina needs to choose between her mortal side and her witch side—"the Path of Night or the Path of Light. But not both."[28] However, the Spellman aunts seem to occupy two spaces—protective surrogate mothers[29] and women who have survived a patriarchal system by learning how to navigate within it (sometimes through complying with its rules).

Zelda seems to struggle between upholding Church of Night traditions and pushing back against her society's norms when it comes to her niece. In "Chapter Fourteen: Lupercalia" (2:3), when Sabrina expresses unease about participating in a festival that ends in an orgy because she is not having sex yet, Zelda says, "What better time to start?"[30] Though on one hand, Zelda is sex-positive, the viewer can assume the good mother archetype probably would not suggest Sabrina lose her virginity via orgy—especially based on Hilda's response of, "How dare you pressure her like that."[31] However, only a few episodes later, Zelda's view on Sabrina having sex or being married shifts; suddenly, her niece is not old enough.[32] After Ambrose confesses Sabrina has placed her powers in a mandrake, which strips the real Sabrina of her witch powers and leaves her completely human, the aunties do not think there could be anything worse than having a mortal child. However, when he adds Sabrina is meant to be the Dark Lord's queen and rule at his side, Zelda says, "How? Wh—As His child bride? Well—Over my dead body. You're too young."[33] Zelda's reaction to the Dark Lord's designs for Sabrina is because beyond the sexual implications of marriage, in *CAoS*, being a wife (often a precursor to being a mother) incites anxiety in Gothic women because of its relation to patriarchal control.

In "Chapter Sixteen: Blackwood" (2:5), Lilith and Adam (Alexis Denisof) discuss matrimony; while Adam is optimistic about their union,[34] Lilith says "marriage is a walk down the primrose path towards a woman's destruction. It's nothing less than the complete obliteration of a woman's personhood. It takes everything from her. Her body, her independence, even her soul, and gives nothing in return. Nothing she'd want at any rate."[35] It is no coincidence that this discussion occurs in the same episode in which Zelda and Faustus marry. Zelda spends much of the second season seeking to replace Constance Blackwood as a teacher at the Academy of Unseen Arts and become surrogate mother to the Blackwoods' infant son, Judas, and Father Blackwood's wife. Though Zelda knows all the mothers of Blackwood's children are dead, she still pursues these roles, not realizing that adjacency to power is not the same as authority of her own. Zelda tells Hilda in "Chapter Fourteen: Lupercalia" (2:3) that she is "going to accept his proposal, but not for love—for power," and "restore our family's luster and seek my own glory in the process."[36] However, Zelda's desire to alter her role is naive. In Gothic narratives, marriage is not a partnership, but as Bienstock Anolik notes, a reflection of coverture.[37] In the case of the Gothic female, and in this case for Zelda as a surrogate mother, marriage is a form of metaphorical and civil death. Though Zelda is a strong-willed woman, the first indicator of this metaphorical death is after her wedding when Blackwood stops in his tracks and tells Zelda, "You forget yourself, my dear. A wife walks behind her husband."[38] Then, when Zelda returns from their honeymoon, she is an entirely different person.

While they are away, for a reason that is not explained, Faustus casts a Caligari spell on Zelda, which Hilda explains is "an old spell warlocks used to on their wives when they got a bit uppity."[39] Knowing Zelda married Blackwood for power, it can be assumed that she attempted to occupy two roles—wife/mother and a woman seeking to elevate her status. The compliant, Stepford Wife-like Zelda who returns to Greendale is nearly unrecognizable.

Prior to her honeymoon, Zelda often wore tight-fitting, 1950s-inspired cloth-ing such as long-sleeve sheath dresses, pencil skirts paired with peplum jackets, lacy blouses, and wiggle dresses in dark colors like black, blood red, leopard, navy, or plum. These "sexy meets business" clothing choices reflect Zelda's personality as a no-nonsense, power-seeking, sex-positive witch. However, after her honeymoon, Zelda returns wearing a cocktail dress that is gold and floral, off-the-shoulder, A-line, and tea length. Her tough-love tone is also replaced with a demure speech and constant smiles. When Hilda calls her "Zelda" or him "Father Blackwood," Zelda is quick to correct her about calling them more formal monikers, such as Lady Blackwood and His Unholy Eminence—which is uncharacteristic of a woman who called her husband-to-be "Faustus" in earlier episodes. The largest indicator that some-thing is amiss is that Zelda is seemingly unconcerned about the fate of her surrogate children. While men in power like Blackwood—now the Interim Anti-Pope—and the Witches' Council debate on Ambrose's execution[40] and what to do about Sabrina's new display of power,[41] Hilda asks her sister, "Are you not worried about Ambrose or Sabrina," to which Zelda answers, "My husband knows best in these matters. He is the Anti-Pope, after all."[42] Once the curse is broken, Zelda reveals she was aware but unable to make choices that were her own. Zelda loses her personhood, body, and independence—the real Zelda is "dead" for a short time. It is an interesting turn in Zelda's char-acter who, earlier in the series, vents to Ambrose about Hilda and Lilith (still pretending to be Mary Wardwell) saying, "For the love of Satan, what have I done to deserve these women in my life?"[43] Initially, Zelda does not want Hilda to change any more than the Church of Night wants women to change, but just because Hilda adheres to more traditionally maternal roles does not mean that is all she is.

Though Hilda is nothing but maternal to the harrowed children, orphaned students, and Sabrina's mortal friends, she is dispossessed of her personhood any time she steps out of the role of a spinster surrogate mother. We see her performing maternal tasks such as doing laundry, cooking dinner, gardening, and tucking Sabrina into bed, but she is deprived of her own life and sexuality by a codependent, strong-willed sister with whom she shares a bedroom. She is also punished by the church if she acts outside its edicts. In "Chapter Three: The Trial of Sabrina Spellman" (1:3), Sabrina receives an Infernal Summons and is tried for breach of promise for not signing her name in the *Book of the Beast*. While the trial is in session, the church strips both Zelda and Hilda of their powers and youth as punishment for not controlling their surrogate daughter. However, the punishment gets worse for Hilda when she reveals to the Church of Night that she and Sabrina's mother, Diana, witnessed Sabrina baptized in a Christian church before her father, Edward Spellman, promised Sabrina to the Dark Lord. Hilda conspiring with Diana adhered to the wishes of the good mother and ultimately saves Sabrina from her threatened punishment in the Pit should she have lost the case, but Hilda is still punished for her role in undermining the Church of Night and is excommunicated. When Zelda informs her sister of the decision, she is callous and takes the side of the church's patriarchal edicts. When Hilda asks if the church can do that to her, Zelda responds, "They most certainly can. And should. You took part in a Catholic baptism. You've cast doubt on our devotion to the Church of Night. And our Dark Lord is a vengeful lord."[44] The message is clear: do not break the rules of the patriarchy.

Unfortunately, this is not the only time that Zelda steps into a patriarchal role that subjugates her sister. In "Chapter Twenty-Three: Heavy Is the Crown," when Zelda takes over the Academy of Unseen Arts, she catches the students reading *Buxom and the Beast*; in this romance novel by Helga Stilwell—Hilda's pen name—a "humble witch and her incubus lover [are] terrorized by the witch's loveless spinster hag of a sister." When Zelda realizes the novel's origins, she chastises Hilda for reinventing herself and says, "your responsibility is to the Academy, and only the Academy."[45] This harkens back to the idea that women can only occupy one role, because when Hilda argues that while she will help the students however she can but that she also deserves to be happy, she is punished. Zelda uses magic to erase the novel, thereby silencing Hilda's voice. Considering what happens to older women when they attempt to occupy more than one space, and that Sabrina is a character that constantly battles what it is like to be half-mortal, half-witch, it begs the question: how do the daughters of the Church of Night break the patriarchal cycle?

THE GOTHIC DAUGHTER

Without a mother figure to guide daughters in the Gothic space, daughters run the risk of repeating the history of the women who came before them—women beholden to the patriarchy and its rules. Prudence learns this when her father hands down gender-specific edicts in "Chapter Nineteen: The Mandrake" (2:8). Blackwood uses her desire to be a faithful daughter to control other women. When Prudence pushes back on edicts that limit only women's ability to cast spells or enroll in classes that cover darker magics, Blackwood informs her that witches should focus on herbs and "fertility," though all the students are minors. She asks if the rules had been handed down by the Dark Lord, but Blackwood admits the tenets are his own and says, "I need you, daughter, to be my strong left hand. To help the other girls understand and accept the Blackwood Doctrine and their vital place in the Church of Judas. Do that for me, and you will be exempt from the strictures.

As Blackwoods, we are beyond censure."[46] However, at this point in the narrative,[47] it is probably difficult for Prudence to believe she would not be punished for acting as anything but a compliant, Gothic daughter since Father Blackwood plans to kill Sabrina for threatening his authority in the same episode that Zelda's body is taken over.

Even if a girl is still in high school, when the men hold positions of power, the series makes evident the danger men pose to women and girls. In "Chapter Eighteen: The Miracles of Sabrina Spellman" (2:7), when Blackwood returns from his honeymoon, he is at the height of his power as Interim Anti-Pope. Even though Sabrina's display of power against the murderous missionaries preserved his congregation, Blackwood fears her. Methuselah, a member of the Witches' Council, initially teases the would-be Anti-Pope for being afraid of "a little schoolgirl like Sabrina Spellman;" however, the Council changes its tune when Blackwood suggests that her powers are a threat if the "younger members started to believe that Sabrina Spellman was more powerful than their High Priest, the Anti-Pope, or worse, the very Council itself."[48] Though baiting Sabrina into performing a miracle to save Ambrose from execution is Prudence's idea, the men leading the church agree to take "definitive, lethal action, against [Sabrina]" if she challenges their authority.[49] This is, of course, not the first—or the last—time Sabrina challenges the rules of her patriarchal society or attempts to subvert the Church of Night's male-centered traditions.

In Eden T. Hade's work on "Gothic Mothers and the Gothic Daughters They Create," she argues that daughters cannot escape cyclical trauma of oppression within the Gothic mode. However, while "a Gothic female cannot escape her Gothic inheritance [. . .] she can find a point of exit from her mother's mistakes and missteps so that the daughter can re-write her narrative as one that deviates from her mother's experiences and patriarchal oppression."[50] Sabrina is a successful example of this, as she breaks the patriarchy's rules at every turn—she runs for Top Boy, suggests that a High Priestess could one day lead the Church of Night, and ensures she can keep one foot in the mortal world and the other in the infernal world. By "Chapter Twenty-Eight: Sabrina Is Legend" (3:8), she is literally split into two versions of herself, Sabrina Spellman and Sabrina Morningstar, to continue her duality. While Sabrina continually frustrates her aunts, her cousin, her friends, and especially the men in power with her plans and actions, it seems that her cycle-breaking behavior influences those around her. It is no coincidence that just after Lilith tells Sabrina Morningstar, "let no man hold power over you," Zelda and Mambo Marie (Skye P. Marshall) discuss renaming the Church of Night after Hecate, who Mambo Marie refers to as a "maternal pouvoir."[51]

SEARCHING FOR HECATE

For much of the series, witches are dominated by male leaders, whether worshiping the Dark Lord or deferring to warlocks in power. However, the largest turn away from a male-led society seems to occur in "Chapter Twenty-Six: All of Them Witches" (3:6). Part of the reason older women in the series cannot establish a foothold to change the system is that, under the rule of the Church of Night, they are divided by their varying roles—monstrous mothers, other mothers, hedge witches, dead mothers, and other outcasts. But when the existence of the witches is threatened by the arrival of Pagans, Zelda summons disenfranchised witches to the Academy of Unseen Arts, and Zelda tells Gryla, Pesta, Sycorax, Dezmelda, Mother Hubbard, and Mambo Marie it is time to unite or die.

Since the series lacks older women and explores complicated identities within motherhood, it is logical that the witches would eventually pursue Hecate. Hecate is a goddess defined by three roles—Maiden, Mother, and Crone. Historically, she is also associated with wilderness, nature, childbirth, fertility, the moon, crossroads, death, and even magic.[52] The moment every witch in Greendale truly realizes her power, a strength that does not come from a patriarchal source, comes after Zelda's first visions of the Maiden, Mother, and Crone—a goddess embodying many roles. Hilda is dead in the Cain Pit, Zelda kneels in grave dirt, and a ring of women has joined hands around them. The men stand off to the side while Zelda pounds her fists onto her womb, calls on Hecate, and realizes the true complexities of what it means to be a mother, a sister, and a witch. Just before Hilda rises, Zelda screams into the wind:

> We call on you, Mother, in all your divine power. We call on you, Crone, in your arcane wisdom. We are descended of all maidens, mothers, and crones. And so, when we call on the Three-in-One, we call on all witches stretching back from the beginning of time to the end of days. We call on ourselves, the powers that have been denied us.[53]

This episode ends season three, and in the eight episodes of season four, the church is renamed, the academy is rededicated, and a statue of the three-faced goddess is placed in the school foyer. Zelda informs the students that to honor the Dark Mother, they will "name a Mother, Maiden, and Crone to embody and exalt her three forms" each year,[54] indicating that the days of women only occupying one role have ended. However, in that same episode, when the first spectral miner appears to Zelda, it says, in a male voice, "You'll never have a child. Sabrina doesn't think of you as a mother," suggesting the anxieties of the Gothic mother still persist even after the witches have found ways to close the rifts the patriarchy forged between them.

The archetype of the Gothic mother has been difficult to define across its long history in literature, film, and television. In some cases, because she is dead, she is an idealized or invented version—a specter in the Greendale woods who urges her daughter not to sign her name away. In other depictions, she is a monstrous, murderous woman willing to kill and cannibalize her own offspring; she is the definition of every horrible attribute that the patriarchy would use as reasoning to control or be rid of women. But perhaps, as *Chilling Adventures of Sabrina* shows us, there is more need for examination when it comes to the surrogate mother in the Gothic and how the behavior of these women informs the cycle-breaking actions of Gothic daughters. While Sabrina refers to Zelda and Hilda as her aunts—or, collectively, as "the aunties"—and they call her "niece," the series finale makes it clear their relationship is much deeper. As Sabrina's life force slips away, the majority of the montage of "her life flashing before her eyes" is spending her birthdays with her family. And when Zelda speaks at the joint funeral of Sabrina Spellman and Sabrina Morningstar, she finally voices the relationship she and Hilda felt all along when she says, "they are both our daughters."[55] Though the series ends with Hilda and Zelda grieving, there is a ray of hope for the Gothic mothers. As they stare at the statues revering Hecate and Sabrina in the foyer of the academy, Hilda offers for her and Dr. Cee to move back in with Zelda since "we Spellmans, we should stick together, I think."[56] With their patriarchal oppressors gone, the pledge to stick together, and Sabrina's visage to remind them, it seems the cycle for Gothic women, at least in Greendale, is finally broken.

BIBLIOGRAPHY

Anolik, Ruth Bienstock. "The Missing Mother: The Meanings of Maternal Absence in the Gothic Mode." *Modern Language Studies* 33, no. 1/2 (2003): 25–43. doi. org/10.2307/3195306.

Chilling Adventures of Sabrina, Season 1, episode 1, "Chapter One: October Country." Directed by Lee Toland Krieger, written by Roberto Aguirre-Sacasa, featuring Kiernan Shipka, Miranda Otto, Lucy Davis, and Chance Perdomo. Released October 26, 2018, Netflix, www.netflix.com/watch/80230071?trackId =200257859.

———, Season 1, episode 2, "Chapter Two: The Dark Baptism." Directed by Lee Toland Krieger, written by Roberto Aguirre-Sacasa, featuring Kiernan Shipka, Miranda Otto, Lucy Davis, and Richard Coyle. Released October 26, 2018, Netflix, www.netflix.com/watch/80230072?trackId=200257859.

———, Season 1, episode 3, "Chapter Three: The Trial of Sabrina Spellman." Directed by Rob Seidenglanz, written by Ross Maxwell, featuring Kiernan Shipka, Miranda Otto, Lucy Davis, and Ross Lynch. Released October 26, 2018, Netflix, www.netflix.com/watch/80230073?trackId=200257859.

———, Season 1, episode 6, "Chapter Six: An Exorcism in Greendale." Directed by Rachel Talalay, written by Joshua Conkel and MJ Kaufman, featuring Kiernan Shipka, Miranda Otto, Lucy Davis, and Michelle Gomez. Released October 26, 2018, Netflix, www.netflix.com/watch/80230072?trackId=200257859.

———, Season 1, episode 10, "Chapter Ten: The Witching Hour." Directed by Rob Seidenglanz, written by Roberto Aguirre-Sacasa and Ross Maxwell, featuring Kiernan Shipka, Miranda Otto, Lucy Davis, and Chance Perdomo. Released October 26, 2018, Netflix, www.netflix.com/watch/80230080?trackId=200257859.

———, Season 1, episode 11, "Chapter Eleven: A Midwinter's Tale." Directed by Jeff Woolnough, written by Roberto Aguirre-Sacasa and Donna Thorland, featuring Kiernan Shipka, Miranda Otto, Lucy Davis, and Chance Perdomo. Released December 14, 2018, Netflix, www.netflix.com/watch/80230081?trackId=200257859.

———, Season 2, episode 3. "Chapter Fourteen: Lupercalia." Directed by Salli Richardson-Whitfield, written by Oanh Ly, featuring Kiernan Shipka, Miranda Otto, Lucy Davis, and Chance Perdomo. Released April 5, 2019, Netflix, www.netflix.com/watch/80230084?trackId=200257859.

———, Season 2, episode 5, "Chapter Sixteen: Blackwood." Directed by Alex Pillai, written by Matthew Barry, featuring Kiernan Shipka, Miranda Otto, Lucy Davis, and Richard Coyle. Released April 5, 2019, Netflix, www.netflix.com/watch/80230086?trackId=14170289.

———, Season 2, episode 7, "Chapter Eighteen: The Miracles of Sabrina Spellman." Directed by Antonio Negret, written by Christianne Hedtke and Lindsay Calhoon Bring, featuring Kiernan Shipka, Miranda Otto, Lucy Davis, and Chance Perdomo. Released April 5, 2019, Netflix, www.netflix.com/watch/80230088?trackId=200257859.

———, Season 2, episode 8, "Chapter Nineteen: The Mandrake." Directed by Kevin Sullivan, written by Joshua Conkel, featuring Kiernan Shipka, Miranda Otto, Lucy Davis, and Chance Perdomo. Released April 5, 2019, Netflix, www.netflix.com/watch/80230089?trackId=14277283.

———, Season 2, episode 9, "Chapter Twenty: The Mephisto Waltz." Directed by Rob Seidenglanz, directed by Roberto Aguirre-Sacasa, featuring Kiernan Shipka, Miranda Otto, Lucy Davis, Luke Cook, and Gavin Leatherwood. Released April 5, 2019, Netflix, www.netflix.com/watch/80230090?trackId=200257859.

———, Season 3, episode 2, "Chapter Twenty-Two: Drag Me to Hell." Directed by Alex Pillai, written by Ross Maxwell, featuring Kiernan Shipka, Miranda Otto, Lucy Davis, and Chance Perdomo. Released December 31, 2020, Netflix, www.netflix.com/watch/81062653?trackId=14277283.

———, Season 3, episode 3, "Chapter Twenty-Three: Heavy Is the Crown." Directed by Rob Seidenglanz, written by Oanh Ly, featuring Kiernan Shipka, Miranda Otto,

Lucy Davis, and Chance Perdomo. Released January 24, 2020, Netflix, www
.netflix.com/watch/81062654?trackId=200257859.

———, Season 3, episode 6, "Chapter Twenty-Six: All of Them Witches." Directed
by Michael Goi, written by Joshua Conkel, featuring Kiernan Shipka, Miranda
Otto, Lucy Davis, and Sam Corlett. Released January 24, 2020, Netflix, www
.netflix.com/watch/81062660?trackId=200257859.

———, Season 3, episode 8. "Chapter Twenty-Eight: Sabrina Is Legend." Directed
by Rob Seidenglanz, written by Roberto Aguirre-Sacasa and Daniel King, featuring
Kiernan Shipka, Miranda Otto, Lucy Davis, and Sam Corlett. Released January 24,
2020, Netflix, www.netflix.com/watch/81062659?trackId=200257859.

———, Season 4, episode 1, "Chapter Twenty-Nine: The Eldritch Dark." Directed
by Jeff Woolnough, written by Roberto Aguirre-Sacasa and Gigi Swift, featuring Kiernan Shipka, Miranda Otto, Lucy Davis, and Chance Perdomo.
Released December 31, 2020, Netflix, www.netflix.com/watch/81062660?trackId
=200257859.

———, Season 4, episode 2, "Chapter Thirty: The Uninvited." Directed by Alex
Pillai, written by Katie Avery, featuring Kiernan Shipka, Miranda Otto, Lucy
Davis, and Sam Corlett. Released December 31, 2020, Netflix, www.netflix.com/
watch/81062661?trackId=200257859.

———, Season 4, episode 5, "Chapter Thirty-Three: Deus Ex Machina." Directed
by Amanda Tapping, written by Eleanor Jean, featuring Kiernan Shipka, Miranda
Otto, Lucy Davis, and Lachlan Watson. Released December 31, 2020, Netflix,
www.netflix.com/watch/81062664?trackId=200257859.

———, Season 4, episode 6, "Chapter Thirty-Four: The Returned." Directed by
Catriona McKenzie, written by Oanh Ly and Ross Maxwell, featuring Kiernan
Shipka, Miranda Otto, Lucy Davis, and Christine Willes. Released December 31,
2020, Netflix, www.netflix.com/watch/81062665?trackId=200257859.

———, Season 4, episode 8, "Chapter Thirty-Six: At the Mountains of Madness."
Directed by Rob Seidenglanz, written by Roberto Aguirre-Sacasa, featuring Kiernan
Shipka, Miranda Otto, Lucy Davis, and Gavin Leatherwood. Released December
31, 2020, Netflix, www.netflix.com/watch/81062667?trackId=200257859.

Douglas, Susan, and Meredith Michaels. *The Mommy Myth: The Idealization of
Motherhood and How It Has Undermined All Women.* New York: Free Press, 2005.

Godwin, Victoria L. "Love and Lack: Media, Witches, and Normative Gender Roles."
In *Media Depictions of Brides, Wives, and Mothers*, edited by Alena Amato
Ruggerio, 91–102. Lanham, MD: Lexington Books, 2012.

Gustafson, Diana. "The Social Construction of Maternal Absence." In *Unbecoming
Mothers: The Social Production of Maternal Absence*, 23–50. New York:
Routledge, 2011.

Hade, Eden T. "Gothic Mothers and the Gothic Daughters They Create." PhD diss.
Indiana University of Pennsylvania, 2022.

"Hecate." *New World Encyclopedia* (September 22, 2022). https://www
.newworldencyclopedia.org/entry/Hecate.

Horner, Avril and Zlosnik, Sue. *Women and the Gothic: An Edinburgh Companion.* Edited by Avril Horner and Sue Zlosnik. Edinburgh University Press: Edinburgh, UK, 2016.

Ledoux, Ellen. "Was there ever a 'Female Gothic'?" *Palgrave Communications* 3, no. 17042 (June 2012): 2–7. doi.org/10.1057/palcomms.2017.42

Moers, Ellen. *Literary Women.* New York, NY: Doubleday, 1976.

Rock, Lindsey. "The 'Good Mother' vs. the 'Other Mother': The Girl-Mom." *Journal of the Motherhood Initiative for Research and Community Involvement* 9 (2007): 23, core.ac.uk/download/pdf/234568914.pdf.

Spore, Mary Beth, Marsha Dianne Harrison, and Nelson L. Haggerson. "Chapter One: The Good Mother Archetype in Myth: Substantive Characteristics of Mytho-Poetics." *Counterpoints* 187 (2002): 5–11. www.jstor.org/stable/42977917.

"Symbolic, The (Lacan)." *International Dictionary of Psychoanalysis.* Encyclopedia. com. (September 22, 2022). www.encyclopedia.com/psychology/dictionaries -thesauruses-pictures-and-press-releases/symbolic-lacan.

NOTES

1. *International Dictionary of Psychoanalysis*, s.v. "Symbolic, The (Lacan)."

2. Ellen Moers, *Literary Women* (New York: Doubleday, 1976).

3. Ellen Ledoux, "Was there ever a 'Female Gothic'?," *Palgrave Communications* 3, no. 17042 (June 2012): 2, doi.org/10.1057/palcomms.2017.42.

4. Avril Horner & Sue Zlosnik, *Women and the Gothic: An Edinburgh Companion* (Edinburgh: Edinburgh University, 2016), 1–15.

5. Ruth Bienstock Anolik, "The Missing Mother: The Meanings of Maternal Absence in the Gothic Mode," *Modern Language Studies* 33, no. 1/2 (2003): 30. www .jstor.org/stable/3195306.

6. *Chilling Adventures of Sabrina*, season 1, episode 1, "Chapter One: October Country," directed by Lee Toland Krieger, written by Roberto Aguirre-Sacasa, featuring Kiernan Shipka, Miranda Otto, Lucy Davis, and Chance Perdomo, released October 26, 2018, on Netflix, www.netflix.com/watch/80230071?trackId=200257859: 00:44:42.

7. Anolik, "The Missing Mother," 25.

8. Though Theo Putnam starts the series named Susie, this chapter will use the character's chosen name.

9. *Chilling Adventures of Sabrina*, season 1, episode 10, "Chapter Ten: The Witching Hour," directed by Rob Seidenglanz, written by Roberto Aguirre-Sacasa and Ross Maxwell, featuring Kiernan Shipka, Miranda Otto, Lucy Davis, and Chance Perdomo, released October 26, 2018, on Netflix, www.netflix.com/watch/80230080 ?trackId=200257859: 00:52:34.

10. *Chilling Adventures of Sabrina*, season 4, episode 2, "Chapter Thirty: The Uninvited," directed by Alex Pillai, written by Katie Avery, featuring Kiernan Shipka, Miranda Otto, Lucy Davis, and Sam Corlett, released December 31, 2020, on Netflix, www.netflix.com/watch/81062661?trackId=200257859.

11. Mary Beth Spore, Marsha Dianne Harrison, and Nelson L. Haggerson, "Chapter One: The Good Mother Archetype in Myth: Substantive Characteristics of Mytho-Poetics," *Counterpoints* 187 (2002): 5–11. www.jstor.org/stable/42977917.

12. *Chilling Adventures of Sabrina*, season 1, episode 2, "Chapter Two: The Dark Baptism," directed by Lee Toland Krieger, written by Roberto Aguirre-Sacasa, featuring Kiernan Shipka, Miranda Otto, Lucy Davis, and Richard Coyle, released October 26, 2018, on Netflix, www.netflix.com/watch/80230072?trackId=200257859: 00:26:10.

13. Victoria L. Godwin, "Love and Lack: Media, Witches, and Normative Gender Roles," Media Depictions of Brides, Wives, and Mothers, edited by Alena Amato Ruggerio (Lanham, MD: Rowman & Littlefield, 2012): 94.

14. *Chilling Adventures of Sabrina*, "Chapter Two: The Dark Baptism," 00:08:03.

15. *Chilling Adventures of Sabrina*, "Chapter Two: The Dark Baptism," 00:29:08.

16. Diana Gustafson, "Chapter 2. The Social Construction of Maternal Absence," in *Unbecoming Mothers: The Social Production of Maternal Absence* (New York, NY: Routledge, 2011), 23–50.

17. *Chilling Adventures of Sabrina*, season 4, episode 8, "Chapter Thirty-Six: At the Mountains of Madness," directed by Rob Seidenglanz, written by Roberto Aguirre-Sacasa, featuring Kiernan Shipka, Miranda Otto, Lucy Davis, and Gavin Leatherwood, released December 31, 2020, on Netflix, www.netflix.com/watch /81062667?trackId=200257859: 00:56:57.

18. For good reason, since Blackwood tells Prudence in "Chapter Nineteen: The Mandrake" (2:8, 00:42:44) that he intends for her twin siblings Judith and Judas to be married and continue the purity of their bloodline.

19. In "Chapter Twenty-Six: All of Them Witches" (3:6), Lilith makes a deal with Father Blackwood, while he is possessed by the Dark Lord, to father Lucifer and Lilith's child. Lilith plans to raise the child to battle Lucifer for the throne.

20. *Chilling Adventures of Sabrina*, season 4, episode 5, "Chapter Thirty-Three: Deus Ex Machina," directed by Amanda Tapping, written by Eleanor Jean, featuring Kiernan Shipka, Miranda Otto, Lucy Davis, and Lachlan Watson, released December 31, 2020, on Netflix, www.netflix.com/watch/81062664?trackId=200257859: 00:33:57.

21. *Chilling Adventures of Sabrina*, season 4, episode 6, "Chapter Thirty-Four: The Returned," directed by Catriona McKenzie, written by Oanh Ly and Ross Maxwell, featuring Kiernan Shipka, Miranda Otto, Lucy Davis, and Christine Willes, released December 31, 2020, on Netflix, www.netflix.com/watch/81062665?trackId =200257859: 00:27:02.

22. *Chilling Adventures of Sabrina*, "Chapter Thirty-Four: The Returned," 00:27:09.

23. Though Bates is a fictional character, John E. Douglas, the first to profile serial killers and author of *Mindhunter: Inside the FBI's Elite Serial Crime Unit*, finds killers like Edmund Kemper also had abusive, overbearing mothers.

24. *Chilling Adventures of Sabrina*, "Chapter Thirty-Four: The Returned," 00:29:04.

25. Susan Douglas and Meredith Michaels, *The Mommy Myth: The Idealization of Motherhood and How It Has Undermined All Women* (New York: Free Press, 2005), 5.

26. A reference to Neil Gaiman's 2002 book, *Coraline,* where a demonic, shape-shifting entity named Bedlam, also referred to as the "Other Mother," entices children into an alternate dimension to consume their flesh and rob them of their souls.

27. Lindsey Rock. "The 'Good Mother' vs. the 'Other Mother': The Girl-Mom," *Journal of the Motherhood Initiative for Research and Community Involvement* 9, no. 1 (2007).

28. *Chilling Adventures of Sabrina*, season 1, episode 1, "Chapter One: October Country," 00:43:28.

29. Not to be confused with the evil stepmother trope.

30. *Chilling Adventures of Sabrina*, season 2, episode 3, "Chapter Fourteen: Lupercalia," directed by Salli Richardson-Whitfield, written by Oanh Ly, featuring Kiernan Shipka, Miranda Otto, Lucy Davis, and Chance Perdomo, released April 5, 2019, on Netflix, www.netflix.com/watch/80230084?trackId=200257859: 00:04:18.

31. *Chilling Adventures of Sabrina*, "Chapter Fourteen: Lupercalia," 00:04:21.

32. At this point in the narrative, they do not realize the Dark Lord is Sabrina's father, though it is revealed later in this episode.

33. *Chilling Adventures of Sabrina*, season 2, episode 9, "Chapter Twenty: The Mephisto Waltz," directed by Rob Seidenglanz, directed by Roberto Aguirre-Sacasa, featuring Kiernan Shipka, Miranda Otto, Lucy Davis, Luke Cook, and Gavin Leatherwood, released April 5, 2019, on Netflix, www.netflix.com/watch/80230090?trackId=200257859: 00:02:90–00:04:30.

34. Though he thinks she is still Mary Wardwell, the teacher's body is inhabited by Madam Satan.

35. *Chilling Adventures of Sabrina*, season 2, episode 5, "Chapter Sixteen: Blackwood," directed by Alex Pillai, written by Matthew Barry, featuring Kiernan Shipka, Miranda Otto, Lucy Davis, and Richard Coyle, released April 5, 2019, on Netflix, www.netflix.com/watch/80230086?trackId=14170289: 00:33:18.

36. *Chilling Adventures of Sabrina*, "Chapter Fourteen: Lupercalia," 00:48:15–00:48:32.

37. A now abolished common law that rendered a married woman's legal existence as merged with her husband's. When referencing coverture, many scholars, including Bienstock Anolik, cite William Blackstone's *Commentaries on the Laws of England*– an 18th-century treatise on English common law.

38. *Chilling Adventures of Sabrina*, "Chapter Sixteen: Blackwood," 00:55:37.

39. *Chilling Adventures of Sabrina*, season 2, episode 7, "Chapter Eighteen: The Miracles of Sabrina Spellman," directed by Antonio Negret, written by Christianne Hedtke and Lindsay Calhoon Bring, featuring Kiernan Shipka, Miranda Otto, Lucy Davis, and Chance Perdomo, released April 5, 2019, on Netflix, www.netflix.com/watch/80230088?trackId=200257859: 00:34:27.

40. Under the control of his mouse familiar, Leviathan, Ambrose kills the former Anti-Pope. Ambrose then attempts to kill Blackwood for orchestrating these events

to gain power, yet another example of Blackwood controlling the bodies of his congregation.

41. In "Chapter Eighteen: The Miracles of Sabrina Spellman," Sabrina is killed, reanimates, destroys "avenging angel" witch hunters, and raises the dead in a display Harvey compares to Dark Phoenix/Jean Grey from Marvel's *X-Men* comics.

42. *Chilling Adventures of Sabrina*, "Chapter Eighteen: The Miracles of Sabrina Spellman," 00:21:19–00:21:28.

43. *Chilling Adventures of Sabrina*, season 1, episode 6, "Chapter Six: An Exorcism in Greendale," directed by Rachel Talalay, written by Joshua Conkel and MJ Kaufman, featuring Kiernan Shipka, Miranda Otto, Lucy Davis, and Michelle Gomez, released October 26, 2018, on Netflix, www.netflix.com/watch/80230072?trackId=200257859: 00:35:33.

44. *Chilling Adventures of Sabrina*, season 1, episode 3, "Chapter Three: The Trial of Sabrina Spellman," directed by Rob Seidenglanz, written by Ross Maxwell, featuring Kiernan Shipka, Miranda Otto, Lucy Davis, and Ross Lynch, released October 26, 2018, on Netflix, www.netflix.com/watch/80230073?trackId=200257859: 00:52:59.

45. *Chilling Adventures of Sabrina*, "Chapter Three: The Trial of Sabrina Spellman," 00:19:38–00:21:07.

46. *Chilling Adventures of Sabrina*, season 2, episode 8, "Chapter Nineteen: The Mandrake," directed by Kevin Sullivan, written by Joshua Conkel, featuring Kiernan Shipka, Miranda Otto, Lucy Davis, and Chance Perdomo, released April 5, 2019, on Netflix, www.netflix.com/watch/80230089?trackId=14277283: 00:16:54.

47. While she struggles to earn her father's acceptance at this point in the series, Prudence later hunts Blackwood, and in varying but impermanent timelines, they kill each other.

48. *Chilling Adventures of Sabrina*, "Chapter Eighteen: The Miracles of Sabrina Spellman," 00:26:13–00:26:35.

49. *Chilling Adventures of Sabrina*, "Chapter Eighteen: The Miracles of Sabrina Spellman," 00:27:18.

50. Eden T. Hade, "Gothic Mothers and the Gothic Daughters they Create" (PhD diss., Indiana University of Pennsylvania, 2022), www.proquest.com/openview/2e01952cc5d47dacd221f5fe6d2c757a.

51. *Chilling Adventures of Sabrina*, season 3, episode 8, "Chapter Twenty-Eight: Sabrina Is Legend," directed by Rob Seidenglanz, written by Roberto Aguirre-Sacasa and Daniel King, featuring Kiernan Shipka, Miranda Otto, Lucy Davis, and Sam Corlett, released January 24, 2020, on Netflix, www.netflix.com/watch/81062659?trackId=200257859: 00:48:42–00:49:12.

52. *New World Encyclopedia*, s.v. "Hecate."

53. *Chilling Adventures of Sabrina*, "Chapter Twenty-Eight: Sabrina Is Legend," 00:26:18.

54. *Chilling Adventures of Sabrina*, season 4, episode 1, "Chapter Twenty-Nine: The Eldritch Dark," directed by Jeff Woolnough, written by Roberto Aguirre-Sacasa and Gigi Swift, featuring Kiernan Shipka, Miranda Otto, Lucy Davis, and Chance Perdomo, released December 31, 2020, on Netflix, www.netflix.com/watch/81062660?trackId=200257859: 00:10.

55. *Chilling Adventures of Sabrina*, "Chapter Thirty-Six: At the Mountains of Madness," 00:57:33.

56. *Chilling Adventures of Sabrina*, "Chapter Thirty-Six: At the Mountains of Madness," 00:58:19.

Chapter 12

Devouring Women, Consuming Men

Cats, Mice, and the World of Sabrina Spellman

David Rosen

The first image in the Netflix traum-com[1] *Chilling Adventures of Sabrina* (hereafter *CAoS*; 2018–20) is a jaw full of bloody teeth unattached to a head. The jagged chompers, devouring the first words in the opening credits, set one of the important themes for the entire series. The viewer who is looking at the hazy sepia that pervades every bit of Greendale's interiors and exteriors, waiting for the action to ratchet up, trying to identify with characters, and attending to the witchy bits of anti-patriarchal dialogue, might miss how much eating takes place in the show from the outset. At the beginning of "Chapter One: October Country" (1:1), Sabrina (Kiernan Shipka) and her friends see a movie about a flesh-eating zombie, then retire to an eatery named after a flesh-eating dog.[2] Of course, the episode contains numerous kitchen table scenes as well as the worm-filled *malum malus*, which Sabrina eats while the apple is being eaten by worms, and so eats the eaters, which of course, eat humans as well. Then there is the quip by Zelda (Miranda Ott) about a male witch's corpse in the family mortuary. "Shame they decided against a closed casket," she says wistfully. "We haven't had long pig for dinner in ages."[3] Yes, it is good to have a man around the house when you can eat him.

The eating/eaten motif is just one aspect of the show's interest in liminality, the setting of boundaries, and the repeated transgression of those boundaries. All those transgressions link to the broader interest that *CAoS* has in the unstable relationship of sex and gender and a hermeneutic approach to the

215

subject. Semiotics, one approach to how meaning is created within texts, suggests a stable relationship between signs and what they signify in a constellation of relationships. It thus implies strong boundaries between signs and significations. On the other hand, hermeneutics suggests that the relationships among signs and what they signify are constantly changing, modified through context and transaction—boundaries between signs and meanings are continuously crossed and reimagined. The relationship of the eater to the eaten, of male to female, and of other binarisms is part of a tricky reality in which every piece may seem locked into a stable antithesis. But to the hermeneutician, every event modifies and sometimes moves meaning into a new position of relationship. It is not simply that meanings will not stay put, but once they start to move, everything around them moves as well. As noted by Roberta Gilchrist,[4] a man's masculine strength is differentially defined in relation to other men and to women. This means that every time one moves, the other moves as well. As I have observed elsewhere, the portrayal of what it is to be masculine, which is unsteady at any moment, shifts radically from the fourteenth to the nineteenth centuries. Men identifying themselves as a civilizing force and women as a natural force gave way to men identifying themselves as a natural force and women as a civilizing one.[5] In the politics of sex and gender, every move in any spot on the continuum causes a repositioning of other aspects. That repositioning preserves aspects of a binarism that inform the dichotomy while complicating and preserving aspects of power in the previous relationships. To return to the metaphor, the eater is always becoming the devoured and the devourer the eaten. Each serves as food for the other.

   Among the many delectable aspects of *CAoS* is the relationship of Ambrose (Chance Perdomo) to his familiar, Leviathan the mouse. Probably every viewer will remember that Ambrose, unbeknownst to himself, consumed his familiar, an incident that reframed Sabrina's world and created the first major re-signification of that world.[6] What every viewer will not know is the long association of mice with the male and cats with the female that informs that episode and can help illuminate the hermeneutics of *CAoS* and their connection with themes of sex, gender, and power.

A HERMENEUTIC HISTORY OF CATS AND MICE AS CULTURAL CONTEXT

Cats and mice are paradigmatically emblems of predator and prey, devourer and devoured. They are both linked to a gendered sexual relationship that has changed over time. Understanding the hermeneutics of the shifting gendered relationships of cats and mice is useful. More important, in the world of witches—and, in particular, of Sabrina and Ambrose, one of whom is associated with a cat and the other with a mouse—the lesson may shed light on the complications of gender and sexual relations in *CAoS*.

It may surprise a modern reader of cultural texts like *CAoS* that the mouse was associated with the phallus in early representations of masculinity. Perhaps the most famous instance occurs in an engraving of Adam and Eve by Dürer in 1504 (see figure 12.1).[7] In that work, a mouse crouches between the feet of Adam and the cat between the feet of Eve.

According to the noted art historian Erwin Panofsky, who devoted his research and writing to iconography in Western art, the mouse in Dürer's engraving portrays male weakness. The picture, which draws its symbols from "the fall," is filled with depictions of the predatory nature of the female and the weakness of the male when confronted by female power. The female's sexual nature is associated with that power.[8] Dürer's symbols themselves rely in part on a long-standing and, at the time, well-known connection of mice and men. The etymology of the word "mouse" is from a Greek diminutive form of the word "muscle." For the Greeks, that little muscle was, of course, the penis.

In the Renaissance, many examples exist of the cat-woman devouring mice-men, for example, the 1584 satire *Beware the Cat*[9] or the sixteen-century poem "Proper Sonet, Intituled, Maid wil you marrie."[10] In Greece, however, the antithesis had been between mice and snakes—another animal that, like cats, eats mice. For instance, when Hercules strangled Python, he freed the mouse.[11] According to the third-century Roman author Claudius Aelian, mice were a "priapic symbol,"[12] and mice revered Hercules.[13] In contrast, the python was associated with Gaia. The serpent in Eden is likewise identified with the female, although now the symbol of the snake has shifted from being plain nature to being pure evil. And although the snake still has female associations, it also has taken on a male one—the phallus. The shift is a characteristic example of substitution and displacement common in language and culture. When the snake can serve as either male or female, when both claim the position of devourers of the other, all meaning will shift to make room for that contest.[14] However, the symbols are merely surrogates for a contest between men and women for dominance, which often requires redefining what constitutes power itself. That is, the symbols serve as replacements for real social and cultural contestation and conform to the purposes of those who use them. The symbols are not just some interesting fiction; they are the weapons men and women use in a battle for power. In the case of *CAoS,* we would expect to see the use of such antithetical images in the contestations for power between Sabrina and Blackwood (Richard Coyle) or Lucifer (Luke Cook) and Lilith (Michelle Gomez), and that is true—up to a point.

However, those symbols begin to shift in the Renaissance and continue to do so into our current age. While the mouse continued to be identified with

Figure 12.1. Albrecht Dürer (1504). *Adam and Eve* **[Engraving].**
Source: Rijksmuseum. www.rijksmuseum.nl/en/collection/RP-P-OB-1155.

male sexual fear based on the predatory and consuming nature of female sexuality, something else was happening in Edward Gosynhyll's poem "The Schole-house of Women," where this famous question makes its first known appearance: "Are you man or a mouse?"[15] In this work, man is a mouse and possibly not a mouse, a state over which he has no agency because, according to the poem, the wife must help the man become one or the other. It is a woman's role to keep a man from being a mouse since as the author states, to escape mousedom, a husband "[m]ust nedes be ruled, by his wife."[16] Note that the man becoming a non-mouse, that is, becoming a "real" man, does not put him in a position of power, since the woman controls the relationship. Manhood, like mousehood, is dictated by the female's power. A man can be a man, or a man can be a mouse. From the standpoint of female power, the shift is inconsequential. However, in the world of Gosynhyll, the male now has a doubled identity as a mouse or a non-mouse.

It is good to keep this doubling of man-as-mouse and non-mouse in mind since Ambrose has a mouse as his familiar. But before we turn to Ambrose, it is also noteworthy that as masculinity tries to escape its muscine nature, the mouse lingers to create instability. "Men" and "mice" occupy the concept of masculinity simultaneously. If this reminds one of Sabrina's binary choice to be a witch or a mortal, that is not accidental.[17] It is the precipitating dilemma of *CAoS*—in fact, the show approaches a solution over and over again, even splitting Sabrina into two Sabrinas.[18] In the end, it is neither possible to choose both nor compromise between them. The show's narrative chronicles the possible options and the problems this choice invariably leads to. We can view that as a problem of female identity trying to contain all aspects of itself. However, we can also say that in the hermeneutics of gender identity and power, mutual destruction is assured, because every solution proposed by one party that emphasizes one aspect of identity over another leaves a space that can be compromised and occupied, starting the perpetual dance of power again.

By the twentieth century, the mouse-man became associated with deviations from virile masculinity, the code for "normal" at the time. In the Monty Python sketch "The Mouse Problem," a group of men emphatically deny that they are mice. Yet their noses twitch, and when the interviewer holds up a piece of cheese, the mice-men become uncomfortable and fearful because they cannot keep their longing in check. The double entendre makes it clear that the mice-men are homosexuals trying to masquerade as straight.[19] The conjunction of mice and men may seem purely accidental, yet the antithesis of virile man and non-virile mouse had been established in previous centuries, just not as a homosexual signifier. Another example of the drift of signs and significance associated with the sexualization of the cat and mouse can be found in Günter Grass's *Cat and Mouse*, where the protagonist Mahlke has an enormous penis (and Adam's apple) and an insatiable sexual appetite, which becomes involved in the imagery of cats and mice. According to one critic, "[t]he cat symbolizes society and mouse ([Mahlke's] Adam's apple), which symbolizes the oppressed people, also refers to the male sexual organ."[20] Moreover, Mahlke finds the mouse-hole, which in the work both explicitly

and implicitly symbolizes the female genitalia, a place of loathing and pesti-
lence where virility is lost. The connection of the pansexual Ambrose with the
mouse seems to rise partly from this latest cultural re-configuration.

Finally, to understand the contestation for power that lives inside these
symbolic shifts, we find in the twentieth century that it is no longer men
(mice) who fear women (cats). It is now women who fear mice. This is not
just true of the *Tom and Jerry* cartoons. In the mid-twentieth century, images
circulated of women climbing on chairs and shrieking when they saw a
rodent—a clear inversion of the earlier relationship. As parapsychologist
Nandor Fodor noted in 1947, "Women who grow hysterical at the sight of
a mouse and jump on a chair disclose the phallic acceptance of the mouse.
They are really frightened of sexual attack: of the mouse running up under
the skirt into the genitalia."[21] How far does this idea permeate our culture? In
2014, a research article purported to scientifically explain women's irratio-
nal fear of mice.[22] Newspapers published their account of the research, and
one exterminating company used the news piece as a reason for husbands to
protect their wives from mice by hiring an exterminator, an interesting solution given the masculine identity of the mouse.[23] However, the study that the
news stories were based on had not shown or concluded that women feared
mice. It instead had shown that mice feared men, but not women. According
to the research, when women lab technicians handled mice in a laboratory setting, the mice remained calm. When male techs handled the same mice, they
became agitated. The study concluded that tests performed with mice handled
by males could not be trusted to have valid results.[24] There can be no surprise
that the facts were distorted. The contest between men and women is played
out through the symbols that signify male and female. Mice and men. Cats
and women. The relationship remains, although the dichotomies of power
shift—or at least become strangely nuanced—with webs of contradiction as
the mice try to become the apex predators and the object of feminine fear.[25]

WHO IS EATING WHOM IN SABRINA'S WORLD?

That Sabrina has a cat as her familiar and Ambrose a mouse seems perhaps
a little too on the nose. In the hermeneutics of Ambrose's mouse Leviathan,
the relationship of Ambrose to the mouse is loaded from the previous hand-
ing of the symbol through historical-cultural shifts. The writers do not need
to consciously understand those shifts because they are stored in the symbols
themselves. That symbolism becomes more fraught when Ambrose enters the
service of Father Blackwood and Blackwood gives Ambrose the mouse as a
gift.[26] Then the mouse mysteriously disappears.

It is during the episodes surrounding the betrothal and marriage of Blackwood and Zelda that Ambrose's mouse vanishes. Early in "Chapter Sixteen: Blackwood" (2:5), the viewer sees Ambrose throwing things at Sabrina's cat familiar Salem, believing that the cat has eaten his mouse.[27] Sabrina protests that Salem never touched Leviathan.[28] If all things had a steady binary relationship regarding sex and gender in the world of *CAoS*, Sabrina's cat would have eaten Ambrose's mouse, since such an event would respond not only to the predator-prey relationship of cats to mice but also to past gendered use of the animals as symbols. In many regards, Ambrose has been serving Sabrina, but not in the "consuming" sense of the word, so the relationship of cat to mouse has some weak significance. But in this case, Ambrose has eaten his own mouse, although unwittingly. "The damn mouse was never missing," Ambrose announces after vomiting its corpse onto the bartop of the establishment belonging to Dorian Gray (Jedidiah Goodacre). "It climbed inside of me. But why?" he asks. "To control you, perhaps," Dorian speculates.[29] That is one way to look at it, and from the standpoint of the plot, Dorian's surmise is true. Somehow Blackwood controlled the mouse and, through the mouse, controlled Ambrose. How that worked or why it worked is unclear. The viewers simply accept that eating the mouse would lead to Blackwood's controlling Ambrose. Ambrose's final statement, however, returns the focus to the aberrant nature of the sexual relations: "I've been fucked."[30] Sure, Ambrose simply means that something bad has happened that will produce an even worse consequence for him. Strikingly, however, this is the only use of the phrase or the word in *CAoS*. If Leviathan holds the traditional symbolism, then Ambrose has been fucked in more than the idiomatic sense.

When we consider the meaning of Ambrose eating his mouse, beyond the awkward plot mechanism that it is, and view it from the standpoint of sexual symbolism, we are confronted with a hermeneutic puzzle, since definitions of sexuality and gender are created through relationships that arise from difference. Is Ambrose a man or a mouse? That is difficult to know since as he guards the Anti-Pope (Ray Wise), Ambrose's stomach rumbles, and Ambrose says that he has a craving for cheese.[31] At this moment, he is both the mouse and not the mouse. But as Sabrina so rightly points out at the opening of the first show and as the history of mice and men shows, one cannot be both woman and witch, man and mouse. The zero-sum game of meaning-making is exactly what *CAoS* delights in playing with. For instance, Ambrose's homoerotic desire is fulfilled by his affair with Luke (Darren Mann), who, like Ambrose, is a witch. Unknown to Ambrose, Luke has disappeared on a mission for Father Blackwood almost the same time Leviathan disappears inside Ambrose.[32] We also learn (vaguely) that Luke was part of the plot to get Ambrose in the right spot near the Anti-Pope at the wrong time, just as

Leviathan was part of the same plot. The viewer will remember that the mouse becomes Ambrose's gift when Ambrose returns to the Academy of Unseen Arts with Luke. So, are Luke and the mouse the same? Maybe. Because once both Luke and Leviathan have been killed and Lucifer has freed Ambrose, Ambrose enters a torrid relationship with one of the strongest female characters in the Greendale coven, Prudence Blackwood (Tati Gabrielle).[33]

These events, like so many others in the show, emphasize the point that an aspect of identity cannot be both present and absent. Therefore, a new position must be taken when one crosses over into the absence that had defined one's presence. For instance, Lilith cannot be both herself and Ms. Wardwell. As Wardwell, she falls in love with Adam Masters (Alexis Denisof). As a result, Satan feeds Adam to Wardwell much as Blackwood fed Leviathan to Ambrose. It is not that Lilith has never tasted human flesh; after all, she orders pizza for the side of delivery boy.[34] It is what eating Adam means in this case. Her relationship to Adam had kept her Wardwell identity in place. Eating Adam unhinges her identity and forces her to assume a new role.[35] Lines have been crossed, and Lilith must find a new position.

In its exploration of gender and sexuality, then, the series continues to create displacement after displacement in which people wind up, to put it simply, eating themselves or others. This leads to continuous dislocation and redefinition. Susie Putnam (Lachlan Watson), for instance, can become Theo, but he winds up, in a twist right out of Caryl Churchill's *Cloud Nine*, in a romantic and sexual relationship with Robin Goodfellow (Jonathan Whitesell), who is a hobgoblin and so is part of a continuum of supernatural beings from which familiars come. It is difficult to unpack the relationship between Theo to Robin. However, it is not unlike Ambrose's relationship to his own familiar, which is charged at the symbolic level with sexual ambiguities and ultimately part of a world of messy repositioning.

THE OUROBOROIC FEAST

This brings us full circle back to the opening. The opening makes sense because *CAoS* is a television series that literally consumes itself. In an homage to the original 1990s version of the show,[36] the penultimate episode of *CAoS* creates a recursive loop that ends in a void.[37] Sabrina Morningstar travels to the parallel world brought near by her very creation and encounters another Salem. Here, the goblin-cat familiar—revealed to be the Endless, the seventh of the eighth Eldritch Terrors—is an animatronic cat and head writer of a *Sabrina* television series who seems to be controlling Sabrina, as Leviathan had controlled Ambrose. As Salem and Sabrina are being pursued by others who want to cast them into The Void, Salem tries to save Sabrina by spitting out ideas that their pursuers are forced to enact because it is in the script. Unfortunately, that does not work in either the episode or the entire series. The writers are out of ideas, so The Void eventually consumes Sabrina, and the show ends. In the playful hermeneutics of the series, the truth emerges: the writers are not really in charge of reality. They are, like so many of the characters, conduits for various words, tropes, and symbols that preexist them and come to trap them in their realities. The question that is raised, then, is to what extent do we control our words, symbols, and spells, and to what extent do those control us? We can shift their meanings, but we never rid ourselves of them. They are always with us, like the many horror writers, supernatural characters, and Gothic stories that keep returning to Sabrina's world. For this reason, the series never provides a clear picture of what form sex, gender, and power might assume in the future—it does not show a political, social, or cultural way forward. Instead, it decides that such a path is an illusion because in the reality we inhabit, which is chilling and cannibalizing, there is no escape. We retell the same stories in which sometimes the good thing is evil and the evil thing is good, but in which, always, the thing is just not stable. Are the "devouring women" and "consuming men" the devoured or the consumed? Apparently, both and neither.

In this thematic, *CAoS* may, in fact, come closest to the roots of horror as a genre. Much critical discourse about the horror genre rests on Sigmund Freud's "The Uncanny," where he describes *unheimlich* as the unfamiliar that is recognized as familiar—the thing that is simultaneously family member and stranger.[38] For the French psychologist Jacques Lacan, Freud's return of the repressed, in which the familiar takes an unfamiliar form, is an externalization of what is always already present.[39] For Lacan, every sign always has shadows of past, associative, and ambiguous meaning attached to it. So, the repressed is always already present and never actually returns per se. As Derek Hook notes in writing about Lacan's view of the return of the repressed in "Tracking the Lacanian Unconscious in Language," a lover's gift of a bouquet may raise doubts about fidelity, whether or not such infidelity exists.[40] The repressed returns because that is the nature of every sign. Itzhak Benyamini, borrowing from Lacan, examines the relationship of men and women, noting that men do not fear castration. They are born powerless. For Benyamini, masculine sexual politics is based on recognition of that powerlessness.[41] Similarly, the relationship of the cat to the mouse is trapped in an associative web in which men are always at a disadvantage so that the act of the mouse being eaten (intercourse) is translated into an act of eating (conquering). In such a world, who is the eater and who is the eaten is continuously contested, and each social, economic, cultural, and political move by one group requires a compensatory move by the other so that the roles of masculine and feminine continually shift.[42] *CAoS* captures this continuous repositioning of signifiers and significance and so can never truly serve a feminist cause, a point which some studies of *CAoS* have suggested.[43] Instead, the show reveals the emptiness (The Void) of any dominance politics. That it does so is independent of any intention of the writers because as they play with the signs, they are trapped in them.

Those entering Sabrina's world looking for resolution will find none. As Blair Speakman points out, when Batibat, a dream-shaping demon, is released and painfully contorts the Spellmans' dreams, each member of the family is doomed to live in a loop, repeating past trauma. Such a loop allows a dreamer to reconsider that past in the present.[44] This temporal ouroboros also has the past eating the present, which is a familiar recursive, destructive pattern in the world of Sabrina that *CAoS* depicts. However, unlike Speakman, who sees dreams as "a space outside of time, where the past and present are blurred," the point the show makes over and over is the Lacanian one—the space where past and present blur is our space and the dream simply reflects that.[45] Theo gets it right in the first episode when he presciently states that the zombie thriller is a Cold War allegory. The two realities inhabit the same set of signs. So do men and women, cats and mice.

BIBLIOGRAPHY

Aelian, Claudius. *On the Nature of Animals.* Translated by A. F. Scholfield, Cambridge, MA: Harvard University Press, 1958–59.

Baldwin, William. *Beware the Cat.* New London, CT: Connecticut College, 1963.

Benyamini, Itzhak. "Woman as Man's Uncanny Object: A Discussion Following Freud and Lacan." *The Undecidable Unconscious: A Journal of Deconstruction and Psychoanalysis* 3 (2016): 67–92. doi.org/10.1353/ujd.2016.0004.

Brüning, Kristina. "'I'm Neither a Slut, Nor Am I Gonna Be Shamed': Sexual Violence, Feminist Anger, and Teen TV's New Heroine." *Television & New Media* 23, no. 7 (May 2021): 1–16. doi.org/10.1177/15274764211015307.

Chilling Adventures of Sabrina. Season 1, episode 1, "Chapter One: October Country." Directed by Lee Toland Krieger, written by Roberto Aguirre-Sacasa, featuring Kiernan Shipka, Miranda Otto, Lucy Davis, and Chance Perdomo. Released October 26, 2018, Netflix, www.netflix.com/watch/80230071?trackId =200257859.

———, Season 1, episode 5, "Chapter Five: Dreams in a Witch House." Directed by Maggie Kiley, written by Matthew Barry, featuring Kiernan Shipka, Miranda Otto, Lucy Davis, and Chance Perdomo. Released October 26, 2018, Netflix, www .netflix.com/watch/80230075?trackId=200257859.

———, Season 1, episode 7. "Chapter Seven: Feasts of Feasts." Directed by Nguyen Viet, written by Oanh Ly, featuring Kiernan Shipka, Miranda Ott, Lachlan Watson, Richard Coyle, Ross Lynch. Lucy Davis. Chance Perdomo, and Michelle Gomez.

Released October 26, 2018, Netflix, www.netflix.com/watch/80230077?trackId =200257859.

———, Season 1, episode 9, "Chapter Nine: The Returned Man." Directed by Craig William Macneill, written by Axelle Carolyn and Christina Ham, featuring Kiernan Shipka, Miranda Otto, Ross Lynch, and Jazz Sinclair. Released October 26, 2018, Netflix, www.netflix.com/watch/80230079?trackId=200257859.

———, Season 2, episode 3. "Chapter Fourteen: Lupercalia." Directed by Salli Richardson-Whitfield, written by Oanh Ly, featuring Kiernan Shipka, Miranda Ott, Lachlan Watson, Richard Coyle, Ross Lynch. Lucy Davis. Chance Perdomo, and Michelle Gomez. Released April 5, 2019, Netflix, www.netflix.com/watch /80230084?trackId=200257859.

———, Season 2, episode 4, "Chapter Fifteen: Doctor Cerberus's House of Horror." Directed by Alex Garcia-Lopez, written by Ross Maxwell, featuring Kiernan Shipka, Miranda Ott, Lachlan Watson, Richard Coyle, Ross Lynch. Lucy Davis. Chance Perdomo, and Michelle Gomez. Released April 5, 2019, Netflix, www .netflix.com/watch/80230085?trackId=200257859.

———, Season 2, episode 5, "Chapter Sixteen: Blackwood." Directed by Alex Pillai, written by Matthew Barry, featuring Kiernan Shipka, Miranda Otto, Lucy Davis, and Richard Coyle. Released April 5, 2019, Netflix, www.netflix.com/watch /80230086?trackId=14170289.

———, Season 2, episode 6. "Chapter Seventeen: The Missionaries." Directed by Rob Seidenglanz, written by Donna Thorland, featuring Kiernan Shipka, Miranda Ott, Lachlan Watson, Richard Coyle, Ross Lynch. Lucy Davis. Chance Perdomo, and Michelle Gomez. Released April 5, 2019, Netflix, www.netflix.com/watch /80230087?trackId=200257859.

———, Season 3, episode 3, "Chapter Twenty-Three: Heavy Is the Crown." Directed by Rob Seidenglanz, written by Oanh Ly, featuring Kiernan Shipka, Miranda Ott, Lachlan Watson, Richard Coyle, Ross Lynch. Lucy Davis. Chance Perdomo, and Michelle Gomez. Released January 24, 2020, Netflix, www.netflix.com/watch /81062654?trackId=200257859.

———, Season 3, episode 8. "Chapter Twenty-Eight: Sabrina Is Legend." Directed by Rob Seidenglanz, written by Roberto Aguirre-Sacasa and Daniel King, featuring Kiernan Shipka, Miranda Otto, Lucy Davis, and Sam Corlett. Released January 24, 2020, Netflix, www.netflix.com/watch/81062659?trackId=200257859.

———, Season 4, episode 7. "Chapter Thirty-Five: The Endless." Directed by Kevin Sullivan, written by Donna Thorland and Matthew Barry, featuring Kiernan Shipka, Miranda Ott, Lachlan Watson, Richard Coyle, Ross Lynch. Lucy Davis. Chance Perdomo, and Michelle Gomez. Released December 31, 2020, Netflix, www.netflix.com/watch/81062666?trackId=200257859.

Cleese, John, and Chapman, Graham. *Monty Python's Flying Circus,* Season 1, episode 2, "The Mouse Problem." Directed by John Davies and Ian MacNaughton. Aired October 12, 1969, BBC.

Dürer, Albrecht. *Adam and Eve*, 1504. Engraving, 9.8″ × 7.5″. Amsterdam. Rijksmuseum. www.rijksmuseum.nl/en/collection/RP-P-OB-1155. PD-1995.

Feldman, S. S. "Fear of Mice." *The Psychoanalytic Quarterly* 18, no. 2 (1949): 227–30. doi.org/10.1080/21674086.1949.11925757.

Freud, Sigmund. "The Uncanny" (1919). web.mit.edu/allanmc/www/freud1.pdf.

Gilchrist, Roberta. "Ambivalent Bodies: Gender and Medieval Archaeology." In *Invisible People and Processes: Writing Gender and Childhood into European Archaeology*, ed. J. Moore and E. Scott. London: Leicester University Press, 1997: 42–58.

Gosynhyll, Edward. *The Schole-house of Women*. London: Thomas Peyt, 1541. www.otago.ac.nz/english-linguistics/tudor/schole_house12104-5.html.

Hack, Robert. "Opening Credits." *Chilling Adventures of Sabrina.* Netflix, 2018–20.

Hook, Derek. "Tracking the Lacanian Unconscious in Language." *Psychodynamic Practice* 19, no. 1 (2013): 38–54. doi.org/10.1080/14753634.2013.750094.

Juranovszky, Andrea. "Trauma Reenactment in the Gothic Loop: A Study on Structures of Circularity in Gothic Fiction." *Inquiries Journal* 6, no. 5 (2014). www.inquiriesjournal.com/articles/898/3/trauma-reenactment-in-the-gothic-loop-a-study-on-structures-of-circularity-in-gothic-fiction.

Knight, Richard Payne. *An Inquiry into the Symbolical Language of Ancient Art and Mythology*. London: Black and Armstrong, 1836.

Lacan, Jacques. "The Instance of the Letter in the Unconscious, or Reason Since Freud." In *Écrits: A Selection*. Translated by Bruce Fink, 412–44. New York: W. W. Norton, 2002.

Opie, David. "Sabrina Season 4 Takes Aim at The Show's Biggest Criticism: Cat Got Your Tongue?" *DigitalSpy.* December 31, 2020. www.digitalspy.com/tv/ustv/a35057111/sabrina-season-4-salem-talking-cat/.

Panofsky, Erwin. *The Life and Art of Albrecht Dürer*. Princeton, NJ: Princeton University Press, 1955.

Quamar, Farah. "Symbolic Significance of Religious Objects with Reference to Social Strata in Gunter Grass' *Cat and Mouse." Journal of Research and Reviews in Social Sciences Pakistan* 2, no. 2 (2019): 461–65.

Raider Wildlife Control. "Why are People Afraid of Mice?" Advertisement. August 13, 2018, raiderwildlife.ca/why-are-people-afraid-of-mice/.

Raisin, Ross. "Men or Mice: Is Masculinity in Crisis." *The Guardian* (London, UK). October 6, 2017. www.theguardian.com/inequality/2017/oct/06/men-or-mice-is-masculinity-in-crisisross-raisin.

Robinson, Clement. "A Proper Sonet, Intituled, Maid, Wil you Marrie." *A Handful of Pleasant Delights,* edited by Edward Arber. London: The English Scholar's Library of Old and Modern Works, 1878.

Rosen, David. *The Changing Fictions of Masculinity*. Champaign-Urbana, IL: University of Illinois Press, 1993.

Rosen, David. "The Volcano and the Cathedral: Muscular Christianity and the Origins of Primal Manliness." *Muscular Christianity: Embodying the Victorian Age*, edited by Donald Hall. Cambridge: Cambridge University Press, 1994: 17–44. doi.org/10.1017/CBO9780511659331.

Speakman, Blair Ian. "'Poor Creature, Trapped in Existential Solitude Forever': Gothic Dreams of the Uncanny, Repetition, Temporal Loops, and the Double in The Chilling Adventures of Sabrina." *M/C Journal* 23, no. 1 (2020). doi. org/10.5204/mcj.1642.

Sorge, Robert E., et al. "Olfactory Exposure to Males, Including Men, Causes Stress and Related Analgesia in Rodents." *Nature Methods* 11, no. 6 (2014): 629–32. doi. org/10.1038/nmeth.2935.

Staff. "Scientists Find Explanation for Why Women May Seem More Scared of Mice Than Men." *Independent* (London, UK). April 29, 2014. www.independent.co.uk /news/science/scientists-find-explanation-for-why-women-may-seem-more-scared -of-mice-than-men-9299600.html.

Zwissler, Laurel. "'I Am That Very Witch': On the Witch, Feminism, and Not Surviving Patriarchy." *Journal of Religion & Film* 22, no. 3 (2018): 1–33. www .proquest.com/scholarly-journals/i-am-that-very-witch-on-feminism-not-surviving /docview/2214900918/se-2?accountid=30659.

NOTES

1. In my view *CAoS* has no exact generic counterpart. Hence the neologism "traum-com," which is a play on the phrase "rom-com" or romantic comedy. The phrase carries those meanings, as well as two other meanings that are unrelated etymologically: "trauma"—a psychic wound—and "traum"—a dream. *CAoS* combines all four elements into a generic form that blends romance, comedy, traumatic/horrific experiences, and a dream-like quality.

2. Cerberus in *Chilling Adventures of Sabrina*, season 1, episode 1, "Chapter One: October Country."

3. *Chilling Adventures of Sabrina*, season 1, episode 1, "Chapter One: October Country," directed by Lee Toland Krieger, written by Roberto Aguirre-Sacasa, released October 26, 2018, on Netflix, www.netflix.com/watch/80230071?trackId =200257859: 00:51:34.

4. Roberta Gilchrest, "Ambivalent Bodies: Gender and Medieval Archaeology," in *Invisible People and Processes: Writing Gender and Childhood into European Archaeology*, ed. J. Moore and E. Scott (London: Leicester University Press, 1997), 42–58.

5. David Rosen, *The Changing Fictions of Masculinity* (Champaign-Urbana, IL: University of Illinois Press, 1993); David Rosen, "The Volcano and the Cathedral: Muscular Christianity and the Origins of Primal Manliness," in *Muscular Christianity: Embodying the Victorian Age*, edited by Donald Hall (Cambridge: Cambridge University Press, 1994), 17–44. doi.org/10.1017/CBO9780511659331.

6. *Chilling Adventures of Sabrina*, season 2, episode 5, "Chapter Sixteen: Blackwood," directed by Alex Pillai, written by Matthew Barry, released April 5, 2019, on Netflix, www.netflix.com/watch/80230086?trackId=14170289.

7. Albrecht Dürer, *Adam and Eve*, 1504. Engraving, 9.8″ × 7.5″. Amsterdam. Rijksmuseum. www.rijksmuseum.nl/en/collection/RP-P-OB-1155. PD-1995.

8. Erwin Panofsky, *The Life and Art of Albrecht Dürer* (Princeton, NJ: Princeton University Press, 1955).

9. William Baldwin, *Beware the Cat* (New London, CT: Connecticut College, 1963).

10. Clement Robinson, "A Proper Sonet, Intituled, Maid, Wil You Marrie," *A Handful of Pleasant Delights,* edited by Edward Arber (London: The English Scholar's Library of Old and Modern Works, 1878).

11. Richard Payne Knight, *An Inquiry into the Symbolical Language of Ancient Art and Mythology* (London: Black and Armstrong, 1836), 38.

12. Knight, *An Inquiry into the Symbolical Language,* 38.

13. Claudius Aelian, *On the Nature of Animals,* translated by A. F. Scholfield (Cambridge, MA: Harvard University Press, 1958–59), Book 5, Chapter 40.

14. In this regard, Nagaina the snake headed/snake dancer is interesting. Introduced in "Chapter Twenty-Three: Heavy Is the Crown," she is connected with sexual activity, particularly female sexual activity. In the comic, Nagaina was also the name of one cobra that was Ambrose's familiar; *Chilling Adventures of Sabrina*, season 3, episode 3, "Chapter Twenty-Three: Heavy Is the Crown," directed by Rob Seidenglanz, written by Oanh Ly, featuring Kiernan Shipka, Miranda Ott, Lachlan Watson, Richard Coyle, Ross Lynch, Lucy Davis, Chance Perdomo, and Michelle Gomez, released January 24, 2020, on Netflix, www.netflix.com/watch/81062654?trackId=200257859.

15. Edward Gosynhyll, *The Schole-house of Women* (London: Thomas Peyt, 1541), lines 385–91.

16. Gosynhyll, *The Schole-house of Women,* line 380.

17. *Chilling Adventures of Sabrina,* season 1, episode 1, "Chapter One: October Country."

18. *Chilling Adventures of Sabrina*, season 3, episode 8, "Chapter Twenty-Eight: Sabrina Is Legend," directed by Rob Seidenglanz, written by Roberto Aguirre-Sacasa and Daniel King, featuring Kiernan Shipka, Miranda Ott, Lachlan Watson, Richard Coyle, Ross Lynch, Lucy Davis, Chance Perdomo, and Michelle Gomez, released January 24, 2020, on Netflix, www.netflix.com/watch/81062659?trackId=200257859.

19. *Monty Python's Flying Circus,* season 1, episode 2, "The Mouse Problem," directed by John Davies and Ian MacNaughton, written by John Cleese and Graham Chapman, Graham, aired October 12, 1969, on BBC.

20. Farah Quamar, "Symbolic Significance of Religious Objects with Reference to Social Strata in Gunter Grass' *Cat and Mouse,*" *Journal of Research and Reviews in Social Sciences Pakistan* 2, no. 2 (2019), 461.

21. S. S. Feldman, "Fear of Mice," *The Psychoanalytic Quarterly* 18, no. 2 (1949), 27, doi.org/10.1080/21674086.1949.11925757.

22. Staff, "Scientists Find Explanation for Why Women May Seem More Scared of Mice Than Men," *Independent* (April 29, 2014), www.independent.co.uk/news/science/scientists-find-explanation-for-why-women-may-seem-more-scared-of-mice-than-men-9299600.html.

23. Raider Wildlife Contro, "Why Are People Afraid of Mice?" Advertisement (August 13, 2018), raiderwildlife.ca/why-are-people-afraid-of-mice/.

24. Robert E. Sorge, Loren J. Martin, Kelsey A. Isbester, Susana G. Sotocinal, Sarah Rosen, Alexander H. Tuttle, Jeffrey S. Wieskopf, et al. "Olfactory Exposure

to Males, Including Men, Causes Stress and Related Analgesia in Rodents," *Nature Methods* 11, no. 6 (2014), 629–32, doi.org/10.1038/nmeth.2935.

25. Ross Raisin, "Men or Mice: Is Masculinity in Crisis," *The Guardian* (October 6, 2017), www.theguardian.com/inequality/2017/oct/06/men-or-mice-is-masculinity -in-crisisross-raisin.

26.*Chilling Adventures of Sabrina*, season 1, episode 9, "Chapter Nine: The Returned Man," directed by Craig William MacNeill, written by Axelle Carolyn and Christina Ham, featuring Kiernan Shipka, Miranda Ott, Lachlan Watson, Richard Coyle, Ross Lynch, Lucy Davis, Chance Perdomo, and Michelle Gomez, released October 26, 2018, on Netflix.

27. *Chilling Adventures of Sabrina*, season 2, episode 5, "Chapter Sixteen: Black-wood," directed by Alex Pillai, written by Matthew Barry, featuring Kiernan Shipka, Miranda Ott, Lachlan Watson, Richard Coyle, Ross Lynch, Lucy Davis, Chance Perdomo, and Michelle Gomez, released April 5, 2019, on Netflix, www.netflix.com /watch/80230086?trackId=14170289.

28. *Chilling Adventures of Sabrina*, season 2, episode 5, "Chapter Sixteen: Black-wood," 00:02:15.

29. *Chilling Adventures of Sabrina*, season 2, episode 5, "Chapter Sixteen: Black-wood," 00:44:51–00:44:56.

30. *Chilling Adventures of Sabrina*, season 2, episode 5, "Chapter Sixteen: Black-wood," 00:45:52.

31. *Chilling Adventures of Sabrina*, season 2, episode 5, "Chapter Sixteen: Blackwood."

32. *Chilling Adventures of Sabrina*, season 2, episode 4, "Chapter Fifteen: Doctor Cerberus's House of Horror," directed by Alex Garcia-Lopez, written by Ross Max-well, featuring Kiernan Shipka, Miranda Ott, Lachlan Watson, Richard Coyle, Ross Lynch, Lucy Davis, Chance Perdomo, and Michelle Gomez, released April 5, 2019, on Netflix, www.netflix.com/watch/80230085?trackId=200257859.

33. *Chilling Adventures of Sabrina*, season 2, episode 3, "Chapter Fourteen: Luper-calia," directed by Salli Richardson-Whitfield, written by Oahn Ly, featuring Kiernan Shipka, Miranda Ott, Lachlan Watson, Richard Coyle, Ross Lynch, Lucy Davis, Chance Perdomo, and Michelle Gomez, released April 5, 2019, on Netflix, on www .netflix.com/watch/80230084?trackId=200257859. Although Ambrose is introduced as pansexual, bisexual would be the best way to describe him since his romantic attractions and attachments are all male or female and his sexual encounters are com-partmentalized in the series. In fact, despite the presence of the idea that witches and warlocks are sexually fluid, almost all the relationships in *CAoS* are binary, with the possible exception of Theo, who is transgender and gay, although what that means in terms of his relationship with Robin Goodfellow is not clear. It could be argued that binarism, although a complex one, is dominant even in the non-binary aspects of the series.

34. *Chilling Adventures of Sabrina*, season 1, episode 7, "Chapter Seven: Feasts of Feasts," directed by Nguyen Viet, written by Oahn Ly, featuring Kiernan Shipka, Miranda Ott, Lachlan Watson, Richard Coyle, Ross Lynch, Lucy Davis, Chance

Perdomo, and Michelle Gomez, released October 26, 2018, on Netflix, www.netflix
.com/watch/80230077?trackId=200257859.

35. *Chilling Adventures of Sabrina*, season 2, episode 6, "Chapter Seventeen: The
Missionaries," directed by Rob Seidenglanz, written by Donna Thorland, featuring
Kiernan Shipka, Miranda Ott, Lachlan Watson, Richard Coyle, Ross Lynch, Lucy
Davis, Chance Perdomo, and Michelle Gomez, released April 5, 2019, on Netflix,
www.netflix.com/watch/80230087?trackId=14277283.

36. David Opie, "Sabrina Season 4 Takes Aim at The Show's Biggest Criticism:
Cat Got Your Tongue?" *DigitalSpy* (2020), www.digitalspy.com/tv/ustv/a35057111/
sabrina-season-4-salem-talking-cat/.

37. *Chilling Adventures of Sabrina*, season 4, episode 7, "Chapter Thirty-Five: The
Endless," directed by Kevin Sullivan, written by Donna Thorland and Matthew Barry,
featuring Kiernan Shipka, Miranda Ott, Lachlan Watson, Richard Coyle, Ross Lynch,
Lucy Davis, Chance Perdomo, and Michelle Gomez, released December 31, 2020, on
Netflix, www.netflix.com/watch/81062666?trackId=200257859.

38. Sigmund Freud, "The Uncanny" (1919), web.mit.edu/allanmc/www/freud1
.pdf.

39. Lacan, Jacques. "The Instance of the Letter in the Unconscious, or Reason
Since Freud," in *Écrits: A Selection,* trans. Bruce Fink. (New York: W. W. Norton,
2002).

40. Derek Hook, "Tracking the Lacanian Unconscious in Language," *Psychodynamic Practice* 19, no. 1 (2013), 38–54, doi.org/10.1080/14753634.2013.750094.

41. Itzhak Benyamini, "Woman as Man's Uncanny Object: A Discussion Following
Freud and Lacan," *The Undecidable Unconscious: A Journal of Deconstruction and
Psychoanalysis* 3 (2016), 67–92, doi.org/10.1353/ujd.2016.0004.

42. David Rosen, *The Changing Fictions of Masculinity* (Champaign-Urbana, IL:
University of Illinois Press, 1993).

43. See, for instance, Kristina Brüning, "'I'm Neither a Slut, Nor Am I Gonna
Be Shamed': Sexual Violence, Feminist Anger, and Teen TV's New Heroine," *Television & New Media* 23 no. 7 (May 2021), doi:10.1177/15274764211015307.
Brüning argues persuasively that the representations of women's anger, alliance, and
fourth-wave feminist intersectionality is never really fulfilled in a concrete vision of
a different world and so remains hollow and trapped in premises it fails to cancel or
overcome. See also Laurel Zwissler, "'I Am That Very Witch': On the Witch, Feminism, and Not Surviving Patriarchy," *Journal of Religion & Film* 22, no. 3 (2018),
1–33, www.proquest.com/scholarly-journals/i-am-that-very-witch-on-feminism-not
-surviving/docview/2214900918/se-2?accountid=30659. Zwissler offers the view
that the witch as feminist is trapped within the structures of a patriarchal society that
it ultimately cannot escape.

44. Blair Ian Speakman, "'Poor Creature, Trapped in Existential Solitude Forever':
Gothic Dreams of the Uncanny, Repetition, Temporal Loops, and the Double in *The
Chilling Adventures of Sabrina*," *M/C Journal* 23, no. 1 (2020), doi.org/10.5204/
mcj.1642; *Chilling Adventures of Sabrina*, season 1, episode 5, "Chapter Five:
Dreams in a Witch House," directed by Maggie Kiley, written by Matthew Barry,
featuring Kiernan Shipka, Miranda Ott, Lachlan Watson, Richard Coyle, Ross Lynch,

Lucy Davis, Chance Perdomo, and Michelle Gomez, released October 26, 2018, on Netflix, www.netflix.com/watch/80230075?trackId=200257859; Andrea Juranovszky, "Trauma Reenactment in the Gothic Loop: A Study on Structures of Circularity in Gothic Fiction," *Inquiries Journal* 6, no. 5 (2014), www.inquiriesjournal.com/articles/898/3/trauma-reenactment-in-the-gothic-loop-a-study-on-structures-of-circularity-in-gothic-fiction.

   45. Speakman, "Gothic Dreams," para. 11.

PART 5

"Where it always feels like Halloween"

Style and Form

Chapter 13

"What's needed here is a fundamental shift in thinking"

Chilling Adventures of Sabrina *and the Complexities of the Teen Drama*

Cori Mathis

Netflix's *Chilling Adventures of Sabrina* (2018–20), the latest interpretation of the iconic Archie Comics character introduced in 1962, is, in many ways, the complete opposite of what many viewers would expect. The series' target audience is ostensibly made up of millennials and Gen Z, the former of which likely grew up watching *Sabrina the Teenage Witch* (ABC, 1996–2000/The WB, 2000–03) or otherwise encountered Sabrina Spellman in more traditional, wholesome representations. However, Gen Z's first exposure to the character would have probably come from investigating the darker world of *Riverdale* (The CW, 2017–present), which centers around Archie Andrews (K. J. Apa) and his friends, occasionally refers to Greendale, and eventually brings in Sabrina Spellman (Kiernan Shipka) as a guest star during season six, beginning with its "Rivervale" arc. As a result, one might assume that *Chilling Adventures of Sabrina* (*CAoS*) functions similarly to *Riverdale*; if it did not, how would the two blend so easily? However, upon close analysis, it becomes clear that while *CAoS* shares some generic elements with *Riverdale*, it differs in some key ways as well, highlighting an emerging concern within teen television studies: as the catalog of teen dramas continues to expand—especially since the recent explosion of original content produced for streaming services—a reconsideration of the ways in which these series function and work in the world becomes vital. *CAoS* is a fruitful site for this type of study, as it is indicative of the complexity of the contemporary teen drama;

at once a dark, soapy exploration of the supernatural and a coming-of-age melodramatic narrative about a teen girl unable to decide where she belongs in the world, the series speaks to an increasing transgenericism in the genre that makes easy categorization difficult.

GENRE AND THE TEEN DRAMA

To situate this examination, it would be helpful to explore the complexities that lie underneath the umbrella term of "teen drama." Any significant study of television genre by necessity begins with genre theory based in literature and film, but, as Jane Feuer reminds us, it is not sufficient for the examination of television, as these genres work differently than film genres—and especially literary genres, which are longer lasting and not "culturally specific or temporally limited."[1] Jason Mittell has provided much of the nuance surrounding how television genres work through his re-conception of genre as a whole, particularly in *Genre and Television*, his seminal examination of the intersections of production, text, and reception and their impact on televisual practices. As he argues, we should:

> examine genres as *discursive practices*. By regarding genre as a property and function of discourse, we can examine the ways in which various forms of communication work to constitute generic definitions, meanings, and values within particular historical contexts. [. . .] the discourses surrounding and running through a given genre are *themselves* constitutive of that generic category; they are the practices that define genres and delimit their meanings, not media texts themselves.[2]

A genre is not determined by the texts that are or are not in it because genre practices shift over time. Genre is a large concept and formed by a variety of factors, so we must also consider the thematic concerns and perspectives privileged, as well as industrial and reception practices. When applied to teen dramas, this idea becomes even more obvious; for a target audience whose interests quickly wane and who can choose from any number of offerings in what often feels like a flooded market, teen dramas must adapt to the teenagers and young adults of the time in which they air. Considering that the genre only truly began to coalesce in the American context a little over thirty years ago, it has become incredibly diverse in approach in that short period of time.[3]

As a genre, the teen drama can be broadly defined as a series in which the majority of the central characters are going through a period of prolonged adolescence and liminality in their attempt to transition to adulthood. This liminal space is a key element of the teen drama; it opens up a variety of transgeneric possibilities and thus expands the idea of "teen" to "young adult,"[4] an allowance that includes speculative narratives, which appear early in the genre's development and include significant series like *Buffy the Vampire Slayer* (The WB, 1997–2001/UPN, 2001–03). In addition, teen characters in this genre spend a great deal of time working through emotional angst, often as a result of parental expectations or romantic and platonic relationships. As Ien Ang proposes in her study of *Dallas* (CBS, 1978–91), melodrama and soap intersect here, where "what is recognized as real is not knowledge of the world, but a subjective experience of the world: a 'structure of feeling.' It is emotions which count [. . .] In the tragic structure of feeling emotional ups and downs occupy a central place."[5] Under the tragic structure of feeling, characters must explore their emotions to effectively exist in the world. Additionally, teen dramas conceive of their audiences as primarily comprised of teen girls, even after many years of data showing teen boys and women eighteen to thirty-four as a significant component of their market share. This gendered idea of spectatorship leads to narratives that both inscribe and deconstruct ideas of gender performance—sometimes all at once—by providing their imagined teen viewers with multiple points of identification through a variety of "types" who may or may not adhere to what is culturally dominant or perceived as acceptable beyond their age group.

The teen drama as a whole is indebted to serial drama, particularly soap operas, for its narrative structure, but as it has grown in popularity—especially as the streaming era has allowed for more varied approaches and types of stories—its complexity has increased, as well, leading to distinct subgenres. Some critics prefer to discuss teen television as a supergenre, which in some ways is useful for the ideological approaches that permeate recent scholarship but also leads to elisions regarding key thematic and formal differences, especially between comedy and drama. Among those who do focus on the teen drama itself, there have been attempts to mark the distinctions within the larger genre,[6] but these tend to rely on genre perspectives that arise from literary studies, something to be expected in television studies, a field with a large proportion of scholars who have at least some training in English departments. However, using only narrative typing to determine a series' formal elements and cultural work is an incomplete approach, ignoring the different types of interiority allowed in television narratives and deep characterization made possible by its differing potential lengths and delivery formats. Under the model I have proposed elsewhere, the genre can be divided first by separating those series which utilize the melodramatic mode from those with a soap opera approach; too often, the two are conflated, but while they do have some elements in common, they differ both aesthetically and thematically.[7] Additional distinctions can be drawn based on a series' centralized perspectives or narrative focus: teen-centered series wherein the adolescent viewpoint is privileged and very few adults appear regularly as anything but antagonists and, as a rule, tend to lack well-developed internal lives; multigenerational series that split the privileged perspective between teens and a few key adults, giving those adults a rich interior life and motivations—namely, lives outside of their children; and speculative series, which generally build their worlds via elements of science fiction, horror, or fantasy. *CAoS* falls within this last category, but the question is whether or not it uses the melodramatic or soap opera approach.

DISTINGUISHING BETWEEN THE YA SPECULATIVE DRAMA AND THE YA SPECULATIVE SOAP

In some ways, *Chilling Adventures of Sabrina* functions as a young adult speculative drama, which includes such foundational texts as *Buffy the Vampire Slayer* (The WB, 1997–2001/UPN, 2001–03), *Roswell* (The WB, 1999–2001/UPN, 2001–02), and *Smallville* (The WB, 2001–06/The CW, 2006–11), as well more recent offerings, such as *Stranger Things* (Netflix, 2016–present). Young adult speculative dramas, regardless of their mythologies or monsters, are concerned with mostly everyday teenage concerns and in many ways seem otherwise indistinguishable from coming-of-age or multigenerational dramas like *Dawson's Creek* (The WB, 1998–2003), *Gilmore Girls* (The WB, 2000–06/The CW 2006–07), or *All American* (The CW, 2018–present) in how they explicitly engage concerns of gender, class, race, and other identity factors. These are coming-of-age narratives in which the young adult characters experience the significant markers and traditions tied to socially acknowledged maturity and emerging adulthood in a contemporary American cultural context—events like prom and graduation as well as more internal and potentially private experiences like first love, virginity loss, first heartbreak, and the deaths of those close to them—the results of which provide a path to emotional maturity and adult identity formation. At the end of these narratives, should they stay on the air long enough to be complete, the protagonists have moved firmly into a more mature perspective on their interpersonal relationships, the world, and their place in it, often reflected by the slow but continuous realignment of their priorities toward community and social justice.

The melodramatic mode is especially apropos for these types of stories; sentimental and sometimes nostalgic, melodrama, as defined by Linda Williams in her early examinations of the genre, is "a filmic mode of stylistic and/or emotional excess that stands in contrast to more 'dominant' modes of realistic, goal-oriented narrative"[8] that relies on pathos and privileges the suffering and sacrifice of mothers—and by extension, women, whose subject positions seem to offer a way of gaining "a modicum of power and pleasure within the given limits of patriarchal constraints on women."[9] The element of "goal-oriented" is key here in addressing the typical charge labeled against all teen dramas: namely, that they are unrealistic. Teen melodramas do not privilege the traditional external goals of Hollywood narrative that can be easily isolated and used to determine the plot and characterization; instead, they attach their protagonists to internal drives of emotional attachment/ security and a strong sense of justice, the effects of which can vary widely from character to character. As Williams later reflects, "melodrama's drive is ultimately to reveal a good or to condemn an evil,"[10] an element demonstrated particularly well in this approach and that reflects characters' core selves rather than the front they design for others. This valuation of the inner life is a key element of the YA speculative drama, which creates plot in response to character; conversely, the YA speculative soap develops character in reaction to the events of the narrative.

By extension, the YA speculative drama privileges sacrifice over selfish-ness, particularly for its female protagonists and their primary love interests. In these series, romantic love is often presented as a barrier to protecting the universe, as it splits one's focus between their own personal needs and those of others. Instead, these girls are marked as "good" because they use their power for the betterment of others, even if it is to their detriment or even their own death. Judith Clemens-Smucker has marked this tendency toward sacrifice by young women in *Stranger Things*, arguing that it is an attempt to disrupt the ways in which horror traditionally represents "girls [. . .] as abject: monstrous, dangerous, and unknowable by parents, boys, other girls, and even themselves."[11] Eleven (Millie Bobby Brown) certainly follows the path of rejection of comfort, love, and other human pleasures in her attempts at living into the superhero identity Mike Wheeler (Finn Wolfhard) and her other friends have laid on her, and she is just one in a long line of other female YA speculative drama protagonists to do so. Ultimately, these young women's suffering reinforces the genre's habit of equating maturity with self-denial, since their decisions literally impact the universe in ways they may not be able to undo. This is the reason I term this subgenre and its companion group-ing "young adult" and not "teen." In the teen soap, characters may physically age while their emotional intelligence does not significantly increase—allow-ing the more unrealistic elements of the genre to feel possible in the series' narrative universe—but the teens of the young adult speculative drama are burdened with the weight of the knowledge that their decisions affect the world, not just themselves. As a result, these teens age emotionally much faster than most others within the larger genre.

Part of the reason that emotional maturity is both possible and necessary is that the young people of this genre effectively function as adults, protecting and sometimes policing their worlds. The young adult speculative drama makes a place for itself within the teen drama genre by featuring a space where teens exert power over adults, not the other way around. Though these series feature some adults that can be trusted—often in the role of a knowledgeable elder in the supernatural element of the protagonist's life, like *Buffy the Vampire Slayer*'s Rupert Giles (Anthony Stewart Head), or a parent who learns of the teens' secret and supports them as they attempt to navigate that inescapable duality, such as Sheriff Jim Valenti (William Sadler) in *Roswell*—most adults serve as antagonists. YA speculative dramas have a great deal of interest in the authority system the protagonist and their friends are held under; the adult or two they can trust allows them to retain some hope, but overall, the system is clearly corrupt. More to the point, these young people are the only ones who can dismantle it because of their particularly impressive powers and the expanded perspectives they are granted as occupants of yet another liminal space. Their supernatural powers or identities also function as a metaphor to explore power and difference for those who are traditionally marginalized and Othered,[12] which is why so many of these protagonists are young women, BIPOC individuals, from low socioeconomic statuses, or otherwise marked as "different."[13]

However obvious it might seem to align the series with YA speculative drama, *CAoS* also features elements that attach it to the young adult speculative soap. A key element of soap is its status as descendent of the sensation novel, which Kathleen Tillotson has termed "novels with a secret" because the narrative structure is deliberately designed to keep readers hanging on by "withholding information."[14] Teen dramas that function as soap operas rather than melodramas are also structured in this way—information is doled out in small doses to keep the audience guessing and compelled to come back the next week (or binge the next episode, as is increasingly common) to learn the rest of the story, making the anticipation of both its resolution and the next exciting incident a key element in the audience's pleasure in the text.[15] Additionally, sensation novels are concerned with uncovering the "extreme evil behind fair appearances" as a way of exposing the hypocrisy so commonly found among those who cited the superiority of the middle-class, pious values of Victorian life.[16] Teen dramas in the soap opera tradition typically utilize this component of sensationalism, as well. The characters may be involved in "scandalous" plotlines, but the function of those stories is to trouble the audience's perceptions of what is "normal" in contemporary life. By operating outside of cultural norms, these televisual teens make space for the questioning of social systems put in place without their input, sometimes long before their births, that they are expected not only to comply with but perpetuate. Young adult speculative soaps often marry this element with the larger genre's general lack of parental presence; while teen soaps set in our reality typically just erase parents from the narrative and characterize many of them as morally grey at best, these series go one step further and make most living parents (and adults overall) completely untrustworthy—and sometimes, outright evil. *The Secret Circle* (The CW, 2011–12) might be the most horrifying example of this tendency, as the Chance Harbor coven must worry about more than their parents aligning with oppressive systems. If they are not neglectful, alcoholic bullies, like Adam Conant's (Thomas Dekker) father, Ethan (Adam Harrington), they want to steal the teens' powers for themselves, like Charles Meade (Gale Harold) and Dawn Chamberlain (Natasha Henstridge)—condemning their children to, at best, the half-life they themselves have lived since having their powers stripped from them, and allowing dangerous forces to pursue their children in the hopes that the stress and pain will activate a power transfer—or are revealed to have manipulated dozens of lives and led fellow witches to their deaths in their pursuit of the ultimate dark power, as in the case of Cassie Blake's (Britt Robertson) father, John Blackwell (Joe Lando).

This sensational element of the soap opera means that its plot can, and typically does, become quite complex, with an extensive recurring cast that weaves in and out of the narrative as needed and a large number of central characters whose intersecting storylines mean more than a simple A, B, and C plot structure. In a storytelling framework in which plot comes first, characterization takes a backseat as the many main characters compete for narrative attention. While the complex and quickly moving plots of soaps can be difficult to puzzle through for those who may not be paying close attention, they do offer a particular pleasure for those who are: multiple sites of identification. As soaps also privilege the external—the shiny, aspirational lives of those who occupy rarified spaces in society, whether that is based in wealth and class, some sort of exceptional talent, or supernatural origins and/or powers—these chances to "try on" another life are especially compelling for teen viewers who are still in the middle of their own identity formation. Recent examinations of the soap audience show that it is not just women who watch these series—though they may be their primary target—and teen dramas reflect this knowledge, offering "test drive" options across gender. *Teen Wolf* (MTV, 2011–17) featured nine young adult characters in the main cast during its run; when one includes the series' many recurring roles, a wide variety of possibilities are offered to its audience, regardless of gender: they can be the ever-loyal best friend; the popular beauty with hidden intelligence; the emerging hero; the socially awkward introvert; the battle-scarred veteran; or the compelling cool girl, among many others. Still, YA speculative soaps must walk a fine line in the details of these alternative lives to avoid tipping the scale from "aspirational" to "impossible," since this market share shows little patience for what they can no longer identify with.

Interestingly, a number of characters available for audience appropria-tion are, in many ways, not that different from some of their less experi-enced viewers; while the young adults of this genre have seen and done a great deal—and have much larger concerns than the average person—they typically exist in a state of arrested development enabled by the soap form's open-ended narrative structure. With no end in sight, why would they change or grow significantly? Their usual dysfunction feeds the plot monster, so to speak, and without it, the series cannot continue. This is particularly evident in the male romantic leads of the YA speculative soap. Because the supernatural worlds these characters inhabit privilege individualism, many characters work from self-interest as they attempt to reach goals and advance agendas, perpetually delaying their emotional maturation. Consider Damon Salvatore (Ian Somerhalder) of *The Vampire Diaries* (The CW, 2009–17) or Klaus Mikaelson (Joseph Morgan) of the series' first spin-off, *The Originals* (The CW, 2013–18). Both Damon and Klaus are central characters whose decisions reverberate throughout the narrative, but each routinely puts their own interests first, even to the detriment of those they hold dear, positioning Damon and Klaus as antiheroes and sometimes antagonists while they remain viable, often preferred, candidates for their respective heroine's heart. While both Damon and Klaus would (and do) argue that their toxic and sometimes abusive behavior is for the benefit of their beloved,[17] they rarely take these women's preferences or skills into consideration, plotting and manipulating those around them to reach their goals. They each have a foil in a "good brother"—Stefan Salvatore (Paul Wesley) and Elijah Mikaelson (Daniel Gillies)—who is positioned as being "forced" to act in harmful ways to pro-tect those around them, emphasizing that selfishness is at the core of Damon and Klaus's characters, a characteristic shared by most primary love interests of female protagonists in YA speculative soaps.

Additionally, the toxicity and functional amorality of their love interests seemingly infects these young women, who become increasingly mor-ally grey as the YA speculative soap continues to grow in popularity. In an uneven attempt to reflect contemporary feminism's argument that acting in one's own self-interest is not necessarily a betrayal of community, these are not girls who sacrifice themselves for the world, though they might do so for love. No, characters such as *Shadowhunters'* (Freeform, 2016–19) Clary Fairchild (Katherine McNamara) might be brave and devoted to their friends and family, but love conquers all, even if their choices negatively impact others. Clary is so desperate to be with Jace Herondale (Dominic Sherwood) that she refuses to allow him to die, using the one wish granted to the entire Shadowhunter population by the angel Raziel—their "break in case of emer-gency" tool—to resurrect Jace after her father, Valentine Morgenstern (Alan Van Sprang) kills him to gain access to that very wish and set in motion his plans to rid the earth of all Downworlders.[18] Like other heroines in YA speculative soaps, Clary, when confronted with the possibility of loss, cannot be trusted to make a decision that benefits the larger community or world as a whole, an aspect of her character that can be traced back to the early days of the series, such as when she prioritizes rescuing her mother over making progress in the war against Valentine, or brings her dead best friend, Simon (Alberto Rosende), back to life as a vampire without his prior knowledge or permission. Much like her fellow heroines in this genre, Clary does not learn and grow in a significant, long-lasting way. Again, this perpetual state of emotional immaturity is connected to the potentially unending nature of soap opera. Typically, at the end of YA speculative soaps, the protagonists may be in a happy place, but they are still essentially incomplete, unformed in some key way. They have not truly reached adulthood due to their ongoing inability or outright refusal to learn from the mistakes they have made in the past—which means an abrupt move toward maturity in the final few episodes would be unearned and therefore ring false in terms of characterization, so it is rarely attempted.

CHILLING ADVENTURES OF SABRINA AS TRANSGENERIC AND TRANSITIONAL TEXT

Taking these aspects of the genre into consideration, I contend that *Chilling Adventures of Sabrina* is both a young adult speculative drama and a young adult speculative soap, depending on the character and storyline under examination, which means it occupies a particularly interesting space as a transgeneric text and is part of a transitional moment for the teen drama genre. Recent series such as *Euphoria* (HBO, 2019–present) and *The Umbrella Academy* (Netflix, 2019–present) refuse easy categorization; in the case of *Euphoria*, critics are divided as to the actual intended audience of the series: adults who want confirmation of the assumed depravity of Gen Z, teens who know that some lives in the twenty-first century are truly this bleak, or those across both groups who just want to be titillated. *The Umbrella Academy*'s interest in the trauma responses of adults with dysfunctional childhoods seemingly keeps it from being a teen drama at all, but the characterization, tropes, and journey of the protagonists almost demand its inclusion. This expansion of what a teen drama is and can be is a clear effect of the proliferation of streaming services, which, in the absence of broadcast limitations of form and content, have much more freedom to experiment and expand our understanding of the genre. As a Netflix series, *CAoS* certainly occupies this position.

How, then, does *CAoS* function as a YA speculative drama? First, the series obviously adheres to the idea of chronicling key moments in a young person's life that mark the transition to adulthood. As the narrative begins, Sabrina is faced with the most important choice a witch can make: formalizing her allegiance to the Dark Lord (Luke Cook) and his Church of Night through the ritual of Dark Baptism.[19] In "Chapter One: October Country" (1:1), as Sabrina discusses the upcoming event with her aunts, their dialogue could refer to any number of culminating rituals, such as graduation; after Sabrina explains the baptismal name she will be taking as a memorial to her parents, Hilda (Lucy Davis) bursts into tears: "I wasn't gonna cry. And . . . I just wish your mom and dad were here to see this, to see you [. . .] They would be so proud of you. They would be so proud of the young woman you've become." Later, as Sabrina talks to Ambrose (Chance Perdomo) about her reluctance to put the mortal world fully behind her, she references the nostalgia characteristic of the melodramatic mode, explaining that she already misses her mortal life, even before she has moved past it.[20] After Sabrina rejects the ritual of the Dark Baptism, she continues to move through significant adolescent experiences that anticipate the move to adulthood: the first time she experiences the unnatural death of a friend; her first love, and her first heartbreak, with Harvey Kinkle (Ross Lynch); and her first romantic betrayal, and later, first sexual experience with Nick Scratch (Gavin Leatherwood). Because Sabrina Morningstar, as Sabrina's double, both is and is not Sabrina Spellman,[21] her experiences could be pulled under this banner, too; the narrative traces her struggles as the newly-crowned Queen of Hell, mirroring the young adult's foray into career, and she is the first among Sabrina's compatriots to get married, to Sabrina Spellman's former challenger for the throne, Caliban, the Prince of Hell (Sam Corlett).[22]

The series also privileges sacrifice, particularly on the part of women and Sabrina herself. Much like her forerunner Buffy Summers, Sabrina consistently puts others' well-being in front of her own, rushing into situations she might not be completely prepared for in an attempt to save family, friends, and even complete strangers; also like Buffy, she dies more than once in these attempts. As Buffy's tombstone reminds viewers, the superpowered girls of YA speculative dramas "[save] the world. A lot."[23] However, they do so at their own expense. Sabrina has no interest in halving herself through Dark Baptism and leaving her friends, boyfriend, and life in Greendale behind, but she is continually told that she must accept the necessary sacrifice of what she loves to gain something far greater, an element of women's membership in the Church of Night that echoes a number of contemporary Christian perspectives on biblical messages of love and unselfish, unbounded giving of oneself for the betterment of others. Building on that positioning of women under Lucifer's rule—and, by extension, Father Faustus Blackwood's (Richard Coyle)—it is no surprise that Sabrina's natural caretaking and managing tendencies are amplified into a need to save those under threat, even at the risk of her own life. While Sabrina is naturally talented in many ways, she is still a teenage girl rushing off to fight the forces of darkness, some of whom predate recorded history and have powers that supersede not only hers but those of the one who bestowed them on her. As she prepares for the fight to save her coven from Jerathmiel (Spencer Treat Clark) and the other avenging angels in "Chapter Seventeen: The Missionaries" (2:6), even Harvey, normally Sabrina's champion, tells her that she is undertaking a "suicide mission,"—and he is right, as the angels kill her almost immediately—but Sabrina refuses to listen.[24]

Not long after this, in "Chapter Nineteen: The Mandrake" (2:8), Sabrina attempts to release the dark energies that resurrected her via the creation of a mandrake double; however, in doing so, she will lose her original powers, too, and turn fully mortal. Ambrose pleads with her to reconsider, but Sabrina insists she must sacrifice her own needs to protect the world from Lucifer's plans:

> Sabrina: [. . .] My life is not my own. Again. I'm a pawn in the Dark Lord's sick, perverse game. Again. This isn't a decision I'm making lightly, Ambrose. Believe me. I love you. I love our aunties. I think I maybe even love Nick. And I know that by going through with this, I will, one day, lose all of you. But this prophecy is real. The End of Days is coming. Unless . . .
>
> Ambrose: Unless you relinquish your powers.[25]

Though Sabrina ultimately regains her powers, she continues on this path of martyrdom, which culminates in the fourth season storyline in which both Sabrina Morningstar and Sabrina Spellman die for the greater good: Morningstar sacrifices the life she so cherishes by entering the portal to the parallel universe—one brought into existence by the time vortex that arose when Sabrina did not close the time loop she created at the end of the previous season—unknowing if she will be able to return, and finally, in the series' penultimate episode, she dies as she returns to warn Spellman of the threat of the Void. In the finale, "Chapter Thirty-Six: At the Mountains of Madness" (4:8), Sabrina risks her life multiple times in an attempt to save everyone else, something she sees as necessary because she believes herself to blame for the release of the Eldritch Terrors; ultimately, Sabrina dies a slow, painful death as she yet again martyrs herself for the greater good. Though she is shown to have been resurrected in *Riverdale*, as a complete narrative, *CAoS* reinforces the necessity of feminine sacrifice for the good of others.

Sabrina must save the world because, like other YA speculative drama heroines, she exists under a corrupt authoritarian system informed and supported by patriarchy; in fact, one could argue that both the mortal world of Greendale and the infernal world of the Church of Night function this way, putting Sabrina under a double subjugation. As Madam Satan (Michelle Gomez)—newly in the body of Sabrina's favorite teacher, Mary Wardwell—explains to Sabrina in "Chapter One: October Country" (1:1), Baxter High exists in a state of "puritanical masculinity" under the direction of Principal Hawthorne (Bronson Pinchot), "the most intolerant, the most buffoonish, the most misogynist of all."[26] However, as the Dark Lord's handmaiden, Madam Satan—typically called Lilith—also works toward patriarchal ends throughout the first two seasons, delicately manipulating Sabrina to perform the acts that will confirm her as Lucifer's Herald of Hell and allow him to walk the earth in his angelic form, ushering in the Apocalypse. Even worse, if the prophecy is fulfilled, Sabrina will have to rule Hell alongside him as his queen. With the exception of her aunties—who, as a result of internalizing the Church of Night's patriarchal dogma, are sometimes complicit in the oppression of other witches—Sabrina can trust none of the adults in her world, mortal or infernal.

While *CAoS* does, in many ways, fit the young adult speculative drama genre, it can also be viewed as a young adult speculative soap. Though the series utilizes the melodramatic mode as it validates Sabrina and her friends' interiorities—perhaps best exemplified in Theo Putnam's (Lachlan Watson) storyline of gender transition—*CAoS* is simply too focused on the wildness of its plot to spend much time developing its characters. The sensational aspects of the story—Satan worship, cannibalism, human sacrifice, the vaguely incestuous interest Lucifer has in Sabrina, and even the more progressive sexual attitudes and practices of the members of the Church of Night—mean that these teens spend their time reacting to what takes place around them rather than preparing for it, and by the end of the series, they remain much as they began. The narrative is also interested in the concept of hypocrisy and the beauty that can hide true evil, that element of sensational literature that has transferred so well to soap opera. *CAoS* spends the majority of its four seasons interrogating organized religion and the misogyny that is often inscribed into the more recognizable of the Abrahamic faith traditions. In the Church of Night's worship of Satan, they have perhaps too deeply internalized his selfish perspective on the world, wherein all mortals and witches were created for his pleasure. As Lucifer explains to Sabrina in "Chapter Twenty: The Mephisto Waltz" (2:9), he does not believe in free will or choice for anyone but himself, and even if that contradicts the doctrine he has laid out, Lucifer still expects his worshipers to fall in line with this dictate to serve him.

Perhaps the best example of the exposure of hidden evil in *CAoS* comes from the leaders of the church themselves, all of whom are revealed to be some combination of hypocritical, predatory, revenge-obsessed, and misogynistic—utterly unworthy of their leadership and pastoral positions. In the beginning of the series, Blackwood is presented as a scholarly, pious old friend of and former mentor to Sabrina's adoptive father, Edward Spellman, but as the story unfolds, he is revealed to be deeply corrupt on every level, even outpacing his Dark Lord in his efforts to subjugate women when he establishes the Church of Judas, an extremist sect of the Church of Night, in season two. Blackwood's Five Facets of Judas make plain his misogyny and its place at the forefront of his vision of the church, even in his revelation of this so-called "New Testament":

> "One. The Sons of Satan are the heirs of the earth. Take what thou wilt, as is your right, by fire, blood, or deceit. [. . .] Two. Mortals are the swine of the earth. We must not lay with them. [. . .] Three. The Sons of Satan are the swineherds of man. [. . .] Four. As Lilith served Satan, so must witches serve warlocks. [. . .] And five. Warlocks shall claim dominion in the Church of Night, just as their Father rules over Hell!"[27]

It is no surprise when Blackwood is revealed to have arranged the death of Sabrina's parents in his attempt to suppress Edward's progressive interpretation of the Satanic Bible—which, among other things, advocates for the equality of mortals and the recognition of witches as matriarchs in the Church of Night—and become High Priest in Edward's place, ushering in the church's current retrogressive era. For the most part, the adults Sabrina and her friends encounter on a regular basis reinforce the idea found throughout teen media that adulthood leads to a loss of innocence and, sometimes, facilitates a dark turn in one's spirit.

With this kind of example, it is no surprise that Greendale's teens are arrested in their emotional development. While some progress is made in each of their moves to full emotional maturity, it is debatable whether or not we should believe these characters to have exited the liminal space of adolescence. Nick Scratch is a particularly good example of the illusion of maturity and moral goodness. Playing on elements of idealized heroes in teen dramas and romance fiction,[28] Nick is bold, confident, sexy, and talented, but he is also deeply damaged and, as revealed in "Chapter Twenty: The Memphisto Waltz" (2:9), was planted in Sabrina's life by the Dark Lord to keep an eye on her. Though he initially befriends Sabrina because he is entranced by her, Nick resists a true emotional union for some time, flirting with Sabrina and often asking her out—even knowing she has a boyfriend—while still enjoying sex with a variety of partners, which he makes no attempt to hide from the monogamous Sabrina. Overall, while Nick becomes a good friend and eventual partner to Sabrina, he is not characterized as especially caring toward mortals—one of the ways the series separates the heroic witches from those who are just especially gifted—and is in many ways fairly emotionally stunted. As a result, he often stops short of the heroics Sabrina expects of him and makes some ethically questionable or otherwise troubling, selfish choices. While he does sacrifice himself at the end of season two, volunteering his body as an Acheron Configuration to imprison Lucifer, it is clear he does so to prove his love to Sabrina and show her he is worthy of her love in return, making it a self-centered choice indicative of the soap rather than the sacrificial one privileged by melodrama.

Later, when Sabrina sacrifices herself for the world at the end of the series, Nick decides soon afterward to walk into the Sea of Sorrows so that he can meet Sabrina in the Sweet Hereafter. In the soap mode, this decision is romantic, positioning Sabrina and Nick as eternal, destined lovers who cannot bear even an instant of separation, but from the melodramatic perspective, the series' previous themes of heroism and sacrifice mean that Nick's perception of death as better than a life without her is another example of the series marking him as less heroic than she is. Considering the way *CAoS* has previously affirmed the importance of leveraging one's talents for the good of all rather than self-interest, with Nick long established as the warlock whose natural gifts might match Sabrina's own, under the heroic archetype provided in the text, Nick should offer a memorial to their relationship and Sabrina's passion for protecting others by using his knowledge and talents to contribute to and improve witch society—and she should recognize this. Instead, Sabrina offers very little in the way of regret for his death and accepts Nick's presence as part of her reward for her sacrifice, even though heroism by definition in this genre does not anticipate reward. The four seasons of the series—and, arguably, the continuation of Sabrina and Nick's story on *Riverdale*—reflect this push-and-pull between the two of them: while Sabrina inarguably makes Nick a better, more heroic man, he drags her down occasionally, encouraging Sabrina to charge forward in her belief that she is right, even if it might backfire, and muddying her pure intentions with self-interest when helping others. This tendency reflects the incomplete endings of YA speculative soaps. Though she experiences many events that lead to adult identity formation, Sabrina resists that call, and though the series—via its characters' perception of Sabrina—likes to claim that she is maturing as a result of these situations and the mistakes she sometimes makes during them, that is not born out; Sabrina routinely reflects the perpetual emotional immaturity of her YA speculative soap counterparts.

In *Genre and Television*, Jason Mittell writes that as genre scholars, "we should collect many discursive instances surrounding a given instance of generic process. By viewing the discourses of genre clusters, larger scale patterns and meanings will emerge [. . .] out of detailed research and specific cultural articulations of definition, interpretation, and evaluation."[29] If we pay close attention in collecting and analyzing these televisual texts, we will notice divergences, but instead of terming them "outliers" and dismissing their importance, we should use these cultural shifts to begin to chart paths of new growth in particular genres. As one of these divergences, *CAoS* denies easy categorization, occupying multiple generic spaces at once and making stylistic and thematic choices that sometimes align it with and sometimes separate it from both its predecessors and its peers. Part of the reason for this transgeneric status may lie in the multiplicity of influences on the series; somehow, *CAoS* combines the styles of melodrama and soap in a Gothic atmosphere with characters and plot points drawn from horror and even superhero narratives in a postmodern pastiche that reveals a truly dazzling number of references, even in a single episode. The text's complexities reflect that of the contemporary teen drama, which continues to evolve as new generations cycle through its target audience, but many scholars continue to work under conceptions of the genre that are not evident in its most current offerings, often as a result of dipping in and out of teen dramas in the service of research outside of television or media studies, which limits the growth of the field. To borrow from Father Blackwood, "what's needed here is a fundamental shift in thinking."[30] Like its intended audience, the teen drama is continually growing and changing, and our scholarship must be similarly flexible.

BIBLIOGRAPHY

All American. Created by April Blair. Aired beginning in 2018 on The CW. www.netflix.com/title/81012998.

Ang, Ien. *Watching Dallas: Soap Opera and the Melodramatic Imagination*, trans. Della Couling. New York: Methuen & Co., 1985.

Brantlinger, Patrick. "What Is 'Sensational' about the 'Sensation Novel'?" *Nineteenth-Century Fiction* 37, vol. 1 (June 1982): 1–28. JSTOR.

Brunsdon, Charlotte. "*Crossroads*: Notes on Soap Opera." *Screen* 22, no. 4 (1981): 32–37. MLA International Bibliography.

Buffy the Vampire Slayer. Created by Joss Whedon. Aired 1997–2001 on The WB and 2001–03 on UPN. www.hulu.com/series/buffy-the-vampire-slayer.

———, Season 5, episode 22, "The Gift." Directed by Joss Whedon, written by Joss Whedon, featuring Sarah Michelle Gellar, Nicholas Brendon, Alyson Hannigan, and Michelle Trachtenberg. Aired May 22, 2001, The WB, www.hulu.com/watch/eb714538-93c4-43ab-b1e8-7775ea1194c8.

Chilling Adventures of Sabrina, Season 1, episode 1, "Chapter One: October Country." Directed by Lee Toland Krieger, written by Roberto Aguirre-Sacasa, featuring Kiernan Shipka, Miranda Otto, Lucy Davis, and Chance Perdomo. Released October 26, 2018, Netflix, www.netflix.com/watch/80230071?trackId=200257859.

———, Season 1, episode 2, "Chapter Two: The Dark Baptism." Directed by Lee Toland Krieger, written by Roberto Aguirre-Sacasa, featuring Kiernan Shipka, Miranda Otto, Lucy Davis, and Richard Coyle. Released October 26, 2018, Netflix, www.netflix.com/watch/80230072?trackId=200257859.

———, Season 2, episode 5, "Chapter Sixteen: Blackwood." Directed by Alex Pillai, written by Matthew Barry, featuring Kiernan Shipka, Miranda Otto, Lucy Davis, and Richard Coyle. Released April 5, 2019, Netflix, www.netflix.com/watch/8023 0086?trackId=14170289.

———, Season 2, episode 6, "Chapter Seventeen: The Missionaries." Directed by Rob Seidenglanz, written by Donna Thorland, featuring Kiernan Shipka, Miranda Otto, and Lucy Davis, and Spencer Treat Clark. Released April 5, 2019, Netflix, www.netflix.com/watch/80230087?trackId=14277283.

———, Season 2, episode 8, "Chapter Nineteen: The Mandrake." Directed by Kevin Sullivan, written by Joshua Conkel, featuring Kiernan Shipka, Miranda Otto, Lucy Davis, and Chance Perdomo. Released April 5, 2019, Netflix, www.netflix.com/ watch/80230089?trackId=14277283.

———, Season 2, episode 9, "Chapter Twenty: The Mephisto Waltz." Directed by Rob Seidenglanz, directed by Roberto Aguirre-Sacasa, featuring Kiernan Shipka, Miranda Otto, Lucy Davis, Luke Cook, and Gavin Leatherwood. Released April 5, 2019, Netflix, www.netflix.com/watch/80230090?trackId=200257859.

———, Season 3, episode 8. "Chapter Twenty-Eight: Sabrina Is Legend." Directed by Rob Seidenglanz, written by Roberto Aguirre-Sacasa and Daniel King, featuring Kiernan Shipka, Miranda Otto, Lucy Davis, and Sam Corlett. Released January 24, 2020, Netflix, www.netflix.com/watch/81062659?trackId=200257859.

———, Season 4, episode 8, "Chapter Thirty-Six: At the Mountains of Madness." Directed by Rob Seidenglanz, written by Roberto Aguirre-Sacasa, featuring Kiernan Shipka, Miranda Otto, Lucy Davis, and Gavin Leatherwood. Released December 31, 2020, Netflix, www.netflix.com/watch/81062667?trackId=200257859.

Clemens-Smucker, Judith. "Stranger Teens: Eleven Transforms the Monstrous Symbolism of Adolescence through a Contemporary Narrative Arc." *Journal of Popular Film and Television* 50, vol. 2 (2022): 60–68. Arts and Humanities Citation Index.

Cook, Pam. "Melodrama and the Women's Picture." In *Gainsborough Melodrama*, edited by Sue Aspinall and Robert Murphy, 14–28. London: BFI, 1983.

Davis, Glyn and Kay Dickinson, eds. *Teen TV: Genre, Consumption, and Identity.* London: BFI, 2004.

Dallas. Created by David Jacobs. Aired 1978–91 on CBS. Warner Brothers, 2013, DVD.

Dawson's Creek. Created by Kevin Williamson. Aired 1998–2003 on The WB. www .hulu.com/series/dawsons-creek.

Driscoll, Catherine. "Teen Types and Stereotypes." In *Teen Film: A Critical Introduction*, 83–100. New York: Berg, 2011.

Euphoria. Developed by Sam Levinson. Aired beginning in 2019 on HBO. play. hbomax.com/page/urn:hbo:page:GXKN_xQX5csPDwwEAAABj:type:series

Feuer, Jane. "Genre Study and Television." In *Channels of Discourse, Reassembled: Television and Contemporary Criticism*, 2nd ed., edited by Robert C. Allen, 138–160. Chapel Hill: University of North Carolina Press, 1992.

———. "Melodrama, Serial Form, and Television Today." *Screen* 25, no. 1 (1984): 4–17. MLA International Bibliography.

Gilmore Girls. Created by Amy Sherman-Palladino. Aired 2000–06 on The WB and 2006–07 on The CW. www.netflix.com/title/70155618.

Kearney, Mary Celeste. "The Changing Face of Teen Television, or Why We All Love *Buffy*." In *Undead TV: Essays on Buffy the Vampire Slayer*, edited by Elana Levine and Lisa Parks, 17–41. Durham: Duke University Press, 2007.

Kuhn, Annette. "Women's Genres." *Screen* 25, no. 1 (1984): 18–28. MLA International Bibliography.

Lipsett, Joe. "Defining Success in the Era of Peak TV: A Case Study of *The Nine Lives of Chloe King* on ABC Family and *Shadowhunters* on Freeform." In *ABC Family to Freeform TV: Essays on the Millennial-Focused Network and Its Programs*, edited by Emily L. Newman and Emily Witsell, 15–32. Jefferson, NC: McFarland, 2018.

Mittell, Jason. *Genre and Television: From Cop Shows to Cartoons in American Culture*. New York: Routledge, 2004.

Modleski, Tania. "The Search for Tomorrow in Today's Soap Operas," in *Loving with a Vengeance: Mass-Produced Fantasies for Women*, 2nd edition, 77–101. New York: Routledge, 2008.

Riverdale. Created by Roberto Aguirre-Sacasa. Aired beginning in 2017 on The CW. www.netflix.com/title/80133311.

Ross, Sharon Marie and Louisa Ellen Stein, eds. *Teen Television: Essays on Programming and Fandom*. Jefferson, NC: McFarland, 2008.

Roswell. Developed by Jason Katims. Aired 1999–01 on The WB and 2001–02 on UPN. www.hulu.com/series/roswell.

Sabrina the Teenage Witch. Created by Nell Scovell. Aired 1996–2000 on ABC and 2000–03 on The WB. www.hulu.com/series/sabrina-the-teenage-witch.

The Secret Circle. Developed by Andrew Miller. Aired 2011–12 on The CW. www.cwtv.com/shows/the-secret-circle.

Smallville. Developed by Alfred Gough and Miles Millar. Aired 2001–06 on The WB and 2006–11 on The CW. www.hulu.com/series/smallville.

Stranger Things. Created by The Duffer Brothers. Aired beginning in 2016 on Netflix. www.netflix.com/title/80057281.

Tillotson, Kathleen. Introduction to *The Woman in White*, by Wilkie Collins, ix–xxvi. Edited by Kathleen Tillotson. Boston: Houghton, 1969.

The Umbrella Academy. Developed by Jeremy Slater and Steve Blackman. Aired beginning in 2019 on Netflix. www.netflix.com/title/80186863.

Williams, Linda. "Film Bodies: Gender, Genre, and Excess." In *Film Quarterly* 44, no. 4, (Summer 1991): 2–13. JSTOR.

———. "Mega-Melodrama! Vertical and Horizontal Suspensions of the 'Classical.'" In *Modern Drama* 55, no. 4 (Winter 2012): 523–543. Project MUSE.

NOTES

1. Jane Feuer, "Genre Study and Television," in *Channels of Discourse, Reassembled: Television and Contemporary Criticism*, 2nd ed., ed. Robert C. Allen (Chapel Hill: University of North Carolina Press, 1992), 139.

2. Jason Mittell, *Genre and Television* (New York: Routledge, 2004), 12–13.

3. As I have argued elsewhere, while teen dramas across the world have some similar characteristics, each country or region's style can vary greatly from another due to the cultural moment from which they arise and the work the series perform. However, like interdisciplinary scholarship, the literature on international series provides useful lenses for examining American teen dramas.

4. This increased inclusion of those over eighteen years old under the umbrella of "adolescent" is, as Mary Celeste Kearney has pointed out in her analysis of *Buffy the Vampire Slayer*, is not just related to social and economic factors that delay formal adulthood but to those individuals that actively reject leaving this liminal space for the traditions and middle-class limitations of adult American society.

5. Ien Ang, *Watching Dallas: Soap Opera and the Melodramatic Imagination*, trans. Della Couling (New York: Methuen & Co., 1985), 45–46.

6. See *Teen TV: Genre, Consumption, and Identity*, eds. Glyn Davis and Kay Dickinson, (London: BFI, 2004); *Teen Television: Essays on Programming and Fandom*, eds. Sharon Marie Ross and Louisa Ellen Stein (Jefferson, NC: McFarland, 2008); and Joe Lipsett's "Defining Success in the Era of Peak TV: A Case Study of *The Nine Lives of Chloe King* on ABC Family and *Shadowhunters* on Freeform," in *ABC Family to Freeform TV: Essays on the Millennial-Focused Network and Its Programs*, eds. Emily L. Newman and Emily Witsell, (Jefferson, NC: McFarland, 2018), 15–32.

7. For more on the connections and divergences of melodrama and soap opera, see Charlotte Brunsdon, "*Crossroads*: Notes on Soap Opera," *Screen* 22, no. 4 (1981): 32–37; Pam Cook, "Melodrama and the Women's Picture," in *Gainsborough Melodrama*, ed. Sue Aspinall and Robert Murphy (London: BFI, 1983), 14–28; Jane Feuer, "Melodrama, Serial Form, and Television Today," *Screen* 25, no. 1 (1984): 4–17; and Annette Kuhn, "Women's Genres," *Screen* 25, no. 1 (1984): 18–28.

8. Linda Williams, "Film Bodies: Gender, Genre, and Excess," in *Film Quarterly* vol. 44, no. 4, (1991): 3.

9. Williams, "Film Bodies," 8.

10. Linda Williams, "Mega-Melodrama! Vertical and Horizontal Suspensions of the 'Classical,'" in *Modern Drama* vol. 55, no. 4 (Winter 2012): 524.

11. Judith Clemens-Smucker, "Stranger Teens: Eleven Transforms the Monstrous Symbolism of Adolescence through a Contemporary Narrative Arc," *Journal of Popular Film and Television* 50, vol. 2 (2022): 61.

12. For many scholars, like Catherine Driscoll—though she is primarily examining teen film, not television—these are metaphors for puberty, and though I do not deny the connections between the process of sexual maturation and monstrous and otherwise supernatural young adult characters, I would argue that the ideas of difference are much more typical of this type of teen drama; in the YA speculative soap, sex and the supernatural are much more closely linked.

13. It should be noted that, until the past few years, these series have privileged a White, middle-class, straight, cisgender perspective through the constructions of their protagonists—even if the "Chosen One" is a young woman—and by surrounding them with similar people, *Buffy the Vampire Slayer* being one of the best examples of this tendency. Increasingly, however, these series not only feature other marginalizations in their main characters but position those other differences as key to the development and success of their protagonists.

14. Kathleen Tillotson, introduction to *The Woman in White*, by Wilkie Collins, ed. by Kathleen Tillotson (Boston: Houghton, 1969), xv.

15. Tania Modleski, "The Search for Tomorrow in Today's Soap Operas," in *Loving with a Vengeance: Mass-Produced Fantasies for Women*, 2nd ed. (New York: Routledge, 2008), 80.

16. Patrick Brantlinger, "What Is 'Sensational' about the 'Sensation Novel'?" *Nineteenth-Century Fiction* 37, vol. 1 (June 1982): 11.

17. The toxicity and abuse that underlies much of supernatural romance has been commented on in multiple areas of inquiry, and while there is not enough space to focus on that issue here, it remains an element that has not received significant challenges within these texts, though other feminist arguments have led to some key revisions of the form.

18. In the *Shadowhunters* universe, the Downworlders are any supernatural beings that are part demon and part human—as opposed to the part angel, part human Shadowhunters, also called Nephilim—but many of them are not evil or antagonists; the source material, which consists of fifteen novels across four connected series and a variety of other stories set in the Mortal Instruments universe, is clear that Downworlders have souls and are victims of institutional and intersecting oppressions from a dominant group.

19. Lucifer is the deity of the Church of Darkness, of which the Church of Night seems to be a type of denomination, based on asides and insinuations throughout the series.

20. *Chilling Adventures of Sabrina*, season 1, episode 1, "Chapter One: October Country," directed by Lee Toland Krieger, written by Roberto Aguirre-Sacasa, released October 26, 2018, on Netflix, www.netflix.com/watch/80230071?trackId =200257859.: 00:13:23, 00:15:29.

21. *Chilling Adventures of Sabrina*, season 3, episode 8, "Sabrina Is Legend," directed by Rob Seidenglanz, written by Roberto Aguirre-Sacasa and Daniel King, released January 24, 2020, on Netflix, www.netflix.com/watch/81062659?trackId =200257859.

22. Admittedly, Sabrina Spellman also marries in the same episode as her double does, but as it is a strategy to trap The Uninvited, I am not counting it toward her coming-of-age experiences.

23. *Buffy the Vampire Slayer*, season 5, episode 22, "The Gift," directed by Joss Whedon, written by Joss Whedon, aired May 22, 2001, on The WB, www.hulu.com/watch/eb714538-93c4-43ab-b1e8-7775ea1194c8: 00:43:30.

24. *Chilling Adventures of Sabrina*, season 2, episode 6, "Chapter Seventeen: The Missionaries," directed by Rob Seidenglanz, written by Donna Thorland, released

April 5, 2019, on Netflix, www.netflix.com/watch/80230087?trackId=14277283: 00:45:45.

25. *Chilling Adventures of Sabrina*, season 2, episode 8, "Chapter Nineteen: The Mandrake," directed by Kevin Sullivan, written by Joshua Conkel, released April 5, 2019, on Netflix, www.netflix.com/watch/80230089?trackId=14277283: 00:11:24.

26. *Chilling Adventures of Sabrina*, season 1, episode 1, "Chapter One: October Country," 00:21:07.

27. *Chilling Adventures of Sabrina*, season 2, episode 5, "Chapter Sixteen: Blackwood," directed by Alex Pillai, written by Matthew Barry, released April 5, 2019, on Netflix, www.netflix.com/watch/80230086? trackId=14170289: 00:20:23.

28. The teen drama as a form has much in common with romance fiction, reflecting the ways in which women's popular culture genres often develop in response to each other.

29. Mittell, *Genre and Television*, 25.

30. *Chilling Adventures of Sabrina*, season 1, episode 2, "Chapter Two: The Dark Baptism," directed by Lee Toland Krieger, written by Roberto Aguirre-Sacasa, released October 26, 2018, on Netflix, www.netflix.com/watch/80230072?trackId =200257859: 00:03:49.

Chapter 14

The Legacy, Liberation, and Limitations of Gender and Genre in *Chilling Adventures of Sabrina*

Lori Bindig Yousman

Over the past thirty years, teen television has become a wildly popular genre, with characters and storylines entering mainstream culture. Though people of all ages and genders watch teen TV, the genre has been particularly successful in drawing 12-to-34-year-old female viewers, a demographic that had been largely unreachable through other programming.[1] Because teen television features young women more centrally and seriously than other genres, it has played a significant role in shaping the portrayal of young femininity.[2] In fact, as Rachel Mosley notes, teen television shows "have been profoundly engaged in the policing of difference and the construction and validation of hegemonic femininities, in the correcting of 'aberrant' femininity."[3] This chapter examines how the legacies of teen television are at play in *Chilling Adventures of Sabrina* (Netflix, 2018–20) and explores how representations of young femininity in the series are both liberated from and limited by genre conventions.

LEGACY

Genre

As Sharon Marie Ross and Louisa Ellen Stein note, the origins of teen television as a genre are often associated with the 1980s, when scholars began focusing on the aesthetics of teen media.[4] However, the roots of teen television can be traced back to 1949, when a struggling ABC affiliate in

Philadelphia aired a local teen variety show, *Teen TV Club* (1949–54), in hopes of drawing a then-untapped market of young viewers.[5] The strategy proved successful and paved the way for iconic teen-oriented programs such as *American Bandstand* (1952–89), *Leave it to Beaver* (1957–63), and *The Adventures of Ozzie and Harriet* (1952–56).[6] Although teen characters were present on television in the 1970s and 1980s, shows marketed to teen audiences that centered around teenagers were extremely rare until the 1990s, when the rise in the teen population coupled with the proliferation of new cable television networks made it profitable to revisit teen programming. Under this new approach to series development, FOX found success with *Beverly Hills, 90210* (1990–2000), leading other networks such as The WB, UPN, The CW, ABC Family, and Freeform to repeat the same strategy—offering a lineup of shows to cater to young female viewers, which, according to Ross and Stein, "have shaped (and continue to shape) the predominant perception of Teen TV."[7] More recently, this strategy has seemingly been embraced by streaming services, which, in addition to providing access to past teen dramas, are also airing original teen programming, as exemplified by HBO Max's *Gossip Girl* reboot (2021–present) and *Pretty Little Liars: Original Sin* (2022-present) and Netflix's *Outer Banks* (2020–present) and *Chilling Adventures of Sabrina*. This new platform impacts the genre because teen series developed for streaming services have greater narrative freedom than their network counterparts—they do not need to adhere to stringent broadcast standards in terms of episode length or content.

Scholars have acknowledged the difficulty of defining "teen television," as there are a wide range of shows that could be included within the broader genre, such as episodic sitcoms like *Saved by the Bell* (NBC 1989–93), half-hour dramedies like *Reservation Dogs* (Hulu, 2021–present), hour-long dramas like *My So-Called Life* (ABC, 1994–95), and even reality television like *Teen Mom* (MTV, 2009–12).[8] Within those categories, additional subgenres can also be identified. Despite these distinctions, teen television is indebted to the 1980s films of John Hughes—*Sixteen Candles* (1984), *The Breakfast Club* (1985), and *Pretty in Pink* (1986), to name a few—which established character archetypes and a set of stock expectations while introducing newfound depth and dimension.[9] These characters and storylines focused not only on love and friendship, but also on timely social issues and struggles with identity.[10] Along with these more nuanced characters and stories, Hughes has been credited with shifting the focus of teen narratives by moving young women into central roles.[11] The characters and storylines of the contemporary teen canon, which consists of shows like *Beverly Hills, 90210*, *Dawson's Creek* (The WB, 1998–2003), *One Tree Hill* (The WB, 2003–06/The CW, 2006–12), *The O.C.* (FOX, 2003–07), *Gossip Girl* (The

CW, 2007–12), *Pretty Little Liars* (ABC Family/Freeform, 2010–17), and *Riverdale* (The CW, 2017–present), embody many of the tropes and conventions established by Hughes.

For this analysis, the series identified above as part of the canon are used to exemplify the broader teen television genre. This admittedly narrow definition of teen television focuses on serialized hour-long scripted programs marketed to young viewers, which air during primetime and feature young ensemble casts in coming-of-age stories that are both quippy and emotional as well as self-referential. While parents and familial conflict may play a role in these stories, the focal point are the teens and their relationships with each other. As a result, these series may be classified as "teen drama" or "teen soaps." While the former term is used by critics to acknowledge "quality" programming and helps legitimize teen television, the latter links the shows to daytime soap operas, which are often dismissed as frivolous melodrama.[12] In both cases, the terms speak to the emotional and serialized nature of the stories, which contributes to the feminization of teen TV.[13] Overall, these series adhere to the conventions established by the touchstone *Beverly Hills, 90210* and have shared similar commercial success and widespread popularity. While these shows fall within the subset of the "melodramatic teen serial," they are highly recognizable as, and representative of, "teen TV" in general, making them ideal points of comparison to the more specific teen horror subgenre.[14]

While the teen TV shows mentioned above are primarily set in the "real world,"[15] there is a subgenre of teen programs that incorporate the supernatural known as "teen horror." In series such as *Buffy the Vampire Slayer* (The WB, 1997–2001/UPN, 2001–03), *Charmed* (The WB, 1998–2006), and *The Vampire Diaries* (The CW, 2009–17), teens and young adults must face the trials of adolescence and burgeoning adulthood while also battling evil forces. Though the inclusion of the supernatural may appear to stray from the traditional teen "drama" or "soap opera," the prevailing metaphor of "high school as hell" anchors these shows within the broader genre. As Sara Magee explains, high school represents a time when teenagers face numerous challenges, and "while demons and monsters might not physically appear in those forms, many teenagers find themselves likening these emotions and experiences to going through hell."[16] Thus, teen television shows that fall within the category of teen horror still deal with the same issues as the programs in the broader genre, but may do so under the guise of young people negotiating magical powers and facing occult beings.

Young Femininity in Teen TV

In a discussion of "teen girl" shows from the 1950s and 1960s, Bill Osgerby notes that these shows "could be interpreted as offering representations of femininity that were passive, conformist, and subordinate through their emphasis on the importance of 'winning a man' and their depiction of a woman's place as being 'in the home.'"[17] While these representations may seem archaic, they are nonetheless present in teen dramas from the 1990s like *Beverly Hills, 90210* and *Dawson's Creek*.[18] In fact, as Jenny Bavidge explains, "The vicissitudes of girlhood, particularly the distinction between good and bad girls, is notably present in much contemporary teen TV."[19] However, over the years, young femininity in teen television evolved. In addition to the wholesome "good girls," the genre also idealizes self-destructive "troubled girls" and post-feminist "bad girls."[20] Regardless of whether they are "good," "troubled," or "bad," these constructions of the broader genre tend to focus predominantly on traditionally attractive cisgender, White, middle- to upper-class, heterosexual young women who have stereotypical storylines that revolve around romance and resolve with marriage and motherhood.[21]

In contrast, the teen horror subgenre has been lauded for offering an alternative version of young femininity—one that portrays "free-thinking, independent-minded young women" who are responsible for saving the world.[22] Teen horror moves beyond simply featuring young women in leading roles and depicts them as empowered heroines due to their magical birthrights. According to Catherine Driscoll and Alexandra Heatwole, heroic young women are more likely to appear in teen horror rather than the broader genre because "a speculative girl hero can act more violently and still remain both heroic and girl-like, given that neither her skills nor the dangers she must confront are checked by realist believability."[23] In other words, teen horror allows for an expanded representation of young femininity—one that highlights strong and intrepid young women—because of its deviation from "reality."

Just as the conventions and characters of the broader genre have grown out of the films of John Hughes, the depictions of young femininity, particularly those situated within in teen horror, owe much to *Buffy the Vampire Slayer*—with the titular character being one of the most iconic female characters of the subgenre.[24] First appearing in a 1992 film and then returning in a long-running television series, Buffy Summers (Sarah Michelle Gellar) challenged preconceived notions of young femininity by showing a beautiful, petite, blonde cheerleader who cracks jokes while saving the world from vampires and demons. Buffy subverted gender expectations of what it meant to be a young woman because, as Marnina Gonick suggests, rather than being "vulnerable, voiceless, and fragile," she embodied "girl power" or a "more positive version of girlhood, one that is assertive, dynamic, and unbound from the constraints of passive femininity."[25] Although Buffy is undeniably powerful, she still adheres to traditional femininity through her appearance and pursuit of heterosexual romance. Therefore, critics have problematized shows like *Buffy* for their underlying post-feminist sensibilities (and their notion of "girl power"), which imply that gender equality has been achieved.[26] Nevertheless, as Jennifer Stuller notes, *Buffy* was responsible for "flipping the script on the damsel in distress," and particularly in the final season, offered a vision of female community and shared power that has been celebrated for its feminist approach.[27]

Despite being placed within the teen horror subgenre, Catherine Driscoll explains, "*Buffy* is as much about feminine adolescence as it is about monsters."[28] Though unique, Buffy, as a representation of young femininity, is not completely divorced from the broader genre. Megan Hensey posits that for young women in teen horror, although "their primary interest is saving the world, finding 'the right man' comes a close second."[29] Thus, Buffy's heroism is dependent upon storylines that still rely on stereotypical feminine plots revolving around romance.[30] Yet, Driscoll points out that "one way in which *Buffy* exceeds the teen TV genre, though, is in its use of this central narrative of frustrated romance [. . .] The destiny articulated for Buffy is magical and deathly rather than heteronormative bliss."[31] In other words, though the series ends with Buffy saving the world, she is not ensconced in romance or motherhood, radically deviating from the resolutions of most young women in teen television. Overall, *Buffy* offers a more complicated depiction of young femininity in teen television by speaking to both feminist and post-feminist sensibilities.

Situating Sabrina

Chilling Adventures of Sabrina (Netflix, 2018–20) follows the journey of Sabrina Spellman (Kiernan Shipka), a half-witch, half-mortal sixteen-year-old girl, as she navigates the "witch world of her family and the human world of her friends."[32] Thus, *Chilling Adventures of Sabrina* (*CAoS*) features many of the hallmarks of teen dramas such as stories about first love, burgeoning sexuality, friendship, and the challenges of growing up. At the same time, Hensey acknowledges that "*Chilling Adventures* has been compared to *Buffy the Vampire Slayer* [. . .] due to shared generic codes and conventions, such as characterization, setting, and narrative. Both protagonists are supernatural, blonde teenage girls who fight monsters to protect the underdog."[33] By associating itself with *Buffy,* Hensey explains, *CAoS* is "aligning itself with quality examples of the horror teen genre" while at the same time establishing "a playful intertextual relationship with another genre; that is, the coming-of-age drama."[34] Though clearly situated in the occult, *CAoS* is a contemporary of The CW's *Riverdale* with both shows sharing the same showrunner (Roberto Aguirre-Sacasa) and source material (*Archie* comic books), making it an ideal case study to interrogate the show's construction of young femininity as a legacy of both the broader genre and the subgenre.

LIBERATION

Chilling Adventures of Sabrina diverges from past teen television programs in a number of ways. Most significantly, the show features a powerful female protagonist that is explicitly feminist and includes feminist storylines. *CAoS* is also far more inclusive in terms of the depiction of its female characters. Beyond identity and appearance, the series offers a more nuanced approach to female sexuality and eschews one of the traditional tropes of female relationships that consist of catfights among "frenemies."

A Feminist Witch

Though contemporary teen television has long been critiqued for its post-feminist sensibilities, Rosalind Gill notes that there has been increased attention to some feminist issues in popular media.[35] Historically, teen television has incorporated some feminist issues in both the broader genre and within the teen horror subgenre.[36] However, there is a distinct difference between having an isolated episode or storyline that features a feminist issue and having an unabashedly feminist protagonist. *CAoS* moves the genre forward by establishing and sustaining a clear feminist ideology throughout the series.

In its very first episode, "Chapter One: October Country" (1:1), *CAoS* addresses hostile environments and the all-too-common indifferent response to sexual harassment when four football players pull up Susie Putnam's (Lachlan Watson) shirt at school. Sabrina brings the incident to the principal's attention in hopes of recourse. Despite sharing concern for her friend's safety, Principal Hawthorne (Bronson Pinchot) dismissively responds that Sabrina should "suggest that Miss Putnam find another school."[37] Rather than give up, Sabrina decides to fight back by forming a club "for young women to meet and bolster each other."[38] Sabrina explains to her friends that the club is a place "where we can discuss issues and problems we're facing and come up with proactive solutions."[39] While organizations can provide a sense of community and support, Sabrina's vision of sisterhood includes actively challenging the status quo. She elaborates that the club will allow young women "to mobilize and protest if we need to get political, to fight when we need to fight, to defend each other" in an effort to "topple the White patriarchy."[40] Therefore, Sabrina moves beyond simply expressing individual empowerment (i.e., "girl power") and instead addresses systemic injustice and acknowledges that direct collective action may be necessary. By naming the club "WICCA," which stands for "the Woman's Intersectional Cultural and Creative Association," the series nods to Rachel Moseley's understanding of "the witch" as "a metaphor for female resistance" that "departs from the hegemonic ideal."[41] Thus, with the pilot the series establishes not just a strong female protagonist but one that is aware of and engaged in feminist activism.

For the rest of the series, *CAoS* continues to feature feminist storylines. As Hensey notes, in "Chapter Three: The Trial of Sabrina Spellman" (1:3), when Sabrina is on trial for promising to sign her name in the *Book of the Beast* and then changing her mind, the episode functions "as case study of how the series explores contemporary issues of consent and choice."[42] In "Chapter Twelve: The Epiphany" (2:1), Sabrina confronts institutionalized sexism once again, this time at the Academy of Unseen Arts, when she vies for the position of "Top Boy"—who is "traditionally a male student" (00:08:44)—to ensure that "all students, regardless of gender, feel like they have a voice" (00:09:14). In "Chapter Twenty-Eight: Sabrina Is Legend" (3:8), Roz Walker (Jaz Sinclair) saves Harvey Kinkle's (Ross Lynch) life, which challenges gender norms by demonstrating female strength and cunning as well as depicting a young woman of color as the hero. More broadly, throughout the series, Sabrina constantly battles powerful men like the Dark Lord (Luke Cook) and Faustus Blackwood (Richard Coyle), as well as men who desire power like Caliban (Sam Corlett)—which aligns evil with the patriarchal forces and offers feminist action as the solution.

Perhaps the most obvious example of the feminist sensibilities of the series occurs in "Chapter Thirty-Two: The Imp of the Perverse" (4:4), when Sabrina and Roz run as co-presidents of Baxter High's Student Council. While distributing campaign flyers featuring the slogan "Witches United," Sabrina makes an impromptu speech explaining:

> It means Roz and I are running as witches. It means we are powerful, disruptive women, champions of the oppressed, supporters of the other, unapologetic feminists, allies to all those who live in the shadow of the patriarchy, reminders that the shadow has its own power. We will speak the truth and we will fight injustice. So, in other words . . . we are Sabrina Spellman and Rosalind Walker. We are teenage witches and we will be your next student council co-presidents.[43]

Like the pilot, here Sabrina acknowledges the need to "fight injustice" that comes from "the patriarchy."[44] However, unlike the pilot, Sabrina does more than just allude to the metaphor of witches as resistant women; this time she makes it explicit along with her "unapologetic" feminist identity.[45] The cheers that Sabrina elicits from the gathering crowd of students affirms that her perspective is not marginal, but rather is readily accepted as the way things should be. Rather than presenting Sabrina and her friends as frivolous young women, the series presents them as thoughtful and eloquent when fighting for fairness and equality.[46] Furthermore, Sabrina and her friends go beyond mere lip service to feminist ideals and instead demonstrate authentic engagement with feminist identities and action—suggesting that *CAoS* has eschewed the post-feminism of past teen television shows.

Inclusive Depictions of Young Femininity

While there is no doubt that Sabrina is the central focus of the series (after all, the show's title clearly indicates it is about her adventures) and she is a young, able-bodied, cis-gender, heterosexual White woman, the series includes characters and storylines that are far more inclusive than past teen TV. For instance, teen dramas tends to feature predominantly White casts as illustrated by *Beverly Hills, 90210*; *Dawson's Creek*; *The O.C.*; and *One Tree Hill*. In fact, these series did not include any non-White lead female characters until Emily in *Pretty Little Liars* in 2010, and the teen horror sub-genre did not feature non-White lead female characters until Bonnie in *The Vampire Diaries* in 2009. This is not to say that there was a complete absence of people of color in these programs; they were present, albeit peripheral. Similarly, teen television by and large adopts compulsory heterosexuality. As both *Dawson's Creek* and *Buffy the Vampire Slayer* progressed, they did include the "coming out" narratives of Jack McPhee (Kerr Smith) and Willow Rosenberg (Alyson Hannigan), but neither were initially introduced as LGBTQ+ characters. Although *Pretty Little Liars* was among the first teen shows that featured a lead lesbian character from the start of the series and incorporated bisexual characters, its portrayal of CeCe Drake (Vanessa Ray), the show's only transgender character, as a mentally deranged villain complicates the series' contributions to increasing diversity within the genre.

In contrast, *CAoS* meaningfully engages in inclusive representation, which broadens the depictions of young femininity in teen television. In the pilot episode, the series establishes Sabrina's two closest friends at Baxter High, Roz and Susie, as individuals who are different from her. Instead of simply being Sabrina's sidekicks, the series also follows Roz, a young Black woman, as she deals with the loss of her vision and the emergence of her own super-natural powers, and Susie, who transitions to Theo in "Chapter Twelve: The Epiphany" (2:1) and finds love with Robin Goodfellow (Jonathan Whitesell). Both Roz and Theo are given their own stories that not only go beyond their relationship with Sabrina, but also go beyond their gender, race, or (dis) ability. Throughout the series both Roz and Theo are involved in romantic relationships even when Sabrina, the protagonist, is not. By showing Roz and Theo as worthy of love, and Sabrina as (temporarily) marginalized, the series works to decenter the hegemonic status quo. At the Academy of Unseen Arts, Sabrina also encounters Prudence Night (Tati Gabrielle), the illegitimate daughter of Faustus Blackwood. Although Prudence is initially antagonistic towards Sabrina, the pair eventually become friends. While Taylor Crumpton rightfully acknowledges that Prudence is portrayed as "an angry Black woman" at the start of the series,[47] like Roz and Theo, she has her own story arc. Instead of simply serving as a foil for Sabrina, Prudence has her own journey—coming to terms with Faustus and holding him accountable for his crimes against the coven. Prudence is also multidimensional as depicted through her caring relationship with her adopted sister Agatha (Adeline Rudolph) and twin half-siblings as well as in her romance with Ambrose Spellman (Chance Perdomo).

Admittedly, Sabrina, Roz, Susie, and Prudence all have thin, fit bodies, which is commonplace for teen TV. However, unlike the hypersexualized femininity of Buffy or *Riverdale*'s Veronica Lodge (Camila Mendes), Betty Cooper (Lili Reinhart), and Cheryl Blossom (Madeline Petsch), *CAoS* offers a range of what is considered acceptable in terms of young female appearance. For instance, before Susie transitions to Theo, Roz and Sabrina think nothing of her ambiguous appearance—they never question it, and the boys at Baxter High that tease Susie are portrayed as wrong for doing so. Likewise, throughout the series Roz appears with glasses and natural hair, which is not the norm in teen television. For the most part, Sabrina and Roz avoid revealing clothing and heavy makeup—a standard for young women in teen television—and although their outfits nod to 1960s fashion, they are not unstylish. Even when dressed in their Baxter High cheerleading uniforms or formal dresses, Sabrina and Roz are not subjected to an objectifying gaze. Although Sabrina and Roz's appearances are not sexualized, they are never presented as undesirable or unattractive. In contrast, Prudence's bold makeup, short blond hair, and more provocative clothing offers a different approach to feminine style. Even when Sabrina is at odds with her, Prudence's look is never commented upon, which is unusual given critiquing the appearance of perceived adversaries is commonplace for female characters throughout teen TV. Thus, *CAoS* offers a broader range of identities for young women and expands perceptions of "acceptable" female appearances.

Nuanced Sexuality

Over the years, teen television has offered a bifurcated depiction of young women's sexuality. At one extreme, in shows like *Beverly Hills, 90210* and *Dawson's Creek,* young women are punished for having sex with pregnancy scares or "bad" reputations.[48] Even Buffy, a character who is celebrated for her "empowered" femininity, is traumatized by her first sexual experience. At the other extreme, the young women of *Gossip Girl* (The CW, 2007–12) and *Riverdale* are shown as in control and aggressive, and sex rarely has consequences. Rather than play to either extreme, *CAoS* takes a new approach to young women and sex where the characters exist as sexual beings without being shamed or overly sexualized. This is not to suggest the series avoids sex altogether or is never exploitative. After all, sex is central to "Chapter Two: The Dark Baptism" (1:2), when Sabrina and the Weird Sisters use the promise of sex to punish Susie's tormentors, and is the foundation of the Lupercalia festival in "Chapter Fourteen: Lupercalia" (2:3). However, what makes *CAoS* unique is the way the characters thoughtfully address sex and sexuality.

In "Chapter Fourteen: Lupercalia" (2:3), prompted by the upcoming Lupercalia celebration—which climaxes in an orgy—Sabrina discusses sex with her aunts, Zelda (Miranda Otto) and Hilda Spellman (Lucy Davis), as well as her best friend Roz. In her conversation with her aunts, Sabrina openly expresses reservations about having sex, to which Zelda responds that the festival "is a symphony of sensuality and pleasure, not shame and regret," while Hilda validates Sabrina's uncertainty.[49] Although Hilda and Zelda have different stances on whether their niece is ready for sex, both are united in wanting Sabrina to have a positive experience. Later, Sabrina asks Roz, "How did you know when you were ready?" and Roz shares that when she lost her virginity to Jordan Bixby she was initially "super scared" but she "really liked him." Roz explains, "I remember this sensation, like a tingling up my spine. And even though I was scared, my body just took over and knew what to do."[50] Although Roz's sexual history is new to the audience, it is presented as natural and positive—she is not ashamed, nor does she feel conflicted about her experience. Yet Roz does not trivialize sex, as demonstrated by her gently asking if Sabrina really cares for Nick Scratch (Gavin Leatherwood) and confirming that he is not pressuring her. Perhaps most importantly, Roz affirms Sabrina by reiterating that her best friend will know when she is ready. Although Sabrina does not have sex with Nick until "Chapter Thirty-Three: Deus Ex Machina" (4:5), when she does, she is confident about her actions. Consequently, through the sex-positive conversations Sabrina has with Hilda, Zelda, and Roz, *CAoS* removes the stigma around sexual activity for young women by normalizing sex and the pleasure it can bring and encouraging them to trust their instincts about their bodies and desires.

Friendship Over Frenemies

Although the stories of teen television and teen horror are constructed around a group of friends, these series often show young women in conflict over power, prestige, and most often, male attention. When the genre presents female characters as "frenemies" rather than actual friends, it upholds age-old gender stereotypes of young women as catty, competitive, and untrustworthy.[51] Fortunately, *CAoS* breaks free from the frenemy trope by depicting an honest and supportive friendship between Sabrina and Roz.

When Roz has a vision that she will kiss Harvey, Sabrina's former boyfriend, she is unsettled despite her growing feelings for him. Likewise, when Harvey asks Roz to the Valentine's Day dance, she does not immediately accept his invitation. Rather than pursue Harvey unbeknownst to Sabrina, which she could easily do due to Sabrina's commitments at the Academy, Roz chooses to be up front with her best friend. In "Chapter Fourteen: Lupercalia" (2:3), Roz directly addresses the issue with Sabrina when she says:

> I had to ask you something and I wanted it to be face-to-face [. . .] Over the last few weeks, Harvey and I have been hanging out. And well, he asked me to go to the Sweethearts Dance with him. And I haven't said yes yet, because we're still friends.[52]

Instead of storming out or getting angry, Sabrina calmly explains that her relationship with Harvey is over. Although Sabrina's response opens the door for a relationship with Harvey, Roz double checks that Sabrina is "100 percent" sure.[53] Admittedly, Sabrina's burgeoning relationship with Nick helps make the situation less fraught, but their conversation suggests that Sabrina and Roz prioritize and value their friendship over male affection. By communicating openly and respectfully with each other, Sabrina and Roz do not engage in the cliched teen TV tropes of backstabbing, insults, and physical attacks. Because this toxic behavior is such an anathema, when a mandrake manifests as Sabrina and cruelly tells Roz that Harvey will always love her in "Chapter Nineteen: The Mandrake" (2:8), Roz quickly realizes it is not her best friend. By avoiding the stereotype of catty teen girls competing for the attention of a man, *CAoS* offers a new model for female friendships.

LIMITATIONS

As highlighted above, there are depictions of young femininity in *Chilling Adventures of Sabrina* that have pushed the boundaries of the teen television genre. At the same time, the series is also limited by its reprisal of tired gendered tropes. *Chilling Adventures of Sabrina* echoes teen television of the past by depicting strong young women as disobedient and unable to control their power. Likewise, in keeping with genre conventions, the series celebrates young women's sacrifices and emphasizes romance.

Personal Failings and Power

As a genre, teen television offers highly gendered depictions of power and obedience. For example, in *One Tree Hill,* Lucas Scott (Chad Michael Murray) deliberately forsakes his heart medication before the state championships because it interferes with his ability to play basketball, yet he is rewarded for his actions by making the game-winning shot. In contrast, both the broader genre and the teen horror subgenre suggest that power is unmanageable for young women, as illustrated by Blair Waldorf's (Leighton Meester) utter failure at her magazine internship in *Gossip Girl* and Willow's dangerous addiction to dark magic that devolves into madness in *Buffy the Vampire Slayer*. Similarly, a running theme throughout *CAoS* is the protagonist's inability to appropriately use her magical powers and heed advice. As a result, Sabrina unintentionally unleashes harm on her loved ones as well as herself.

In "Chapter Eight: The Burial" (1:8), a well-intentioned Sabrina attempts necromancy in hopes of easing Harvey's grief by resurrecting his deceased brother, Tommy Kinkle (Justin Dobies). Hilda explicitly tells Sabrina that "bringing back the dead is by and large a no-no. Easier done with witches and never-ever to be tried with mortals." Sabrina not only ignores Hilda but baldly lies to her when she claims, "Don't worry, Aunt Hilda. I haven't got any ideas."[54] Sabrina then seeks help from Ms. Wardwell (Michelle Gomez) who also warns that "necromancy is the darkest and most dangerous of sacred magics" and that "it's a treacherous business. Life. Death. The Afterlife. These are not things to be trifled with."[55] As with her aunt, Sabrina ignores Ms. Wardwell and proceeds to resurrect Tommy even though it requires her schoolmate Agatha's death, which Sabrina also presumes she can undo. Upon realizing what his cousin has done, Ambrose chastises Sabrina:

> Why must you always insist that the universe grant you special privileges? You've upset the natural order. You do realize that, don't you? There is no cheating fate [. . .] You've crossed a line this time [. . .] No, you've completely erased it![56]

And though she resurrects both Tommy and Agatha, as "Chapter Nine: The Returned Man" (1:9) chronicles, Sabrina is far from successful. Agatha is vomiting dirt, a result of coming back to life too soon, and Tommy is a zombie—a body without a soul. When Hilda discovers what Sabrina has done, she exclaims, "You did the one thing I told you not to do! Incorrectly to boot!" and Zelda rebukes, "no one in their right mind would do what you did [. . .] all you did was make things worse [. . .] there's nothing to fix, and he can't be saved." Although Sabrina naively insists that she can "fix this,"[57] Hilda, Ambrose, and Zelda are eventually proven right, forcing Harvey to kill his resurrected brother to correct Sabrina's actions and bringing him more pain.

Even when Sabrina can control her magic, her poor judgment and self-interest undercut her power. At the end of the third season, Sabrina creates a time paradox which enables her to pursue two paths by having a version of herself (Sabrina Morningstar) rule Hell while she (Sabrina Spellman) continues her life in Greendale. In "Chapter Twenty-Eight: Sabrina Is Legend" (3:8), Ambrose discovers what Sabrina has done and explains that the two Sabrinas must limit their contact because "the ramifications of this are horrifying at best."[58] When his cousin brushes him off, he cautions "everything has consequences."[59] Later in "Chapter Twenty-Nine: The Eldritch Dark" (4:1), Ambrose reiterates that the Sabrinas interacting "could precipitate a cataclysm [. . .] that could snuff out both timelines completely."[60] Nevertheless, Sabrina Spellman fails to heed these dire warnings and chooses to visit Sabrina Morningstar to ease her loneliness and regret. As predicted, Sabrina's selfish actions eventually result in the death of Sabrina Morningstar, making it impossible for Sabrina Spellman to ignore the inherent truth of the Eldritch Dark's accusation, "You put your family in danger. You put your friends in danger."[61] Thus, rather than praising Sabrina's headstrong behavior as tenacious and determined, her actions are portrayed as self-centered and reckless.

Sabrina and Sacrifice

Sacrifice permeates stories about women—with cultural expectations valorizing women who put the needs of others before themselves.[62] Teen television is no exception—from Joey Potter (Katie Holmes) choosing to stay in Capeside with Dawson Leery (James Van Der Beek) instead of going to Paris in the first season finale of *Dawson's Creek* to Buffy dying in the first and the fifth season finales of *Buffy the Vampire Slayer*. Although Sabrina is depicted negatively when it comes to her ineptitude and disobedience, she is portrayed positively when it comes to sacrifice, reinforcing the gendered stereotype that women are supposed to be selfless.

Sabrina's first sacrifice occurs in "Chapter Nineteen: The Mandrake" (2:8), when she is faced with her role in the Dark Lord's prophecy that would bring about the End of Days. Her only recourse is to relinquish her power and become fully mortal. Sabrina's friends and family implore her to consider alternatives since relinquishing her powers is equivalent to "witch suicide," leading her to "age, wither, and die."[63] However, Sabrina accepts her fate bravely stating, "I couldn't let my legacy be the destruction of the world."[64] Unlike other instances when she disregards the perspectives of her loved ones, in this case, Sabrina's actions appear noble because she is placing the greater good before her own self-interest. Although Lilith (Michelle Gomez)[65] eventually restores Sabrina's "witch abilities"[66] and grants her freedom in "Chapter Twenty: The Mephisto Waltz" (2:9), Sabrina has no idea this will occur, making her decision truly altruistic.

In the final season, *CAoS* revisits the idea of sacrifice, this time requiring it of both Sabrina Morningstar and Sabrina Spellman. "Chapter Thirty-Three: Deus Ex Machina" (4:5) reveals that the existence of the two Sabrinas has resulted in a parallel cosmos hurtling towards the earth, and the only way to avert impact is to send one Sabrina to the alternate universe. Though both Sabrinas are willing, a game of "rock, paper, scissors" determines that Sabrina Morningstar will go. Responding to the Dark Lord's objections, she states, "You always said you wanted me to bring honor to the house of Morningstar. What kind of queen would I be if I let my subjects die?" and courageously enters the portal to the other realm—giving up her husband, throne, and life in Hell.[67] As if sacrificing love and power were not enough, in "Chapter Thirty-Five: The Endless" (4:7), Sabrina Morningstar makes the ultimate sacrifice—her life—when she tries to warn Sabrina Spellman of the impending doom of the Void. In the final episode, "Chapter Thirty-Six: At the Mountains of Madness" (4:8), Sabrina Spellman acknowledges the selflessness of her doppelgänger, "Thanks to Sabrina Morningstar. She gave up her life for us, and now my soul is in her body. How many sacrifices does she have to make for us? For me?"[68]

Just as Sabrina Morningstar sacrifices her life, so does Sabrina Spellman. In "Chapter Thirty-Six: At the Mountains of Madness" (4:8), Sabrina is willing to sacrifice herself not once, but twice, for others. Sabrina's first sacrifice takes place when she journeys to the Void in an attempt to save the world. She tells her familiar, "It has to be me, Salem. It's my life weighted against billions. And even though people say it's not my fault, I feel like it is."[69] Not only does Sabrina feel responsible for the encroaching Void, but she feels guilt over the death of Sabrina Morningstar. Thus, she decides to trap the Void in Pandora's box—despite the risk of getting trapped herself. Sabrina's willingness to put herself in danger demonstrates that she believes the lives of others take precedence over her own.

Although Sabrina teleports back to Earth before being engulfed, she unintentionally begins manifesting the Void's properties—making objects and people disappear. Because she cannot control these newfound powers, Sabrina exiles herself to the Mountains of Madness where she plans to drain the Void out of her body, releasing those who disappeared. Sabrina tells her loved ones to allow the bloodletting to go on for "as long as it takes" in order to get everyone out, even though it may kill her.[70] The painful process takes a physical and emotional toll on Sabrina—she whimpers, pants, and tearfully bids farewell to her loved ones as the life drains out of her. The series leaves no room for doubt that Sabrina was well-aware of the sacrifice she was making; in grief over her niece's death, Hilda sobs, "She knew! She knew what she had to do to save everyone."[71]

In the finale, the sacrifices of Sabrina Spellman and Morningstar are not just depicted but also honored as Zelda memorializes both young women at their funeral, where a mourning crowd of loved ones surround the graves in which the two Sabrinas are buried. In addition, Sabrina is immortalized with a life-sized bronze statue that stands in the center of the Academy's foyer. Not only does Sabrina's monument replace the once revered statues of the Dark Lord and Faustus Blackwood, but Sabrina's literally appears on a pedestal with a spotlight shining down upon it and candles surrounding it to commemorate her life and actions. The homage paid to the Sabrinas after their deaths valorizes and venerates female sacrifice. However, unlike Buffy, there is no resurrection for either Sabrina—the series ends, and though their actions are portrayed as heroic, they are nevertheless dead.

To be fair, Nick also sacrifices himself twice throughout the series—first, when he acts as a flesh Acheron, thus imprisoning the Dark Lord inside himself, and is relegated to Hell in "Chapter Twenty: The Mephisto Waltz" (2:9), and second, at the end of "Chapter Thirty-Six: At the Mountains of Madness" (4:8), when he drowns in the Sea of Sorrows. In both cases, Nick makes these choices not for others, but for Sabrina. To be clear, Sabrina never asks or expects Nick to make these sacrifices; in the former, Nick is trying to prove that he does truly love Sabrina (after it is revealed that he had ulterior motives at the start of their relationship), and in the latter, Nick wants to be with Sabrina, so he opts to join her in the Sweet Hereafter. Though the series frames Nick's choices positively, it is obvious that his sacrifices satisfy his own needs while Sabrina's sacrifices are made in the interest of others.

Romantic Resolution

Although *CAoS* is framed as Sabrina's exploration of her identity (both witch and mortal), the series emphasizes and then resolves with romantic love, like other teen series of the past.[72] Throughout the series, Sabrina is involved in heterosexual romantic relationships—first with Harvey and then with Nick. In the few episodes when Sabrina is not in a romantic relationship, she is extremely unhappy to the point where, in "Chapter Twenty-Nine: The Eldritch Dark" (4:1), Ambrose tells her, "Buck up cousin, being single is not the end of the world."[73] Despite being surrounded by friends, in "Chapter Thirty: The Uninvited" (4:2), Sabrina is so jealous of all the couples she proceeds to get drunk at her aunt's wedding and make an inappropriate speech. Later, in "Chapter Thirty-One: The Weird" (4:3), Sabrina even contemplates conjuring her own boyfriend to alleviate her loneliness and only stops due to the arrival of an Eldritch Terror. Sabrina's ongoing relationships and preoccupation with romance suggests that it is essential to her happiness and self-fulfillment.

Sabrina's other self, Sabrina Morningstar, is also focused on romance. In "Chapter Twenty-Nine: The Eldritch Dark" (4:1), when Sabrina Spellman questions her involvement with Caliban, Morningstar admits, "I mean, yes, he tried to trap us in the Ninth Circle for all of eternity, but he is totes sorry about it."[74] Later, in "Chapter Thirty: The Uninvited" (4:2), Sabrina Morningstar confirms that Caliban is "the one" and announces that they will be getting married.[75] Sabrina Spellman believes she is "too young" and this "too fast," but Morningstar is confident about her decision, explaining, "Every day is a new adventure, and tomorrow I get to marry the man I'm crazy about."[76] Compelled by envy, Sabrina Spellman attempts to sabotage the relationship, but her plan backfires when Caliban proves he truly loves Sabrina Morningstar. Though Sabrina's doubts initially serve as a critique of the relationship, the episode endorses the romance by ending with Sabrina Morningstar and Caliban as a happy couple.

More than her friends, family, or ruling Hell, the series presents Sabrina's relationship with Nick as the most important aspect of her life. In "Chapter Thirty-Six: At the Mountains of Madness" (4:8), as the life drains out of her, Sabrina tearfully says goodbye to her loved ones in her mind. As she cycles through her family, friends, schools, and familiar, her final farewell, which she lingers on, is reserved for Nick. By leaving her goodbye to Nick for last, Sabrina suggests that their romance was the most significant relationship that she had and the most difficult to let go. However, despite her death, Sabrina avoids the frustrated romance of *Buffy*, when Nick joins her in the Sweet Hereafter. Although Sabrina questions Nick's decision, he explains, "What's important is that we're together here forever and ever," and she replies, "That is a plus."[77] With Nick's return in the final moments of the series, *CAoS* once again engages in the cliché of "saving the best for last" and privileges Sabrina's romantic relationship above all others. By reuniting the couple, the series undercuts the tragedy of Sabrina's untimely death and instead reframes it as a happy ending because she has found eternal love. Likewise, through the finale, *CAoS* not only reaffirms that Nick and Sabrina are "endgame," but for Sabrina, in both life and death, romantic love is the ultimate goal.

As a legacy of teen television and teen horror, *Chilling Adventures of Sabrina* simultaneously embraces and challenges the tropes about young femininity that have been previously established by the genre and subgenre.

Most notably, the series is liberated from the past by offering explicitly feminist characters, greater inclusivity, more nuanced approaches to sexuality, and mature female friendships. At the same time, the series also relies on gendered stereotypes about young women when it comes to power, sacrifice, and romance. Therefore, like the genre and subgenres it has emerged from, *CAoS* contains both moments of hegemonic capitulation and moments of resistance. Thus, the series reflects the complicated—and, at times, contradictory—representations of young femininity which enthusiastically promote empowered young women embracing their gifts, engaging in self-definition, and challenging oppressive social forces while at the same time reinforcing conventional gender norms through plot resolution.[78] However, rather than argue that the series simply presents "good" or "bad" depictions of young femininity, it is far more useful to consider how shows like *CAoS* function within the genre and subgenre. If, as Maggie Nelson suggests, liberation is about "making space, of increasing degrees of possibility and decreasing degrees of domination," *CAoS* certainly does just that in terms of how young women are represented.[79] Thus, this chapter seeks to understand continuity and change within teen television and the integral role *CAoS* plays within it.

Ultimately, this chapter suggests that much like its titular character, *CAoS* is presented with two paths, and like Sabrina, attempts to travel both, with mixed results. Though there are moments the series blazes an exciting new trail for representations of liberated young femininity, it also simultaneously follows the chillingly conventional road paved by the female protagonists of past teen television programs. Nevertheless, *Chilling Adventures of Sabrina* pushes at the limits of gender and genre and will undoubtedly impact future teen television programs and their representations of young femininity.

BIBLIOGRAPHY

Bavidge, Jenny. "Chosen Ones: Reading the Contemporary Teen Heroine." In *Teen TV,* edited by Glyn Davis and Kay Dickinson, 41–53. London: British Film Institute, 2004.

Berridge, Susan. "Empowered Vulnerability? A Feminist Response to the Ubiquity of Sexual Violence in the Pilots of Female-Fronted Teen Drama Series." In *Feminist Erasures,* edited by Kumarini Silva and Kaitlynn Mendes, 91–105. New York: Palgrave McMillan, 2015.

Bindig Yousman, Lori. "Same Girl, Different Show: Representations of Young Femininity in Teen TV." In *Women in Media,* edited by Amy Damico, 144–48. Westport, CT: ABC-CLIO/Greenwood, 2022.

———. "Good Girls Go Bad: The Transformation of Young Femininity in Contemporary Teen TV." In *Gender, Race and Class in Media: A Critical Reader,*

6th edition, edited by Bill Yousman, Lori Bindig Yousman, Gail Dines, and Jean M. Humez, 209–17. Thousand Oaks, CA: Sage, 2021.

Chilling Adventures of Sabrina, Season 1, episode 1, "Chapter One: October Country." Directed by Lee Toland Krieger, written by Roberto Aguirre-Sacasa, featuring Kiernan Shipka, Miranda Otto, Lucy Davis, and Chance Perdomo. Released October 26, 2018, Netflix, www.netflix.com/watch/80230071?trackId =200257859.

———, Season 1, episode 8, "Chapter Eight: The Burial." Directed by Maggie Kiley, written by Christianne Hedtke and Lindsey Calhoon Bring, featuring Kiernan Shipka, Ross Lynch, Jaz Sinclair, and Tati Gabrielle. Released October 26, 2018, Netflix, www.netflix.com/watch/80230078?trackId=200257859.

———, Season 1, episode 9, "Chapter Nine: The Returned Man." Directed by Craig William Macneill, written by Axelle Carolyn and Christina Ham, featuring Kiernan Shipka, Miranda Otto, Ross Lynch, and Jazz Sinclair. Released October 26, 2018, Netflix, www.netflix.com/watch/80230079?trackId=200257859.

———, Season 2, episode 3. "Chapter Fourteen: Lupercalia." Directed by Salli Richardson-Whitfield, written by Oanh Ly, featuring Kiernan Shipka, Miranda Otto, Lucy Davis, and Chance Perdomo. Released April 5, 2019, Netflix, www .netflix.com/watch/80230084?trackId=200257859.

———, Season 2, episode 8, "Chapter Nineteen: The Mandrake." Directed by Kevin Sullivan, written by Joshua Conkel, featuring Kiernan Shipka, Miranda Otto, Lucy Davis, and Chance Perdomo. Released April 5, 2019, Netflix, www.netflix.com/ watch/80230089?trackId=14277283.

———, Season 3, episode 8. "Chapter Twenty-Eight: Sabrina Is Legend." Directed by Rob Seidenglanz, written by Roberto Aguirre-Sacasa and Daniel King, featuring Kiernan Shipka, Miranda Otto, Lucy Davis, and Sam Corlett. Released January 24, 2020, Netflix, www.netflix.com/watch/81062659?trackId=200257859.

———, Season 4, episode 1, "Chapter Twenty-Nine: The Eldritch Dark." Directed by Jeff Woolnough, written by Roberto Aguirre-Sacasa and Gigi Swift, featuring Kiernan Shipka, Miranda Otto, Lucy Davis, and Chance Perdomo. Released December 31, 2020, Netflix, www.netflix.com/watch/81062660?trackId =200257859.

———, Season 4, episode 2, "Chapter Thirty: The Uninvited." Directed by Alex Pillai, written by Katie Avery, featuring Kiernan Shipka, Miranda Otto, Lucy Davis, and Sam Corlett. Released December 31, 2020, Netflix, www.netflix.com/ watch/81062661?trackId=200257859.

———, Season 4, episode 4, "Chapter The Imp of the Perverse." Directed by Antonio Negret, written by Christianne Hedtke, featuring Kiernan Shipka, Miranda Otto, Ross Lynch, and Jaz Sinclair. Released December 31, 2020, Netflix, www.netflix .com/watch/81062663?trackId=200257859.

———, Season 4, episode 5, "Chapter Thirty-Three: Deus Ex Machina." Directed by Amanda Tapping, written by Eleanor Jean, featuring Kiernan Shipka, Miranda Otto, Lucy Davis, and Lachlan Watson. Released December 31, 2020, Netflix, www.netflix.com/watch/81062664?trackId=200257859.

————, Season 4, episode 8, "Chapter Thirty-Six: At the Mountains of Madness." Directed by Rob Seidenglanz, written by Roberto Aguirre-Sacasa, featuring Kiernan Shipka, Miranda Otto, Lucy Davis, and Gavin Leatherwood. Released December 31, 2020, Netflix, www.netflix.com/watch/81062667?trackId=200257859.

Coulter, Natalie. *Tweening the Girl.* New York: Peter Lang, 2013.

Crumpton, Taylor. "How 'Chilling Adventures of Sabrina' Failed Prudence Night." *Teen Vogue,* November 1, 2018. www.teenvogue.com/story/chilling-adventures-of -sabrina-failed-prudence-night.

Driscoll, Catherine. *Girls.* New York: Columbia University Press, 2002.

Driscoll, Catherine and Heatwole, Alexandra. *The Hunger Games.* London: Routledge, 2018.

Gill, Rosalind. "Post-postfeminism? New Feminist Visibilities in Postfeminist Times." *Feminist Media Studies* 16, no. 4 (2016): 610–30.

Golden, Stephanie. *Slaying the Mermaid.* New York: Harmony Books, 1998.

Gonick, Marnina. "Between 'Girl Power' and 'Reviving Ophelia': Constituting the Neoliberal Girl Subject." *NWSA Journal* 18, no. 2 (2006): 1–23.

Henesy, Megan. "'Leaving my girlhood behind': Woke Witches and Feminist Liminality in *Chilling Adventures of Sabrina.*" *Feminist Media Studies* 21, no. 7 (2021): 1143–1157. doi.org/10.1080/14680777.2020.1791929.

Kaklamaniduou, Betty and Tally, Margaret. *The Millennials on Film and Television.* Jefferson, NC: McFarland, 2014.

Magee, Sara. "High School is Hell: The TV Legacy of *Beverly Hills, 90210* and *Buffy the Vampire Slayer.*" *Journal of Popular Culture* 47, no. 4 (2014): 877–94.

Martin, Jeff. "*TV Teen Club:* Teen TV as Safe Harbor." In *Teen Television,* edited by Sharon Marie Ross and Louisa Ellen Stein, 27–42. Jefferson: NC: McFarland, 2008.

Mosely, Rachel. "Glamorous Witchcraft: Gender and Magic in Teen Film and Television." *Screen* 43, no. 4 (2002): 403–22.

Murphy, Bernice. *The Suburban Gothic in American Popular Culture.* New York: Palgrave McMillian, 2009.

Nash, Ilana. *American Sweethearts.* Bloomington, IN: Indiana University Press, 2006.

Nelson, Maggie. *On Freedom.* Minneapolis, MI: Graywolf Press, 2021.

Newman, Michael Z. and Levine, Elena. *Legitimating Television.* New York: Routledge, 2012.

Osgerby, Bill. *Youth Culture and the Media.* New York: Routledge, 2021.

Osgerby, Bill. "'So Who's Got Time for Adults!': Femininity, Consumption and the Development of Teen TV—From *Gidget* to *Buffy.*" In *Teen TV,* edited by Glyn Davis and Kay Dickinson, 71–86. London: British Film Institute, 2004.

Ross, Sharon Marie and Stein, Louisa Ellen. "Introduction." In *Teen Television,* edited by Sharon Marie Ross and Louisa Ellen Stein, 3–26. Jefferson, N.C.: McFarland, 2008.

Shary, Timothy. *Teen Movies.* London: Wallflower Press, 2005.

Stuller, Jennifer K. "'Buffy the Vampire Slayer' Celebrated the Joy of Female Power." *Bitch Media,* March 6, 2017. www.bitchmedia.org/article/20-years-buffy-letters -vampire-slayer/joy-female-power.

NOTES

1. Betty Kaklamaniduou and Margaret Tally, *The Millennials on Film and Television* (Jefferson, NC: McFarland, 2014).

2. Illana Nash, *American Sweethearts* (Bloomington, IN: Indiana University Press, 2006).

3. Rachel Mosley, "Glamorous Witchcraft: Gender and Magic in Teen Film and Television," *Screen* 43, no. 4 (2002): 405.

4. Sharon Marie Ross and Louisa Ellen Stein Ross, "Introduction," in *Teen Television,* ed. Sharon Marie Ross and Louisa Ellen Stein (Jefferson, NC: McFarland, 2008), 3–26.

5. Jeff Martin, *"TV Teen Club:* Teen TV as Safe Harbor," in *Teen Television,* ed. Sharon Marie Ross and Louisa Ellen Stein, (Jefferson, NC: McFarland, 2008), 27–42.

6. Bill Osgerby, *Youth Culture and the Media* (New York: Routledge, 2021).

7. Ross and Stein, "Introduction," 17.

8. Ross and Stein, "Introduction," 3–26.

9. Timothy Shary, *Teen Movies* (London: Wallflower Press, 2005).

10. Albeit Hughes' films predominantly privilege cisgender, White, middle class, heterosexual identities.

11. Natalie Coulter, *Tweening the Girl* (New York: Peter Lang, 2013).

12. Ross and Stein, "Introduction," 17–18.

13. Michael Z. Newman and Elena Levine, *Legitimating Television* (New York: Routledge, 2012), 99.

14. Ross and Stein, "Introduction," 15–18.

15. In 2021, *Riverdale* aired a five-episode arc under the name "Rivervale," which was set in an alternative/parallel universe. Interestingly, Sabrina Spellman from *Chilling Adventures of Sabrina* makes an appearance in *Riverdale*'s Rivervale in "Chapter 99: The Witching Hour(s)" (6:4).

16. Sara Magee, "High School is Hell: The TV Legacy of *Beverly Hills, 90210* and *Buffy the Vampire Slayer,*" *Journal of Popular Culture* 47, no. 4 (2014): 885.

17. Bill Osgerby, "'So Who's Got Time for Adults!': Femininity, Consumption and the Development of Teen TV—From *Gidget* to *Buffy,*" in *Teen TV,* ed. Glyn Davis and Kay Dickinson (London: British Film Institute, 2004), 75–76.

18. Lori Bindig Yousman, "Good Girls Go Bad: The Transformation of Young Femininity in Contemporary Teen TV," in *Gender, Race and Class in Media: A Critical Reader, 6th edition,* ed. Bill Yousman, Lori Bindig Yousman, Gail Dines, and Jean M. Humez (Thousand Oaks, CA: Sage, 2021), 209–17.

19. Jenny Bavidge, "Chosen Ones: Reading the Contemporary Teen Heroine," in *Teen TV,* ed. Glyn Davis and Kay Dickinson (London: British Film Institute, 2004), 42.

20. Bindig Yousman, "Good Girls Go Bad," 209–17.

21. Lori Bindig Yousman, "Same Girl, Different Show: Representations of Young Femininity in Teen TV," *Women in Media* (Westport, CT: ABC-CLIO/Greenwood, 2022), 144–48.

22. Bernice Murphy, *The Suburban Gothic in American Popular Culture* (New York: Palgrave McMillian, 2009), 67.

23. Catherine Driscoll and Alexandra Heatwole, *The Hunger Games* (London: Routledge, 2018), 121–22.

24. Given the sheer volume of work dedicated to *Buffy the Vampire Slayer* it could be argued that Buffy is not just one of the most iconic female characters of the sub-genre or teen TV, but television as a whole.

25. Marnina Gonick, "Between 'Girl Power' and 'Reviving Ophelia': Constituting the Neoliberal Girl Subject," *NWSA* Journal 18, no. 2 (2006): 199.

26. Roslind Gill, "Post-postfeminism? New Feminist Visibilities in Postfeminist Times," *Feminist Media Studies* 16, no. 4 (2016): 610–30.

27. Jennifer Stuller, "'Buffy the Vampire Slayer' Celebrated the Joy of Female Power." *Bitch Media* (March 6, 2017) www.bitchmedia.org/article/20-years-buffy -letters-vampire-slayer/joy-female-power.

28. Catherine Driscoll, *Girls* (New York: Columbia University Press, 2002), 233.

29. Megan Hensey, "'Leaving my girlhood behind' Woke witches and feminist liminality in Chilling Adventures of Sabrina," *Feminist Media Studies* 21, no. 7 (2020): 4, doi.org/10.1080/14680777.2020.1791929.

30. Driscoll and Heatwole, *The Hunger Games,* 122.

31. Driscoll, *Girls*, 233.

32. As noted by Sabrina in her opening dialogue in "Chapter One: October Country"; *Chilling Adventures of Sabrina*, season 1, episode 1, "Chapter One: October Country," directed by Lee Toland Krieger, written by Roberto Aguirre-Sacasa, featuring Kiernan Shipka, Miranda Otto, Lucy Davis, and Chance Perdomo, released October 26, 2018, on Netflix, www.netflix.com/watch/80230071?trackId=200257859: 00:02:01.

33. Hensey, "Leaving My Girlhood Behind," 7.

34. Hensey, "Leaving My Girlhood Behind," 8.

35. Gill, "Post-postfeminism? New Feminist Visibilities in Postfeminist Times," 615.

36. Susan Berridge, "Empowered Vulnerability? A Feminist Response to the Ubiquity of Sexual Violence in the Pilots of Female-Fronted Teen Drama Series," in *Feminist Erasures*, ed. Kumarini Silva and Kaitlynn Mendes (New York: Palgrave McMillan, 2015), 91–105.

37. *Chilling Adventures of Sabrina*, "Chapter One: October Country," 00:20:07.

38. *Chilling Adventures of Sabrina*, "Chapter One: October Country," 00:22:46.

39. *Chilling Adventures of Sabrina*, "Chapter One: October Country," 00:22:49.

40. *Chilling Adventures of Sabrina*, "Chapter One: October Country," 00:22:54–00:22:59.

41. Moseley, "Glamorous Witchcraft," 410.

42. Hensey, "Leaving My Girlhood Behind," 11.

43. *Chilling Adventures of Sabrina*, season 4, episode 4, "Chapter Thirty-Two: The Imp of the Perverse," directed by Antonio Negret, written by Christianne Hedtke, featuring Kiernan Shipka, Miranda Otto, Ross Lynch, and Jaz Sinclair, released December 31, 2020, on Netflix, www.netflix.com/watch/81062663?trackId=200257859: 00:56:29.

44. *Chilling Adventures of Sabrina*, "Chapter Thirty-Two: The Imp of the Perverse," 00:56:53–00:56:42.

45. *Chilling Adventures of Sabrina*, "Chapter Thirty-Two: The Imp of the Perverse," 00:56:38.

46. Hensey, "Leaving My Girlhood Behind," 5.

47. Taylor Crumpton, "How 'Chilling Adventures of Sabrina' Failed Prudence Night." *Teen Vogue* (November 1, 2018): www.teenvogue.com/story/chilling -adventures-of-sabrina-failed-prudence-night

48. Bindig Yousman, "Good Girls Go Bad," 211.

49. *Chilling Adventures of Sabrina*, season 2, episode 3, "Chapter Fourteen: Lupercalia," directed by Salli Richardson-Whitfield, written by Oanh Ly, featuring Kiernan Shipka, Miranda Otto, Lucy Davis, and Chance Perdomo, released April 5, 2019, on Netflix, www.netflix.com/watch/80230084?trackId=200257859: 00:04:26.

50. *Chilling Adventures of Sabrina*, "Chapter Fourteen: Lupercalia," 00:51:12–00:51:30.

51. Bindig Yousman, "Good Girls Go Bad," 214.

52. *Chilling Adventures of Sabrina*, "Chapter Fourteen: Lupercalia," 00:13:33.

53. *Chilling Adventures of Sabrina*, "Chapter Fourteen: Lupercalia," 00:14:05.

54. *Chilling Adventures of Sabrina*, season 1, episode 8, "Chapter Eight: The Burial," directed by Maggie Kiley, written by Christianne Hedtke and Lindsey Calhoon Bring, featuring Kiernan Shipka, Ross Lynch, Jaz Sinclair, and Tati Gabrielle, released October 26, 2018, on Netflix, www.netflix.com/watch/80230078?trackId =200257859: 00:16:12–00:16:33.

55. *Chilling Adventures of Sabrina*, "Chapter Eight: The Burial," 00:25:58–00:26:39.

56. *Chilling Adventures of Sabrina*, "Chapter Eight: The Burial," 00:44:26.

57. *Chilling Adventures of Sabrina*, season 1, episode 9, "Chapter Nine: The Returned Man," directed by Craig William Macneill, written by Axelle Carolyn and Christina Ham, featuring Kiernan Shipka, Miranda Otto, Ross Lynch, and Jazz Sinclair, released October 26, 2018, on Netflix, www.netflix.com/watch/80230079 ?trackId=200257859: 00:26:33–00:34:43.

58. *Chilling Adventures of Sabrina*, season 3, episode 8, "Chapter Twenty-Eight: Sabrina Is Legend," directed by Rob Seidenglanz, written by Roberto Aguirre-Sacasa and Daniel King, featuring Kiernan Shipka, Miranda Otto, Lucy Davis, and Sam Corlett, released January 24, 2020, on Netflix, www.netflix.com/watch/81062659 ?trackId=200257859: 00:53:42.

59. *Chilling Adventures of Sabrina*, "Chapter Twenty-Eight: Sabrina Is Legend," 00:56:20.

60. *Chilling Adventures of Sabrina*, season 4, episode 1, "Chapter Twenty-Nine: The Eldritch Dark," directed by Jeff Woolnough, written by Roberto Aguirre-Sacasa and Gigi Swift, featuring Kiernan Shipka, Miranda Otto, Lucy Davis, and Chance Perdomo, released December 31, 2020, on Netflix, www.netflix.com/watch/81062660 ?trackId=200257859: 00:12:48.

61. *Chilling Adventures of Sabrina*, "Chapter Twenty-Nine: The Eldritch Dark," 00:47:25.

62. Stephanie Golden, *Slaying the Mermaid* (New York: Harmony Books, 1998).

63. *Chilling Adventures of Sabrina*, season 2, episode 8, "Chapter Nineteen: The Mandrake," directed by Kevin Sullivan, written by Joshua Conkel, featuring Kiernan Shipka, Miranda Otto, Lucy Davis, and Chance Perdomo, released April 5, 2019, on Netflix, www.netflix.com/watch/80230089?trackId=14277283: 00:10:47–00:10:51.

64. *Chilling Adventures of Sabrina*, "Chapter Nineteen: The Mandrake," 00:29:04.

65. Michelle Gomez plays Ms. Wardwell, Sabrina's favorite teacher at Baxter High, as well as Lilith.

66. *Chilling Adventures of Sabrina*, "Chapter Twenty: The Mephisto Waltz": 00:54:17.

67. *Chilling Adventures of Sabrina*, season 4, episode 5, "Chapter Thirty-Three: Deus Ex Machina," directed by Amanda Tapping, written by Eleanor Jean, featuring Kiernan Shipka, Miranda Otto, Lucy Davis, and Lachlan Watson, released December 31, 2020, on Netflix, www.netflix.com/watch/81062664?trackId=200257859: 00:54:17.

68. *Chilling Adventures of Sabrina*, season 4, episode 8, "Chapter Thirty-Six: At the Mountains of Madness," directed by Rob Seidenglanz, written by Roberto Aguirre-Sacasa, featuring Kiernan Shipka, Miranda Otto, Lucy Davis, and Gavin Leatherwood, released December 31, 2020, on Netflix, www.netflix.com/watch /81062667?trackId=200257859: 00:19:08.

69. *Chilling Adventures of Sabrina*, "Chapter Thirty-Six: At the Mountains of Madness," 00:11:36.

70. *Chilling Adventures of Sabrina*, "Chapter Thirty-Six: At the Mountains of Madness," 00:49:16.

71. *Chilling Adventures of Sabrina*, "Chapter Thirty-Six: At the Mountains of Madness," 00:55:51.

72. Bindig Yousman, "Same Girl, Different Show," 147.

73. *Chilling Adventures of Sabrina*, "Chapter Twenty-Nine: The Eldritch Dark," 00:05:07.

74. *Chilling Adventures of Sabrina*, "Chapter Twenty-Nine: The Eldritch Dark," 00:38:56.

75. *Chilling Adventures of Sabrina*, season 4, episode 2, "Chapter Thirty: The Uninvited," directed by Alex Pillai, written by Katie Avery, featuring Kiernan Shipka, Miranda Otto, Lucy Davis, and Sam Corlett, released December 31, 2020, on Netflix, www.netflix.com/watch/81062661?trackId=200257859: 00:09:40.

76. *Chilling Adventures of Sabrina*, "Chapter Thirty: The Uninvited," 00:29:52.

77. *Chilling Adventures of Sabrina*, "Chapter Thirty-Six: At the Mountains of Madness," 01:00:43.

78. Driscoll and Heatwole, *The Hunger Games*, 148.

79. Maggie Nelson, *On Freedom* (Minneapolis, MI: Graywolf Press, 2021), 77.

Chapter 15

The Anachronistic Bricolage and Eternal Autumn Aesthetic in *Chilling Adventures of Sabrina*

Daria Romanova and Maggie Webster

This chapter focuses on the different ways the fragmented vintage aesthetic manifests itself in *Chilling Adventures of Sabrina* (Netflix, 2018–20), a remake of the *Sabrina the Teenage Witch* (ABC, 1996–2000/The WB, 2000–03) sitcom, both of which are based on the Archie Comics series. After a brief introduction to the notion of contemporary witch identities and the application of vintage within the context of film studies, we propose a theoretical background of retro, faux-vintage, and anachronism, which may be suitable for analyzing modern film productions that cannot be strictly attributed to period films. This study explores fashion and film elements such as colors and historical inspirations for characters' styles in the first season of *Chilling Adventures of Sabrina*, which creates a unique, anachronistic, vintage-inspired look of the show.[1]

WE NEED TO TALK ABOUT VINTAGE

Originally used to label predominantly fashion, the term "vintage" has become increasingly widespread and usually denotes the re-appearance of former styles and tastes in the contemporary fashion context. Scholars such as Angela McRobbie and Alexandra Palmer note that the consumption of past fashion gains an increasing volume due to an overall shift of the general public's interest in the aesthetic of bygone eras.[2] According to Jussi Parikka, vintage nowadays is considered almost better than the new.[3] Heike Jenss states that the popularity of vintage reflects "an expanding memory culture propelled through the accumulation and circulation of the past in material and visual culture."[4] Moreover, Elizabeth E. Guffey calls this contemporary trend of re-evaluating previously used clothing the "symbol of fashion independence."[5]

The booming popularity of everything vintage inevitably sprawls a certain terminological confusion among fashion jargon related to the phenomenon. Due to this widespread trend, the word "vintage" has been adopted as an umbrella term that includes a multitude of contemporary fashion trends that recycle certain elements of the styles from bygone eras. However, in its original meaning, vintage refers specifically to garments and accessories that are between twenty and one hundred years old (the latter is traditionally attributed as antique) and connected to the historical period during which they came into vogue. Therefore, the term vintage can be defined as a consumer practice of collecting and using original items at least twenty years old.

The deliberate inclusion of various anachronistic elements in the show reflects the recent trend of conscious style recycling within popularized witchcraft. In their article "Hooked on Vintage!" Marilyn DeLong, Barbara Heinemann, and Kathryn Reiley notice that vintage style consumers use original garments and mix them with contemporary apparel to create a unique style and, consequently, new identities through altering the original historical motifs to suit their taste and the impression they would like to convey.[6] Many contemporary twenty-first century witches use vintage style, specifically the historic and Gothic horror aesthetic, when presenting their witch identities.[7] Douglas Ezzy argues that the aesthetic is what makes witchcraft popular.[8] Notably, the so-called vintage look does have to be comprised of pieces of clothing produced twenty or more years ago, and as Jenss notes in her study of second-hand fashion cultures, vintage is a "construction of past images and historic looks which can be achieved with original objects as well as new ones that look historic."[9] Hence, a person can put together several pieces of modern clothing and accessories but arrange and pair them with something truly vintage so that the ensemble would create a compelling historical or vintage-inspired look. Contemporary witches play with the dichotomy of old and new through the use of clothing and objects which support the creation of witch identities that not only reify witch heritage but also simultaneously create a modern witch identity. They use vintage as a script or wardrobe to represent what a witch is.[10] The modern approach to bygone styles, therefore, is far from being a re-enactment but is rather a re-imagination of the past in the new modern light. Witches play with various clothing to reinforce the witch they feel they are and, in doing so, cultivate their witch identity.[11]

Some scholars, including Tracy Cassidy and Hannah Rose Bennett, attribute widespread bygone fashion aesthetics to the rise of the idealistic vision of the past in the form of nostalgia as a result of the current economic climate, change in attitudes to old items (from disdain to appreciation), as well as an overall reaction to the fast fashion industry and its lack of individuality.[12] Furthermore, the ethical and moral beliefs about the use and reuse of vintage clothing marries the performativity of contemporary witches within popularized forms of witchcraft, such as Neo-Paganism and earth-based witchcraft, while also supporting environmental ethics.

Similarly, the term "retro" is somewhat consonant with the term "vintage" but is more obscure and does not apply any specific time frame to an object. Usually, it is used to refer to the mainstream phenomenon of reproducing old designs and garments with contemporary materials. In her study, Guffey proposes understanding *retro* as a dualism that "revisits the past with acute ironic awareness" and "pillages history with little regard for moral imperatives or nuanced implications."[13] Notably, the terms *retro* and *vintage* are often used interchangeably even in some academic studies. Stefano Baschiera and Elena Caoduro argue that the term vintage is "applied indiscriminately to a multitude of cultural practices (such as antique, retro, and even second-hand), thus destabilizing its meaning and significance."[14] The definitions of these terms are different somewhat from each other; however, this study makes a conscious choice to adopt vintage as an umbrella term that refers to a multi-faceted notion of bygone aesthetics that relates to the re-imagination, revitalization, and re-creation of styles with fashion trends from the past. The first season of *Chilling Adventures of Sabrina* (*CAoS*) uses a bricolage of vintage aesthetics to create an ethereal atmosphere that provides a stage for oxymoronically anachronistic contemporary witch characters. Originally developed by Claude Levi-Strauss, the concept of bricolage was contextualized in a contemporary style analysis by Dick Hebdige in *Subculture: The Meaning of Style*. They both refer to bricolage as the act of displacing items in comparison with their original practical meaning and therefore breaking with the origin of things in order to give them new meanings.[15] The term bricolage, therefore, is adopted here to denote the multi-faceted kaleidoscope of items from different fashion eras that constitute an overall visual aesthetic of the show. Moreover, the identities of the *CAoS* characters are formed through a "polyphonic bricolage"[16] where visual discourses about the witches in the show are amalgamated to become a performance of that character's identity within specific scenes.

NOSTALGIA IN POPULAR CULTURE

It is impossible to discuss vintage and retro aesthetics without touching upon the notion of nostalgia. Originally, the term nostalgia (from the Greek *nostos,* a return home, and *algia,* longing) was used to denote a pathological mental condition of homesickness similar to melancholy or depression.[17] With time, the term has lost its predominantly medical usage and transcended into the cultural terrain to denote what Philip Drake terms a romanticized "yearning for a better but irretrievable past."[18]

In recent decades, nostalgia has acquired much critical attention as a way of understanding how we relate to time, place, and the media. Often seen as an inhibiting and emotional phenomenon that reacts against change and modernity, nostalgia not only represents a longing for the past but also manifests dissatisfaction with the present. There are two major views on nostalgia: one is represented by Simon Reynolds's argument that nostalgia is "thoroughly entwined with the consumer-entertainment complex: we feel pangs for the products of yesteryear, the novelties, and distractions that filled up our youth."[19] It seems, therefore, that historical artifacts and personal possessions act as a time machine capable of evoking past eras, lives, and narratives. The counterargument, supported by a number of scholars such as Susan Stewart, Henry Jenkins, and Justin Smith, is built on Boym's concepts of "reflective nostalgia," which is a longing for a mythical golden age that is thought to have existed in the past but was lost—a longing for objects and qualities from the past which are impossible in the contemporary world.[20] This idea is further developed in the works of Jenkins, who argues that for nostalgia to work, the aspects of the actual past have to be forgotten and substituted with a "sentimental myth about how things might have been" or "objects we never possessed."[21]

From that point of view, media that utilize vintage aesthetics to evoke a sense of nostalgia, create a depersonalized, romanticized image of the past that does not connect to viewers' memories. As Stewart puts it, nostalgia re-constructs the past that "has never existed except as narrative."[22] Analyzing British cult cinema, Smith argues that nostalgia is a "retrospective fantasy, the memory's utopia" that is "forever-unobtainable."[23] The above-mentioned terms and concepts shared by Smith and Stewart are vitally important for the present analyses of *CAoS,* as they facilitate the exploration of the meaning, purpose, and effects of the anachronistic inaccuracies presented as the norm.

HOW FILM REWORKS THE PAST

Taking into account the ever-growing popularity of vintage both in fashion and lifestyle, it seems reasonable and timely to address the issues of reconstruction and manifestation of the past in contemporary cinema. The term "film aesthetic" refers to the overall look and feel, including visual style, costumes, motifs, and symbols. The vintage discourse opens up more nuanced perspectives on bricolage and how objects, images, and styles of the past are used in a variety of practices and contexts. *CAoS* creates a certain diegetic space that is difficult to locate at a specific time due to the many anachronistic elements presented in the frame; hence, the indeterminacy creates a certain effect on viewers by employing various nostalgic cues.

The theory proposed by Baschiera and Caoduro problematizes the application of the notion of vintage to film theory with the goal of troubling the discursive field of aesthetics.[24] The authors present a taxonomy based on three categories (faux-vintage, retro, and anachronistic) under the rubric of vintage cinema. They mark distinctions based on the temporal placement of the films in question and on the techniques being adopted to represent the historical period. Baschiera and Caoduro's theory aims to promote a new reflection on the ways contemporary cinema represents and embodies infatuation with widespread nostalgia and the past, hence is a useful theoretical framework for this chapter. By focusing on the fascination for these "fragmentary aesthetics" and the different ways in which contemporary cinema continues to build "artificial ruins," Baschiera and Caoduro argue that the mechanism behind the vintage look creates an "appealing 'cuteness' of the image based on contemporary trends and tastes valued by audiences and consumers."[25] Thus, nostalgia in these circumstances does not directly refer to the image of the past, but rather to the re-imagination of it from the standpoint of the modern viewer. Interpreting the rise of the vintage phenomenon in cinema, Baschiera and Caoduro refer to the work of Katharina Niemeyer, who attributes it to "a reaction to accelerated times and the impact of digital technologies and [. . .] a desire to overcome and cure our 'homesickness' for the past via media itself."[26]

Baschiera and Caoduro's classification of vintage cinema includes the category of "anachronism" and refers to cinema productions that utilize bygone fashion styles or obsolete technologies that may show "signs and indexes of their age or, at the opposite, appear as idealized and mint, preserved forever from usage and time decay."[27] Notably, an anachronistic film is set in a time when the technology or fashion style in question is already outdated, and its presence goes beyond the occasional appearance in the frame.[28] Furthermore, the faux-vintage category defines cinema productions that are created with a conscious visual archaism in mind. The latter can be obtained through various digital interventions (such as cigarette burns, visible grain, gritty images, scratches, and vignettes) or the employment of analog technologies (videotape or 8mm film). The film productions in this category try to "hide their digital status, pretending to be from a different decade."[29]

Finally, Baschiera and Caoduro's *retro* category defines cinema products that aim to reach a deliberate archaism (by playing with props, costumes, and set design) in a form of pastiche[30] that involves self-conscious simulations as well as reinterpretations of past visual styles."[31] In these films, vintage objects are often "on display," meticulously arranged to cater to a beautiful, clean, and highly fetishized depiction of a particular era, which is not necessarily true to what the time looked like but rather to the audience's image of it. They acknowledge that the taxonomy is not comprehensive but can reasonably synthesize different trends in utilizing the decorative function of vintage in a film aesthetic.

We use Baschiera and Caoduro's theoretical frame within this chapter to analyze *CAoS* and evaluate whether the TV series creates a certain diegetic space that is difficult to locate at a specific time due to its many anachronistic elements. The relative indeterminacy has a certain effect on viewers through various nostalgic cues. We focus on visual analysis of the show's aesthetic alongside fashion performances that present a polyphonic bricolage that forms the identities of some of the main characters. Moreover, it seeks to define whether *CAoS* can be categorized as anachronistic within Baschiera and Caoduro's taxonomy. Upon defining the problem and proposing a possible theoretical framework for its study, we utilize the methodological device of visual analysis to identify and understand how the elements of the environment and the material culture surrounding the characters are strongly connected with an idea of *pastness*. An image or visual aesthetic can be considered "third-dimensional" data that can represent cultural discourses.[32]

ANALYSIS OF SEASON ONE OF *CAOS*

The Netflix show's temporal setting is purposefully vague. The events of *CAoS* take place in contemporary times, which is reflected by the use of the latest models of gadgets; however, the characters still use rotary dial phones, listen to old radios, and drive vintage cars. An occasional appearance of a smartphone or a laptop brings dissonance into this seemingly retro-looking show, whose aesthetic vibe hints at the 1960s with a modern twist.

In the opening scene of *CAoS,* the titular heroine describes her hometown of Greendale, where "it always feels like Halloween."[33] These words set the mood of the "eternal autumn" that is reflected in the title of the first episode, "Chapter One: October Country." Furthermore, according to the main production designer, Lisa Soper, each of *CAoS'*s main characters was assigned a personal color palette, which was adjusted "depending on the mood, using color to isolate characters, keeping them emotionally apart from the world that surrounds them."[34] Hence, splashes of color are utilized to create the anachronistic atmosphere and polyphonic bricolage of character identity.

Indeed, the use of colors, both subliminal and explicit, has a subtle effect on how the audience perceives the mood of the show. The world of Greendale is built around the autumnal palette that is traditionally attributed to the harvest season, and as Rosemary Radford Ruether argues, in feminist witch-craft these colors can represent divine femininity and the symbolic decay of nature before the long winter season.[35] Moreover, Samhain (Halloween) is the Wiccan's New Year. This balance between the light and the darkness poetically reflects the choice between the worlds of mortals and witches that Sabrina Spellman (Kiernan Shipka) has to face. Coincidentally, the warm, autumnal shades of orange and maroon as well as the use of rich corduroy and wool work as an ode to 1960s fashion, turning *CAoS* into an ultimate almanac of retro Halloween aesthetic.

ANACHRONISTIC BRICOLAGE IN COSTUME DESIGN

Angus Strathie, an Academy Award-winning costume designer who worked on such feature films as *Moulin Rouge* (2001), *A Series of Unfortunate Events* (2017), and *The Age of Adaline* (2015), was responsible for the characters' wardrobes in *CAoS*. Strathie's choice of costumes for the show pays homage to the original Archie Comic series (which dates back to 1962) and skillfully blends various fashion eras into an anachronistic bricolage. Although the producers were not aiming at doing a traditional period drama, the principle of mixing different eras and fashion styles lies at the core of the show's aes-thetic; Strathie noted in an interview that "we were informed by the 1960s and this timeless, country America feeling."[36] Strathie explains that it was not easy to create the wardrobe for the main characters as the plot took place in Greendale, where the weather lingered on the eternal autumn and hence needed "a venerable fall foliage of burgundies, browns, greens, and oranges."[37] The wardrobes of the main characters draw inspiration from vari-ous fashion époques (including strong reminiscences of 1950s, 1960s, and 1970s fashion) and blend vintage with retro and modern, emulating a form of nostalgia for the observer.

Strathie was inspired by the autumn weather to create most of Sabrina's everyday looks in warm colors with the occasional use of various shades of red, green, and brown. The color red was reserved for the most part for Sabrina as an homage to *Little Red Riding Hood,* as she often wandered into the woods where many magical scenes took place, seemingly naive of her vul-nerability to imminent danger. In the first episodes, she appeared in a bright red trapezoidal coat with a round collar, while the rest of the characters wore neutral shades. Most of Sabrina's apparel choices can be described as part of preppy style (popular in the 1950s), characterized by pleated skirts, blazers, headbands, berets, loafers, ballet flats, detachable collars, and knee-high socks. Another vital element in most of Sabrina's looks is a black headband. Notably, during the first important encounter with the world of witchcraft (the Dark Baptism ceremony) in "Chapter One: October Country" (1:1), Sabrina wears a white lace wedding dress formerly belonging to her mother, which is in a style that is pronouncedly 1950s, but the dress changes to black when she moves from the mortal world into the supernatural world. The costume choices and use of colors are examples of anachronistic bricolage, with the aim to establish the polyphonic nature of Sabrina's identity.

Sabrina's cousin Ambrose (Chance Perdomo) lives with Sabrina in the Spellman household, and his costume design has a strong 1970s vibe. He wears thin scarves, printed shirts, and leather jackets which give a relaxed boho feel. The 1970s fashion references to floral prints, sweaters, shoes with small heels, and cropped trousers are a tribute to the first comics about Sabrina, published during the heyday of hippie culture. Furthermore, the styles of Sabrina's aunts, Zelda Spellman (Miranda Otto) and Hilda Spellman (Lucy Davis), have a particular inclination to the late 1920s to 1950s fashion. Strathie said he took into account the 1930s fashion trends for the aunts' looks. It is assumed that the sisters have already lived for over a century, which implies that they must have accumulated a lot of clothes. The clothes not only bring a timeless, vintage vibe associated with the eras in which the witches have lived but also highlight their characters' identities. For instance, Zelda's character is cold, calculating, and pragmatic. She therefore wears dark shades, fur, and corseted clothing in accordance with the timeless elegance of period fashion. She accents these with a large brooch or leopard print, which catapults a retro look from the back of Grandma's closet to the forefront of the modern runway shows. Strathie comments that he liked the idea that something died in the process of dressing Zelda.[38] This is in stark contrast to Zelda's sister, Hilda, who is softer and more indecisive. She is a "Mother Earth" archetype and a kitchen witch, which is reflected in her wardrobe through the green and brown color palette, floral prints, knitted clothing, and baggy silhouettes.

THE ETERNAL AUTUMN ANACHRONISTIC AESTHETIC

Production designer Lisa Soper, who worked on a number of horror films such as *Awakening the Zodiac* (2017) and *House at the End of the Street* (2012), said that the aim of the film set was to reflect the autumnal mood and the vintage nature of the show's aesthetic. Nathaniel Hawthorne's *The House of the Seven Gables* served as the inspiration for the atmosphere of the Spellman house, while the actual House of the Seven Gables that stands in Salem, Massachusetts, influenced its appearance.[39] Soper lists *Rosemary's Baby* (1968) and *The Exorcist* (1973) as sources of inspiration,[40] hence offering a visual narrative that links the Gothic horror genre to the established perception that witches are evil. The film set reflects the autumnal mood and the vintage nature of the show's aesthetic. Aligning *CAoS* with iconic cinematic productions, the creators place the show within the intertextual discourse between its predecessors and contemporaries, expanding beyond merely teen TV and horror genres.

The Spellman house contains many objects and elements of decoration from different decades and styles. This feature falls into Marc Le Sueur's concept of "deliberate archaism," which considers the role of props and digital intervention in creating "new-old films" and was thoroughly explored in Christine Sprengler's *Screening Nostalgia*.[41] Following Walter Benjamin's argument on the revolutionary power of the "outmoded," Le Sueur argues that there is a general agreement in granting the analog object (in particular analog media) an "aura," unlike the "simulation" or its digital counterpart—meaning that a vintage or retro object within the film is more interesting to view and experience on-screen than something more modern. In the case of *CAoS,* we can see the application of this approach explained in the work of Baschiera and Caoduro:

> One could provocatively state that a character browsing a collection of vinyl records is more "cinematographic" than one scrolling through a playlist on iTunes or Spotify. With several media objects now existing digitally and the new miniaturization of technology, there are fewer opportunities to organize the cinematic space using these elements of material culture which, working as a synecdoche, can succinctly offer much information about the characters portrayed and the world they inhabit.[42]

In another essay, Baschiera suggests that nostalgia is created when objects, technology, and clothing disconnect from the era of the film and soundtrack.[43] Thus, a typewriter, a vintage car, or a record player in the frame facilitates the creation of a unique space. With regard to *CAoS*, the director's use of color, soundtrack, vintage clothing, and retro artifacts creates an anachronistic ambiance. The retro appearance of the props in *CAoS* may be explained by the show's focus on characters who are engaged with supernatural powers and how they age differently from mortals. The same principle can be found in Jim Jarmusch's *Only Lovers Left Alive* (2014), which acts as an emblematic example of the anachronistic amalgam of old and new that utilizes old technologies such as musical instruments, recording devices, valve amplifiers, and old television sets to indicate that the main characters (a vampire couple) live beyond the irreversibility of time.

There seems to be a certain parallel between the renewed fascination in popular culture for mythical creatures such as witches, zombies, and vampires with anachronism and analog nostalgia pervading contemporary culture.[44] Amanda Howell notes that vampires act as the perfect mediator for expressing "longing for a relation to the past unbroken by loss" as they "collect, curate, and celebrate remnants of past human creativity."[45] This view is shared by scholars such as Andrzej Marzec, who connects this phenomenon to Boym's notion of "reflective nostalgia."[46] According to Howell, the nostalgic appeal of supernatural fiction deliberately focuses more on "*algia*" (longing) than "*nostos*" (home), and therefore offers a restorative relation to the past that, in return, fuels the "power and persuasiveness of the [nostalgic] fantasy."[47]

The aim of *Chilling Adventures of Sabrina* is not to consistently represent a specific period, but to produce a fluid retro aesthetic that is timeless. The production is inspired by many different elements that refer to 1950s, 1960s, and 1970s aesthetics. Clothing styles as well as outdated gadgets shift the aesthetic vector towards nostalgia, bringing about a touch of mystery. It seems that a nostalgia for the romanticized past collides here with the melancholy of a small town and the Gothic vibe of the witch world. The vintage/retro look with a modern twist is utilized in the creation of the world of *CAoS* because it allows producers to transform the original comics series into a visual kaleidoscope of the vintage aesthetic. The outdated media technologies, fashion garments, and furniture organically coexist with modern-day technologies and together create a unique visual feature of the show. It is noteworthy that the nostalgic feeling does not aim to evoke certain personal recollections, however, because the intended audience of *CAoS* is younger than the vintage era that is being utilized. Yet the creators make allusions to the past through objects associated with a certain time period that indicate an aspect of a character's identity or situation.

These elements of bygone aesthetics qualify *Chilling Adventures of Sabrina* as an anachronistic show in which elements are consciously misplaced in comparison to their original time period in order to create a distinct visual text that facilitates character, plot, or witch narratives. Due to the various levels of visual and narrative readings, *CAoS* can offer fruitful material for further studies on the use of vintage aesthetics as well as the notion of nostalgia in recent film productions in an attempt to theorize the shifting relationship between art, media, and artifacts.

BIBLIOGRAPHY

Abrams, Bryan. "How Chilling Adventures of Sabrina's Production Designer Creates the Occult." *The Credits,* January 5, 2022. www.motionpictures.org/2019/04/how-the-chilling-adventures-of-sabrinas-production-designer-creates-the-occult/.

Baschiera, Stefano, and Elena Caoduro. "Retro, Faux-vintage, and Anachronism: When Cinema Looks Back." *NECSUS: European Journal of Media Studies* 4 (Autumn 2015): 143–163. doi.org/10.25969/mediarep/15202.

Baschiera, Stefano. "'Nostalgically Man Dwells on this Earth': Objects and Domestic Space in *The Royal Tenenbaums* and *The Darjeeling Ltd.*" *New Review of Film and Television Studies* 10, no. 1 (2012): 118–131. doi.org/10.1080/17400309.2011.633030.

Baudrillard, Jean. *Simulacra and Simulation.* Ann Arbor: University of Michigan Press, 1994.

Belk, Russell W. "Halloween: An Evolving American Consumption Ritual." In *NA - Advances in Consumer Research Volume 17*, edited by Marvin E. Goldberg, Gerald Gorn, and Richard W. Pollay, 508–517. Provo, UT: Association for Consumer Research, 1990.

Boym, Svetlana. "Ruinophilia: Appreciation of Ruins." *Atlas of Transformation,* November 23, 2021. monumenttotransformation.org/atlas-of-transformation/html/r/ruinophilia/ruinophilia -appreciation-of-ruins-svetlana-boym.html/.

Boym, Svetlana. *The Future of Nostalgia.* New York: Basic Books, 2001.

Butler, Judith. *Gender Trouble: Feminism and the Subversion of Identity.* 2nd ed. New York: Routledge, 1999.

Cassidy, Tracy Diane, and Hannah Rose Bennett. "The Rise of Vintage Fashion and the Vintage Consumer." *Fashion Practice* 4, no. 2 (2012): 239–261. doi.org/10.2752/175693812X13403765252424.

DeLong, Marilyn, Barbara Heinemann, and Kathryn Reiley. "Hooked on Vintage!" *Fashion Theory* 9, no. 1 (2005): 23–42. doi.org/10.2752/136270405778051491.

Drake, Philip. "Mortgaged to Music': New Retro Movies in 1990s Hollywood Cinema." In *Memory and Popular Film*, edited by Paul Grainge, 183–201. Manchester, UK: Manchester University Press, 2003.

Dyer, Richard. *Pastiche.* London-New York: Routledge, 2007.

Emmison, Michael. "Visual Research: Issues and Developments." In *Qualitative Research*, edited by David Silverman, 297–310. London: SAGE Publications Ltd., 2016.

Ezzy, Douglas. "White Witches and Black Magic: Ethics and Consumerism in Contemporary Witchcraft." *Journal of Contemporary Religion* 21, no. 1 (2006): 15–31. doi.org/10.1080/13537900500381609.

Fachin, Fernando F., and Eduardo Davel. "Reconciling Contradictory Paths." *Journal of Organizational Change Management* 28, no. 3 (2015): 369–392. doi.org/10.1108/JOCM-01-2014-0012.

Freiburger, Calvin, "Netflix 'Sabrina' Reboot Has Real Wiccans Fact-Checking the Details of Witchcraft, Star Tells Kimmel." *LifeSite* November 11, 2021. www

.lifesitenews.com/news/netflix-sabrina-reboot-has-real-wiccans-fact-checking-the
-details-of-witchcraft-star-tells-kimmel/.

Friedlander, Whitney. "Chilling Adventures of Sabrina Costumes Evoke an 'Eternal Autumn,' Says Designer." *The Hollywood Reporter*, October 26, 2021. www .hollywoodreporter.com/lifestyle/style/chilling-adventures-sabrina-costumes -evoke-an-eternal-autumn-says-designer-1154868/.

Geraghty, Lincoln. "Nostalgia, Fandom and the Remediation of Children's Culture." In *A Companion to Media Fandom and Fan Studies,* edited by Paul Booth, 161–174. John Wiley & Sons, Inc. 2018.

Grainge, Paul. "Nostalgia and Style in Retro America: Moods, Modes and Media Recycling." *Journal of American Culture* 23, no. 1 (2000): 27–34. doi. org/10.1111/j.1537-4726.2000.2301_27.x.

Guffey, Elizabeth. *Retro: The Culture of Revival*. London: Reaktion Books, 2006.

Hebdige, Dick. *Subculture: The Meaning of Style*. London: Methuen, 1979.

Holland, Samantha. *Alternative Femininities: Body, Age and Identity*. Oxford: Berg, 2004.

Howell, Amanda. "Vampire Nostalgia." *Continuum* 35, no. 2 (2021): 258–269. doi. org/10.1080/10304312.2021.1936830.

Jenkins, Henry. "Introduction: Childhood Innocence and Other Modern Myths." In *The Children's Culture Reader*, edited by Henry Jenkins, 1–37. New York: New York University Press, 1998.

Jenkins, Henry. *The WOW Climax: Tracing the Emotional Impact of Popular Culture*. New York: New York University Press, 2007.

Jenss, Heike. "Sixties Dress Only." In *Old Cloth, New Looks: Secondhand Fashion*, edited by Alexandra Palmer and Hazel Clark, 177–196. Oxford: Berg, 2005.

Jenss, Heike. *Fashioning Memory: Vintage Style and Youth Culture*. London; New York: Bloomsbury Academic, 2017.

Lukszo Klein, Ula. "Noir Fashion and Noir *as* Fashion." In *Fashion in Film*, edited by Adrienne Munch, 54–80. Bloomington, IN: Indiana University Press, 2011.

Marzec, Andrzej. "Zombie Characters and Hollywood's Second Life-Nostalgia." *Contemporary Cinema* 33, no. 2 (2018): 30–40.

McColl, Julie, Catherine Canning, Louise McBride, Karina Nobbs, and Linda Shearer, "'It's Vintage Darling!': An Exploration of Vintage Fashion Retailing." *The Journal of the Textile Institute* 104, no. 2 (2013): 140–150. doi.org/10.1080/00405000.2012. 702882.

McRobbie, Angela. *Postmodernism and Popular Culture*. England: Psychology Press, 1994.

Moseley, Rachel. "Glamorous Witchcraft: Gender and Magic in Teen Film and Television." *Screen* 43, no. 4 (2002): 403–422. doi.org/10.1093/screen/43.4.403.

Munich, Adrienne, ed. *Fashion in Film*. Bloomington: Indiana University Press, 2011.

Niemeyer, Katharina, ed. *Media and Nostalgia: Yearning for the Past, Present and Future*. New York: Palgrave Macmillan, 2014.

Palmer, Alexandra, and Hazel Clark, eds. *Old Clothes, New Looks, Second Hand Fashion*. Oxford: Berg, 2005.

Palmer, Alexandra. "Vintage Whores and Vintage Virgins, Second Hand Fashion in the Twenty-first Century." In *Old Clothes, New Looks, Second Hand Fashion*, edited by Alexandra Palmer and Hazel Clark, 197–213. Oxford: Berg, 2005.

Parikka, Jussi. *What is Media Archaeology?* Cambridge: Polity Press, 2012.

Reynolds, Simon. *Retromania: Pop Culture's Addiction to its Own Past*. London: Faber and Faber, 2011.

Ruether, Rosemary Radford. *Goddesses and the Divine Feminine: A Western Religious History*. University of California Press, 2005.

Schmidt, Bettina. "Polyphonic Bricolage—Caribbean Cultures in New York." Paper presented at the 2003 meeting of Latin American Studies Association, Dallas, Texas, March 27–29, 2003. moam.info/polyphonic-bricolage-latin-american-studies-association_5995c8021723ddcf69a41513.html.

Sedikides, Constantine, and Tim Wildschut. "Nostalgia across Cultures." *Journal of Pacific Rim Psychology* 16, no. 2 (2022): 1–16. doi.org/10.1177/18344909221091649.

Smith, Justin. *Withnail and Us: Cult Films and Film Cults in British Cinema.* London: IB Tauris, 2010.

Sprengler, Christine. *Screening Nostalgia: Populuxe Props and Technicolor Aesthetics in Contemporary American Film*. Oxford: Berghahn, 2009.

Stewart, Susan. *On Longing: Narratives of the Miniature, the Gigantic, the Souvenir, the Collection*. Durham, NC: Duke University Press, 1993.

Villarreal, Yvonne. "Here's How 'Chilling Adventures of Sabrina' Achieved its 'Suspiria'-Inspired Look." *Los Angeles Times*, October 31, 2021. www.latimes.com/entertainment/tv/la-et-st-chilling-adventures-sabrina-netflix-20181031-story.html/.

Warkander, Philip. "'This Is All Fake, This Is All Plastic, This Is Me': A Study of the Interrelations Between Style, Sexuality and Gender in Contemporary Stockholm." PhD diss., Stockholm University, 2013.

Webster, Maggie. "Becoming Witch: Creating and Confirming Witch Identities Within Social Networking Spaces*.*" PhD diss., University of Wales Trinity Saint David, Lampeter, 2021.

NOTES

1. In this study, the term "style" is understood as a range of actions related to corporal adornment such as dressing, adding accessories, and modifying the body through make-up, hairstyle, etc. Therefore, style is perceived as a multitude of elements: the dress, the dressed body, and the way the clothing is worn to articulate a particular identity and constitute the production of a certain impression, the so-called "look."

2. Angela McRobbie, *Postmodernism and Popular Culture* (England: Psychology Press, 1994); Alexandra Palmer, "Vintage Whores, and Vintage Virgins, Second Hand Fashion in the Twenty-first Century," in *Old Clothes New Looks, Second Hand Fashion*, eds. Alexandra Palmer and Hazel Clark (Oxford: Berg, 2005), 197.

3. Jussi Parikka, *What is Media Archaeology?* (Cambridge: Polity Press, 2012), 3.

4. Heike Jenss, *Fashioning Memory: Vintage Style and Youth Culture* (London: Bloomsbury Academic, 2017), 1.

5. Elizabeth E. Guffey, *Retro: The Culture of Revival* (London: Reaktion Books, 2006), 8, 58.

6. Marilyn DeLong, Barbara Heinemann, and Kathryn Reiley, "Hooked on Vintage!" *Fashion Theory* 9, no. 1 (2005): 25–26, doi.org/10.2752/136270405778051491.

7. Maggie Webster, "Becoming Witch: Creating and Confirming Witch Identities Within Social Networking Spaces" (PhD diss., University of Wales Trinity Saint David, Lampeter, 2021), 257.

8. Douglas Ezzy, "White Witches and Black Magic: Ethics and Consumerism in Contemporary Witchcraft," *Journal of Contemporary Religion* 21, no. 1 (2006): 15–31. doi.org/10.1080/13537900500381609.15-31.

9. Jenss, *Fashioning Memory*, 1.

10. This type of identity cultivation and projection recalls Judith Butler's concept of gender performance, in which what constitutes gender is not internal or essential, but "a stylized repetition of acts" dependent on external efforts, including clothing choices, among other elements. Judith Butler, *Gender Trouble: Feminism and the Subversion of Identity*, 2nd ed. (New York: Routledge, 1990), 179.

11. Fernando F. Fachin and Eduardo Davel, "Reconciling Contradictory Paths," *Journal of Organizational Change Management* 28, no. 3 (2015): 369–392.

12. Tracy Diane Cassidy and Hannah Rose Bennett, "The Rise of Vintage Fashion and the Vintage Consumer," *Fashion Practice* 4, no. 2 (2012): 239–261.

13. Guffey, *Retro: The Culture of Revival*, 163.

14. Stefano Baschiera and Elena Caoduro, "Retro, Faux-vintage, and Anachronism: When Cinema Looks Back," *NECSUS: European Journal of Media Studies* 4, no. 2 (2015): 145–146.

15. Philip Warkander, "'This Is All Fake, This Is All Plastic, This Is Me' A Study of the Interrelations Between Style, Sexuality and Gender in Contemporary Stockholm" (PhD diss., Stockholm University, 2013), 242.

16. Bettina Schmidt, "Polyphonic Bricolage—Caribbean Cultures in New York" (paper presented at the 2003 meeting of Latin American Studies Association, Dallas, Texas, March 27–29, 2003).

17. Constantine Sedikides and Tim Wildschut, "Nostalgia across Cultures," *Journal of Pacific Rim Psychology* 16, no. 2 (2022): 2. doi.org/10.1177/18344909221091649.

18. Philip Drake, "'Mortgaged to Music: New Retro Movies in 1990s Hollywood Cinema," in *Memory and Popular Film*, ed. Paul Grainge, (Manchester, UK: Manchester University Press, 2003), 190.

19. Simon Reynolds, *Retromania: Pop Culture's Addiction to its Own Past* (London: Faber and Faber, 2011), xxix.

20. Svetlana Boym, *The Future of Nostalgia* (New York. Basic Books, 2001), 41.

21. Henry Jenkins, "Introduction: Childhood Innocence and Other Modern Myths," in *The Children's Culture Reader*, ed. Henry Jenkins (New York: New York University Press, 1998), 4.

22. Susan Stewart, *On Longing: Narratives of the Miniature, the Gigantic, the Souvenir, the Collection* (Durham, NC: Duke University Press, 1993), 47.

23. Justin Smith, *Withnail and Us: Cult Films and Film Cults in British Cinema* (London: IB Tauris, 2010), 218.

24. Baschiera and Caoduro, "Retro, Faux-vintage, and Anachronism," 143–163.

25. Baschiera and Caoduro, "Retro, Faux-vintage, and Anachronism," 144.

26. Katharina Niemeyer, ed., *Media and Nostalgia: Yearning for the Past, Present and Future* (Basingstoke-New York: Palgrave Macmillan, 2014), 2.

27. Baschiera and Caoduro, "Retro, Faux-vintage, and Anachronism," 153.

28. This is often the case with Wes Anderson's films, in which objects appear to be displaced in time rather than belonging to a real, specific past and yet are absolutely vital for the distinct visual look of the film.

29. Baschiera and Caoduro, "Retro, Faux-vintage, and Anachronism," 148.

30. The concept of pastiche was defined by Richard Dyer in *Pastiche* as "a kind of imitation that you are meant to know is an imitation" (Dyer 2007, 1). In her chapter, "Noir Fashion and Noir *as* Fashion," Ula Lukszo Klein uses the term *pastiche* retrospectively in order to characterize the film noir genre as such (Lukszo Klein 2011).

31. Richard Dyer, *Pastiche* (London-New York: Routledge, 2007), 1.

32. Michael Emmison, "Visual Research: Issues and Developments," in *Qualitative Research*, ed. David Silverman (London: SAGE Publications Ltd., 2016), 297–310.

33. *Chilling Adventures of Sabrina*, season 1, episode 1, "Chapter One: October Country," directed by Lee Toland Krieger, written by Roberto Aguirre-Sacasa, aired 2018, on Netflix: 0:00:01:50. www.netflix.com/title/80223989.

34. Bryan Abrams, "How Chilling Adventures of Sabrina's Production Designer Creates the Occult," *The Credits*, January 5, 2019, www.motionpictures.org/2019 /04/how-the-chilling-adventures-of-sabrinas-production-designer-creates-the-occult/.

35. Rosemary Radford Ruether, *Goddesses and the Divine Feminine: A Western Religious History* (University of California Press, 2005), 17.

36. Whitney Friedlander, "'Chilling Adventures of Sabrina' Costumes Evoke an 'Eternal Autumn,' Says Designer," *The Hollywood Reporter*, October 26, 2021, www .hollywoodreporter.com/lifestyle/style/chilling-adventures-sabrina-costumes-evoke -an-eternal-autumn-says-designer-1154868.

37. Friedlander, "'Chilling Adventures of Sabrina' Costumes Evoke an 'Eternal Autumn,' Says Designer."

38. Friedlander, "'Chilling Adventures of Sabrina' Costumes Evoke an 'Eternal Autumn,' Says Designer."

39. Yvonne Villarreal, "Here's How 'Chilling Adventures of Sabrina' Achieved its 'Suspiria'-Inspired Look," *Los Angeles Times*, October, 31, 2018. www.latimes.com/ entertainment/tv/la-et-st-chilling-adventures-sabrina-netflix-20181031-story.html.

40. Bryan Abrams, "How Chilling Adventures of Sabrina's Production Designer Creates the Occult," *The Credits*, January 5, 2019. www.motionpictures.org/2019 /04/how-the-chilling-adventures-of-sabrinas-production-designer-creates-the-occult.

41. Christine Sprengler, *Screening Nostalgia: Populuxe Props and Technicolor Aesthetics in Contemporary American Film* (Oxford: Berghahn, 2009), 86.

42. Baschiera and Caoduro, "Retro, Faux-vintage, and Anachronism," 154.

43. Stefano Baschiera, "'Nostalgically Man Dwells on This Earth': Objects and Domestic Space in *The Royal Tenenbaums* and *The Darjeeling Ltd*," *New Review of Film and Television Studies* 10, no. 1 (2012): 129.

44. Paul Grainge, "Nostalgia and Style in Retro America: Moods, Modes, and Media Recycling," *Journal of American Culture* 23, no. 1 (2000): 27.

45. Amanda Howell, "Vampire Nostalgia," *Continuum* 35, no. 2 (2021): 266–267.

46. Andrzej Marzec, "Zombie Characters and Hollywood's Second Life-Nostalgia," *Contemporary Cinema* 33, no. 2 (2018): 30.

47. Howell, "Vampire Nostalgia," 267.

Chapter 16

Intersecting Narratives and the *Book*(s) *of the Beast*

The Multiplicity of Textual Engagements and Chilling Adventures of Sabrina

Alissa Burger

The Netflix series *Chilling Adventures of Sabrina* (2018–20) functions effectively as a standalone narrative, with a wide range of themes and representations deserving of critical engagement, including gender, sexuality, race, and power. However, the series is also situated at the nexus of a wide range of intersecting and overlapping texts, each of which provides a new perspective on and enables a range of dynamic negotiations with the Netflix series. *Chilling Adventures of Sabrina* (*CAoS*) is an adaptation of Roberto Aguirre-Sacasa and Robert Hack's comic series of the same name (2014–present).[1] Sabrina also appears in another horror iteration of the Archie universe, *Afterlife with Archie*, by Aguirre-Sacasa and Francesco Francavilla (2013–present).[2] While these two comics versions of Sabrina's story predate and serve as a foundation and inspiration for the Netflix series, the series itself has also resulted in further intertextual engagement, including three young adult tie-in novels by Sarah Rees Brennan; a crossover event with *Riverdale* (2017–present), a CW series also developed by Aguirre-Sacasa; and a new comic series that will continue Sabrina's adventures beyond the Netflix series' finale, titled *The Occult World of Sabrina* (forthcoming).

This intersection of the multiple textual engagements surrounding *CAoS* transcends any consideration of adaptation in the traditional sense and instead demands a multifaceted approach to *CAoS*, its characters, and its narratives.

This creates a complex situation in which readers and viewers are provided with significant variation in worlds, narratives, and character identities in a schema that engages with notions of the multiverse, parallel worlds, and the richness of what Mary S. Gossy refers to as "the untold story"[3] through new stories in which characters who are peripheral in other iterations take a privileged narrative position. Through this complicated reading and viewing experience, consumers are immersed in a narrative in which notions of objective, verifiable "truth" are called into question, as they instead must contend with multiple—and at times conflicting—realities and interpretations. In embracing this multiplicity, viewers and readers must actively negotiate and navigate these liminal spaces in order to reflect on how they know what they know, how new information shifts perspective, how contrasting and even contradictory narratives can be productively brought into conversation with one another, and how it is possible to read the same text in dramatically different ways in light of these multiple narratives. While one could look at any single iteration of this narrative and take that as the central, core text against which they measure all others—Aguirre-Sacasa and Hack's comic or the Netflix series as the privileged, authoritative text, for example—reading these texts in combination with one another opens up a far more compelling and multifaceted way of engaging with Sabrina's world, one that interrogates narrative construction, enables the reader or viewer to consider the same character from multiple perspectives, and amplifies voices that might be marginalized or peripheral in one of the other texts.

In this chapter, I will explore the textual intersections surrounding *CAoS* and the dynamically engaged reading these intersections make possible. While Sabrina makes her first appearance in *Archie's Mad House* #22 in 1962, has had several comics incarnations in the intervening decades, and was at the center of the popular 1990s sitcom *Sabrina the Teenage Witch* (ABC, 1996–2000/The WB, 2000–03), this analysis will focus on the intertextual engagements of *CAoS* as a horror genre narrative. This will include Aguirre-Sacasa and Hack's *Chilling Adventures of Sabrina* comics (both those issues published prior to the Netflix series and the comic's recent resumption), Aguirre-Sacasa and Francavilla's *Afterlife with Archie*, Brennan's trio of Netflix series tie-in novels, and *Riverdale*'s season six five-episode "Rivervale" crossover event, as well the anticipation of Aguirre-Sacasa's continuation of Sabrina's story in *The Occult World of Sabrina*.

HORROR COMICS: *CHILLING ADVENTURES OF SABRINA* AND *AFTERLIFE WITH ARCHIE*

There is a long and well-established connection between horror and the comics genre, from the pulps to EC Comics and beyond. Several key elements of comics' form and structure make this format an ideal fit for horror. Julia Round points out that "thematically, Gothic is characterized by a tendency toward inversion, parody, subversion and doubling,"[4] a combination of approaches that could be similarly applied to comics' negotiation and rewriting of dominant narratives. Both comics and the Gothic mode also overtly engage with temporality and perspective, with Round writing that Gothic narratives "can tell dis-located, timeless tales, or the narrative itself may be disrupted, atemporal, or circular. Even if a linear temporal structure is used, multiple voices or perspectives may destabilize this."[5] In short, the comics format offers writers, artists, and readers the opportunity for a new perspective—or intersection of perspectives—that not only combines image and text but blurs the lines between past and present, multiple points of view, and familiar tales that become suddenly and unexpectedly reinvented, all of which are the case with *Chilling Adventures of Sabrina* and *Afterlife with Archie*.[6]

Aguirre-Sacasa and Hack's *Chilling Adventures of Sabrina* has the most direct influence on the Netflix series, laying its narrative foundation. Aguirre-Sacasa and Hack's comic is populated with a range of faces familiar to the series's viewers, including Sabrina, Hilda, Zelda, Salem, Ambrose, and Harvey, though many of these characters take on different roles or relationship dynamics. Aguirre-Sacasa and Hack's comic is also steeped in nostalgia, set in the 1960s, which makes for an interesting—and notably whitewashed—version of Greendale, particularly when considered in contrast to the diverse range of race, gender identity, and sexuality in the Netflix series in both characterization and casting.

However, the most significant and notable differences between the Netflix series and Aguirre-Sacasa and Hack's comic are each respective work's tone and the nature of the relationships presented within them. While Lisa Soper, production designer for the Netflix series, "bathed the show in the colors of fall; yellows, oranges, reds, and greens,"[7] Hack's comic illustrations adopt a "scratched filmstrip style, set in sepia tones, [which] makes the inevitable violent splashes of red provocatively grotesque."[8] This visual distinction between these two iterations of Sabrina—the warmth of Soper's design vs. the more faded aesthetic of Hack's—echoes the tone of each narrative itself. Netflix's *CAoS* is playfully nostalgic, combining a modern perspective with midcentury vibes, while Aguirre-Sacasa and Hack evoke the nightmares of the past. This exploration of the past is central to Aguirre-Sacasa and Hack's comic, not just in the 1960s setting of the story but in narrative off-shoots that take the reader further back to Edward Spellman, including stories of his rise to power in the Church of Night, Edward's relationship with and institutional-ization of Sabrina's mother Diana, Sabrina's early childhood, and backstories for Salem and for Ambrose's familiars, two cobras named Nag and Nagaina. While the horrors of the past play an integral role in the Netflix series, partic-ularly with the violence of "The Harrowing" of new students at the Academy of Unseen Arts[9] and the return of the Greendale Thirteen,[10] the influence of the past on the present is much more insidious in the comic, inextricable from the everyday occurrences and the consequences of Sabrina's actions.

The other major distinction between the Netflix series and Aguirre-Sacasa and Hack's comic that establishes these two versions as taking place in par-allel but very different worlds lies in the relationships Sabrina has with her friends and family. In the Netflix series, Sabrina (Kiernan Shipka) is cared for and well-loved. No matter what nightmares she faces or mistakes she makes, she knows she can turn to Hilda (Lucy Davis), Zelda (Miranda Otto), Ambrose (Chance Perdomo), Harvey (Ross Lynch), Roz (Jaz Sinclair), and Theo (Lachlan Watson). The Sabrina of Aguirre-Sacasa and Hack's comic does not have the reliability of this support system. When Sabrina is trauma-tized, her aunts "talk and talk, but they never ask her if she's alright . . . She can't believe . . . how cold her aunts are about it"[11] and when Sabrina steps out of bounds, they attack her in their monstrous forms, forcing her into a violent confrontation rather than attempting to reason with her.[12] Similarly, while the Sabrina of the Netflix series has friends who not only support her but also work collectively together to make the world a better place as "politically active, outspoken teens"[13] who refuse to accept abuse or injustice in any form, Aguirre-Sacasa and Hack's Sabrina is largely on her own. There is a Rosalind at Sabrina's high school, but she is more of a mean girl than best friend material. Harvey is there, but he is a new love interest and a bit of a jock. He remains a relatively flat character and is insecure enough in his newfound relationship with Sabrina that he is easily tricked into going to the woods, where he expects to find her with another guy but instead stumbles upon her Dark Baptism, which results in him literally being eaten alive by witches.[14] While Edward Spellman's (Georgie Daburas) legacy is a topic of mystery and contention in the Netflix series, the backstory Aguirre-Sacasa and Hack provide for him in their comic presents a darker, more self-serving warlock who deceives the Church of Night and all of its followers, commits murder to seize power, abuses and discards women (including Sabrina's mother Diana as well as Iona, the comic's Madam Satan-type character), and is ultimately imprisoned by his own sisters. The most unsettling development, however, is when Edward is resurrected in Harvey's reanimated body and in a sense, becomes his own daughter's boyfriend, thinking as he embraces her that "it's *less* disturbing than it should be."[15]

Aguirre-Sacasa and Hack's version of Greendale and Sabrina's life is less forgiving and more isolating, full of darker realities and even harsher consequences than Netflix's *CAoS*. When Sabrina makes bad choices or mistakes in the Netflix series, there are people who love her to take care of her and help her put the world back together, even if that world will never quite be what it was before. But in Aguirre-Sacasa and Hack's world, what is broken stays broken. Harvey is not coming back (and the form in which he seems to only promises further horrors), and the safety of Sabrina's home is not always promised, as Zelda follows up Hilda's remark to Sabrina that they will "see [her] at home—" with a curt and dismissive "we will or we won't, and that's on *her*."[16] Aguirre-Sacasa and Hack's world gives readers a glimpse of what Sabrina's life would be like without the love, comfort, and reassurance of her family and friends, a shift that fundamentally changes who Sabrina is, who she could become, what her life is like, and how she sees and engages with the world around her.

Aguirre-Sacasa and Francavilla's *Afterlife with Archie* also imagines a different reality for Sabrina, in this case one of post-apocalyptic horrors, zombies, and Lovecraftian monsters. One common thread uniting all three of these versions—the Netflix series, Aguirre-Sacasa and Hack's *Chilling Adventures*, and *Afterlife with Archie*—is Sabrina's undeniable power and particular flair for necromancy, as she resurrects a character in each of them: Tommy (Justin Dobies), Harvey, and Jughead Jones's dog Hot Dog, respectively. While each of these resurrections has a profound impact on their individual worlds, Sabrina's resurrection of Hot Dog is devastating on the largest scale, a direct cause of the zombie apocalypse and the end of the world. Just as with Sabrina's resurrection of Tommy Kinkle in the Netflix series, her heart is in the right place when she brings back Hot Dog, but interfering with the natural order of life and death has disastrous consequences as the undead Hot Dog bites Jughead, who becomes the first zombie and begins preying on his friends and other Riverdale residents.

In addition to the shared resurrection narrative of the two texts, *Afterlife with Archie* and Netflix's *CAoS* also both engage with H. P. Lovecraft's Cthulhu mythos. In *Afterlife with Archie*, after Sabrina has been exiled to a period "of silent reflection and atonement in the Nether-Realm, away from the mortal world,"[17] she regains consciousness in Issue Six, "Witch in the Dream House,"[18] in a seemingly alternate universe in which her aunts are dead and her witchcraft is only a figment of her imagination. She is being treated for this delusion by a psychiatrist named Doctor Lovecraft and his colleague, Doctor Machen—an allusion to Arthur Machen, the author of *The Great God Pan* (1894), another work that probes the thin boundaries between worlds and the monsters that wait on the other side. In some ways, Sabrina's experience in the asylum where she wakes up is similar to Harvey's vision of the Lovecraftian horrors terrorizing his new friend Howard (Nikolai Witschl) in the Netflix series' "Chapter Fifteen: Doctor Cerberus's House of Horror" (2:4).[19] In Aguirre-Sacasa and Francavilla's comic, Sabrina becomes aware of the thin membrane that separates multiple worlds from one another, particularly in her friendship with a young violinist named Erich and an artist named Richie, whose gifts Lovecraft is using in an attempt to resurrect the Great Old Ones. As Richie tells Sabrina, "Lovecraft's using us to bring them back,"[20] to "serve them—keep them happy—prepare the way for them."[21]

Doctor Lovecraft's arrogant search for power also echoes that of Faustus Blackwood (Richard Coyle) in the Netflix series, who calls upon Lovecraftian gods throughout the series's fourth installment. With these Lovecraftian narratives enfolded into the larger drama of Netflix's *CAoS* and the zombie apocalypse of *Afterlife with Archie*, both texts are expanded to include cosmic horror in addition to the realistic and supernatural threats with which the characters must already contend. In his seminal *Supernatural Horror in Literature*, H. P. Lovecraft defines cosmic horror, explaining that "a certain atmosphere of breathless and unexplainable dread of outer, unknown forces must be present [. . .] [including] a malign and particular suspension or defeat of those fixed laws of Nature which are our only safeguards against the assaults of chaos and the daemons of unplumbed space."[22] This notion of worlds just beyond the boundaries of the characters' own and the horrors that might lurk there evoke the possibility of multiple universes, a reality which is also central to *CAoS*'s conflict between the realms in "Chapter Thirty-Three: Deus Ex Machina" (4:5),[23] and the episodes that follow, as well as the parallel universes explored in *Riverdale*'s five-episode "Rivervale" crossover event.

Sabrina's appearances in *Afterlife with Archie* are few and far between, but they carry great narrative weight and come with dire consequences. She helps Jughead reanimate Hot Dog in the series' first issue, inadvertently causing the zombie apocalypse, and she uncovers Lovecraft's plot to bring back the Great Old Ones in the series' sixth issue only to find out that she has been chosen to be the Bride of Cthulhu. Several characters see Sabrina in their dreams in the next issue, where she is "sitting at a banquet table with these . . . these *inhuman things*,"[24] but she does not physically reappear until Issue Nine, "The Trouble with Reggie," where she is an otherworldly femme fatale with blank, white eyes and a hairband of thorns, to tempt Reggie Mantle to turn on his friends. In these final panels, Sabrina is visually tied to the similarly empty-eyed zombies, while her dialogue—white text within black speech bubbles, as opposed the black text within white speech bubbles of human characters—further sets her apart from being human, marking her as something Othered and monstrous. Netflix's Sabrina is occasionally Othered in a similar fashion, specifically in her Dark Phoenix moment in "Chapter Eighteen: The Miracles of Sabrina Spellman" (2:7),[25] though in that reality, Sabrina's humanity is reclaimed, with this Othering a temporary departure from her everyday life and identity. In *Afterlife with Archie*, there is no such promise, and with the series' stalling out after the tenth issue, readers have no way of knowing what may happen next or if this horror can ever be undone. As with Aguirre-Sacasa and Hack's *Chilling Adventures of Sabrina* comic, *Afterlife with Archie*'s version of Sabrina is that of a young woman with great power but little hope that all will turn out happily in the end.

SARAH REES BRENNAN'S TIE-IN NOVELS: *SEASON OF THE WITCH, DAUGHTER OF CHAOS,* AND *PATH OF NIGHT*

Sarah Rees Brennan has written three tie-in novels in the Netflix *CAoS* universe: *Season of the Witch* (2019), *Daughter of Chaos* (2020), and *Path of Night* (2020), all of which are Archie Comics publications and bear the cover tagline "inspired by the Netflix original series." While iconic series such as *Star Trek* and *Star Wars* had tie-in novels as far back as the mid-twentieth century, in "the mid-1990s, tie-in novels seemed to be pretty standard for most TV shows and some movie series as well,"[26] especially for teen dramas. Tie-in novels and novelizations provide a textual medium and a new opportunity for fans to engage with the film or television series they love, with tie-ins specifically featuring new stories and perspectives.

Brennan's three *Sabrina* novels function to fill gaps of both narrative chronology and characterization. *Season of the Witch* is a prequel whose narrative is situated just before the action of the series' first episode,[27] *Daughter of Chaos* fills the narrative gap between the series' parts one and two, and *Path of Night*'s action takes place between the series' parts two and three. While the Netflix series foregrounds Sabrina's perspective, Brennan's novels privilege multiple points of view, including those of Harvey, Nick, Roz, and Ambrose. In positioning this narrative action in gaps in the existing narrative, Brennan is engaging with the attraction of what Gossy calls "the untold story."[28] Within this paradigm, through narrative framing and engagement, the reader or viewer becomes aware of a perspective that has been previously marginalized or a story that has so far remained untold, either because the character in question is peripheral to the larger narrative or through an intentional act of privileging some narratives while silencing others. Once the reader or viewer recognizes the potential of this untold story or previously unexplored perspective, this creates a curiosity about or desire to know the rest of that story.[29] For example, while viewers are predominantly focused on

Sabrina's perspective in *CAoS*—and understandably so, as she is the eponymous protagonist—the suggestion that Aunt Hilda might have a rich, full life bursting with domestic misadventures, or the question of how Harvey might perceive the growing influence of magic in Sabrina's life from his mortal perspective, gives the reader the opportunity to consider what those stories might look like, how the familiar world of Greendale might look different through new eyes, and how many other diverse perspectives may be going unexplored, along with what new perceptions and insights those points of view might offer.

Brennan's *Season of the Witch* is a prequel to the Netflix series's first season and explores a range of Sabrina's relationships, her own ambitions and misgivings, and the nature of Greendale itself. The novel has two distinct perspectives, as Sabrina's subjective perspective is interspersed with black pages titled "What Happens in the Dark" that provide an omniscient point of view encompassing all of Greendale as well as insights into a range of other characters, including Roz's dreams, Zelda's nostalgic remembrances of caring for Sabrina as a baby, and Ambrose's frustration with his house arrest and even his resentment of Sabrina's freedom. Notably, these moments of insight run counter to the dominant representation in the series, where Zelda is sternly unsentimental and Ambrose adopts a laid back, devil-may-care attitude, with Brennan's descriptions adding a complexity and depth of understanding for the reader, offering them an opportunity to see these characters in a new way and consider what might be going on beneath the surface, the things that have remained unsaid within the action of the series. The conflict between Sabrina and Ambrose is particularly significant, as they are generally shown as affectionate co-conspirators in the Netflix series. Brennan's narrative digs deeper to consider how much Ambrose might envy his cousin's freedom, with their argument reframing their relationship, granting Ambrose heightened agency, and in their reconciliation, actually deepening the understanding and connection between the cousins.

Another character whose perspective is foregrounded in the "What Happens in the Dark" sections in *Season of the Witch* is Mary Wardwell, who only briefly appears as herself in the series' opening episode before being taken over by Madam Satan/Lilith, with Brennan giving readers the chance to know a character whose true identity is largely absent from the series itself. Brennan describes Mary Wardwell as "young and brimful of promise herself, once. She was the only child of elderly parents, growing up bookish and excruciatingly shy, especially with children her own age. She didn't have many friends, but she took long walks in the woods and told herself everything would be different when she grew up."[30] As a young woman, she left Greendale to go to the city, but found the city and its possibilities "so glittering, so exciting, that it was too frightening,"[31] returning to Greendale to care for her parents and never leaving again. Madam Satan (Michelle Gomez) is such a rich and entertaining character in the Netflix series that it can be easy to forget that there is another personality in her body that has been subsumed through Madam Satan's possession, another person's life which she has stepped into and taken over. The fact that viewers know almost nothing about Mary Wardwell before this transformation makes that forgetting even easier, but Brennan's inclusion of just a few small moments of Mary Wardwell's untold story, individual personality, and characterization bring that contrast into stark relief, drawing the reader's attention to a narrative largely missing from the Netflix series, particularly in early seasons.

The inclusion of some of these other untold stories amplifies the relationships and narratives of the series itself, which is the case with *Season of the Witch*'s Tommy Kinkle storyline. In the Netflix series, Tommy and Harvey's relationship is clearly established and significant, though Tommy himself remains a bit underdeveloped: he is a dutiful son and loving brother, and his identity and motivations are filtered through those lenses, informing and demarcating the scope of the audience's understanding of Tommy. These priorities are foundational to Tommy's characterization in *Season of the Witch* as well. However, readers also learn more about Tommy as an individual and see more of his relationship with Harvey, as well as Tommy's interactions with Sabrina, his relationship with a mysterious young woman, and the choices he has made to protect Harvey. While Harvey laments in *Season of the Witch* that Tommy did not get a football scholarship that would have allowed him to go to college and get out of Greendale—a deception and secret which is also addressed in *CAoS*'s "Chapter Eight: The Burial" (1:8),[32] when Harvey finds Tommy's acceptance letter from Notre Dame—Brennan's novel also includes another opportunity for Tommy to get out when the beautiful woman he has been seeing asks him to leave Greendale and go with her to Los Angeles, an adventure he refuses in order to stay and take care of Harvey.

Daughter of Chaos is narratively situated between the Netflix series' first and second parts, as Sabrina leaves Baxter High to devote herself to her studies at the Academy of Unseen Arts. While Sabrina's adjustment to this change and her quest to stop a demon threatening Greendale are the driving narrative, much of the novel focuses on interactions and relationships between other characters, like Nick and Harvey's tentative friendship and the growing romantic feelings between Harvey and Roz. While *Daughter of Chaos* still includes several chapters told from Sabrina's subjective perspective, other chapters foreground a range of different characters' points of view, including those of Roz, Harvey, and Prudence, though these are told through an omniscient third-person perspective rather than the first-person narration of Sabrina's chapters. This distinction allows readers to gain a new, more intimate understanding of these characters while simultaneously maintaining Sabrina's position as the central protagonist of the novels.

Harvey and Nick's growing friendship is one of the dominant narratives in *Daughter of Chaos* and the one that has the greatest potential impact, as these two young men learn to understand one another and work together, transcending their former romantic rivalry and the established divide between witches and mortals. In these interactions, Harvey also serves as a narrative proxy, providing an external perspective on some of the traditions and expectations of witch culture that even Sabrina, as a half-witch who divides her time between her home and the Academy, fails to notice. For example, one of the most important building blocks of Harvey and Nick's growing sense of trust and camaraderie is food, which prompts Sabrina to realize that the students at the Academy are intentionally underfed and kept hungry[33] as a means of demonstrating Father Blackwood's dominance and control. While Nick and Harvey find a lot of common ground and combine their energies for the greater good, there are still moments of violent dissonance when Harvey realizes that he cannot comfortably or safely move between these two worlds, such as in Nick's magical control of Harvey's father and Harvey's discovery that Dorcas was partially responsible for Tommy's death. There is true depth and feeling in Harvey and Nick's friendship, including Nick asking Harvey for mortal relationship advice and Nick supporting Harvey in his grief when he visits Tommy's grave for the first time. In the end, however, after Harvey has stood with the witches to help banish the infernal threat and save Greendale, he asks Nick to perform a memory spell on him to forget the last five days, allying himself exclusively with the mortal world. Harvey tells Nick, "I miss my brother. But it was magic that took him away from me. And I hate that girl, Dorcas. I want to kill her but—I don't want to be someone that angry, someone who wants to hurt someone else that much. I don't want to be reminded of magic and murder at every turn."[34] Though Nick calls Harvey "a coward"[35] for wanting to forget—which is one of Harvey's biggest sources of fear and self-doubt throughout the Netflix series—Harvey is willing to accept this criticism to do what he needs to do for himself and his friends, reflecting that "maybe he had to go through being a coward to become something more."[36] While the friendship between Nick and Harvey in *Daughter of Chaos* is rich and emotionally complex, in the end, it is undone, resetting the world of *CAoS* back to the default of conflict between these two young men and a magic-averse Harvey, which allows the narrative of the series to pick up where it left off when it resumes, while also exploring the relationships, connections, and potential for understanding that could exist if the narrative followed another trajectory.

As with the previous two novels, Brennan's third and final *Sabrina* novel, *Path of Night*, includes multiple perspectives, in this case switching between sections titled "Greendale," "Hell," and "On the Road," which foreground Sabrina and her friends' quest, Nick's imprisonment, and Ambrose and Prudence's pursuit of Blackwood, respectively. While *Daughter of Chaos* built upon and developed Nick's bookish nature and navigation of his growing feelings for Sabrina, *Path of Night* delves deeper into Nick's past and psyche in the representation of the infernal psychological torture he endures while being held captive. While Nick (Gavin Leatherwood) told Sabrina about losing his parents and being cared for by his familiar Amalia in *CAoS*'s "Chapter Fourteen: Lupercalia" (2:3),[37] what he experiences in Hell in *Path of Night* is a reliving of this trauma rather than a narrative recounting of it. Brennan also provides insight into Nick and Amalia's relationship in the time between the death of his parents and his appearance at the Academy, with Nick taken in as part of a wolf pack and isolated from both witches and mortals, who he watches with a mingled sense of curiosity and longing for the affection he sees there. Amalia is violent and possessive, and when Nick becomes enamored with a mortal girl, Amalia kills and dismembers her in front of him.[38] Finally, Nick must flee Amalia:

> His head jerked up, and he thought: *I cannot live like this for a moment longer.*

> He ran. Amalia caught up with him. She tried to drag him back, but he fought. It felt like his last chance. She snarled and hurt him, werewolf red in tooth and claw. For a blurred, desperate moment Nick was sure she'd kill him. His mind seized on a spell he'd read years ago, sitting by his mother.

> With a mouth full of blood and trembling hands, Nick teleported away.[39]

The telling of this story fills in gaps in Nick's characterization, personal history, and motivation, reframing his conversation with Sabrina in the "Lupercalia" episode, and offering a more complicated interpretation of his sense of belonging and the significance of the home he has found at the Academy of Unseen Arts. The experiences recounted here are ones that are largely unspeakable, that cannot be reduced to a simple narrative telling and, in some ways, run counter to Nick's own sense of himself as a result of the love he still feels for Amalia when he tells Sabrina part of his story.

Path of Night also foregrounds the fears and courage of Sabrina's mortal friends, as Harvey, Roz, and Theo choose to join her on a quest in which they are each individually tested to gain artifacts that will help them open the gates of Hell and rescue Nick. Through this testing, Sabrina's friends face their own greatest fears, plumb the depths of their individual and collective strength, and engage in the complex negotiation of accepting and supporting Sabrina while simultaneously remaining outside and critical of the witch world to varying degrees. Roz's Cunning draws her into the liminal space between magic and mortal, as does Theo's affinity with his ancestor Dorothea Putnam, and while Harvey has great empathy for the orphaned witch children (both living and dead) that now reside at the Spellman house, he remains largely anti-magic. While Roz, Theo, and Harvey love and accept Sabrina and will go to any lengths to protect and help her—including undertaking a dangerous quest and storming the very gates of Hell—they also each realize that the witch world is not one they can safely inhabit in the long term and, even more importantly, that they do not wish to do so.

The stories of Sabrina's friends and Nick's imprisonment in Hell lay the narrative groundwork of backstory for the start of the series' third installment and the action of "Chapter Twenty-One: The Hellbound Heart" (3:1).[40] Brennan's *Path of Night* provides insight into how Sabrina's friends have been prepared for the quest they undertake to save Nick and contextualizes the trauma that Nick has endured in Hell, which drives his motivation and actions in the series' third part but remains largely unspeakable and unarticulated onscreen. Brennan's final *Sabrina* novel provides readers with another lens through which they can read and interpret the actions of Sabrina's friends in "The Hellbound Heart,"[41] as well as Nick's self-destructive and isolating behavior in the aftermath of his rescue, which is not the restorative solution that Sabrina has hoped will put everything back the way it was before. Nick has been indelibly marked by the trauma he has experienced in Hell, and while his internalized emotional and psychological processing of this trauma remain largely unarticulated in the Netflix series—which instead foregrounds the effect of that trauma through Nick's externalized actions—Brennan's novel provides some depth and insight into what Nick may be thinking and feeling, but unable to speak aloud.

ARCHIE FOR A NEW AGE: MAYHEM
AND MAGIC IN *RIVERDALE*

In addition to *CAoS*, Aguirre-Sacasa is also the developer and showrunner of *Riverdale*, a series which follows Archie Comics' iconic characters through a contemporary and gritty version of Riverdale bursting with sex, intrigue, and murder. There have been allusions to a significant connection between the towns of Riverdale and Greendale in both series, including the identification of the Blossom family as fellow witches in *CAoS*.[42] However, the two worlds were not brought together until the five-episode "Rivervale" event that kicked off *Riverdale*'s sixth season in late 2021, after Sabrina's death in the final episode of *CAoS*.[43]

Punctuated with *Twilight Zone*-style narration by Jughead Jones (Cole Sprouse), viewers are guided through an alternate universe Riverdale called Rivervale. Sabrina herself plays a relatively minor role, showing up in the final minutes of the fourth episode, "Chapter Ninety-Nine: The Witching Hour(s)" (6:4) to help Cheryl Blossom (Madelaine Petsch) and her Nana Rose (Barbara Wallace) with a transference spell. In addition to featuring a "seemingly older, wiser version of Sabrina,"[44] the *Riverdale* crossover serves to some degree as a corrective to or a reset of *CAoS*'s final episode, which ended with Sabrina's death and her reunion with Nick in the afterlife. As Sabrina says in *Riverdale* shortly following her reintroduction, "there is no death for witches. Only transformation. I mean, I died and came back."[45] No further explanation of how this resurrection occurred is offered in the *Riverdale* episode, but this statement lays some of the groundwork for *The Occult World of Sabrina*, a forthcoming comic series that will resume the story where Netflix's *CAoS* left off, "following Sabrina Spellman's family as they work to get her back to the land of the living."[46]

While fans were thrilled to see Sabrina back, her cryptic explanation leaves some unresolved issues that viewers and critics noted as problematic. Specifically, David Opie points out that the romanticized portrayal of "Nick's suicide remains just as troubling and just as dangerous, particularly for Sabrina fans who wouldn't even make this connection with *Riverdale*'s crossover episode"[47] or do not watch *Riverdale* and thus remain unaware of this development. Sabrina returns to *Riverdale* later in the sixth season to help resurrect some of the gang who have fallen in battle, including Archie and Jughead, and ends up temporarily bringing Nick back in Jughead's body when Jughead is reluctant to leave "the Sweet Hereafter."[48] As Sabrina and Nick talk, viewers learn that Nick sacrificed himself to save Sabrina and return her to the land of the living, to her family and her coven, though he himself cannot return. Nick and Sabrina savor the "borrowed time"[49] they have together and say goodbye once more, and while Sabrina is successful in helping the women of Riverdale reclaim their lost loved ones, Nick is relegated to his fate in the afterlife. While this episode provides some resolution for Nick's story, *CAoS*'s final series image of romanticized suicide remains regrettable and permanent.

Another resonance between *Riverdale*'s "Rivervale" storyline and *CAoS* is the existence of multiple worlds with an endless range of possibilities, which Jughead discovers in the crossover event's final episode, "Chapter One Hundred: The Jughead Paradox,"[50] as he figures out what needs to be done to reestablish the dominant reality. Jughead's exploration of the interconnected realities, the threat they pose, and the action that needs to be taken echoes the intersection of the Prime and Pocket Universes in *CAoS*'s "Chapter

Thirty-Three: Deus Ex Machina" (4:5),[51] while the appearance of familiar characters in different roles in Rivervale continues the multiverse approach and reimagining of familiar Archie Comics characters over the last half century, the most recent of which include the Archie Horror narratives of *Afterlife with Archie* and *Chilling Adventures of Sabrina*, among others. The existence of these multiverses and the range of alternate narratives creates a sort of "all bets are off" world in which anything can happen, including the killing off of beloved characters, in the reassurance that, as Archie (K.J. Apa) tells Jughead, "no one stays dead here [. . .] Everyone comes back to life in this universe."[52] This is a cosmology in which multiple realities are simultaneously possible, opening up a range of potential narratives, shifts in characterization, and paths that draw narratives both forward and together with other, intertwined stories, for an inventive and dynamic range of intertextual engagements.

The Netflix series *Chilling Adventures of Sabrina* takes place at the intersection of multiple narratives, providing a variety of opportunities for reading, negotiating, and interpreting these texts. It is possible—and arguably easier—to fall into a comparative or exclusive pattern of interpretation, where one text is the "true" text or where questions of adaptation are engaged primarily through an assessment of fidelity to a source text. However, the range of intertwined and at times contradictory texts engaged by *CAoS* instead provides readers with diverse and divergent possibilities, multiple ways of reading the same world and knowing its characters. This is a multiverse in which characters can make dramatically different choices and take a new path, where the destroyed world can be restored, and where characters who have died can be brought back to begin a new series of adventures. In addition to the flexible nature of these intersecting stories, these intertextual narratives also allow those same readers and viewers the chance to see a familiar world and the characters who inhabit it through new eyes. No matter how well-known and well-loved a character may be, there are always new depths to explore, new perspectives to consider, and new discoveries to make. The possibilities are endless.

BIBLIOGRAPHY

Abrams, Bryan. "How *Chilling Adventures of Sabrina*'s Production Designer Creates the Occult." *The Credits*, 2019. www.motionpictures.org/2019/04/how -the-chilling-adventures-of-sabrinas-production-designer-creates-the-occult/.

Aguirre-Sacasa, Roberto and Francesco Francavilla. *Afterlife with Archie: Betty: R.I.P.*, no. 6. Pelham, NY: Archie Comic Publications, 2014.

———, *Afterlife with Archie: Betty: R.I.P.*, no. 7. Pelham, NY: Archie Comic Publications, 2014.

———, *Afterlife with Archie: Betty: R.I.P.*, no. 8. Pelham, NY: Archie Comic Publications, 2015.

———, *Afterlife with Archie: Betty R.I.P.*, no. 9. Pelham, NY: Archie Comic Publications, 2016.

———, *Afterlife with Archie, Book One: Escape from Riverdale.* Pelham, NY: Archie Comic Publications, 2019.

Aguirre-Sacasa, Roberto and Robert Hack. *Chilling Adventure of Sabrina: Occult Edition*. Pelham, NY: Archie Comic Publication, 2019.

———, *Chilling Adventures of Sabrina*, no. 9. Pelham, NY: Archie Comic Publications, 2021.

Anders, Charlie Jane. "Untold Adventures: The Complete History of Tie-In Novels." *Gizmodo*, 2009. gizmodo.com/untold-adventures-the-complete-history-of-tie-in-novel-5411331.

Brennan, Sarah Rees. *Daughter of Chaos*. New York: Archie Comics Publications/Scholastic, 2020.

———, *Path of Night*. New York: Archie Comics Publications/Scholastic, 2020.

———, *Season of the Witch*. New York. Archie Comics Publications/Scholastic, 2019.

Chilling Adventures of Sabrina, Season 1, episode 1, "Chapter One: October Country." Directed by Lee Toland Krieger, written by Roberto Aguirre-Sacasa, featuring Kiernan Shipka, Miranda Otto, Lucy Davis, and Chance Perdomo. Released October 26, 2018, Netflix, www.netflix.com/watch/80230071?trackId=200257859.

———, Season 1, episode 4, "Chapter Four: Witch Academy." Directed by Rob Seidenglanz, written by Diana Thorland, featuring Kiernan Shipka, Miranda Otto, Lucy Davis, and Richard Coyle. Released October 26, 2018, Netflix, www.netflix.com/watch/80230074?trackId=200257859.

———, Season 1, episode 5, "Chapter Five: Dreams in a Witch House." Directed by Maggie Kiley, written by Matthew Barry, featuring Kiernan Shipka, Miranda Otto, Lucy Davis, and Chance Perdomo. Released October 26, 2018, Netflix, www.netflix.com/watch/80230075?trackId=200257859.

———, Season 1, episode 8, "Chapter Eight: The Burial." Directed by Maggie Kiley, written by Christianne Hedtke and Lindsey Calhoon Bring, featuring Kiernan Shipka, Ross Lynch, Jaz Sinclair, and Tati Gabrielle. Released October 26, 2018, Netflix, www.netflix.com/watch/80230078?trackId=200257859.

———, Season 1, episode 10, "Chapter Ten: The Witching Hour." Directed by Rob Seidenglanz, written by Roberto Aguirre-Sacasa and Ross Maxwell, featuring Kiernan Shipka, Miranda Otto, Lucy Davis, and Chance Perdomo. Released October 26, 2018, Netflix, www.netflix.com/watch/80230080?trackId=200257859.

———, Season 2, episode 3. "Chapter Fourteen: Lupercalia." Directed by Salli Richardson-Whitfield, written by Oanh Ly, featuring Kiernan Shipka, Miranda Otto, Lucy Davis, and Chance Perdomo. Released April 5, 2019, Netflix, www.netflix.com/watch/80230084?trackId=200257859.

————, Season 2, episode 4, "Chapter Fifteen: Doctor Cerberus's House of Horror." Directed by Alex Garcia-Lopez, written by Ross Maxwell, featuring Kiernan Shipka, Miranda Ott, Lachlan Watson, Richard Coyle, Ross Lynch. Lucy Davis. Chance Perdomo, and Michelle Gomez. Released April 5, 2019, Netflix, www .netflix.com/watch/80230085?trackId=200257859.

————, Season 2, episode 7, "Chapter Eighteen: The Miracles of Sabrina Spellman." Directed by Antonio Negret, written by Christianne Hedtke and Lindsay Calhoon Bring, featuring Kiernan Shipka, Miranda Otto, Lucy Davis, and Chance Perdomo. Released April 5, 2019, Netflix, www.netflix.com/watch/80230088 ?trackId=200257859.

————, Season 3, episode 1, "Chapter Twenty-One: The Hellbound Heart." Directed by Rob Seidenglanz, written by Roberto Aguirre-Sacasa, featuring Kiernan Shipka, Chance Perdomo, Tati Gabrielle, and Michelle Gomez. Released December 31, 2020, Netflix, www.netflix.com/watch/81062652?trackId=200257859.

————, Season 3, episode 8. "Chapter Twenty-Eight: Sabrina Is Legend." Directed by Rob Seidenglanz, written by Roberto Aguirre-Sacasa and Daniel King, featuring Kiernan Shipka, Miranda Otto, Lucy Davis, and Sam Corlett. Released January 24, 2020, Netflix, www.netflix.com/watch/81062659?trackId=200257859.

————, Season 4, episode 5, "Chapter Thirty-Three: Deus Ex Machina." Directed by Amanda Tapping, written by Eleanor Jean, featuring Kiernan Shipka, Miranda Otto, Lucy Davis, and Lachlan Watson. Released December 31, 2020, Netflix, www.netflix.com/watch/81062664?trackId=200257859.

————, Season 4, episode 7, "Chapter Thirty-Five: The Endless." Directed by Kevin Sullivan, written by Donna Thorland and Matthew Barry, featuring Kiernan Shipka, Miranda Ott, Lachlan Watson, Richard Coyle, Ross Lynch. Lucy Davis. Chance Perdomo, and Michelle Gomez. Released December 31, 2020, Netflix, www.netflix.com/watch/81062666?trackId=200257859.

————, Season 4, episode 8, "Chapter Thirty-Six: At the Mountains of Madness." Directed by Rob Seidenglanz, written by Roberto Aguirre-Sacasa, featuring Kiernan Shipka, Miranda Otto, Lucy Davis, and Gavin Leatherwood. Released December 31, 2020, Netflix, www.netflix.com/watch/81062667?trackId=200257859.

Gossy, Mary S. *The Untold Story: Women and Theory in Golden Age Texts.* Ann Arbor: University of Michigan Press, 1989.

Henesy, Megan. "Leaving my girlhood behind": Woke Witches and Feminist Liminality in *Chilling Adventures of Sabrina.*" *Bournemouth University Research Online*, 2020. epr ints.bournemouth.ac.uk/34342/.

Jackson, Matthew. "*Chilling Adventures of Sabrina* to Continue Netflix Saga in Comic Form, 'Archie' Multiverse on the Way." *SyFy.com*, 2021. www.syfy.com/syfy-wire/chilling -adventures-of-sabrina-continue-comic-form.

Lovecraft, H.P. *The Annotated Supernatural Horror in Literature*, Revised & Expanded. Edited S.T. Joshi. New York: Hippocampus Press, 2012.

Murphy, Anna. "Aguirre-Sacasa, Roberto. Chilling Adventures of Sabrina: Vol. 1." *School Library Journal 62, no. 10 (2016): 118.*

Opie, David. "Riverdale's Sabrina Crossover Tackles the Spin-Off's Controversial Ending." *Digital Spy*, 2021. www.digitalspy.com/tv/ustv/a38460462/riverdale-sabrina-crossover-explained/.

Riverdale, Season 6, episode 4, "Chapter Ninety-Nine: Witching Hour(s)." Directed by James DeWille, written by Roberto Aguirre-Sacasa, Arabella Anderson, and Chrissy Maroon, featuring K.J. Apa, Lili Reinhart, Cole Sprouse, Camila Mendes, and Madelaine Petsch. Aired December 7, 2021, The CW, www.netflix.com/watch/81487576?trackId=200257859.

———, Season 6, episode 5, "Chapter One Hundred: The Jughead Paradox." Directed by Gabriel Correa, written by Roberto Aguirre-Sacasa, Chrissy Maroon, and Evan Kyle, featuring K.J. Apa, Lili Reinhart, Cole Sprouse, Camila Mendes, and Madelaine Petsch. Aired December 14, 2021, The CW, www.netflix.com/watch/81487577?trackId=255824129.

———, Season 6, episode 19, "Chapter One Hundred and Fourteen: The Witches of Riverdale." Directed by Alex Pillai, written by Roberto Aguirre-Sacasa, Chrissy Maroon, and Evan Kyle, featuring K.J. Apa, Lili Reinhart, Cole Sprouse, Camila Mendes, and Madelaine Petsch, and Kiernan Shipka. Aired July 9, 2022, The CW, www.netflix.com/watch/81487591?trackId=200257859.

Romano, Nick. "All the *Riverdale* Easter eggs in *Chilling Adventures of Sabrina* Part 3."

Entertainment Weekly, 2020. ew.com/tv/2020/01/24/chilling-adventures-of-sabrina-part-3-riverdale-easter-eggs/.

Round, Julia. *Gothic in Comics and Graphic Novels: A Critical Approach*. Jefferson, NC:McFarland, 2014.

NOTES

1. There was a long hiatus between Issue 8, "Witch War, Part 2: A Serpent's Tooth," which was published in August 2017, and Issue 9, "Witch War, Part 3: The Sacrificial Lamb" in October 2021.

2. While *Afterlife with Archie* is still technically listed as an ongoing series, the most recent issue—Issue 10, "Interlude with the Pussycats"—was published in August 2016. This issue is a Josie and Pussycats-focused side story to the larger *Afterlife with Archie* narrative, with the last *Afterlife*-focused issue, "The Trouble with Reggie," published in May 2016.

3. Mary S. Gossy, *The Untold Story: Women and Theory in Golden Age Texts* (Ann Arbor: University of Michigan Press, 1989), 5.

4. Julia Round, *Gothic in Comics and Graphic Novels: A Critical Approach* (Jefferson, NC: McFarland, 2014), 56.

5. Round, *Gothic in Comics and Graphic Novels*, 56. Netflix's *CAoS* negotiates temporarily in some similar ways in several episodes, reflecting this comic sensibility, including "Chapter Five: Dreams in a Witch House" (season 1, episode 5),

"Chapter Fifteen: Doctor Cerberus's House of Horror" (season 2, episode 4), "Chapter Twenty-Eight: Sabrina Is Legend" (season 3, episode 8), "Chapter Thirty-Three: Deus Ex Machina" (season 4, episode 5), and "Chapter Thirty-Five: The Endless" (season 4, episode 7).

6. The Archie Horror line has a range of other comics as well, including *Jughead: The Hunger* (2017–present), a Jughead werewolf narrative; *Vampironica* (2018–present), featuring a vampire Veronica; the 2019 five-issue crossover event *Jughead: The Hunger vs. Vampironica*; and *Blossoms 666* (2019), a five-issue story in which one of the Blossom twins is the Antichrist.

7. Bryan Abrams, "How *Chilling Adventures of Sabrina*'s Production Designer Creates the Occult," *The Credits* (2019), www.motionpictures.org/2019/04/how-the -chilling-adventures-of-sabrinas-production-designer-creates-the-occult/.

8. Anna Murphy, "Aguirre-Sacasa, Roberto. Chilling Adventures of Sabrina: Vol. 1," *School Library Journal* 62, no. 10 (2016), 118.

9. *Chilling Adventures of Sabrina*, season 1, episode 4, "Chapter Four: Witch Academy," directed by Rob Seidenglanz, written by Diana Thorland, featuring Kiernan Shipka, Miranda Otto, Lucy Davis, and Richard Coyle, released October 26, 2018, on Netflix, www.netflix.com/watch/80230074?trackId=200257859.

10. *Chilling Adventures of Sabrina*, season 1, episode 10, "Chapter Ten: The Witching Hour," directed by Rob Seidenglanz, written by Roberto Aguirre-Sacasa and Ross Maxwell, featuring Kiernan Shipka, Miranda Otto, Lucy Davis, and Chance Perdomo, released October 26, 2018, on Netflix, www.netflix.com/watch/80230080 ?trackId=200257859.

11. Roberto Aguirre-Sacasa and Robert Hack, *Chilling Adventures of Sabrina: Occult Edition* (Pelham, NY: Archie Comic Publications, 2019), 105.

12. Aguirre-Sacasa and Hack, *Chilling Adventures of Sabrina: Occult Edition*, 220–31.

13. Megan Henesy, "'Leaving My Girlhood Behind': Work Witches and Feminist Liminality in *Chilling Adventures of Sabrina*," *Bournemouth University Research Online* (2020), eprints.bournemouth.ac.uk/34342/1/%E2% 80%9CLeaving%20 my%20girlhood%20behind%E2%80%9D%20woke%20witches%20and%20feminist%20liminality%20in%20Chilling%20Adventures%20of%20Sabrina.pdf.

14. Aguirre-Sacasa and Hack, *Chilling Adventures of Sabrina*, 79–102.

15. Aguirre-Sacasa and Hack, *Chilling Adventures of Sabrina*, 214; emphasis original.

16. Aguirre-Sacasa and Hack, *Chilling Adventures of Sabrina*, 231; emphasis original.

17. Roberto Aguirre-Sacasa and Franco Francesco Francavilla, *Afterlife with Archie, Book One: Escape from Riverdale* (Pelham, NY: Archie Comic Publications, 2019), 8.

18. The title is an allusion to and inversion of H.P. Lovecraft's 1933 short story "The Dreams in the Witch House" (which is also invoked in *CAoS* episode "Chapter Five: Dreams in a Witch House" [season one, episode 5]). Much like Netflix's *CAoS*, *Afterlife with Archie* abounds with a range of allusions and references to classic and contemporary horror influences, including Alfred Hitchcock's *Psycho* (1960) and *The*

Birds (1963), George Romero's *Night of the Living Dead* (1968), and Stephen King's *The Shining* (1977) and *Pet Sematary* (1983), among others.

19. *Chilling Adventures of Sabrina*, season 2, episode 4, "Chapter Fifteen: Doctor Cerberus's House of Horror," directed by Alex Garcia Lopez, written by Ross Maxwell, featuring Kiernan Shipka, Miranda Otto, Lucy Davis, Chance Perdomo, and Michelle Gomez, released April 5, 2019, on Netflix, www.netflix.com/watch /80230085?trackId=200257859.

20. Roberto Aguirre-Sacasa and Francesco Francavilla, *Afterlife with Archie: Betty: R.I.P.*, no. 6 (Pelham, NY: Archie Comic Publications, 2014), 15.

21. Aguirre-Sacasa and Francavilla, *Afterlife with Archie: Betty: R.I.P.*, no. 6, 16.

22. H.P. Lovecraft, *The Annotated Supernatural Horror in Literature*, Revised and Expanded, edited by S.T. Joshi (New York: Hippocampus Press, 2012), 28.

23. *Chilling Adventures of Sabrina*, season 4, episode 5, "Chapter Thirty-Three: Deus Ex Machina," by Amanda Tapping, written by Eleanor Jean, featuring Kiernan Shipka, Miranda Otto, Lucy Davis, and Lachlan Watson, released December 31, 2020, on Netflix, www.netflix.com/watch/81062664?trackId=200257859.

24. Roberto Aguirre-Sacasa and Francesco Francavilla, *Afterlife with Archie: Betty: R.I.P.*, no. 7 (Pelham, NY: Archie Comic Publications, 2014), 13; emphasis original.

25. *Chilling Adventures of Sabrina*, season 2, episode 7, "Chapter Eighteen: The Miracles of Sabrina Spellman," directed by Antonio Negret, written by Christianne Hedtke and Lindsay Calhoon Bring, featuring Kiernan Shipka, Miranda Otto, Lucy Davis, and Chance Perdomo, released April 5, 2019, on Netflix, www.netflix.com/ watch/80230088?trackId=200257859.

26. Charlie Jane Anders, "Untold Adventures: The Complete History of Tie-In Novels," *Gizmodo* (2009), gizmodo.com/ untold-adventures-the-complete-history-of-tie-in-novel-5411331.

27. *Chilling Adventures of Sabrina*, season 1, episode 1, "Chapter One: October Country," directed by Lee Toland Krieger, written by Roberto Aguirre-Sacasa, featuring Kiernan Shipka, Miranda Otto, Lucy Davis, and Chance Perdomo, released October 26, 2018, on Netflix, www.netflix.com/watch/80230071?trackId=200257859.

28. Gossy, *The Untold Story*, 5.

29. Gossy, *The Untold Story*, 6.

30. Sarah Rees Brennan, *Season of the Witch* (New York: Archie Comic Publications/Scholastic, 2019), 141–42.

31. Brennan, *Season of the Witch*, 142.

32. *Chilling Adventures of Sabrina*, season 1, episode 8, "Chapter Eight: The Burial," directed by Maggie Kiley, written by Christianne Hedtke and Lindsey Calhoon Bring, featuring Kiernan Shipka, Ross Lynch, Jaz Sinclair, and Tati Gabrielle, released October 26, 2018, on Netflix, www.netflix.com/watch/80230078?trackId =200257859.

33. Sarah Rees Brennan, *Daughter of Chaos* (New York: Archie Comic Publications/Scholastic, 2020), 110–11.

34. Brennan, *Daughter of Chaos*, 336.

35. Brennan, *Daughter of Chaos*, 337.

36. Brennan, *Daughter of Chaos*, 337.

37. *Chilling Adventures of Sabrina*, season 2, episode 3, "Chapter Fourteen: Lupercalia," directed by Salli Richardson-Whitfield, written by Oanh Ly, featuring Kiernan Shipka, Miranda Otto, Lucy Davis, and Chance Perdomo, released April 5, 2019, on Netflix, www.netflix.com/watch/80230084?trackId=200257859.

38. Sarah Rees Brennan, *Path of Night* (New York: Archie Comic Publications/ Scholastic, 2020), 84.

39. Brennan, *Path of Night*, 86; emphasis original.

40. *Chilling Adventures of Sabrina*, season 3, episode 1, "Chapter Twenty-One: The Hellbound Heart," directed by Rob Seidenglanz, written by Roberto Aguirre-Sacasa, written by Roberto Aguirre-Sacasa, featuring Kiernan Shipka, Chance Perdomo, Tati Gabrielle, and Michelle Gomez, released December 31, 2020, on Netflix, www .netflix.com/watch/81062652?trackId=200257859.

41. *Chilling Adventures of Sabrina*, "Chapter Twenty-One: The Hellbound Heart."

42. Nick Romano, "All the *Riverdale* Easter Eggs in *Chilling Adventures of Sabrina*, Part 3," *Entertainment Weekly* (2020), ew.com/tv/2020/01/24/ chilling-adventures-of-sabrina-part-3-riverdale-easter-eggs/.

43. *Chilling Adventures of Sabrina*, season 4, episode 8, "Chapter Thirty-Six: At the Mountains of Madness," directed by Rob Seidenglanz, written by Roberto Aguirre-Sacasa, featuring Kiernan Shipka, Miranda Otto, Lucy Davis, and Gavin Leatherwood, released December 31, 2020, on Netflix, www.netflix.com/watch /81062667?trackId=200257859.

44. David Opie, "*Riverdale*'s Sabrina Crossover Tackles the Spin-Off's Controversial Ending," *Digital Spy* (2021), www.digitalspy.com/tv/ustv/a38460462/riverdale -sabrina-crossover-explained/.

45. *Riverdale*, season 6, episode 4, "Chapter Ninety-Nine: The Witching Hour(s)," directed by James DeWille, written by Roberto Aguirre-Sacasa, Arabella Anderson, and Chrissy Maroon, featuring K.J. Apa, Lili Reinhart, Cole Sprouse, Camila Mendes, and Madelaine Petsch, aired December 7, 2021, on The CW, www.netflix.com/watch/81487576? trackId=200257859: 00:40:27–00:40:35.

46. Matthew Jackson, "*Chilling Adventures of Sabrina* to Continue Netflix Saga in Comic Form, 'Archie' Multiverse on the Way," *SyFy.com* (2021), www.syfy.com/syfy -wire/chilling-adventures-of-sabrina-continue-comic-form.

47. Opie, "*Riverdale*'s Sabrina Crossover Tackles the Spin-Off's Controversial Ending."

48. *Riverdale*, season 6, episode 19, "Chapter One Hundred and Fourteen: The Witches of Riverdale," directed by Alex Pillai, written by Roberto Aguirre-Sacasa, Chrissy Maroon, and Evan Kyle, featuring K.J. Apa, Lili Reinhart, Cole Sprouse, Camila Mendes, and Madelaine Petsch, and Kiernan Shipka, aired July 9, 2022, on The CW, www.netflix.com/watch/81487591?trackId=200257859: 00:04:14–00:04:16.

49. *Riverdale*, "Chapter One Hundred and Fourteen: The Witches of Riverdale," 00:27:53.

50. *Riverdale*, season 6, episode 5, "Chapter One Hundred: The Jughead Paradox," directed by Gabriel Correa, written by Roberto Aguirre-Sacasa, Chrissy Maroon, and Evan Kyle, featuring

K.J. Apa, Lili Reinhart, Cole Sprouse, Camila Mendes, and Madelaine Petsch. Aired December 14, 2021, The CW, www.netflix.com/watch/81487577?trackId =255824129.

51. *Chilling Adventures of Sabrina*, "Chapter Thirty-Three: Deus Ex Machina."

52. *Riverdale*, "Chapter One Hundred: The Jughead Paradox," 00:30:40–00:30:52.

Index

The Coven of Contributors

ABOUT THE EDITORS

Cori Mathis is the director of LIGHT, an intercultural education program, and the Writing Studio at Lipscomb University, where she also teaches undergraduate and graduate courses in film and television studies, cultural analysis, and pedagogy in the Department of Cinematic Arts. She earned her PhD at Middle Tennessee State University, where her dissertation examined the complexities of the teen drama as a narrative form. Her current research centers on questions of genre, form, and representation in teen television and its intersections with other popular culture genres typically directed to women, such as the romance novel and the melodrama. She serves as the area chair of Young Adult Popular Culture for the Popular Culture Association in the South and is the author of "Bringing the Pain: An Examination of Marti Noxon's Contributions to *Buffy the Vampire Slayer*" in *Slayage: The International Journal of* Buffy+.

Stephanie A. Graves, MA, is a PhD candidate in English at Georgia State University, and her scholarship focuses on rhetoric in film, television, and popular culture. With a background in the world of theatrical entertainment and lighting design, her areas of research are primarily bounded by the fields of rhetoric, media, and gender and sexuality. Her publications include contributions to the Bram Stoker Award-nominated collection *Shirley Jackson: A Companion* (Peter Lang); *Transmediating the Whedonverse(s): Essays on Text, Paratext, and Metatext* (Palgrave); *Television Finales: From Howdy Doody to Girls* (Syracuse UP); and *Supernatural Out of the Box: Essays on the Metatextuality of the Series* (McFarland). She has presented research at regional, national, and international academic conferences, is president of the Association for the Study of *Buffy+*, serves as an area chair for the Popular Culture Association in the South, and is a longstanding active member of the Popular Culture Association. She is currently a lecturer in English at Vanderbilt University.

Melissa Tyndall is a two-time Tennessee Press Award winner who has published dozens of poems, most recently with *peculiars magazine, Dark Marrow, Vamp Cat Magazine, Red Tree Review, and Porkbelly Press.* She has presented at a variety of conferences, including PCA/ACA and the Southwest Popular/American Culture Association, about parenting in the *Archie* universe and generational stereotypes in *Supernatural.* She was a professor for fifteen years, during which time she taught communications, English, creative writing, film, and served as advisor of an award-winning student literary magazine. Tyndall is currently a full-time writer and independent scholar. She holds an MFA in creative writing and lives in Nashville with her husband and their two children, who Melissa hopes will prefer terrors over trucks and tiaras. Her fiction is represented by Ann Rose at The Tobias Literary Agency.

CONTRIBUTORS

Lori Bindig Yousman is a professor and chair of the Department of Communication Studies in the School of Communication, Media and the Arts at Sacred Heart University. She earned her doctorate in Communication at the University of Massachusetts Amherst. Her research interests include feminist television studies and critical media literacy. Dr. Bindig Yousman has published three monographs on teen television with Lexington Books. Her media literacy research has appeared in edited volumes and journal articles. She is the co-editor of the award-winning 5th and best-selling 6th edition of *Gender, Race, and Class in Media* published by Sage.

Alissa Burger is an associate professor of English and director of Student Success at Culver-Stockton College. She teaches courses in research, writing, and literature, specializing in gender, horror, and the Gothic. She is the author of *The Quest for the Dark Tower: Genre and Interconnection in the Stephen King Series* (McFarland, 2021), *Teaching Stephen King: Horror, The Supernatural, and New Approaches to Literature* (Palgrave, 2016), and *The Wizard of Oz as American Myth: A Critical Study of Six Versions of the Story, 1900–2007* (McFarland, 2012).

Alice Capstick focuses on the development of alternative heroic archetypes in the Romantic period. In particular, her work traces how the figure of the Satanic hero developed into a fully established archetype in the Romantic period. She examines how Romantic perception of Satan from John Milton's

Paradise Lost and other archetypal heroic figures informed their own experimentation with "dark heroes." Alice is also interested in theories from the field of Literary Darwinism and how they can be used to understand and account for the enduring prevalence of certain types of dark heroes and people's fascination with them. Her broader research interests include early modern poetry, aesthetic theory, gothic studies, and book history.

Katie E. Cline is a PhD student at Bowling Green State University, where her studies include feminism and gender studies, YA literature, witches, cats, and Taylor Swift. She has presented at ChLA, PCA/ACA, and YA Studies Association (YASA), and her article "The Bigger Picture: The Representation of Female Characters in Jim Kay's Illustrated Harry Potter Books" was published in the *Journal of Fantasy and Fan Cultures'* Winter 2020 issue. When not working, she enjoys reading contemporary romance novels and doting on her cats: Minnie, Toothless, and Beanie. She dedicates this publication to her late father, Dr. George R. Cline.

Lisa Delacruz Combs (she/her/siya) is a doctoral candidate at The Ohio State University in the Higher Education and Student Affairs program. She plans to write her dissertation about liminality and multiraciality. Lisa's research interests include identity interconnections, multiraciality in higher education, Filipinx identity development, poststructural feminist perspectives, and Asian American college students. Lisa has published about multiracial topics including two co-edited volumes and multiple journal articles. She received her BA in Political Science and English from The Ohio State University and her MS in Student Affairs in Higher Education from Miami University in Oxford, Ohio.

Tp Coughlin is a PhD student at The University of California Davis. Their work focuses on the intersection of economics, feminism, and gender in speculative fiction.

Laura Davidel defended her thesis entitled "Liminal Creatures: Representations of Monstrosity, Queerness, and Procreation in Anne Rice's *The Vampire Chronicles*" in December 2021. She is an English teacher at the *Université de Lorraine* in Metz, France. Her research focuses on the construction of monstrosity through performativity and performance, aspects of liminality, and queerness in Rice's vampire novels. Her most recent chapter, "Transmedia Vampire Stories and their Consumers in Anne Rice's *The Vampire Chronicles*" has been published in *The Transmedia Vampire: Essays on Technological Convergence and the Undead*, edited by Simon Bacon.

Diana Celeste Etain had her first introduction to occult and Neo-Pagan feminist literature at age ten. She holds a Bachelor of Arts in English from The University of Alabama, where she also completed the requirements for the Blount Scholars Program. She earned her Master of Arts with a specialization in Literary and Textual Studies from Bowling Green State University. She is currently attending Harvard Divinity School to pursue a Master of Theological Studies degree in an effort to further her understanding of religiosity. Her research interests include occultism, comparative theology, the New Age Movement, Neo-Paganism, feminist theology, hermeticism, and mysticism.

Luisa Fernanda Grijalva-Maza has a PhD in Cultural Studies. She is an associate professor at the Department of International Relations, Universidad Popular Autónoma del Estado de Puebla (UPAEP), and she is the managing editor of *Tapuya: Latin American Science, Technology and Society* (Routledge). Her recent research focuses on the movements of hybridity and liminality, their intersections, and their transgressions of the patriarchal-colonial-neoliberal power structure in Mexican horror films and cultural figures, such as Santa Muerte.

Farhana Irshad is a PhD candidate at St Mary's University in London. Her research explores the horror and true crime genres and their evolution to suit the streaming and exhibition practices within the current digital climate. Farhana's broader research areas also explore digital detectives within the true crime spaces, binge-watching, narrative transportation, and audience behavior.

Marc P. Johnston-Guerrero is associate chair of the Department of Educational Studies, associate professor in the Higher Education and Student Affairs (HESA) program, and affiliate faculty in Asian American Studies at The Ohio State University. His research focuses on race and multiraciality within higher education in the United States.

Nicole Neifert is a recent graduate of The Ohio State University, where she studied neuroscience and theatre. After becoming increasingly interested in multiracial identities during the beginning of her undergraduate career, she began conducting critical mixed-race research, particularly focusing on themes of mixedness in supernatural fiction.

Daria Romanova is an independent researcher with a passion for all things immersive. Her MA thesis, "Affiliation with the Past: Narrating Identity Through Neo-Edwardian Style in Digital Era," explores people negotiating their modern identities through an all-encompassing corporeal experience of wearing a vintage wardrobe. Romanova's research interests lie in the nexus of cultural studies, entertainment, and storytelling and include immersive experiences, participatory culture, visual media, narrative design, identity, and spectatorship.

David Rosen holds a doctorate in English Literature from Johns Hopkins and serves as the chair of general studies at South College in Nashville. He has written extensively on gender, primarily examining the construct of masculinity from a social and cultural perspective. His works include *The Changing Fictions of Masculinity* and "The Volcano and the Cathedral" in *Muscular Christianity: Embodying the Victorian Age*.

Shannon Hughes Spence a PhD student at Ireland's South East Technological University, looking at 18–24-year-old women's experiences in the Night Time Economy in Ireland. As a sociologist, her research interests include gender, power, historic witch trials, the occult, and social movements. The results of her interviews with people who identify as Irish, feminist witches can be found on her project's Instagram page, @cailleacha.na.heireann (Cailleacha na hÉireann/Witches of Ireland).

Maggie Webster has been a senior lecturer in Education and Religion at Edge Hill University since 2005 and is course lead in the Department for Secondary and Further Education for the contemporary degree BA (hons) in Religion. During her time at Edge Hill University she has also been a program lead for Primary Initial Teacher Education and a Year Lead for the Part Time program. She has published three books related to the English primary curriculum that are still in print: *Teaching Primary Religious Education* (Pearson Ltd., 2010); *Creative Activities and Ideas for English as an Additional Language Pupils* (Pearson Ltd., 2011), and *Teaching the Primary Foundation Subjects* (Open University Press, 2015) and has published various articles related to education. Her PhD thesis at The University of Wales Trinity St. David, *Becoming Witch: Creating and Confirming Faith Traditions within Social Networking Spaces* explores how people become witches within social media.

Ingram Content Group UK Ltd.
Milton Keynes UK
UKHW011407290623
424273UK00005B/81